OSCAR WILDE

OSCAR WILDE

THE UNREPENTANT YEARS

Nicholas Frankel

Harvard University Press

Cambridge, Massachusetts
London, England
2017

First printing

Library of Congress Cataloging-in-Publication Data

Names: Frankel, Nicholas, 1962– author.

Title: Oscar Wilde : the unrepentant years / Nicholas Frankel.

Description: Cambridge, Massachusetts : Harvard University Press, 2017. |
Includes bibliographical references and index.

Identifiers: LCCN 2017021767 | ISBN 9780674737945 (alk. paper)

Subjects: LCSH: Wilde, Oscar, 1854–1900—Exile—France. | Wilde,
Oscar, 1854–1900—Imprisonment. | Wilde, Oscar, 1854–1900—Death
and burial. | Authors, Irish—19th century—Biography.

Classification: LCC PR5823 .F67 2017 | DDC 828 / .809 [B]—dc23

LC record available at https://lccn.loc.gov/2017021767

For Susan,
With love and gratitude

Contents

The artist must live the complete life, must accept it as it comes and stands like an angel before him, with its drawn and two-edged sword. . . . I have had great success, I have had great failure. I have learned the value of each; and I now know that failure means more—always must mean more than success. Why, then, should I complain? . . . I have at last come to the complete life which every artist must experience in order to join beauty to truth.

—OSCAR WILDE, in conversation with
Laurence Housman, September 1899

Oscar Wilde, 1889. Photograph by W. and D. Downey.

Prologue

A T 6:15 A.M. on Wednesday, May 19, 1897, Oscar Wilde walked through the courtyard of London's Pentonville Prison for the last time and climbed into a waiting horse-drawn carriage. After two years in regulation prison serge, he was now dressed in the same frock coat, silk hat, and patent leather boots he wore the day he was convicted and sentenced to prison with hard labor for the crime of gross indecency with another man.[1] Inside the carriage were his friend More Adey and the radical cleric Stewart Headlam, a fierce campaigner against sexual puritanism who had generously stood bail for Wilde before his conviction. With Wilde aboard, the carriage sped through the gates, observed only by the prison governor and the warders who accompanied Wilde from his cell. Having completed his two-year prison sentence—a sentence that brought him to the point of suicide and insanity, in turn leading the authorities, in an effort to hide his torment from the public, to house him in three different jails—Wilde was at last a free man.

For weeks, Wilde had been nervous about the moment of his release. "I no doubt shall be very much upset and hysterical," he wrote a week earlier.[2] Like the prison authorities, he was keen to avoid the prying eyes of journalists. "Already the American interviewer and the English journalist have arrived," he wrote on May 17. "Is it not appalling? I who am maimed, ill, altered in appearance . . . broken-hearted, ruined, disgraced—a leper, and a pariah to men—I am to be gibbeted for the pleasure of the public of two worlds" (*CL* 829). But Wilde and the authorities feared more than unwanted attention from the press: to prevent demonstrations at Reading Prison, where Wilde had spent the final eighteen months of his sentence, the authorities secretly transferred Wilde, on the day before his official release, to Pentonville Prison in London, where his prison sentence had begun. For the imprisoned aesthete, the move revived painful memories of his transfer to Reading eighteen months earlier when, handcuffed and dressed in prison clothing, he had been spat at and jeered by crowds while changing trains at London's Clapham Junction station. This time, the transfer was handled humanely.

Afraid he would be recognized on London's streets, Wilde asked to be met with "a little brougham with blinds" or "a closed brougham" (*CL* 831, 833). He was no less anxious about the occupants and the destination of the carriage. "A good friend is a new world. I must be with nice sweet real people," he told his friend Reggie Turner two days before his release. Wilde had asked Turner personally "to come to Pentonville Prison . . . to have a carriage waiting for me and to take me to some hotel in the vicinity, or wherever you think there is a quiet place" (*CL* 830), but Turner replied that "More and Headlam are going to do that," that all the necessary arrangements had been put in place, and that "were my presence to be made known by any means to my people my allowance would be stopped, and that I could not afford."[3] As Turner indicated, few individuals living in England were willing and brave enough to welcome Wilde openly upon his release. Many English homosexuals, Turner included, had fled to France around the time of Wilde's arrest for fear of being prosecuted themselves for gross indecency. Adey later stated that Headlam was "the only person I could find both able and willing to accompany me," and it had been decided that Wilde should be taken briefly to Headlam's house in Upper Bedford Place, Bloomsbury.[4] From there he would travel by train and cross-Channel ferry to France, where rooms had been reserved at the Hôtel Sandwich in Dieppe, on the Normandy coast.

Wilde was not keen at all when informed of this plan shortly before his release. He told Turner that he didn't know Headlam very well, that he was "afraid of strangers" and disliked the idea of Dieppe, and that he would vastly prefer some "quiet place"—a hotel in "Euston Road or anywhere like that"—to Headlam's house (*CL* 833). He craved fresh clothes, "a room to dress in, and a sitting-room," and he feared being recognized in the streets of London (*CL* 831). But it was to Headlam's, a relatively short distance of two miles, that he was taken. A hotel, even in the Euston Road "or anywhere like that," was out of the question.

Headlam later expressed surprise and relief that they managed to leave the prison unobserved, but the carriage ride must have been tense nonetheless.[5] If Headlam's presence made Wilde nervous, Adey's presence created a more acute embarrassment. "I am so distressed by the conduct of More Adey towards me . . . that I could not travel with him," Wilde wrote two days earlier (*CL* 832). Wilde had known Adey, a homosexual writer and translator, since at least 1893, but prior to Wilde's imprisonment, relations between them had not been especially close. Before Wilde's arrest, Adey "was not a friend of Oscar's at all," Robert Ross, an intimate friend of both men, wrote. "I do not think he ever liked Oscar particularly. He certainly disapproved of him very much."[6] Perhaps so, but then Adey's behavior after news of Wilde's arrest broke appears all the more remarkable. Adey, who had trained as a barrister although he was never called to the bar, contributed several hundred pounds to Wilde's legal defense, and during Wilde's imprisonment, he had generously taken the management of Wilde's financial and legal affairs upon himself.[7] As Ross recalled, "directly Oscar was in low water, [Adey] became as fond of Oscar, I believe, as any friend of Oscar's could be."[8] At first Wilde welcomed Adey's well-intentioned efforts on his behalf, but by the time of his release, Wilde had come to think that Adey had betrayed his interests and that "he is incapable of managing the domestic affairs of a tom-tit in a hedge for a single afternoon. He is a stupid man, in practical concerns" (*CL* 823). In the days before Wilde's release, as Adey and other friends were making plans to shepherd Wilde into exile, it had been proposed that Adey accompany him to France. But Wilde told Adey personally two days before his release that "I am so hurt with you . . . not so much by what you have done, but by your failing to realise what you have done, your lack of imagination, which shows lack of sympathy, [and] your blindness . . . that if you came abroad with me it would only distress us both: I could talk to you of nothing but of the mode in which you very nearly [destroyed me]" (*CL* 834). It is a mark of Adey's immense generosity of spirit and sensitivity to his friend's suffering that he was willing to overlook these recriminations and meet Wilde at the prison gates two days later.

As the carriage made its way through the misty London streets, Wilde's emotions must have been running high. Years before his arrest, he had written about these very streets in his fiction. In his early story "Lord Arthur Savile's Crime," while London is still asleep, a distraught Lord Arthur Savile stumbles blindly down a silent street that "looked like a long riband of polished silver, flecked here and there by the dark arabesques of waving shadows. Far into the distance curved the line of flickering gas-lamps, and outside a little walled-in house stood a solitary hansom, the driver asleep inside."[9] Similarly, in *The Picture of Dorian Gray,* Wilde's troubled protagonist wanders at daybreak through "dimly-lit streets with gaunt black-shadowed archways and evil-looking houses," conscious of something evil lurking in the air itself.[10] As they proceeded to Headlam's, Wilde and his companions glimpsed a newspaper placard announcing the "Release of Oscar Wilde."[11] The sight must have called to mind how, reeling through the streets in the sure knowledge of his own criminality, Lord Arthur Savile fears seeing "his own name . . . placarded on the walls of London." For Wilde, as for Lord Arthur, there must have been "something in the dawn's delicate loveliness that seemed . . . inexpressibly pathetic."[12]

It was a cold May morning, and if the newspaper placard was a grim reminder of the past, then Wilde was also entering a world that was entirely new to him. At the time of his arrest in April 1895, two of his plays, *An Ideal Husband* and *The Importance of Being Earnest,* had been running to packed houses in London's West End (*The Importance of Being Earnest* was shortly to open in New York too). He was then at the top of his game and one of the most celebrated writers in the English-speaking world. Widely interviewed and photographed, he was as renowned for his wit, charm, elegant appearance, and sparkling conversation as he was for his writings, including his controversial novel *The Picture of Dorian Gray,* published in 1890, nearly two years before his first success as a playwright. Dressed always in the height of fashion, with immaculate coiffure and an orchid or a carnation smartly in his lapel, he had seemed what the poet Charles Baudelaire once called "the supreme embodiment of the idea of Beauty transported into the sphere of material life," and he had frequently been welcomed into the country homes and London townhouses of England's ruling class.[13] More personally, Wilde had spent three years recklessly and passionately in love with the fiery-tempered and preternaturally youthful-looking Lord Alfred Douglas, sixteen years his junior, whom he had first met in 1891.[14] "Your love has broad wings and is strong, your love comes to me through my prison bars and . . . is the light of all my hours," he had written Douglas from Holloway Prison shortly after his arrest (*CL* 646). "In prison . . . I am going to test the power of love," he told Douglas one month later, "to see if I cannot make the bitter waters sweet by the intensity of the love I bear you" (*CL* 651).

But the Wilde who emerged from Pentonville had drunk deeply from bitter waters, and his love for Douglas had failed to make them sweet. His literary and social reputation was now in tatters, and he faced a dispiriting and uncertain future. Doors across London were firmly shut against him, as he had painfully discovered in May 1895, one month after his arrest, when he was finally released on bail during the interim between his two criminal trials.[15] Even before his conviction, his name had been removed from playbills and theater programs, producers had braced for the inevitable boycotting of his plays, and booksellers had withdrawn his books from their shelves. Until his arrest, his plays alone had earned him some £10,000, equivalent to roughly £1 million today.[16] But in April 1895, bailiffs occupied Wilde's house and sold off his family's possessions to meet creditors' bills, and later that year Wilde was officially declared bankrupt. His wife, Constance, who visited him in jail just twice, had legally separated from him; her second prison visit, undertaken compassionately in February 1896 to break the news of his beloved mother's death, was the last occasion Wilde saw her alive. According to the terms of the separation agreement, which Wilde signed two days before his release, she would allow him £150 per year, but this would be forfeit if he ever attempted to communicate with her against her will or without her leave, or if he communicated with Douglas. Similarly, he was legally deprived of any right to see his children, of whom Constance was now sole guardian, and if he ever tried to communicate with them he would be imprisoned for contempt of court. Like their mother, his children had adopted the last name "Holland" and had been taught by Constance and her relatives "to forget that we had ever borne the name of Wilde and never to mention it to anyone."[17] Wilde had "lost wife, children, fame, honour, position, [and] wealth," he wrote six months before his release: poverty was "all that he [could] look forward to [and] obscurity all that he [could] hope for" (*CL* 668).

Only his closest friends might continue to know him as *Oscar Wilde,* he decided from his prison cell, since to the rest of the world his name was so loathsome. Upon his release he would become *Sebastian Melmoth.* There was symbolism in the pseudonym: St. Sebastian, who has been called the patron saint of homosexuals, was an early Christian martyr, persecuted and savagely killed at the hands of the Romans. Even before Wilde adopted his name, St. Sebastian had become a "coded means of articulating same-sex desire," at least among writers with homosexual and Catholic allegiances.[18] In the twentieth century, Sebastian would more widely become a homosexual icon, in part through Wilde's own reverence for him—consider the homosexual characters Sebastian Flyte in Evelyn Waugh's *Brideshead Revisited* and Sebastian Venable in Tennessee Williams's *Suddenly Last Summer.* In his youth, Wilde had fallen in love with one of Guido Reni's seven painted depictions of the martyred saint, on first seeing the painting in Genoa in 1877. In Reni's painting, the dying Sebastian, bound half-naked to a tree and pierced by poisoned arrows, rolls his eyes heavenward. It is easy to see why the painting, with its powerful evocation of pain, beauty, eroticism, and otherworldly transcendence, appealed to Wilde. The second half of the pseudonym, *Melmoth,* alludes to the Gothic novel *Melmoth the Wanderer,* by Wilde's Irish great-uncle Charles Maturin. Maturin's Faust-like protagonist, half hero and half villain, sells his soul to the devil in exchange for an extended, permanently youthful life and, when death finally draws near, wanders the earth in vain, haunting the dreams of men while hoping that one of them will absolve him of his pact. If *Sebastian* suggests Wilde's willingness to cast himself in the role of the martyr, *Melmoth* hints at the fundamentally transgressive nature of his life and art.

In the weeks before his release, Wilde also resolved to have nothing further to do with his lover Lord Alfred Douglas. "Never . . . mention in conjunction with mine that ill-omened and most unfortunate name, so fatal to me and to my house" he wrote about Douglas to a friend in December 1896 (*CL* 674). "By associating with one of [your] nature, I . . . soiled and shamed my life irretrievably," he wrote to Douglas from Reading Prison, in a long unsent letter that unsparingly listed Douglas's personal failings (*CL* 700). On no account should Douglas be informed of Wilde's whereabouts upon release, Wilde told Adey two weeks before he left prison. But Wilde sought to reject more than just Douglas personally; there was something fatal in the very nature of his love, he had begun to think. "Your love is the light of all my hours," he had written to Douglas in April 1895: "our love was always beautiful and noble, and if I have been the butt of a terrible tragedy, it is because the nature of that love has not been understood" (*CL* 646–47). Eighteen months later, desire itself seemed a form of malady or madness: "Tired of being on the heights," he wrote, "I deliberately went to the depths in the search for new sensations" (*CL* 730). In a petition asking the home secretary to commute his sentence on the grounds of incipient insanity, Wilde called his love for men "the most horrible form of erotomania" and a "monstrous sexual perversion," one more properly treated as a disease "to be cured by a physician" than a crime to be punished by a judge (*CL* 656).

In short, Wilde had lost almost everything. Moreover, he had repudiated much of what he had not lost. As they drove off from Pentonville, Wilde's companions doubtless explained the plans that had been made for him to journey to the French coast, after first resting, changing, and breakfasting at Headlam's. But figuratively speaking, where exactly was Wilde headed? What future, if any, did Wilde envision for himself as his carriage transported him toward the center of London, the scene of his greatest successes and deepest disgraces? Would he be able to rebuild his life from the ruins that lay around him? Would he ever again charm audiences with his fecund wit, storytelling, and learning? What effects would poverty and enforced exile have on a psyche already weakened by imprisonment, disgrace, and hard labor? And would Wilde ever again find the love he had found, albeit tempestuously, with Douglas? Relations with his wife had been frosty for years, leading him to remark shortly before his release, when it appeared as if Constance and her lawyers were agitating for a divorce, that "whether I am married or not is a matter that does not concern me. For years I disregarded the tie" (*CL* 785). But it was a different matter with his children and mother, with whom he had cherished close filial kinships that had inspired much of his writing. "Each man kills the thing he loves. . . . / The coward does it with a kiss," Wilde would proclaim in *The Ballad of Reading Gaol,* perhaps thinking of the disastrous effects of his extramarital affairs and his conviction on his immediate family.[19] His staunchly loyal mother—who, refusing to believe in his guilt, had urged him to stand trial when others advised him to flee—had died impoverished and heartbroken while he was in jail. But had Wilde unwittingly "killed" his children too, and if so, how would he channel his guilt and unhappiness at the thought?

––––––––

The pages that follow show how Wilde faced this uncertain and difficult future. Part One lays the groundwork and takes a necessary backward glance: it describes Wilde's dramatic psychological and physical collapse in prison as well as his subsequent, belated efforts in the final months of his sentence to imagine a viable future for himself and to reconstruct himself as both man and writer. Part Two, the core of the book, paints a detailed portrait of the final three-and-a-half years of Wilde's life, following his emergence from prison in 1897. It begins with his departure for France on the day of his release, as he attempted to reconcile himself to a life of self-imposed exile and rebuild his literary career. It describes Wilde's euphoric enjoyment of his new freedom in the days immediately after his release, as well as the disappointment and dejection that followed as Wilde came to realize that exile as Britain's most notorious sex offender meant public insults, long bouts of isolation, loss of livelihood, and eventually a withering of his health and creative faculties. It documents his ill-fated attempt to rebuild his relationship with Douglas anew, despite the bitterness with which he disavowed the friendship in prison, as well as the further breakdown in his already strained relations with his wife, following a failed attempt at reconciliation with her prior to her own premature death in 1898. And it depicts his battles with poverty and social ostracism, particularly after he fulfilled a longstanding desire in February 1898 to make his home in the French capital. It describes his minor and, until recently, largely unacknowledged role in the Dreyfus scandal, which was reaching its peak when Wilde arrived in Paris.

Much of what lay in store for England's most notorious sexual criminal would prove difficult and depressing, but after two bitter years of solitary confinement, Wilde was determined to rebuild his life along lines continuous with the path he had followed in the years before his conviction: unapologetic, unrepentant, and even defiant about the crimes that sent him to prison in the first place. England had already done its worst. Particularly after his arrival in Paris, his pursuit of a series of young men lent joy, passion, and a great deal of good humor to his final years, while his wit, vividly on display in his many surviving letters from this period, was arguably at its sharpest. Although Wilde now lacked for much that he had previously taken for granted—not least money, social success, and an assured audience—he had never been comfortable with the conventional trappings of success. Until his health started to decline sharply in the final year of his life, his mode of living in exile was in many ways an extension of his mode of living before his downfall. Despite the acrimony with which he had written of Douglas while in Reading, for instance, Wilde left prison determined to rid himself of bitterness, to forgive Douglas, and even to reunite with Douglas "in some quiet foreign town" (*CL* 778).

He was equally determined to resurrect his literary career—"to do beautiful work and speak to the world again," as he put it, "on an instrument that has . . . become wider in possibility of range and effect"—even if initially this meant using his talents to advance the cause of prison reform (*CL* 882). Just before leaving prison, he told a friendly warder of his determination henceforth to write "exclusively for those who have suffered or are suffering."[20] Within days of his release, he had not only written a superb polemic about the harsh injustices of the prison system, published in the reform-oriented *Daily Chronicle* and subsequently printed as a penny pamphlet titled *Children in Prison and Other Cruelties of Prison Life,* he had also begun *The Ballad of Reading Gaol,* a poem that proved to be the bestselling of all Wilde's works in his lifetime and that was twice cited in Parliamentary debate in the run-up to the 1898 Prisons Act. Upon his release, Wilde immediately began to forge relations with other writers, dramatists, publishers, poets, and eventually translators. By the time he arrived in Paris in the early spring of 1898, he held serious hopes of resuscitating his literary career. He dined with leading figures in the Parisian avant-garde theater, briefly contemplated writing a new Biblical tragedy and a novel, was active in arranging for the publication of *The Ballad* in French, and spent much of the summer of 1898 revising the text of *The Importance of Being Earnest* for publication. He wanted the book's format to match the format of his earlier plays in order to emphasize the continuities in his life and his work. His revisions to the play were drastic. Many of the witticisms now associated with this glorious comedy date from this period.

Today *The Importance of Being Earnest* is the most collectible of all Wilde's books, and first-edition copies of it sell for exorbitant prices. It was a different story in 1899, however, when the play was first published, without Wilde's name on the title page. Wilde recognized that his name was a liability, and his publisher had followed his own suggestion that rather than giving his name, the title page should state simply that the play was "by the author of *Lady Windermere's Fan.*" Despite the time and care Wilde invested in revision and in plans for publication, sales were extremely poor, and Wilde was disappointed when critics ignored the play.[21] The same proved true of *An Ideal Husband*, which Wilde regarded even more highly than *The Importance of Being Earnest*.[22] It is a sad, inescapable fact that after the publishing failure of *An Ideal Husband* in July 1899, Wilde's creative wellspring seems to have dried up. His brave and loyal publisher Leonard Smithers was one of many who hoped the publication of these great plays would spur Wilde to new feats of creativity. Looking forward to new successes, Smithers went so far as to pay Wilde a regular retainer and commission him to write a new play for the London stage, but Wilde confessed that "it is difficult for me to laugh at life, as I used to" and that the idea of writing comedy "frightens me a little" (*CL* 1150). As he had said shortly before leaving prison, "I am no longer the Sirius of Comedy. If I write any more books, it will be to form a library of lamentations . . . written in a style begotten of sorrow, and in sentences composed in solitude, and punctuated by tears."[23]

If Wilde lost what remained of his creativity after the success of *The Ballad* and after his two last plays failed to find a readership, he remained uncompromising and resolute in his personal life. In the early months of his exile, he was determined to enjoy his new freedom in the company of those brave and loyal enough to flout the general opprobrium, such as Smithers ("a delightful companion" and "the most learned erotomaniac in Europe") and the decadent poet Ernest Dowson (*CL* 924). Until his final illness in the autumn of 1900, he delighted in the pleasures of conversation, sex, companionship, and alcohol, unafraid at the prospect of courting the disapproval of others, especially where it might mean compromising his belief in his right to love whom and how he wanted. In Paris, the poets Jean Moréas, Ernest La Jeunesse, and other denizens of the Calisaya Bar near the Crédit Lyonnais took the place that Ernest Dowson and Leonard Smithers had occupied in the early months of his exile. Some time before this, Wilde had relished the companionship of Major Ferdinand Walsin Esterhazy, the histrionic villain of the Dreyfus Affair. Esterhazy's combination of charm, bravura, and obvious criminal guilt fascinated Wilde, so much so that when criticized for his friendship with Esterhazy, before the latter's own flight into exile in late 1898, Wilde replied that innocence was easy, whereas it required courage and imagination to be a criminal.

If the idea of writing comedy now frightened him, Wilde remained determined to prove in his personal relationships that, as he put it, "laughter is the primaeval attitude towards life" and "where one laughs there is no immorality" (*CL* 1106, 1073). He seized pleasure whenever and wherever he could find it, especially among the bohemian denizens of the bars, cafés, and boulevards of Paris, and his young lovers were numerous by his own reckoning. "In the mortal sphere I have fallen in and out of love," he remarked to his friend Robert Ross, just months before his death in 1900; "[I have] fluttered hawks and doves alike. . . . My mouth is twisted with kissing, and I feed on fevers. The Cloister or the Café—there is my future. I tried the Hearth, but it was a failure" (*CL* 1187). The wit and passion of the remark are typical. When de-

among the French, and if his existence was promiscuous, it was hand-to-mouth as well. Although Wilde often exaggerated his poverty and received regular allowances from a number of friends, he was constantly in debt and, in the words of his first biographer, "spent money with the recklessness of sailors on shore."[26] But it was not a life for which Wilde would have wanted pity. Just as, at the height of his success, Wilde had furtively pursued a decadent existence, so now did Wilde seek passionate experience, living according to what he had once termed "a new Hedonism" sharply at odds with the puritanism of Victorian England.[27] In the earliest weeks of his exile, he struggled between his desire for reconciliation with his wife and children on the one hand and a rapprochement with his ex-lover Lord Alfred Douglas on the other. As we shall see, this struggle was soon decisively settled in Douglas's favor when Wilde shocked even some of his closest friends by suddenly eloping with Douglas to Naples in the late summer of 1897, only to be forcibly and permanently separated from him three months later.

The relationship between Wilde and Douglas is still widely misunderstood. Douglas has too often been represented as a callous and heartless Judas or Iago figure who spurred Wilde on to not one but two disastrous and fateful actions, before abandoning Wilde each time to face the consequences alone.[28] But this view derives partly from the long vituperative letter that Wilde wrote his lover from prison in the concluding months of his sentence, in which Wilde blames Douglas for all of his sufferings and calls Douglas "the true author of [my] hideous tragedy" (*CL* 710). It is not a view that holds up under scrutiny. Wilde had always courted danger and defied the majority, and he later said of his elopement with Douglas to Naples that "my eyes were not blinded" (*CL* 1000). Just as important, as Wilde's surviving letters indicate, when he eloped to Naples he was still deeply and determinedly in love with the man he had once called "the supreme, the perfect love of my life," and equally determined to accept whatever might come from the pursuit of his love (*CL* 652). Within weeks of his release, he was writing to Douglas daily, addressing him as "my darling boy" and "my dear honey-sweet boy," and eagerly making plans for Douglas to visit him in his secluded retreat at Berneval, on the Normandy coast (*CL* 906, 910, 898).

Significantly, Wilde never sent Douglas the letter from prison blaming him for his misfortunes, in part I believe because he knew that his characterizations were shaped by the circumstances of his imprisonment. Indeed, Douglas himself remained ignorant of Wilde's recriminations, despite spending many months in Wilde's company in 1897 and 1898, until he read an allusion to them in Arthur Ransome's book *Oscar Wilde: A Critical Study* twelve years after Wilde's death. (After reading of Wilde's bitter attack, Douglas, in shock and disbelief, unsuccessfully sued Ransome for libel, whereupon Wilde's most damaging accusations were read aloud in court and quoted in the press.) As Wilde himself said in the course of writing his prison letter to Douglas, "we who live in prison and in whose lives there is no event but sorrow have to measure time by throbs of pain, and the record of bitter moments" (*CL* 696). The casting of blame had served a crucial psychological purpose so long as he remained behind bars, since to Wilde and many other prisoners "suffering in the past is necessary to us as the warrant, the evidence, of our continued identity" (*CL* 696). In the days after his release from prison, however, and with his litany of recriminations unsent, Wilde quickly came to view Douglas with a very different cast of mind.

Douglas himself had suffered more greatly during Wilde's prison sentence than Wilde was inclined to realize at the time. Although Douglas possessed many faults, the letters, poems, petitions, and articles that he wrote about Wilde during the latter's imprisonment show that lack of love and failure of sympathy were not among them at this time. These documents provide an important context for Wilde's decision to elope to Naples with Douglas, and the Douglas who emerges from them is a more sympathetic figure than the Douglas who appears in more skeletal form, nakedly self-obsessed, in many previous books, plays, and films about Wilde. "More than two years ago," Douglas told a friend in the summer of 1897, "I was parted from the person I love best in the world and . . . ever since I have waited and hoped and longed to see him again."[29] "I wanted to go back to him, I longed for it and for him," Douglas told his own mother, explaining his reasons for eloping to Naples with Wilde, "because I love him and admire him and think him great."[30] We should recall as well that Douglas was the chief mourner at Wilde's funeral in December 1900, and that once the coffin was lowered, he reportedly threw himself into Wilde's grave, screaming "Oscar! Oscar!" and, besmeared with earth, had to be forcibly removed.

––––––––

In addition to describing the closing years of Wilde's life with fresh clarity and detail, this book represents the first sustained effort to understand Wilde's imagination through the prism of his final years. Wilde's two last great works, *The Ballad of Reading Gaol* and *De Profundis,* the one begun shortly after his release from prison and the other composed shortly before it, belong to this period. Wilde's experience of imprisonment shaped them both closely, and in different ways they attempt to transcend the raw banality of suffering and confinement to find deeper, lasting meaning in the experience of imprisonment and the conduct of life. It is no surprise that both works proved immensely successful upon publication, running into many editions and quickly being translated into foreign languages. Although *De Profundis* was not published till nearly five years after Wilde's death, and then only in a highly redacted form where no trace of the work's origins in a letter to Alfred Douglas remained, both works went some way toward redeeming Wilde as a literary figure and laying the groundwork for the lifting of his estate's bankruptcy in 1906.

Despite the fame the poem would achieve, Wilde was initially circumspect about *The Ballad of Reading Gaol*'s appearing under his own name, as was also the case with his final plays. "I see it is my name that terrifies," he told his publisher, Leonard Smithers, in the weeks before the poem's publication (*CL* 1011). In consequence he adopted his prison cell number, C. 3. 3. (cell block C, landing 3, cell 3), on the title page of early editions of *The Ballad.* Not till the poem's seventh edition, published in June 1899, did Smithers incorporate Wilde's name on the title page, in brackets after the signature "C. 3. 3.," by which time the poem had already sold several thousand copies and been widely reviewed and translated. But nobody was fooled when the poem first appeared without Wilde's name on it. *The Ballad* presupposed Wilde's reputation as Britain's most illustrious and controversial prisoner, and Wilde counted on the public's continued interest in him. The pseudonym "C. 3. 3." was effectively a statement of Wilde's kinship with other "outcast men" and "souls in pain." "Have Smith's bookstalls taken the poem?" Wilde eagerly asked his publisher one month after publication. "Could you have a leaflet . . . put into the leaves of a good magazine? Like Pears soap, and other more useful things" (*CL* 1043). Like *De Profundis, The Ballad* is a work of public self-justification as well as a highly personalized indictment of the society that had convicted and imprisoned Wilde. In its day, it received high praise for being the most genuine, sincere, and truthful of Wilde's works.

The circumstances of Wilde's exile help to illuminate the works he wrote in prison or shortly after his release, but just as importantly, they retrospectively illuminate many works he wrote before his conviction. Wilde had always insisted his writings should be understood as consummate examples of art for art's sake and celebrated for their verbal style, wit, and inherent linguistic beauty. "The artist is the creator of beautiful things," he maintained in the 1891 preface to *The Picture of Dorian Gray,* where he explained that "to reveal art and conceal the artist" is art's aim.[31] "The only beautiful things . . . are the things that do not concern us," he had asserted in "The Decay of Lying," where he explained that art's object "is not simple truth but complex beauty."[32] By the time of his arrest in 1895, Wilde had for years been widely understood as the self-appointed "apostle of aestheticism," and his poems, plays, fictions, and essays alike had been celebrated or condemned on the grounds of their artfulness and verbal wit. This trend culminated over the course of the three years before Wilde's arrest with the run of social comedies for which Wilde is perhaps still best known. These hugely entertaining plays were praised, and continue to be praised, by theatergoers and critics for their witty, epigrammatic dialogue, "perpetual flow of brilliant talk," and "dramatic instinct [of the very] highest potency."[33]

When considered in the retrospective light cast by his years of imprisonment and exile, however, the finely wrought style of Wilde's pre-prison writings begins to appear like a carefully constructed mask, and the plays, poems, and fictions upon which his earlier fame rested seem to have a great deal more to do with the life that lay ahead of him than at first appears the case. For all their witty repartee, the protagonists of Wilde's plays and fictions frequently harbor unspeakable, often criminal personal secrets. Those who pursue illicit love are repeatedly made to suffer a symbolic degradation or fall from grace, and a sense of impending personal tragedy hangs over even the wittiest and most outwardly exuberant of Wilde's social comedies.

When it opened in early January 1895, *An Ideal Husband* seemed merely the latest in a line of "plays which are so unapproachably playful that they are the delight of every theatergoer."[34] But we can now see that the play expresses Wilde's own trepidation at the consequences should his mask as an "ideal husband" be lifted and his secret, illegal life as a lover of young men be revealed. He once told his friend the artist Charles Ricketts that the play "contains a great deal of the real Oscar," and when revising it for publication four years later, Wilde said he found the play "prophetic of tragedy to come."[35] The remark is no less true of the other, perhaps greater of the two comedies running at the time of his arrest, *The Importance of Being Earnest.* When Jack Worthing creates the alter ego Ernest to avoid his social and familial responsibilities and pursue instead a secret life of pleasure in London's West End, a host of farcical complications ensue. Early in the play, Algernon suspects his friend of being "one of the most advanced Bunburyists I know"—of having "invented a very useful younger brother named Ernest" much as he himself had "invented a valuable permanent invalid named Bunbury"—and it is only a matter of hours before Algernon too is masquerading as Ernest in an effort to bring about "the most wonderful Bunbury I have ever had in my life."[36] But in their commitment to Bunburying and their reckless pursuit of gratification, the play's protagonists flirt constantly with the kinds of personal disaster that eventually befell Wilde himself, while their behavior throughout is driven by a fear of public exposure. Even Wilde's own death seems foreshadowed in the sudden reported death of the impoverished, impenitent, pleasure-seeking Ernest in an obscure Parisian hotel.

In *De Profundis,* Wilde observes, "at every single moment of one's life one is what one is going to be no less than what one has been" (*CL* 740). The remark usefully points to the continuities between the different phases of Wilde's life as well as the continuities between his life and his work. The secret transgressions and fears of public exposure driving the plots of *The Picture of Dorian Gray, An Ideal Husband, The Importance of Being Earnest,* and "Lord Arthur Savile's Crime" show that long before his criminal conviction, Wilde was consciously aware of the risks he ran by pursuing a secret life at odds with his public and familial persona, and that he anticipated his own unmasking, at least on an imaginative level. In a sense, the last years of Wilde's life seem to spring from the pages of his earlier written works. "Pen, Pencil and Poison," for instance, Wilde's 1889 memoir celebrating the life of the forger-artist-writer Thomas Wainewright, who died impoverished and disgraced in 1847 after being tried for forgery and transported to Tasmania, reads like an outline of Wilde's own life, from his early years of artistic success and private deception to his premature death in exile, poverty, and disgrace. The memoir is an indispensable reflection on the essential congruity between artistry and crime.

If Wilde's final years illuminate much of what he wrote at the height of his literary and social success, those writings by the same token illuminate our understanding of his years of imprisonment and exile.

From the mid-1880s onward, his writings are inflected by their author's consciousness of the terrible, intertwined, destructive power of England's courts of justice and public opinion. He took many risks in his writings in the face of England's harsh criminal statutes against homosexuality. *The Picture of Dorian Gray, An Ideal Husband, The Importance of Being Earnest,* "Pen, Pencil and Poison," and others of his pre-prison works show that Wilde set himself against the laws and institutions of British justice long before the Crown tried and convicted him for acts of "gross indecency." During the last months of his imprisonment, Wilde accurately described himself as "a born antinomian . . . one of those who are made for exceptions, not for laws," adding that he saw nothing wrong in "what one does" (*CL* 732). He meant that by virtue of his position as an artist and a homosexual, he felt no obligation to submit to conventional laws, stereotyped traditions, or social structures, and that he answered to a morality rooted only in his personal identity or character.

He had articulated the position earlier, politically, in his 1891 essay "The Soul of Man Under Socialism," often reprinted under the simpler and more accurate title "The Soul of Man." In that essay, he calls his philosophy "Individualism," or the perfection and expression of one's inner personality. "The things people say of a man do not alter a man," he writes; "he is what he is. Public opinion is of no value whatsoever. . . . He may keep the law, and yet be worthless. He may break the law, and yet be fine. . . . He may commit a sin against society, and yet realise through that sin his own perfection."[37] This conviction in his own exceptionalism underwrites the unapologetic, frequently defiant spirit in which Wilde conducted his final years, just as it underwrites the unapologetic, seemingly reckless manner in which, at the height of his artistic success in 1895, he brought the full legal machinery of the state down upon himself. When his friend André Gide met Wilde on vacation in Algiers in January 1895, as rumors about his double life were already circulating back home, and asked him whether he knew what he risked by returning to London, Wilde replied uncompromisingly that he "must go as far as possible" and that "something must happen."[38] If ostracism, social and financial collapse, or still worse ensued from his determination to pursue his desires for other men, Wilde implied, they were a price worth paying.

This note of defiance has been largely missing from previous accounts of Wilde's final years. Biographers have been too quick to frame these years as merely the tragic aftermath to Wilde's years of social and literary success. For H. Montgomery Hyde, the author of *Oscar Wilde: The Aftermath* (1963), the only previous book to deal exclusively with the period following Wilde's conviction, Wilde's is "a tragic story of human suffering."[39] While Hyde offers a detailed, invaluable account of Wilde's torments in prison, he gives scant attention to Wilde's often rich and pleasure-filled life after his release. Likewise, Richard Ellmann tells us that "Wilde's situation framed itself in terms of the Greek tragedies that he knew so well."[40] Ellmann calls the period with which I am centrally concerned Wilde's "leftover years," describing it as the tragic postscript to the two decades of clever striving, self-cultivation, and brilliant success that occupy the bulk of his 1987 Pulitzer Prize–winning biography of Wilde.[41] Other, more recent commentators have portrayed Wilde as a martyr or a saint, immolated on the pyre of injustice through his homophobic Victorian accusers' and judges' relentless persecution of him. While it is certainly true that Wilde was the victim of legally sanctioned homophobia, injustice, and a torturous late-Victorian prison system, Wilde did not emerge from prison without ambitions or plans, and he took pleasure where it was to be had. While he faced injury and insult on an almost daily basis, to frame Wilde's story as tragedy or martyrdom is to ignore elements in his makeup at once personal and philosophical that go to the heart of who he was.

Far from being a personal tragedy, Wilde's unrepentant years were the completion of him as a man and as a man of letters. "Still leading his life of pleasure?" inquires Canon Chasuble of "Ernest" when Jack

PART ONE

THE PRISON YEARS
1895–1897

I

Fettered and Chained

WHEN WILDE LEFT Oxford University in late 1878, he quickly became the brightest of London's bright young things: "professional beauties" frequented the cramped apartments that he shared with the society portrait-painter Frank Miles, and he occupied the center of attention at fashionable openings as much for his dandyish appearance and witty *mots* as for his radical ideas about art, beauty, dress, and interior design. Then, in 1882, a widely reported lecture tour throughout North America brought the young aesthete great fame as well as a public on both sides of the Atlantic that was surprisingly receptive to his ideas about the "house beautiful" and what he called "the value of art in modern life." But there was another aspect to his new fame: from virtually the moment his boat docked in New York, accusations of effeminacy dogged him wherever he went, and his first book of poems—which had already caused a breach with Miles, whose father refused to allow his son to remain friends with its author—was widely condemned in America as "unmanly."

In light of Wilde's later life as a lover of men and his proud defense of "Uranian love," his marriage in 1884 to the beautiful Constance Lloyd (whom he had been courting as early as 1881) has excited a great deal of retrospective comment and speculation. The marriage was encouraged, even facilitated, by his match-making mother, and perhaps

Wilde acquiesced partly in an effort to quell the accusations of effeminacy or deny the most important element in his own sexual makeup. Initially, anyway, he seems to have been much in love with Constance— "O execrable facts, that keep our lips from kissing, though our souls are one" (CL 241), he wrote to his wife seven months after their wedding, when away lecturing in Scotland: "I feel incomplete without you." Though Constance quickly bore him two sons, Wilde was sexually and passionately attracted to younger men, as became clear at his trials eleven years later: he had had intense male friendships for many years before his marriage, and within three years of their wedding he had ceased sexual relations with his wife.[1] In 1886 he began a secret, lengthy affair with the clever young Canadian Robert Ross, later a writer, art critic, and gallery owner. The affair with Ross is widely regarded as Wilde's first actively sexual relationship with another man, in part because both Wilde and Ross represented it in this light. But many biographers speculate that, long before 1886, Wilde's earlier, intense friendships with Miles and other men contained at least some sexual element.[2] Fifteen years younger than Wilde, the seventeen-year-old Ross was precocious, sexually experienced, and unashamed about his own homosexuality. Although within a couple of years Ross would become displaced in Wilde's sexual affections by other young men, he remained among the most loyal and devoted of Wilde's friends.

In 1887 Wilde began to hint at the existence of his own double life in a series of increasingly risqué and homoerotic stories, essays, and dialogues that appeared over his name in leading London magazines and journals. But the homoeroticism of his writings was subtly encoded, and as the critic Regenia Gagnier has shown, Wilde wrote at least partly for "an audience of intimates"—for a small circle of highly educated fellow homosexuals who could be expected to appreciate what Gagnier calls his "private art of seduction."[3] To the vast majority of his readers, Wilde was simply the wittiest and most aesthetic of English-language writers. This more widely held view was consolidated as he became more prolific in the early 1890s, especially by the critical and popular acclaim he received as a playwright. Reviewers and audience members alike delighted in the sparkling repartee of the four social comedies with which Wilde took London's West End stage by storm between 1892 and 1895, finding nothing homoerotic or even especially provocative in them except for their willfully paradoxical wit. *The Importance of Being Earnest,* the most frequently performed and best of these comedies, is simply an "iridescent filament of fancy," proclaimed the eminent critic William Archer, while the author himself advertised the play as "exquisitely trivial, a delicate bubble of fancy," although we can now see that the play is carefully layered and loaded with coded allusions to Wilde's own life.[4] Even when his novel *The Picture of Dorian Gray* was attacked by reviewers as indecent, "unclean," and principally of "medico-legal interest," and Wilde himself was threatened with prosecution, he was able to deflect such accusations by forcefully insisting that "the sphere of art and the sphere of ethics are entirely distinct."[5] Upon republishing the novel in 1891, with its most obviously sexual elements newly censored, he attached a brilliant aphoristic preface to it in which he maintains that "the artist is the creator of beautiful things," that "there is no such thing as a moral or an immoral book," and that "those who find ugly meanings in beautiful things are corrupt without being charming."[6]

It should not surprise us that Wilde lived a double life or that his own writings should be so carefully coded. The prim conventions and laws surrounding sexuality, gender, and propriety in Victorian Britain had led many apparently monogamous or celibate Victorian men to pursue a secret sexual life in the margins. As Robert Louis Stevenson's *Dr. Jekyll and Mr. Hyde* dramatizes, upstanding citizens frequently transformed themselves into what the literary critic Steven Marcus once called "Other Victorians," often by crossing rigid demarcation lines between social classes, genders, races, and metropolitan neighborhoods. Like Stevenson's Dr. Jekyll, Dorian Gray, the wealthy eponymous hero of Wilde's only novel, is increasingly given to mysterious and prolonged absences from his Mayfair home, leading to strange conjectures among his friends. Dorian frequents a "sordid room" in London's East End, where he goes repeatedly under an assumed name and in disguise, although this does not prevent him from thinking "of the ruin he had brought upon his own soul."[7]

Homosexuals had particular reasons for pursuing such a furtive, illicit sex life. In 1885, the British Parliament, in a panic at the explosive growth in the white slave trade and spurred on by sensational journalism describing it, had passed The Criminal Law Amendment Act, legislation primarily designed "for the Protection of Women and Girls, the suppression of brothels, and other purposes." Among other things, the Act raised the age of sexual consent from twelve to sixteen. At the eleventh hour, and after hurried Parliamentary debate, a statute was added to this legislation (the so-called Labouchere Amendment, named after Henry Labouchere, the radical MP and journalist who proposed it) outlawing "gross indecency" between men: "any male person who, in public or private, commits, or is a party to the commission of, or procures, or attempts to procure the commission by any male person of, any act of gross indecency with another male person, shall be guilty of a misdemeanour, and being convicted thereof, shall be liable at the discretion of the Court to be imprisoned for any term not exceeding two years, with or without hard labour."[8] This rushed and vaguely worded amendment was to have the most pernicious and longstanding ramifications for British society. By outlawing "gross indecency" rather than any specified sex act, the Act made even the most innocent, private, and consensual actions liable to criminal prosecution. The criminal standard was loosely defined and entirely subjective, and the burden of proof was dangerously low. It has been said that the Act brought the modern male homosexual into being, for it created panic, paranoia, and a new sense of sexual identity among both men with same-sex desires and those most desirous of policing them. The Act quickly became known as the "Blackmailer's Charter": "gross-indecency" was a catch-all phrase, and two years before he fell afoul of the Act in 1895, Wilde himself was subjected to blackmail by virtue of letters that he had recently written to Douglas and that Douglas had incautiously let fall into the hands of the blackmailer Alfred Wood.[9]

One unintended result of the Criminal Law Amendment Act was to exacerbate a suppressed homosexual subculture in London's West End, on the fringes of polite Victorian society. To many well-to-do Victorian men, the gentleman's club and the private home were sacrosanct and sought-after places, but homosexual men were increasingly forced to seek companionship in rented apartments or else in public or semi-public places such as stations, hotels, and the private dining rooms of restaurants—places not easily or obviously accessible to vigorous policing. Knightsbridge Skating Rink and Earls Court Exhibition Hall became popular meeting places, for instance, while Piccadilly Circus developed "a subcultural and more general notoriety for renters and homosexual cruising."[10] London's grand stations, with their lavish interiors and promise of anonymity and speedy travel, became places for chance meetings, while richly appointed new hotels such as the Ritz and the Savoy, where Wilde himself took a number of male sexual partners from 1893 onward, became places for anonymous and extra-marital sex.

As became scandalously clear in late 1889, when the police unearthed a network of "renters" working as telegraph boys at London's Central Post Office by day and as male prostitutes at a brothel in Cleveland Street by night, homosexuals at the very highest levels of the British establishment were driven to seek sexual and social companionship through clandestine, illegal means. The Cleveland Street brothel's customers included many men of high rank, including Lord Arthur Somerset, the Prince of Wales's Equerry, and possibly even the Queen's grandson Prince Albert Victor, although no socially prominent men were prosecuted in the ensuing scandal, and Lord Arthur Somerset was allowed to flee to France.[11] The judicial failure to prosecute any of the high-ranking individuals at the heart of the Cleveland Street Scandal led to lingering resentment in the press and indirectly fueled Wilde's own prosecution five years later.[12] That Wilde had by 1895 become an active participant in this homosexual underworld is seen in the fact that, after failing to convict him at his first criminal trial (and after immediately declaring a mistrial), the Crown obtained Wilde's conviction at a second criminal trial by trying him alongside the procurer and purported brothel-keeper, Alfred Taylor. To his great credit, Taylor refused to mitigate his own sentence by turning witness against Wilde.

In the years leading up to his conviction, the Criminal Law Amendment Act cast its shadow over Wilde's life, just as it did over nearly everything he wrote. It profoundly affected the composition, publication, and critical reception of Wilde's only novel, *The Picture of Dorian Gray*. In the critical reaction to that novel in Britain in 1890, and especially in the suggestion of two reviewers who hinted that Wilde ought to be prosecuted for what he had written, one can hear the baying of the hounds who would chase Wilde to ground five years later. Significantly, *The Picture of Dorian Gray* was used in court against Wilde in 1895, both in the first of his two criminal trials and in the libel trial that preceded it. But it was not the Criminal Law Amendment Act alone that led to Wilde's criminal conviction. From one standpoint, the criminal conviction was self-inflicted, the result of an act of monumental hubris or perhaps willful self-destruction on Wilde's part.

––––––––

Wilde seems initially to have been attracted to artistic young men. During the period running roughly from 1887 to 1891, he pursued ever closer friendships with, among others, the actors Clyde Fitch and Harry Melvill, the stage designer and painter W. Graham Robertson, and the poets Richard Le Gallienne, George Kersley, André Raffalovich, and John Gray (who was widely understood to be the model for "Dorian" Gray). Evidence that there was a sexual basis to Wilde's intimacy with these men is speculative, although Wilde's surviving correspondence with some of them is certainly flirtatious and his sexual fascination can be easily inferred.[13] If he acted on this fascination, he was discreet, and his partners could be relied upon for their discretion too. But in 1891, his double life took a more dangerous turn when he met the brash, unpredictable, and frequently imprudent young aristocrat Lord Alfred Douglas, the youngest son of the ninth Marquess of Queensberry, who introduced the older Wilde to the dangerous and seductive world of male brothels and "rent boys." Wilde was to say in *De Profundis,* "They were to me the brightest of gilded snakes. Their poison was part of their perfection," as he unsparingly detailed how Douglas had "brought the element of Philistinism into a life that had been a complete protest against it" (*CL* 758–59).

Douglas harbored poetic aspirations too, and his literary abilities were both greater and of more direct relevance to Wilde's creativity than they are often held to be. By the summer of 1892, Wilde had fallen in love with Douglas, later telling him that his "slim gilt soul walks between passion and poetry" (*CL* 544). In one another's company, the two became increasingly open and reckless in their behavior, thrilling to the danger of their exploits, careless as to whether some of their more disreputable associates might later prove to be blackmailers too. "Sooner or later," says the blackmailer Mrs. Cheveley in Wilde's play *An Ideal Husband,* in words that were more prophetic than their author knew, "we all have to pay for what we do": if the truth about Wilde's "ideal husband" became publicly known, she says, he would "be hounded out of public life," made to disappear completely, and hypocritical journalists would gleefully drag his name through the mud by making it the centerpiece of leading articles and "the foulness of the public placard."[14] Rumors of Wilde's relationships with Douglas and other young men were already circulating when things came to a crisis in 1895.

Wilde's affair with Douglas—at times intense, passionate, petty, rhapsodic, tender, ill-tempered, and vituperative—was the defining love affair of his life, and it lasted well beyond his imprisonment. The Marquess of Queensberry ("Queensberry") had objected to the friendship between his son and the older Wilde almost from its inception, but from 1894 onward, as the two became inseparable and increasingly careless in their behavior, he threatened to "make a public scandal in a way you little dream of" if Douglas did not end the relationship.[15] In

LORD ALFRED DOUGLAS, AT THE AGE OF TWENTY-ONE, AT OXFORD

Lord Alfred Douglas, around the time Wilde first met him.

June 1894, taking the matter further, Queensberry had appeared un-announced at Wilde's house accompanied by a prizefighter and had to be forcibly ejected, and on February 14, 1895, on the opening night of *The Importance of Being Earnest,* Wilde got wind of and foiled Queensberry's attempt to enter the theater and publicly denounce Wilde from the stage. Four days later, making good on his threat to create a scandal, Queensberry left a calling card at Wilde's West End club on which he had scrawled "For Oscar Wilde, posing somdomite" (in his haste and spleen, Queensberry misspelled *sodomite*).

When the club porter handed Wilde Queensberry's card ten days later, Wilde was left reeling. He must have felt that Queensberry, having attempted to surprise him at his theatre and having already intruded on him in his family home, would never leave him alone. Sodomy (the ancient, biblically derived term for "unnatural" sex) was a criminal of-fence under both the 1885 Criminal Law Amendment Act and the 1861 Offences Against The Person Act.[16] Queensberry's hate-filled scrawl formed the legal basis for libel charges. Encouraged by Douglas and his older brother Percy, who both loathed their father and promised to assist Wilde with the costs, Wilde decided to prosecute Queensberry for criminal libel, in an effort to stop the virulent harassment once and for all. The decision was to prove a fateful and misguided one, and Douglas has sometimes been blamed for the wreckage that followed as a result. But it is important to note that in the run-up to the trial, and even before he made his decision to prosecute Queensberry, Wilde pos-sessed complete conviction in his own success. When pressed by André Gide about whether he knew what he risked, Wilde replied that he was determined to resist the calls of friends who advised prudence. "I don't see anything now but a criminal prosecution," Wilde determined within minutes of receiving Queensberry's fateful card (*CL* 634). ("The only thing for me to do now," says the lawbreaking protagonist of *An Ideal Husband,* when threatened with the public exposure of his crime, "is to fight the thing out . . . [using] any weapon I can find.")[17] Barely a week before the libel trial began, after consulting the fashionable fortune-teller Mrs. Robinson, Wilde felt certain of "complete triumph" (*CL* 636).

But Wilde had seriously misjudged his opponent. In advance of the libel trial, while Wilde and Douglas vacationed in Monte Carlo, Queensberry and his lawyers were employing private detectives to scour London's homosexual underworld to prove that Wilde was not merely a "posing" but a practicing "sodomite." Right up to the commencement of the libel trial, a number of close friends, including Frank Harris, George Bernard Shaw, and George Alexander, urged Wilde to abandon the prosecution. But Wilde's judgment was seriously impaired by his love for Douglas and by the virulence of Queensberry's persecution, and probably no one with the exception of Douglas—who was in no frame of mind to urge caution—could have dissuaded him from proceeding to court: "My whole life seems ruined by this man," he confessed to Ross on the night he read Queensberry's offensive card. "The tower of ivory is assailed by the foul thing. On the sand is my life spilt" (*CL* 634).

Wilde began his libel action in blasé fashion. He arrived at court in an expensive hired carriage (the unpaid bill, a hefty £2 5s 6d, survives among his bankruptcy papers at the UK National Archives), and on his way to court, according to the coachman, he stopped in St. James's Street to buy a "gayer tie."[18] When challenged by Queensberry's counsel, Sir Edward Carson, about his life and writings, Wilde at first thought he could rely on wit and obfuscation alone. But Carson, a brilliant courtroom lawyer, was playing a game of cat and mouse. In the "Plea of Justification" he filed with the court four days before the trial opened, Queensberry hinted at the devastating nature of the evidence his detectives had amassed. When Carson questioned Wilde about whether he had kissed a young male servant named Walter Grainger, prompting Wilde to reply with insouciance "Oh, no, he was a peculiarly plain boy . . . [and] unfortunately . . . very ugly," Carson seized his chance: he pressed Wilde repeatedly about why he had mentioned Grainger's ugliness and whether that was the reason he had not kissed him.[19] Wilde became flustered, confused, and suddenly realized that his wit was misplaced in court. On being confronted with Queensberry's more damaging evidence, he withdrew from his prosecution under advice from his lawyer, Sir Edward Clarke. Following Wilde's withdrawal, Queensberry's description of him as a "posing sodomite" was found by the court to be legally justified, or "true in fact," as well as "published . . . for the public benefit."[20]

By withdrawing from his libel suit, Wilde and his lawyers hoped to avert prosecution under the graver charges to which Queensberry's defense gave rise. Queensberry's evidence was passed immediately to the Director of Public Prosecutions, who later the same day issued a warrant for Wilde's arrest. It has been suggested by many commentators that the government intentionally dragged its feet in issuing an arrest warrant, to afford Wilde adequate time to flee the country. The basis for these suggestions is hearsay, and Wilde's grandson Merlin Holland, who recently edited and published an invaluable transcript of his grandfather's libel trial, finds them "absurd."[21] Certainly, following the collapse of the libel trial on April 5, 1895 at 11:15 a.m., Wilde must have anticipated his arrest as he "hurriedly left the building."[22] When advising his client to withdraw, Sir Edward Clarke had suggested to Wilde not merely that he risked arrest if he allowed the case to continue but also that his presence in court was not legally required. "I hoped and expected that he would take the opportunity of escaping from the country," Clarke later wrote, "and I believe he would have found no difficulty in doing so."[23] The arrest warrant was not issued till 4:55 p.m., and there was a lag of nearly ninety minutes before Wilde was arrested at London's Cadogan Hotel at 6:20 p.m., an event immortalized many years later in John Betjeman's poem "The Arrest of Oscar Wilde at the Cadogan Hotel."[24]

But Wilde was not a man to flee: as he put it to the *Evening News,* explaining his decision not to call Lord Alfred Douglas as a witness against his own father, he was "determined to bear on my own shoulders whatever ignominy and shame might result from prosecuting Lord

Queensberry" (*CL* 637). "I decided that it was nobler and more beautiful to stay," he told Douglas directly, adding "I did not want to be called a coward or a deserter" (*CL* 652). If imprisonment and personal ruin beckoned, they were worth enduring, or were at least endurable, by virtue of his love for Douglas. "If prison and dishonour be my destiny," he wrote to Douglas three weeks later, "my love for you and [the] . . . divine belief that you love me in return will sustain me in my unhappiness and will make me capable . . . of bearing my grief most patiently" (*CL* 646). "In my solitude you will be with me," he told Douglas five days before his conviction on May 25, 1895 (*CL* 651).

————

Until the day of the verdict and sentencing, Wilde put a brave face on the prospect of imprisonment. On the eve of the verdict "he was very fine," his friend and first biographer Robert Sherard says: "his face was calm" and his attitude was heroic.[25] Almost certainly, he still held an exalted and Romantic view of imprisonment: he had once written that "an unjust imprisonment for a noble cause strengthens as well as deepens the nature" while quoting approvingly the words his friend Wilfred Scawen Blunt had written upon being jailed in Kilmainham Prison in 1888, when his support for Irish Home Rule brought him into conflict with England's harsh new Perpetual Crimes Act: "Imprisonment is a reality of discipline most useful to the modern soul. . . . Like a sickness or a spiritual retreat, it purifies and ennobles; and the soul emerges from it stronger and more self-contained."[26]

But within days of his conviction and sentencing, Wilde began a downward spiral that would have far reaching effects, not just on himself personally, but on the administration of British prisons generally. He was imprisoned under the cruel and pitiless prison regime of "hard labour, hard board, and hard fare" mandated in 1877 by the incoming first chairman of the Prison Commission, Major-General Sir Edmund du Cane, following the centralization and standardization of British prisons in the Prison Acts of 1865 and 1877.[27] Even before Du Cane's appointment, the Victorian prison system had been harshly punitive:

in the 1840s, the so-called silent system and separate system, mandating that prisoners remain silent at all times and, still worse, be housed individually in separate cells, were adopted in English prisons. In theory both penal systems were designed to encourage reflection and penitence, but the separate system—ubiquitous in British prisons by the 1890s—amounted to solitary confinement for the full term of a prisoner's sentence, and it was a form of torture that drove many prisoners insane. In order to enforce the separate system, purpose-built penitentiaries were constructed throughout Britain in the 1840s and 1850s using Jeremy Bentham's panopticon as a blueprint. These contained long banks or "blocks" of individual cells arranged in multi-story galleries, radiating like the spokes of a wheel from a central hall: the very architecture was designed to prevent contact between prisoners while maximizing their close supervision by prison staff. (While the separate system has long been discredited, many of the prisons built to facilitate the system are still in use today.) Prisoners were often restricted to their cells for twenty-three hours a day; when parading the prison exercise yard for an hour each day, they were forbidden from communicating with one another, upon pain of further punishment, and in the early days of the system they wore a special mask when exercising or moving about the prison—termed by prisoners a *beak*—to prevent them from recognizing one another.[28] Even on Sundays at chapel, which all prisoners except Jews were mandated to attend, prisoners were kept separated from one another in individual stalls or cubicles. Chapel "was just part of one's punishment," remarked one prisoner: "if one looked either to the right or the left or attempted to whisper to another fellow it meant three days' bread and water in close confinement."[29]

Du Cane, who had seamlessly moved into prison administration after a military career, disbelieved that prisoners could be reformed or rehabilitated, and he took the severity of this regime to a new level, even for the smallest of offences.[30] Under his administration, the prisoner's diet was reduced to the minimum necessary to maintain life: in many cases just bread and thin gruel or "stirabout" (coarse meal, suet, greasy cocoa and water).[31] Du Cane also intensified the severity of hard labor by calculating the maximum that a man could endure walking a treadmill or turning a crank: in 1880, for instance, he mandated that prisoners sentenced to hard labor should ascend 8,640 feet daily on the treadmill, equivalent to six ascents of Chicago's Sears Tower, or that they turn the crank 10,000 times before receiving their final meal of the day.[32] In a particularly cruel extension of this torture, if an inmate was able to turn the crank with relative ease, the screw was tightened so that the work became harder—a practice that gave rise to the modern British slang term of *screw* for a prison warder. If a crank had not been installed in the prisoner's cell, particularly once the treadmill fell into disuse in the closing years of the nineteenth century, hard labor was often performed in the prisoner's own cell through such mind-numbing tasks as sewing mail sacks or "picking oakum" (separating out the strands of old tarry rope with the fingers alone). Prisoners spent their nights on hard plank beds that inevitably produced insomnia, not rest. For the first three months, books were banned except for a Bible, prayer-book, and hymn-book. Thereafter the prisoner might be allowed one book per week from the prison library, which generally consisted of third-rate theological works selected by the prison chaplain. Petty regulations confined the number of visitors (for twenty minutes each) or the writing and receiving of a letter to just once every three months, save in exceptional circumstances.[33] As the prison historian Sean McConville has written, Du Cane "fashioned . . . a national penology for the last quarter of the nineteenth century," refining and legitimizing dietary, labor, and living arrangements that amounted to "scarcely veiled torture."[34] The system—which was to be made more humane by Act of Parliament shortly after Wilde completed his sentence, partly as a result of Wilde's own imprisonment—was designed to break the spirit of even the toughest offenders, and mental breakdowns were a frequent occurrence.

Wilde was sentenced on a Saturday, and because he could not be transferred to a modern prison before the following Monday, he spent the weekend in the old Newgate Prison, adjacent to London's Central Criminal Court, where his trials had taken place. On Monday, May 27, 1895, he was driven through the massive arched entrance of Pentonville Prison in North London to serve his two-year sentence. Pentonville, conceived as a "penitentiary" and not simply a prison, had been constructed in 1842 as the model for future British penal institutions.[35] (Wandsworth and Reading Prisons, where Wilde spent later portions of his sentence, were both modelled on Pentonville.) Here the regime of silence, separateness, and hard labor was enforced by a body of uniformed warders who patrolled the prison's four radiating cellblock wings via a labyrinthine network of cast-iron walkways.

Upon arrival at Pentonville, Wilde was immediately subjected to a number of personal indignities. First his head was shaved to a short stubble. Before his conviction, Wilde had spent substantial amounts of time and money on his renowned and photogenic head of hair, but it took the prison barber just two minutes to cut all the locks off. As a result, one journalist wrote at the time, Wilde now presented "an awful sight, more like a well-to-do butcher who has served a sentence for fraud than the great dramatic genius of the nineteenth century."[36] He was next stripped, weighed, made to get into a filthy bath in which other prisoners had already bathed, and then dressed in the coarse regulation prison-dress, with its distinguishing broad arrows, before being subjected to a medical examination certifying him fit for "first-class hard labour," which meant six hours daily on the treadmill.[37] Like other new prisoners, he was then administered a dose of potassium bromide (a crude sedative, "said to produce in some people extreme melancholia," whose side-effects included nausea and vomiting) and taken to a poorly ventilated, dimly lit cell measuring thirteen feet long by seven wide, containing nothing more than a plank bed, blanket, hard pillow, small table, and small tin chamber pot, which the prisoner was allowed to empty three times per day (but not between the "lock-up" hours of 5:00 p.m. and 5:00 a.m.).[38] Since the prison diet consisted mostly of thin gruel or "stirabout" and prisoners were often subject to diarrhea,

Pentonville Prison, treadmill, 1895.

the stench was frequently overwhelming, and it was not uncommon for warders to be violently sick in the mornings when opening the cells for inspection.

Wilde was to spend longer parts of his sentence in other English prisons, as we shall shortly see, but he never forgot the shock of arriving at Pentonville. "At first it was a fiendish nightmare," he told his friend and biographer Frank Harris,

> more horrible than anything I had ever dreamt of; from the first evening when they made me undress before them and get into some filthy water they called a bath and dry myself with a damp, brown rag and put on this livery of shame. The cell was appalling: I could hardly breathe in it, and the food turned my stomach; the smell and sight of it were enough: I did not eat anything for days and days, I

could not even swallow the bread; and the rest of the food was uneatable; I lay on the so-called bed and shivered all night long. . . . After some days I got so hungry I had to eat a little, nibble at the outside of the bread, and drink some of the liquid; whether it was tea, coffee or gruel, I could not tell. As soon as I really ate anything it produced violent diarrhea and I was ill all day and all night. From the beginning I could not sleep. I grew weak and had wild delusions. . . . The hunger made you weak . . . but the inhumanity was the worst of it; what devilish creatures men are. I had never known anything about them. I had never dreamt of such cruelties.[39]

Within days of his arrival at Pentonville, the British press was reporting that Wilde's condition was rapidly deteriorating and that prison officials were becoming anxious on his account. The *Daily Chronicle* and *The Pall Mall Gazette,* citing the same agency report, reported early in June that Wilde had become violently insane, while *The Morning* clarified that Wilde suffered from acute diarrhea followed by "mental prostration and melancholy," that he had been taken off the treadmill, and was "in such a bad state that he was removed to the infirmary" for a while.[40] Although *The Morning* went on to claim, on the word of the prison doctor, that Wilde's condition was "improving daily," that he had been reassigned only to "second-class hard labour" (i.e., oakum picking), and that he was "treated . . . with the greatest kindness and consideration," these press reports alarmed those in the highest echelons of the British establishment.

Following a series of incendiary articles in the *Daily Chronicle* in early 1894, the cruelty of Victorian prisons had recently been exposed to public light by the Gladstone Committee, set up to inquire into the failures of the prison system, under the chairmanship of Herbert Gladstone, MP, the son of the Liberal leader. The Committee's report of April 1895 had recommended a raft of reforms, causing Du Cane immediately to resign as chair of the Prison Commission. Press accounts of Wilde's deterioration threatened to increase the pressure on already defensive prison administrators, politicians, and government officials. "Please inquire whether there is any foundation for the statement in today's *Chronicle*," inquired the home secretary, Herbert Asquith, on June 5, "that Oscar Wilde . . . has become mentally disordered."[41] As the scholar Montgomery Hyde points out, Asquith had known Wilde during the heyday of his social success—he had been Wilde's host on at least one occasion—so his alarm was motivated at least partly by personal concern. Asquith's inquiry was referred to the prison doctor at Pentonville, who replied formally that Wilde "has not been in hospital or padded cell, and has given no anxiety to any of the officials here," and that "with the exception of a little relaxed throat, for which he has been treated, he is in good health and perfectly sane."[42] That this was far from the case, subsequent events would prove. "Prison doctors have no knowledge of mental disease of any kind," Wilde was to write shortly after his release: "They are as a class ignorant men. The pathology of the mind is unknown to them" (*CL* 854).

A more significant reaction to the press reports of Wilde's insanity came from the Liberal statesman Richard Haldane, QC, MP. Haldane was a man of strong independent mind, widely respected throughout the British establishment, who would later be war minister and twice lord chancellor, being created a viscount in 1911. Like Asquith, he had known Wilde in the days of his social success, but more importantly he had been an active member of the Gladstone Committee and possessed a special warrant allowing his entry into any English prison. He later wrote that "he was haunted by the idea of what this highly sensitive man was probably suffering under ordinary prison treatment."[43] Haldane duly visited Wilde in Pentonville in mid-June to ascertain Wilde's state of mind for himself.[44] At first, Wilde refused to speak, but when Haldane put his hand on Wilde's shoulder, reminded him that they were once acquaintances, and promised to try to obtain books and writing materials, Wilde burst into tears. In the course of the ensuing discussion, Haldane suggested that prison might prove a blessing for Wilde's career "for he had got a great subject."[45]

Haldane seems to have reassured himself and other officials about Wilde's sanity for the time being. But there were two more significant upshots to Haldane's visit. That Wilde sent a copy of *The Ballad of Reading Gaol* to Haldane upon its publication in 1898, one year after his release from prison, shows that the visit was instrumental in Wilde's subsequent efforts to turn his prison experiences to profitable literary and political use: the poem "was the redemption of his promise to me," Haldane later wrote.[46] As important, and more immediate, Haldane's success in procuring books saved Wilde's sanity and established an important precedent in the eyes of prison administrators, who would allow Wilde the privilege of further books and eventually writing materials later in his sentence. Haldane immediately arranged for Wilde to be sent fifteen volumes, including Augustine's *Confessions* and *De Civitate Dei,* Pascal's *Pensées,* Newman's *Apologia Pro Vita Sua* and *Grammar of Assent,* Mommsen's five-volume *History of Rome,* and Pater's *Renaissance,* while another ten volumes, including multiple works by Walter Pater, were to follow in September.

The effect of these gifts on the prisoner's life was profound and immediate. From a literary standpoint, Newman, Augustine, and Pascal constituted important models for the long confessional letter that Wilde was to compose in the last six months of his sentence, which would be published in redacted form five years after his death under the title *De Profundis.* But the psychological and emotional effects of Haldane's gift were at least as important. For a man of Wilde's intellect, exercising the mind and the imagination was no less important than the fresh air in the prison yard. It was with good reason that Wilde later wrote that an adequate supply of good books was critical for every prisoner's mental health: "Deprived of books," Wilde would observe in 1898, "of all human intercourse, isolated from every humane and humanizing influence . . . treated like an unintelligible animal . . . the wretched man who is confined in an English prison can hardly escape becoming insane" (*CL* 1047).

After Haldane's visit in mid-June, Wilde adjusted somewhat to the conditions at Pentonville. But suddenly, on June 25, the prison commissioners ordered Wilde be transferred across London to Wandsworth Prison on the south bank of the Thames. The transfer took place on July 4, 1895. It has been suggested that concern for Wilde's wellbeing was the motivation for the move, and that "the Prison Commissioners may have thought Wilde would benefit from these new surroundings."[47] The chaplain at Wandsworth, the Rev. William Douglas Morrison, author of a number of books of criminology as well as one of the incendiary articles that prompted the government to form the Gladstone Committee, was one of the leading critics of the existing system. The scholar Montgomery Hyde thinks that Haldane and the prison commissioners "may have wished to bring Wilde into touch with this clergyman, on whom they could rely to keep a particular eye on him."[48] But a more compelling reason for the transfer may have been that, rightly or wrongly, the home secretary suspected the warders at Pentonville were unduly influenced by Wilde's friends on the outside to grant him preferential treatment.[49]

Whatever the reasons for the transfer, Wilde found life at Wandsworth far more difficult to bear. "At Wandsworth I thought I should go mad," he told Frank Harris: "I could not sleep, I grew weak and had wild delusions. . . . Wandsworth is the worst. No dungeon in hell could be worse."[50] The food, worse than at Pentonville, "even smelt bad [and] was not fit for dogs." "While I was in Wandsworth I longed to die," he later wrote (*CL* 735): "it was my one desire." Possibly Wilde's deterioration at Wandsworth owed something to the crushing news that he would be a bankrupt when he emerged from prison: he was served with a bankruptcy notice just prior to his removal to Wandsworth, shortly after the Marquess of Queensberry had instigated bankruptcy proceedings against him to recover his heavy legal costs. Possibly it owed something as well to his apprehension that his wife would petition him for divorce and that he would thereby lose custody of his children. In September 1895, when Constance paid the first of her two painful prison visits, Wilde swore that he had "been mad the last three years" and that "if he saw Lord A[lfred Douglas] he would kill him," whereupon Constance temporarily shelved plans for divorce and promised Wilde that he might rejoin herself and the children upon release.[51] "I cannot refuse to him the forgiveness that he has asked," she explained to a friend.[52] But Wilde must have known unconsciously that he could never again be a husband to Constance, and before his jail sentence was over, the marriage would break down irretrievably.

Another visitor to Wandsworth that September, Wilde's old friend (and later biographer) the journalist Robert Harborough Sherard, brought more unwelcome news. Lord Alfred Douglas was on the point of publishing a defense of Wilde, titled "On the Case of Mr. Oscar Wilde," in the Parisian monthly magazine *Mercure de France.* He planned to quote extensively from Wilde's most intimate and personal letters to him. Douglas hoped to prove to the world that Wilde's love for himself was pure and noble, but such a defense could only do more harm than good, especially given the apparent reconciliation between Wilde and his wife. We must keep in mind that Wilde's earlier correspondence with Douglas had been used against him in his legal trials, and before that by blackmailers, as a direct result of Douglas's carelessness in handling it. "The gibbet on which I swing in history now is high enough," Wilde wrote: "there is no need that he of all men should for his own vanity make it more hideous" (*CL* 666). As Wilde later put it in *De Profundis,* "I was greatly taken aback, and much annoyed, and gave orders that the thing was to be stopped at once" (*CL* 716). Sherard conveyed Wilde's wishes to the editor of the *Mercure de France,* who in turn wrote to Douglas asking him to omit the letters. This Douglas refused to do, preferring instead to withdraw the entire defense from publication.[53]

If Douglas had been allowed to proceed as planned, there is little doubt he would have made matters worse for Wilde personally.

Whether the prison authorities intended it or not, Morrison, the reform-minded chaplain, took a great deal of concerned interest in Wilde. "He is now quite crushed and broken," Morrison reported privately to Haldane on September 11: "This is unfortunate, as a prisoner who breaks down in one direction generally breaks down in several. . . . Some of our most experienced officers openly say that they don't think he will be able to go through the whole two years."[54] After a few weeks, "it was easy to see that this man would break down long before his sentence came to an end," Morrison later wrote, "He was losing flesh, he was refusing food, his face was assuming a deathly pallor; he was presenting all the symptoms of an approaching crisis."[55] Sherard, who could find nobody willing to accompany him to visit Wilde in prison ("everybody was unfortunately engaged"), records that Wilde's hands were disfigured and his nails broken and bleeding from picking oakum.[56] By mid-September 1895, Wilde had lost about thirty-two pounds since his initial incarceration, on remand, at Holloway Prison the previous April.[57]

————

By the time he appeared at his first bankruptcy hearing on September 24, he was nearing a complete breakdown. "I was very much shocked at his appearance," reported his trustee and friend Arthur Clifton, who had been present at the hearing: "he looked dreadfully thin . . . and he was very much upset and cried a good deal; he seemed quite broken-hearted, and kept on describing his punishment as savage . . . and said several times that he did not think he would be able to last the punishment out."[58] About ten days later, on a Sunday, utterly weakened by sleeplessness, illness, and semi-starvation, Wilde could no longer get out of bed. Accused by the prison doctor of malingering and threatened with punishment "if you don't get up," he forced himself to rise and dress, only to fall repeatedly.[59] Eventually he made it to the prison chapel for the mandatory prayer service and homily, but there he lost consciousness again, in a fall that did painful and lasting damage to his ear. He awoke with his ear in pain in an infirmary cell, where he was visited by the kindly Morrison but remained isolated from other prisoners. A week later he was transferred to the infirmary ward, where he had the company of other sick prisoners, and remained there until his transfer to Reading in the penultimate week of November.

On November 12 Robert Ross, as one of Wilde's trustees, was allowed a brief interview at the second of Wilde's bankruptcy hearings. "Physically he was worse than anyone had led me to believe," Ross reported. "Indeed I really should not have known him at all. This I know is a figure of speech, but it exactly described what I experienced. His clothes hung about him in loose folds and his hands are like those of a skeleton. The colour of his cheeks is completely changed [and] his slight beard . . . only hides the appalling sunken cheeks. . . . I cannot understand how any human nation . . . can keep him in this condition. He is still in the infirmary, but told me . . . he hoped to die very soon [while] . . . every other subject caused him to break down."[60]

Meanwhile, news of Wilde's deteriorating condition had leaked to the press, causing further consternation to the prison authorities. On September 27, the *Daily Chronicle* reported Wilde's poor health and weight loss, finding these symptomatic of "the way in which our prison system destroys the mind and enfeebles the body of its victims," and on October 15, the same paper reported that Wilde was in the infirmary, stoking fears that the great playwright had suffered a mental collapse. Among government and prison officials, these fears were exacerbated by Morrison's report, in his letter to Haldane of September 11, that Wilde was masturbating in his cell or, as Morrison put it, "perverse sexual practices are again getting the mastery of him."[61]

The upshot was that, in late-September and October of 1895, a series of official inquiries into Wilde's mental and physical condition were undertaken. The first of these, by D. H. M. Gover, the medical inspector to prisons and a trusted lieutenant to Du Cane, brusquely refuted

Morrison's observations, asserting "there is not the slightest reason to suppose that Wilde is 'yielding to perverse sexual practices.' On the contrary . . . under the prison regime he is becoming altogether more healthy, both in body and mind." Gover's report appears to have initially satisfied Sir Evelyn Ruggles-Brise, who had replaced Du Cane as chairman of the prison commissioners the previous April, but it was strongly refuted by Haldane, who commented that upon recently visiting Wilde in Wandsworth, he had been much struck by Wilde's deterioration since he had last seen him in Pentonville. As far as Gover's official assertions of Wilde's good health went, "I myself was painfully struck by the exact contrary." Haldane reported to Ruggles-Brise, "I should think, judging as a layman," he continued, "that his mind is showing symptoms of danger. His utterance was indistinct and confused . . . and he was extremely depressed." It was clear to Haldane that "Dr. Gover has been so set up that he [*sic*] is not a reliable judgment. . . . If you are examining Wilde's condition further, it would be best to have it done by an outsider of eminence in mental disease, who would form his own judgment."[62] Furthermore, if the commissioners were truly concerned to help Wilde, he might be allowed writing materials after a time, the governor keeping what he wrote till his release, since "this would help him most . . . settling him to the occupation which could be of use to him."

Haldane's retort to Gover, along with the press accounts of Wilde's condition, caused yet more consternation at the Home Office. The immediate consequence was that two leading forensic psychologists, David Nicholson (medical superintendent of the state criminal lunatic asylum at Broadmoor) and Richard Brayn (governor and medical officer of the female convict prison at Woking, and later Nicholson's successor as medical superintendent at Broadmoor), were dispatched to Wandsworth to make a fresh, thoroughgoing, independent report. They examined Wilde on October 22, 1895 and reported to the home secretary a week later that they found no indication of mental disease or derangement, that Wilde's "present bodily condition is satisfactory," that Wilde had been treated with "judicious care" at Wandsworth, and that "any to-kens of mental depression . . . [are] due to the natural and not unhealthy operation of circumstances, and to the existence of a limited circle of thoughts which are unusually active in their character."[63] Medically speaking, there was no cause for alarm and Wilde suffered under no form of depressive illness. But it was Nicholson and Brayn's recommendations for Wilde's future treatment that were most striking: "under the circumstances" it might be best to transfer Wilde to "a suitable prison in the country or away from London," especially since "a country prison would suit well for insisting on the prisoner taking outdoor exercise with some garden work"; a cell "larger than the usual size" would be preferable; he should be assigned a "variation of employment" such as "bookbinding or other work . . . enabling the time to pass in a less uninteresting way than a man brooding on his past," and there should be "a continuation of such minor relaxations of the full rigour and discipline of prison life as have already been sanctioned, especially should a freer range of books be allowed and a larger supply."[64]

Given their generally positive conclusions about Wilde's present state of health, as well the role of the press in exacerbating concern for Wilde's health, it appears that Nicholson and Brayn were recommending a transfer to a country prison and a relaxation of the prison rules for mainly political reasons. Wilde was already a poster-boy for the inhumanity of the existing system, and a move to a small country prison would place him out of sight of London-based journalists and prison-reformers. (The proposal to move Wilde to a country prison had in fact been first mooted by a senior official of the Home Office as early as October 1.) Whatever the medical advantages of such a move, "there were distinct secondary advantages for Oscar to be placed in a smaller country prison," and the forensic psychologists' report made the move an easy one to defend administratively.[65] Three weeks after Nicholson and Brayn filed their report, Wilde was transferred to the small regional prison at Reading, in Berkshire, where he was to serve out the remainder of his sentence and where, in the relieved words of Ruggles-Brise to the home secretary, "suitable occupation in the way of gardening and bookbinding and library work will be found for him." Shortly before Wilde's arrival there, Lieutenant-Colonel Henry Isaacson, the governor of Reading, wrote, "I shall be very glad to do anything I can to carry out the Commissioners' wishes as regards prisoner Oscar Wilde."[66]

But if anybody expected the move to Reading to lead to a general improvement in Wilde's mind and wellbeing, they were sorely mistaken. First, there was the move itself, described by biographer Richard Ellmann as "the single most humiliating experience of Wilde's prison life."[67] As Wilde memorably relates in *De Profundis,* on November 20, 1895 he was taken, handcuffed and in prison clothing, from Wandsworth to nearby Clapham Junction Station, to await the next train for Reading: "From two o'clock till half-past two . . . I had to stand on the centre platform . . . in convict dress and handcuffed, for the world to look at. I had been taken out of the Hospital Ward without a moment's notice being given to me. Of all possible objects I was the most grotesque. When people saw me they laughed. Each train as it came up swelled the audience. Nothing could exceed their amusement. That was of course before they knew who I was. As soon as they had been informed, they laughed still more. For half an hour I stood there in the grey November rain surrounded by a jeering mob."[68] The man who loudly informed the mob of his identity, Wilde told Robert Sherard, stepped up to the handcuffed prisoner and spat in his face. In the words of Robert Sherard, this was "a cruel outrage which . . . lent the bitterness of death to that journey."[69] "For a year after that was done to me I wept every day at the same hour and for the same space of time," Wilde was to write (*CL* 757).

Wilde arrived at Reading so traumatized that the prison governor promised Wilde he would not be submitted to so terrible an experience again under any circumstances, and Wilde later anxiously petitioned the home secretary, toward the very end of his sentence, requesting that he not be transferred to another prison prior to his release. But his trauma was not due to the transfer alone. The previous day had seen the official conclusion of Wilde's bankruptcy proceedings, in the course of which details of his reckless extravagance had been exposed to public light. "Step by step with the Bankruptcy Receiver I had to go over every item of my life. It was horrible," he later wrote, recalling bitterly that he had spent "£5000 in actual money" (roughly equivalent to $700,000 or £460,000 today) on Lord Alfred Douglas alone (*CL* 688). Wilde knew by this time that his life-interest in his wife's marriage settlement was to be sold by the official receiver as one of his assets. The sale would become a bone of bitter contention between Wilde's representatives and Constance, contributing ultimately to the couple's legal separation, but even at this date Wilde knew that he must relinquish his legal rights over his children and a share in his wife's property if he was to avoid painful divorce proceedings.

When Robert Sherard visited Wilde at Reading, roughly two weeks after his arrival there, he was shocked at what he found: "it was a painful interview in a degrading setting. He was in a kind of rabbit-hutch, over which wire-grating was nailed, as though for the caging of an animal. . . . The hutch was almost in complete darkness, and of my friend's presence I perceived little beyond his hesitating and husky voice."[70] It was at this meeting that Sherard informed Wilde that his wife and children had relinquished his name and taken the surname *Holland*. All through the winter following Sherard's visit, Wilde's ear ached and discharged fluid, and although it was syringed on three occasions for the purposes of examination, the prison doctor was either unable or unwilling to recognize that Wilde suffered from an underlying medical condition, which would ultimately contribute to his death from meningoencephalitis five years later. When Frank Harris asked him nine months later why the prison authorities didn't give him some cotton wool or something to put in it, Wilde replied, "If you think one dare disturb a doctor or a warder for an earache, you don't know much about prison. You would pay for it."[71]

At Christmas he gathered himself sufficiently to write "a very beautiful letter" to his mother.[72] Two months later, in February 1896,

Constance made a special trip from her new home near Genoa, Italy, to break the news that his beloved mother had died. "Her death was so terrible to me," Wilde later wrote, "that I, once a lord of language, have no words in which to express my anguish and my shame. . . . She and my father had bequeathed me a name they had made noble and honoured not merely in Literature, Art, Archaeology and Science, but in the public history of my own country in its evolution as a nation. I had disgraced that name eternally. I had made it a low byword among low people. I had dragged it through the very mire. I had given it to brutes that they might make it brutal, and to fools that they might turn it into a synonym for folly. What I suffered then, and still suffer, is not for pen to write or paper to record" (*CL* 721).

Bankruptcy, illness, grief, and the threat of divorce exacerbated the torments of the separate system, but Wilde's sufferings in his first eight months at Reading were made worse by the prison governor, Lieutenant-Colonel Henry Isaacson—like Du Cane, an ex-army officer—whom Wilde was later to describe, after Tennyson, as "a mulberry-faced dictator" (*CL* 983). Isaacson was "not able to enjoy his breakfast unless someone was punished before he ate it," Wilde related after his release.[73] "I am perpetually being punished for nothing," Wilde told Harris seven months after his transfer to Reading: "this governor loves to punish, and he punishes by taking my books away from me."[74] Wilde's testimony is borne out by numerous other accounts of Isaacson as well as by the number of punishments awarded by Isaacson for petty breaches of prison regulations, a number that fell by two-thirds under his immediate successor.[75] One of Wilde's warders later recorded that, for at least the first eight months of his incarceration in Reading Prison, "all the rigours of the system were applied to him relentlessly," and that Wilde "had to pick his quantity of oakum . . . [and] turn the monotonous crank, along with his fellows."[76] Another testified that Wilde was "no good for anything," that he failed to accomplish even the most basic tasks, and that he "seldom followed the prison regulations with regard to scrupulously cleansing his cell daily."[77] Many prison rules were made with no other object than to be broken, one of Wilde's warders later said, so that an excuse might be found for inflicting additional punishments such as the withdrawal of Wilde's reading privileges, the restriction of his already limited diet to just coarse bread and water, or an increase in the required amount of hard labor.[78] But these were not the worst additional punishments: "there is a punishment here more terrible than the rack," Wilde told Frank Harris. "[T]hey can drive you mad in a week." Harris understood Wilde to be alluding to solitary confinement in a darkened cell, a punishment "as terrible as any of the tortures of the past."[79]

By the first anniversary of his imprisonment, in May 1896, Wilde's physical condition was no better than at Wandsworth in October 1895; psychologically it was far worse. During a joint visit from Robert Ross and Sherard that month, he cried the whole time and hardly talked at all. Asked by Ross to list his complaints, Wilde replied "they treat me cruelly," that the doctor was very unkind to him, that he had only been admitted to the infirmary for two days in six months, and that he was not allowed pencil or paper.[80] "Did we think his brain seemed all right?" Ross records Wilde poignantly asking. During this visit, Ross and Sherard broke the news that Douglas was going to dedicate to Wilde his first volume of poems, to be published in France by the *Mercure de France.* Wilde found this prospect "revolting and grotesque" (*CL* 654), doubtless in part because he still harbored hopes of reconciling with his wife. He instructed Ross to write at once to Douglas saying he must do nothing of the kind. Douglas must surrender also any letters or gifts from Wilde in his possession: "the thought that they are in his hands is horrible to me. . . . If I get out of this loathsome place I know that there is nothing before me but a life of a pariah—of disgrace and penury and contempt—but at least I will have nothing to do with him nor allow him to come near me" (*CL* 654–55). Wilde's eyes were horribly vacant during the interview, recorded Ross, and he had lost a great deal of hair, while Sherard, who had visited Wilde at Reading the previous winter, "was nearly breaking down all the time and . . . was much shocked by the change for the worse." "He is simply wasting and pining away," concluded Ross. "I should be less surprised to hear of Oscar's death than Aubrey Beardsley's and you know what he looks like."[81] Sherard concurred: "His state under the circumstances is really alarming."[82]

By the middle of 1896, Wilde's condition had come to such a pass that something had to be done. Wilde's friend Frank Harris, editor of *The Saturday Review* and ex-editor of the highly respected *Fortnightly Review* (in which he had published Wilde's "Pen, Pencil, and Poison," "The Soul of Man Under Socialism," and Wilde's artistic credo, the aphoristic Preface to *The Picture of Dorian Gray*), was so alarmed by Ross's and Sherard's accounts of their visit that he sought an interview with Ruggles-Brise, the new chairman of the Prison Commission. Ruggles-Brise, who has been called "the very model of a Victorian public servant," was more liberal and reform-minded than his predecessor, the draconian Edmund Du Cane.[83] To Harris's surprise and gratification, Ruggles-Brise immediately dispatched Harris to Reading to ascertain how Wilde was being treated for himself and to make recommendations to the commission upon his return.

Harris interviewed Wilde at Reading on June 16, 1896, out of earshot of any warders, where Wilde movingly recounted the cruelty of his treatment, though not without fear that Isaacson would punish him if Harris were to report what he had told him. "They punish me on every pretext," Wilde told Harris, and "want to make my life here one long misery."[84] Wilde, "beside himself with dread," insisted that Harris treat his revelations as confidential and purely private.[85] According to his own account, Harris assured Wilde that his treatment would change as a result, that "you shall not be harassed every moment by punishment" and that "you shall have books and things to write with." Whilst at the prison, Harris also met with Isaacson, who bragged that he was "knocking the nonsense out of Wilde," as well as with the prison doctor.[86] He later wrote that from this meeting with the two prison officials, he learned for the first time "the full, incredible meaning of 'man's inhumanity to man.' "[87] Much affected, Harris made his report to a sympathetic Ruggles-Brise upon returning to London, in the express hope that it would contribute to changes to the manner of Wilde's treatment. Without some radical change in his treatment, Wilde would surely lose his mind.

2

From the Depths

H ARRIS'S VISIT OF June 1896 was a turning point in Wilde's treatment during his two years in prison; it contributed at least partly to changes in Wilde's circumstances that in turn enabled him to consider the prospect of exile, poverty, and isolation upon his release with something approaching equanimity. Wilde would later write that, had he been released around the time of Harris's visit, he would have "left this place loathing it and every official in it with a bitterness of hatred that would have poisoned my life" (*CL* 754). But the changes that ensued in the wake of Harris's visit ensured Wilde completed the remainder of his sentence in a very different spirit. The immediate result was that, at Harris's prompting, Wilde drafted the first and lengthiest of several petitions to the home secretary seeking an early release.

One of the most remarkable documents he composed during his imprisonment, running to nearly two thousand words, the petition is Wilde's first effort while in jail to take stock of his life as a whole and project a possible future. It begins by observing that, while he had no wish to palliate the "terrible offences" of which he had "rightly been found guilty," those offences were "forms of sexual madness" and "diseases to be cared for by a physician, rather than crimes to be punished by a judge" (*CL* 656). Eminent men of science—here Wilde cited the work of the criminologist Cesare Lombroso and the Austro-Hungarian medic and cultural critic Max Nordau—"specially insisted on . . . the intimate connection between madness and the literary and aesthetic temperament." For three years prior to his conviction, he had been one of the intellectual luminaries of Europe, his plays staged throughout Europe, North America, and Australia, but the entire time he was "suffering from the most horrible form of erotomania, which made him forget his wife and children, his high social position . . . his European distinction as an artist, the honour of his name and family, his very humanity itself." Wilde now feared, he wrote, that "this insanity," which had before been "confined to one portion of his nature" and displayed itself "in monstrous sexual perversion," might presently extend to his "entire nature and intellect" were his imprisonment to continue along the same lines (*CL* 657).

Wilde went on to detail the privations and torments he suffered in prison. The fearful system of solitary cellular confinement "without human intercourse of any kind, without writing materials . . . without suitable and sufficient books" was torture to a man of his education, creativity, and imagination. He was conscious of the privilege extended to him the previous summer, as a result of Haldane's intervention, of being allowed two books a week to read. But "the prison library . . . hardly contains a score of books suitable for an educated man" and "the books kindly added at the prisoner's request he has read and re-read till they have become almost meaningless to him" (*CL* 657). Horrible as all the physical privations of modern prison life are, "they are nothing compared to the entire privation of literature to one to whom Literature was once the first thing of life, the mode by which perfection could be realized, by which, and by which alone, the intellect could feel itself alive" (*CL* 657). The mind is forced to think, Wilde went on, but "when it is deprived of the conditions necessary for healthy intellectual activity, such as books, writing materials, companionship, [and] contact with the living world . . . it becomes . . . the sure prey of morbid passions, and obscene fancies, and thoughts that defile, desecrate and destroy." And thus "vices live on," making "their dwelling house in him who by horrible mischance or fate has become their victim . . . embedded in his flesh . . . spread over him like a leprosy . . . feed[ing] on him like a strange disease" so that they become "an essential part of the man" and "no remorse however poignant can drive them out" (*CL* 658). If the justice system truly wanted Wilde to repudiate the "insanity" for which he had been convicted, Wilde implied, the administration of his punishment was hardly conducive to this end.

He had borne all this for more than a year, but he could bear it no longer, he said. Convinced that his reason would be permanently wrecked otherwise, the prisoner begged the home secretary "that his sentence may be remitted now, so that he may be taken abroad by his friends and . . . put . . . under medical care so that the sexual insanity from which he suffers may be cured" and "balance . . . restored to a shaken mind" (*CL* 658). He entreated the home secretary to seek expert opinion from recognized medical authorities on the effects of silence and isolation "on one already suffering from sexual monomania or a terrible character" (*CL* 659). He ended his appeal by detailing the inadequate medical treatment he had received in Reading Prison for the painful and persistent ear condition he had mentioned to Harris and for the marked deterioration in his eyesight that had resulted from living, working, and reading in semidarkness.

These self-representations need to be taken with caution, given their intended recipient and the urgency with which Wilde needed to plead his case, but even so this petition is a remarkable document. On the surface, Wilde repudiates the crimes for which he had been imprisoned as forms of madness, perversion, and monomania. (In admitting to a "monstrous sexual perversion," he echoes the tragic hero of his story "The Birthday of the Infanta," a love-besotted and kindly dwarf—a "misshapen thing that Nature . . . had fashioned for others to mock at"—whose generous heart breaks when he realizes that he is himself the "grotesque monster" whose face leers at him from a mirror.)[1] But the petition is hardly one of repentance, and Wilde subtly, even defiantly, alludes to the inescapable and essential aspects of his sexuality while

Reading Prison, c. 1900.

implicating the justice system by implying that the solitary and isolated nature of Victorian imprisonment turns the mind in on itself and hardens any existing tendency to "sexual perversity." Even still, the document eloquently testifies to the effects of solitary and silent confinement while implicitly condemning the lack of attentive care he had received under Isaacson's governorship at Reading. Most important, perhaps, it shows that the wish to die was no longer Wilde's "one desire." Wilde now imagined a possible future for himself, albeit as an exile much weakened and debilitated by the painful experience of prison.

Before dispatching Wilde's petition to Ruggles-Brise, Isaacson requested and attached a short, fresh medical report in which the prison doctor asserted, "The health of the prisoner . . . has improved considerably since he came to Reading" and "I see no . . . evidence of his mind giving way." Upon receipt of both documents and realizing that he needed independent advice, Ruggles-Brise dispatched the Visiting Committee, a statutory body of five officials charged with inspecting conditions in British prisons, to visit Reading and ascertain the truth for themselves. On July 10, 1896, following an official visit to Reading, this committee reported that Wilde was being well treated and that they saw no danger of his becoming insane, though they suggested that an expert medical inquiry into Wilde's case be held nonetheless, including a thoroughgoing examination of his hearing and eyesight. Wilde was later to write that "no prisoner has ever had the smallest relief, or attention, or care from any of the official visitors. The visitors arrive not to help the prisoners, but to see that the rules are carried out. Their object in coming is to ensure the enforcement of a foolish and inhuman code" (*CL* 1045). The home secretary evidently considered acting on the visitors' recommendation of an expert medical inquiry, but first Wilde's file was forwarded to David Nicholson, who had visited Wilde at Wandsworth and who was now officially the lord chancellor's visitor in lunacy. Nicholson, who did not visit Wilde this time and instead judged his case simply on the paperwork, responded "there is no indication of insanity or approaching insanity," and it was "hardly necessary to call in further medical assistance at present."[2] He advised the home secretary against establishing an independent medical inquiry, whereupon the visitors' recommendation was dropped.

But Wilde had made much in his petition of his intellectual suffering and his need for books and writing materials, implying that by such means he might once again be restored to literary creativity. To this element of his petition, Nicholson, like Haldane before him, responded positively—indeed he and Brayn had themselves advised the previous October that Wilde be allowed a freer range and a larger supply of books. So he advised the home secretary "it would be well to give him increased and exceptional facilities as to books and writing materials."[3] The upshot was that, while Wilde received no official reply to his petition, and his plea for an early release fell on deaf ears,[4] Ruggles-Brise instructed the governor of Reading Prison on July 27 to provide Wilde with foolscap paper, pen, and ink, "for use in his leisure moments in his cell," and also to ask Wilde "to name any work with which he desires to be provided."[5] More generally, the governor was instructed to relax in Wilde's case the rules limiting the issue of books to two per week and to "use your discretion as to allowing to the prisoner sufficient books to occupy his mind, always provided that any indulgence granted in this respect is not extravagant, and does not interfere with the ordinary labour required of the prisoner in fulfillment of his sentence." In addition, the prison medical officer was authorized to obtain an outside second opinion, so that the prognosis for Wilde's eyesight and hearing could be confirmed.

These instructions were dispatched to Reading Prison, where Wilde speedily drew up a list of possible new book acquisitions, including a Greek Testament, Milman's *History of the Jews,* Farrar's *St. Paul,* a prose translation of Dante's *Divine Comedy,* Renan's *Vie de Jésus* (in French), essays by Newman, Carlyle, and Emerson, and poetry by Tennyson, Keats, Chaucer, Spenser, and Marlowe. The list was vetted and approved on July 29, 1896, not by Isaacson but by the far more kindly and humane Major James O. Nelson, who had replaced Isaacson as governor a few days prior. As Ashley Robins writes, the timing of Isaacson's replacement suggests that "the Prison Commissioners engineered the switch in governorship because they recognized that the continuing conflictual relations between Isaacson and Wilde were a bad omen for the uneventful completion of Oscar Wilde's sentence."[6] That Wilde was later to describe Nelson publicly as "a man of gentle and humane character, greatly liked and respected by all the prisoners," and privately as "the most Christ-like man I ever met," is an indication of how radical an alteration of the regime at Reading was in store.[7]

Although these administrative changes had been prompted partly through the agency of Frank Harris in June, two other events in the first half of 1896 had a bearing on how Wilde approached the remainder of his sentence. In February, Wilde's play *Salomé*, banned from stage production in Britain by fiat of the censor in 1892, had its premiere in Paris at the Théâtre de L'Œuvre under the direction of the actor-manager Aurélien-Marie Lugné-Poe. The event, attended by Ernest Dowson and Aubrey Beardsley, and reviewed by the eminent French critic Henri Bauër among others, was reported in the English press, and while he always remained grateful for Harris's intervention, Wilde himself believed that Lugné-Poe's production "was the thing that turned the scale in my favour, so far as my treatment in prison by the Government was concerned" (*CL* 872). Wilde was deeply conscious of the artistic compliment paid to him by Lugné-Poe, Bauër, and other members of the French artistic elite, and the event shored up what remained of Wilde's artistic self-conviction.

The second event did not have any impact on Wilde's personal treatment, but it had a lasting effect on Wilde's sense of himself and other prisoners as the victims of a cruel, inhumane machine. In the spring of 1896, Charles Thomas Wooldridge, a thirty-year-old guardsman, arrived at Reading on remand for the murder of his wife on March 29. Following his conviction and sentencing at the Berkshire Assizes in mid-June, Wooldridge was hanged and buried within the prison walls on July 7, 1896. Wooldridge's imprisonment and execution were to inspire the only literary work Wilde would complete following his emergence from prison: *The Ballad of Reading Gaol.* Notwithstanding the terrible nature of Wooldridge's crime, the event crystallized for Wilde the savagery of the prison regime, implacable in its judicially sanctioned violence. After Wooldridge's execution, Wilde's writings from and about prison are notable for the clarity with which Wilde sees—as he put it to the home secretary in another petition seeking early release—that "modern modes of punishment . . . desecrate and destroy whatever good, or even desire of good, there may be in a man" (*CL* 668). When the prison chaplain patronizingly told the prisoners each Sunday "how thankful they should all be that they lived in a Christian country where a paternal Government was as anxious for the welfare of their souls as for the safe-keeping of their miserable bodies," Wilde told a sympathetic warder, he "long[ed] to rise in my place, and cry out . . . and tell the poor, disinherited wretches . . . that it is not so [and] . . . that they are society's victims."[8]

––––––––––

From any objective standpoint, the most important change in the summer of 1896 was Isaacson's replacement by Nelson, to whom Wilde near the end of his sentence would refer as "my good and kind friend" (*CL* 826). "The Home Office has allowed you some books," Nelson announced upon introducing himself to Wilde. "[P]erhaps you would like to read this one? I have just been reading it myself."[9] One of Nelson's first acts was to propose that Wilde be issued a strongly bound manuscript notebook rather than the loose foolscap sheets recommended by Nicholson. "I take notes of books I read. . . . I cling to my notebook," Wilde wrote in September 1896. "[I]t helps me: before I had it my brain was going in very evil circles" (*CL* 666). Soon after Nelson's arrival, Wilde started making full use of his right to call on the new governor, and according to a mourner at the time of his death, Nelson himself took great pleasure when Wilde exercised this right on a daily basis: "I looked forward to those morning talks [and] always allowed Wilde to stay the full quarter of an hour to which a prisoner was entitled . . . or rather I kept him the full time. For it was a pleasure to me."[10] Four months after Nelson's arrival, Wilde wrote that "there are . . . kinder elements in this evil prison air than there were before: sympathies have been shown to me, and I no longer feel isolated from humane influences. . . . And it seems as if I were better in many ways" (*CL* 669).

Under Nelson's governorship, Wilde experienced a sudden decline in the number of petty punishments, a cessation of onerous forms of manual labor, and an elevation to the role of "schoolmaster's orderly," meaning that he was in charge of the prison library. About five months before his release, he was also allowed to grow his hair back rather than

keeping it closely cropped.[11] But the chief effects of the new prison regime on Wilde were literary. With the conspicuous exception of Dante's
Divina Commedia, which More Adey had persuaded the prison commissioners to allow Wilde the previous winter, Wilde had received no
books that interested him since the last of Haldane's purchases the previous fall. However, as we have seen, Nelson approved the acquisition
of the bulk of the books Wilde requested in July, and he was to approve
numerous further book requests in December 1896 and March 1897
(*CL* 673 and 682). Had Nelson not done this, Wilde "would . . .
have pined away and died," testified one of his jailers.[12] For a voracious
reader such as Wilde, books were a lifeline. When he had cleaned his
cell and performed his rounds as schoolmaster's orderly, he occupied
himself reading, and by the end of his sentence his cell contained many
books. Under Nelson's governorship, Wilde was also allowed the extraordinary privilege of having his gas-jets kept lit so that he might read
late into the night, notwithstanding that the other prisoners retired
at eight.[13]

The books Wilde read during his imprisonment possess considerable interest in their own right: although he was reading Newman and
Pater as early as August 1895, these authors recur in later book requests
alongside collected editions of the chief English poets. "I thought at
first that what would please me most would be Greek literature," Wilde
told André Gide, "but I couldn't take to it."[14] The Church Fathers
"didn't interest me either."[15] Later lists are conspicuous for the inclusion of very recent novels such as Stevenson's *Treasure Island,* Hardy's
The Well-Beloved, Meredith's *The Amazing Marriage,* and Huysmans's
En Route, as well as the posthumously published correspondence of
Dante Gabriel Rossetti and Robert Louis Stevenson. "Meredith's novel
charmed me," Wilde was to write from prison in April 1897, but
"Rossetti's letters are dreadful," Stevenson's letters "most disappointing
also," and Huysmans's novel "most-overrated . . . sheer journalism . . .
worthless, slipshod, [and] flaccid" (*CL* 789–90). As the end of his sentence approached, Wilde's book requests are conspicuous too for the

inclusion of dictionaries and guides to Italian and German, indicating that he was giving thought to life in exile on the European Continent.

But among the plethora of literary authors, classic and contemporary, British and European, that Wilde requested be sent him in Reading Prison, the most important, along with a Greek Testament, is undoubtedly Dante, who recurs in list after list, and whom Wilde was in 1899 to call "the supreme modern poet" (*CL* 1129). Wilde had first been sent the *Divina Commedia* in February 1896 after More Adey persuaded the prison authorities to allow him access to Dante. "You can imagine how I tasted every word," he later told Wilfred Chesson.[16] He compared his personal inferno to Dante's, complaining to Frank Harris that in Dante's lowest circle at least "people could move about; could see each other, and hear each other groan. There was some change, some human companionship in misery."[17] In July 1896, he requested a prose translation of Dante's *Divine Comedy;* in December 1896 he requested *Dante and Other Essays,* by Dean Church, *An Introduction to Dante,* by John Addington Symonds, and *A Companion to Dante,* by A. J. Butler; and in the following March he requested *La Vita Nuova* in both Italian and English editions. By November of 1896, he could write to Robert Ross that "I read Dante, and make excerpts and notes for the pleasure of using a pen and ink" (*CL* 669).

In a fresh (unanswered) appeal to the home secretary for an early release, also written in November 1896, Wilde emphasized that he hoped "to recreate the life of a student of letters" and to "find in literature an anodyne from pain, first, and afterwards a mode by which sanity and balance and wholesomeness might be restored" (*CL* 668). In fact, Wilde had begun to resume a writing life. In September 1896, he informed Adey that he copied out "lines and phrases in the poets" and that he had tried to remember and write down *A Florentine Tragedy,* upon which he had been working at the time of his arrest, "but only bits of it remain with me, and I find that I cannot invent" (*CL* 666). Wilde's manuscript prison notebook has regrettably not survived, so it is impossible to see his unsuccessful efforts at playwriting or know which lines and phrases from the poets he was keen to copy, but it is clear that at some point in the late summer and autumn of 1896, he started using writing materials to take stock of—and ultimately make meaning of—his own life. He wrote mostly in the evenings, placing his plank bed across two wooden trestles for a makeshift writing-table.[18] His manuscript book was always on his table, one warder recalled, "and in it he kept writing and writing. The Chief Warder took it to the Governor's office every morning, and after the Governor had glanced over it, the prisoner's book was taken back to his cell again."[19]

The writing privileges Nelson extended to Wilde included some that had not been sanctioned by his superiors.[20] As well as allowing Wilde the special privilege of a notebook in his cell, he encouraged Wilde to correspond regularly with his friends outside prison, either stretching or ignoring regulations that strictly limited Wilde to writing and receiving just one letter per quarter.[21] Nelson believed that if penitence and reflection were the prime objectives of the silent system, in Wilde's case they could be achieved by allowing him to write to his friends. Within weeks of his arrival as governor, for instance, Nelson responded to Wilde's evident disappointment at news that Robert Sherard would not be granted visitation rights by allowing Wilde "as a favour" to write to Sherard (*CL* 662).[22] Further acts of generosity followed. In February 1897, for instance, Wilde began a letter to his friend More Adey saying "the Governor has kindly allowed me to see your letter, and to answer it at once" (*CL* 677), and similarly in May 1897, two days before his release, he began a letter to Reginald Turner saying "I write to you by kind permission of the Governor" (*CL* 831). Only four letters by Wilde survive from May 1895 to Nelson's appointment in late July of 1896, and two of these are petitions to the home secretary written during July 1896.[23] But some twenty-nine letters, occupying nearly two-hundred pages of Wilde's collected correspondence, survive from the nearly ten months when Wilde was under Nelson's jurisdiction.

The number alone testifies to the change the new governor wrought in Wilde's circumstances. To be sure, some of these twenty-nine letters address legal and financial matters or arrangements for his release, and two are notes written on scraps of paper to a gentle and sympathetic warder, Thomas Martin, and passed surreptitiously by hand. But even allowing for these facts, twenty-nine letters represents an unusual relaxation of the prison regulations. The vast majority of them are signed "Oscar," "Oscar Wilde," or simply "O. W." Within the circumscribed freedom of these letters, prisoner C. 3. 3. was not "merely the figure and letter of a little cell in a long gallery, one of a thousand lifeless numbers, as of a thousand lifeless lives" (*CL* 717). Letter writing was a reassertion of the prisoner's humanity as well as a bridge between the past and future. For as Wilde writes, "one of the tragedies of prison life is that it turns a man's heart to stone. The feelings of natural affection, like all other feelings, require to be fed. They die easily of inanition. A brief letter, four times a year, is not enough to keep alive the gentler and more humane affections by which ultimately the nature is kept sensitive to any fine or beautiful influences that may heal a wrecked and ruined life" (*CL* 1048).

Over the remaining months of his sentence, Wilde would write to his friends More Adey (ten times), Robert Ross (five times), Reginald Turner (twice), and Robert Sherard, expressing among other things his newfound joy in "handling pen and ink," the folly of his past life, his concern over the future of his two children, his gratitude for the kindness shown by his friends, and his relief at "kinder elements in this evil prison air" (*CL* 666, 669). Conspicuously, Wilde did not write to his wife, or at least no letter written from prison to her survives, and in settling legal arrangements for the future of their marriage and their children during his final year in prison, Wilde relied upon Adey and Ross as his agents.

––––––––––

The most important and unusual letter that Wilde would write would be life-changing—the long, 50,000-word document addressed to Lord Alfred Douglas now known and frequently republished as *De Profundis,* the title Robert Ross gave it in 1905. Wilde began this letter, almost certainly with no intention or expectation that it would ever be published, in the closing months of 1896, possibly as early as September, and he continued working on it till early April 1897.[24] By the time he finished it to his satisfaction, his intentions had changed drastically, and it had morphed into something very different from purely a letter. While he certainly began and ended it with Douglas in mind, large swathes did not concern Douglas directly or even appear to be addressed to him. Instead they concerned the radically new spirit in which Wilde intended to live and write upon his release. Over the months of its composition, the letter became a more purely autobiographical and meditative document, oriented to the future as much as to the past, in which Wilde laid out the preconditions and terms on which he intended to face the world once again.

In fact, this vital letter was never to be "sent" to Douglas in any conventional sense, and is today treated by scholars as one of Wilde's most enduring and important literary works. The day after his release from prison, upon arriving in Dieppe, Wilde handed the manuscript to Robert Ross. Explaining that he was "not prepared to sit in the grotesque pillory they put me into, for all time," and that "the truth will have to be known, not necessarily in my lifetime or Douglas's," he told Ross to have the letter reproduced in typescript, and parts of it immediately distributed to sympathetic readers, because "I want you to be my literary executor . . . and would like you to have all my works" (*CL* 780). He even playfully suggested a possible title for the letter, *Epistola: in Carcere et Vinculis* (Letter: In Prison and Chains), and hinted that its future publication might generate income for his children. It is true that Wilde instructed Ross to send the original to Lord Alfred Douglas, after first having typewritten duplicates made, "so that you should have a copy as well as myself" (*CL* 781). But Ross retained the manuscript, realizing its literary value, and eventually deposited it in the British Library in 1909. To his dying day, Lord Alfred Douglas, who only became aware of the manuscript's existence in 1912, when Arthur Ransome alluded to it in his book *Oscar Wilde: A Critical Study,* maintained that Ross had never sent him a copy.[25] Five years after Wilde's death, in the belief that he was honoring his friend's wishes, Ross published a heavily redacted version of the manuscript to great acclaim, with the title *De Profundis* (meaning "From the Depths," from Psalm 130), having first carefully removed all references to Douglas or his family as well as all traces of the document's origins as a letter. Tellingly, when Douglas reviewed this 1905 publication for the *Motorist and Traveler,* he was unable to recognize the work's origins in a letter to himself.[26]

Wilde's evolving sense of the work, and the length of time its composition took, created an unusual problem for Nelson. In allowing Wilde access to writing materials, the Prison Commission had stipulated that Wilde should "not employ these materials to communicate with outside persons otherwise than consistently with the ordinary rules," that Nelson should "supervise the provision of writing materials, with discretion as to the time during the day when the privilege may be exercised," and that all writing materials were "to be withdrawn at lock-up and all matter written by Wilde made subject to the Governor's inspection, ensuring that no improper use was made of this privilege."[27] But study of Wilde's manuscript makes clear that Nelson stretched these regulations in order to accommodate Wilde's evolving sense of his own work. The manuscript is composed of twenty folio sheets of ruled blue prison notepaper, embossed in blind on the front with the Royal Arms, each lined on both sides and folded in two, so as to make eighty pages in total.[28] When Nelson requested official permission for Wilde to be allowed to send the finished manuscript by mail in early April 1897, he stated that each sheet was carefully numbered before being issued to Wilde each morning, then withdrawn each evening at lock-up and placed before him the next morning with his other official papers. The arrangement, if true, calls to mind Samuel Beckett's Molloy, who writes for a man who "comes every week . . . and takes away the pages. So many pages. . . . When he comes for the fresh pages, he brings back the previous week's. They are marked with signs I don't understand."[29]

One of the most striking features of Wilde's manuscript, however, is that most of its twenty sheets are continuous: only two of them finish at the end of a sentence, implying that Wilde had access to multiple sheets at once. When instructing Ross to distribute parts of the letter to sympathetic readers, moreover, Wilde specified exact sheet and page numbers, and even quoted the exact phrases where Ross was to begin and end.[30] He can hardly have been citing from memory. Finally, while some of Wilde's sheets are clearly rough drafts, containing erasures, emendations, blottings, and a spontaneous, hard-to-decipher script, others are neatly handwritten fair copy, again suggesting that Wilde had access to multiple sheets at once and that he revised the text considerably. The evidence that Wilde was trying to bring coherence and continuity to the manuscript, in a manner reminiscent of his previous literary works, is hard to dispute.[31]

Wilde's sense of his manuscript's permanent literary value likely came late in the composition process, and if Douglas was unable to recognize in 1905 that *De Profundis* originated in a letter to himself, Wilde had nonetheless originally conceived at least parts of it as a personal letter to him. Douglas's destructive role in his own life had become increasingly apparent ever since he had told his wife, during her visit to Wandsworth in September 1895, that he would "kill" Douglas if he saw him again. Although Wilde had begun his sentence vowing undying love for Douglas, over the ensuing months he became increasingly angry, alienated, and depressed at the thought of his lover. This change owes more to Wilde's isolation and depression in the first year of his sentence, when he harbored hopes of reconciliation with his wife and children, than it does to any slights or neglect on Douglas's part. As Wilde biographer Rupert Croft-Cooke writes, "a man in prison is perpetually seeking objects for his resentment. . . . The smallest incident of his past or present may become exaggerated into an affront, a wound, a contemptuous and heartless attack or a cruel humiliation. Some trivial story from the world in which he has no part may be enough to reduce him to impotent fury or grinding despair. Wilde, already in a state of tearful self-pity and remorse, needed only an apparently casual reference to Bosie, who was the one human being he loved, to sink into hatred and malice."[32] Moreover, Wilde relied for news of the exiled Douglas upon his friends Robert Ross, More Adey, and Robert Harborough Sherard, all of whom fanned the flames of his displeasure: all were keen to effect Wilde's reconciliation with his wife. And Ross, who considered Douglas to have supplanted himself in Wilde's affections, frequently misrepresented Douglas, while simultaneously deluding the latter into believing that Wilde wished to receive neither a visit nor a letter from him.

For the first six months of Wilde's sentence, Douglas for his part had little inkling that Wilde's feelings about him had begun to change. In the early autumn of 1895, he proposed risking a return to England expressly to visit Wilde in prison, and he was "very much upset" when Ross told him "that he had just come from Wilde and that, as his correspondence and visitors were strictly limited, he desired that I should neither write to him nor visit him." Accordingly Douglas "determined to follow out [Wilde's] wishes and to wait until he could write or send to me."[33] As Douglas later pointed out, Wilde "either did not know, or pretended not to know, that Ross had given me most positive instructions, purporting to come from Wilde himself, that I was on no account to write to him or to attempt to visit him."[34] By November 1895, however, Douglas had begun to sense that Wilde's feelings about him had changed and, vowing that "I shall kill myself if Oscar throws me over," he implored More Adey, whom he knew to be managing Wilde's financial affairs, to ask Wilde "to send me some message."[35] Adey replied by advising Douglas to "show the love which I know you have for him by the most difficult of all ways—*waiting*."[36]

By May 1896, when Ross told Wilde that Douglas wished to dedicate his first volume of poems to him, Wilde felt that Douglas had ruined his life and wanted nothing more to do with him. Six months later, in November 1896, having been told (inaccurately) by Ross and Adey that Douglas angrily resented being asked to remove Wilde's name from the dedication and surrender the love letters that Wilde had written him, Wilde gave in to stronger emotions.[37] Now he blamed Douglas for "not appreciating the man he ruined," while cursing himself for his folly in allowing Douglas to dominate his life (*CL* 670). "By what you have done . . . and left undone, [you have] made every day of my long imprisonment still more difficult to live through," Wilde writes unfairly near the beginning of *De Profundis* (*CL* 728). Nearly consumed with bitterness, he needed to repudiate Douglas by making him conscious of the injustice (as Wilde saw it) of what he had done and also by exacting some emotional reparation. "One cannot always keep an adder in one's breast to feed upon one," he remarked (*CL* 729). By the end of 1896, Wilde had begun what he would describe as "the most important letter of my life" (*CL* 678).

Wilde's bitterness toward his ex-lover can be detected even between the innocent-sounding lines of the manuscript's opening sentence: "Dear Bosie, After long and fruitless waiting I have determined to write to you myself, as much for your sake as for mine, as I would not like to think I had passed through two long years of imprisonment without ever having received a single line from you, or any news or message even, except such as gave me pain" (*CL* 683–84). On the surface, after waiting in vain for Douglas to write, Wilde renews an intimate conversation that Douglas has heartlessly and abruptly let drop, hoping that he might thereby prompt a "line" from Douglas in return. But as Wilde was well aware, Douglas had in fact attempted to send a line and a message. In August 1895, three months after Wilde's incarceration, when prison regulations dictated that Wilde might be allowed the first of four quarterly personal letters, Douglas had applied from France to be allowed to write to Wilde directly. In the same month, he had attempted to communicate with Wilde through a solicitor's clerk who had visited Wandsworth to prepare Wilde for the bankruptcy proceedings. As he acknowledges later in *De Profundis,* Wilde had rejected Douglas's application to be allowed to correspond, wanting to reserve for family business his first opportunity of receiving a letter, and he had felt

Letter to Lord Alfred Douglas from Reading Prison, published as *De Profundis*. Opening page.

nothing but scorn and bitterness for the surreptitious way in which his prison visitor had communicated Douglas's cryptic message to him ("Prince Fleur-de-Lys wishes to be remembered to you").

The first third of Wilde's manuscript is filled with barely concealed rage as Wilde recounts, in deceptively meticulous detail, the central events of his life to date with Douglas. Often taken as being a factual account of how Wilde allowed himself to be depraved and destroyed by his hot-headed friend, these sections of *De Profundis* in fact constitute a highly partial and frequently unfair attack on the man whom Wilde described as "the true author of [my] hideous tragedy" (*CL* 710). For the most part, he represents Douglas as his annihilator and himself as Douglas's unwitting and powerless victim. "During the whole time we were together I never wrote one single line," Wilde bluntly and inaccurately tells his ex-lover: "my life, as long as you were by my side, was entirely sterile and uncreative" (*CL* 685).[38] His will had become absolutely subject to Douglas's, he writes, while the younger man's own "meanest motive . . . lowest appetite, [and] most common passion became . . . laws by which the lives of others were to be guided . . . and . . . sacrificed" (*CL* 689–90). Not understanding the conditions necessary for art's creation, Douglas had insisted upon being constantly entertained, Wilde claims, usually by taking long expensive meals, often lasting till well past midnight, when Wilde's time had far better been devoted to completing his plays *An Ideal Husband* or *A Florentine Tragedy*. According to Wilde, Douglas had made incessant demands for money and insisted on a life of reckless profusion, making Wilde pay for all his pleasures because he believed that he "had a sort of right to live at my expense and in a profuse luxury to which you had never been accustomed" (*CL* 688). Recalling the exact prices paid for "luncheons, dinner, supper, amusements, hansoms, and the rest of it," Wilde says that in the two-and-a-half years of their relationship, he had spent "with you and on you more than £5000 in actual money, irrespective of the bills I incurred" (*CL* 688).[39] Only weakness of will had kept him from making the permanent break he knew he ought make.[40]

The recriminations continue for many pages: Wilde holds Douglas responsible for his imprisonment, castigates him for recklessness and insensitivity in writing to the press in Wilde's defense, and lambasts him for doing nothing to prevent the sale of Wilde's most prized possessions, just days after his arrest, by bailiffs seeking payment for Wilde's debts. Douglas's indifference to the sale was, according to Wilde, worse for the fact that "it was to pay for some gifts of mine to you that the bailiffs had entered the house where you had so often dined" (*CL* 713). Wilde also damns Douglas for his behavior following Wilde's conviction—for ham-fistedly attempting to defend Wilde in the *Mercure de France* by publishing extracts of Wilde's personal letters; for allowing his father to take legal action in the summer of 1895 to recover his court costs (an action that resulted in Wilde's bankruptcy), when Douglas himself was "absolutely responsible" for these costs; for attempting to communicate with Wilde via the solicitor's clerk under the absurd pseudonym "Prince Fleur de Lys" (Wilde had in fact encouraged Douglas's adoption of the pseudonym "Fleur-de-Lys," writing in early May 1895 that "I have not had a line today from Fleur-de-Lys. . . . I am so wretched when I don't hear from him," just as he was later to urge Douglas to adopt the pseudonym "Jonquil du Vallon"); for his failure to communicate and commiserate with Wilde upon the death of his mother in early 1896; for his ill-considered efforts later that year to dedicate his first volume of poems to Wilde; and finally, for "allowing [Wilde] to eat [his] heart away in darkness and solitude without trying in some way, however, slight, to help . . . bear the bitter burden of [his] disgrace" (*CL* 648, 898, 726). Whatever Wilde's feelings for Douglas might have been in the past, he concludes, "it would be impossible for me now to have for you any feeling other than that of contempt and scorn" (*CL* 727).

———

If it is not entirely clear why, upon leaving jail in May 1897, Wilde immediately handed the manuscript of *De Profundis* to Ross in his capacity as Wilde's literary executor, it is nonetheless clear why Wilde had decided against sending the manuscript to Douglas directly. The notes of scorn and anger could not be more marked, nor Wilde's attack upon Douglas's character more complete. Douglas's "imagination" had been "as much in prison as I was," Wilde writes: "Vanity had barred up the windows, and the name of the warder was Hate" (*CL* 720). Midway through its composition, Wilde must have realized that, even if prison regulations had allowed it, this was not a document that could be delivered into Douglas's hands without risk. It would cut him to the quick, and he was more likely than not to destroy it upon receipt.

But Wilde's motive in writing was not simply to express his contempt for Douglas or to remove the "poisonous adder" from his breast. Although *De Profundis* opens by giving every sign of being a personal letter to Douglas, and although Wilde refers self-consciously to it as a letter on multiple occasions, it bears the stamp of the spiritual autobiographies that Wilde read in the first year of his imprisonment, and this results in the unmistakable tension between a letter as a communicative medium and something more purely expressive or private. Large parts of it are governed by the need to disburden the self of thoughts, ideas, and feelings, as is also the case with Franz Kafka's long recriminatory letter to his father. "For nearly two years I had within me a growing burden of bitterness," Wilde was to remark upon concluding the letter, "much of which I have now got rid of. On the other side of the prison-wall there are some poor black soot-smirched trees that are just breaking out into buds of an almost shrill green. I know quite well what they are going through. They are finding expression" (*CL* 783). In the course of composing the letter, Wilde had come to realize that he needed to get beyond simple expressions of contempt and rage. What mattered was the future and not the past. If hatred was Douglas's "warder," still more was it the warder of his own imagination.

Paradoxically, repudiating Douglas would become the means for Wilde to return to him without rancor at some point in the future. The very intensity of his attack on Douglas's character, in the earlier parts of the letter, is a clue that Wilde still loved him and intended some kind of reconciliation with him upon release. That this was the case becomes especially clear toward the end where, having now acknowledged his own culpability, Wilde plans the conditions, circumstances, and even place in which he might meet Douglas again once his prison term were over. Upon release, he would spend at least a month in the company of friends, he writes, "to gain, in their healthful and affectionate company, peace, and balance, and a less troubled heart, and a sweeter mood" (*CL* 776). But at the end of a month, he tells Douglas, "when the June roses are in all their wanton opulence, I will, if I feel able, arrange through Robbie to meet you in some quiet foreign town like Bruges" (*CL* 778). Douglas would have to come incognito, abandoning his own name and aristocratic title. Still Wilde hoped that this reconciliation "will be what a meeting between you and me should be, after everything that has occurred. In old days there was always a wide chasm between us, the chasm of achieved Art and acquired culture: there is a still wider chasm between us now, the chasm of Sorrow: but to Humility there is nothing that is impossible, and to Love all things are easy" (*CL* 778).

These notes of personal longing and forgiveness—which foreshadow Wilde's actual reunion with Douglas in late August 1897, roughly three months after his release—represent a remarkable turnaround in a document that began with such bitterness and recrimination. But the revolution in Wilde's attitude to Douglas is not the only important turn that took place in the course of writing *De Profundis*. For if he was to emerge from prison as anything more than a pariah, Wilde needed to reconstruct *himself* imaginatively too, not least as an artist. He would never again be widely accepted as the person or the writer he had been before his conviction. He needed to reinvent himself as someone who could live and write unapologetically in spite of the poverty, ostracism, and isolation that he already knew he would face upon release. He wanted to reach a point, to use his own immortal phrase, when he would be able "to say, simply and without affectation, that the two great turning-points of my life were when my father sent me to Oxford, and when society sent me to prison" (*CL* 732).

The second of these "turning-points" is heralded by the memorable, oft-quoted indictment Wilde brings against his past life, roughly midway through *De Profundis:*

> I let myself be lured into long spells of senseless and sensual ease. I amused myself with being a *flâneur,* a dandy, a man of fashion. I surrounded myself with the smaller natures and the meaner minds. I became the spendthrift of my own genius, and to waste an eternal youth gave me a curious joy. Tired of being on the heights I deliberately went to the depths in the search for new sensations. What the paradox was to me in the sphere of thought, perversity became to me in the sphere of passion. Desire, at the end, was a malady, or a madness, or both. I grew careless of the lives of others. I took pleasure where it pleased me and passed on. I forgot that every little action of the common day makes or unmakes character, and that therefore what one has done in the secret chamber one has some day to cry aloud on the housetops. I ceased to be Lord over myself. I was no longer the Captain of my Soul, and did not know it. (*CL* 730)

In the face of this pitiless indictment, Wilde says, "there is only one thing for me now, absolute Humility. . . . I find hidden away in my nature something that tells me that nothing in the whole world is meaningless, and suffering least of all. That something . . . like a treasure in a field is Humility" (*CL* 730). Although his sufferings in prison had been great, they had been no greater than those of his fellow-prisoners. In the midst of suffering and recrimination, he says, the sudden discovery of humility had triggered new hope and a recognition that he had to free himself from bitterness.

for his rediscovery of himself as an artist: "there is before me so much to do," he writes, "that I would regard it as a terrible tragedy if I died before I was allowed to complete at any rate a little of it" (*CL* 736). He now saw new developments for himself as both a person and an artist, and contrary to the suicidal impulses that were coursing through him in late 1895, he ends *De Profundis* longing to live "so that I can explore what is no less than a new world to me" (*CL* 736). As Haldane had prophesied back in the early summer of 1895, Wilde had found in prison perhaps his greatest subject—"Sorrow . . . and all that it teaches one"—and henceforth it would be the cornerstone of his art (*CL* 736).

For a writer who had once written that "to love oneself is the beginning of a lifelong romance," this emphasis upon humility and sorrow represents nothing less than a revolution in Wilde's ideas about artistry.[41] Humility and a frank acceptance of suffering were indispensable to the artist, Wilde now insisted, and he hoped henceforth to attain "the ultimate realisation of the artistic life" (*CL* 740). In this respect, he would look to Christ as his example, since Christ above all others "realized in the entire sphere of human relations that imaginative sympathy which in the sphere of Art is the sole secret of creation" (*CL* 741). This is not to say that Wilde wished to become more *Christian:* "the faith that others give to the unseen, I give to what one can touch, and look at," he wrote (*CL* 752). Spirituality could only be found within the self, and "if I may not find its secret within myself, I shall never find it" (*CL* 752). Rather, Christ stood as an example for humanity and a model for how the artist might absorb humility and suffering into his personal vision, for Christ "understood the leprosy of the leper, the darkness of the blind, the fierce misery of those who live for pleasure, the strange poverty of the rich. . . . With a width and wonder of imagination, that fills one almost with awe, he took the entire world of the inarticulate, the voiceless world of pain, as his kingdom, and made of himself its eternal mouthpiece" (*CL* 741, 746). In one of the most remarkable, sustained, and heavily revised passages in all of *De Profundis,* Wilde extends the argument that he had first made six years previous, in *The Soul of Man,* that "he who would lead a Christ-like life must be entirely and absolutely himself," that "Christ's place is . . . with the poets" and that Christ's "whole conception of Humanity sprang right out of the imagination and can only be realized by it" (*CL* 740–41).[42] In his personal identification with the broader suffering and pain of humankind, says Wilde, Christ was both "the true precursor of the romantic movement," possessed like the artist of "an intense and flamelike imagination," and "the most supreme of Individualists," who realized what he called *God's Kingdom* by "getting rid of all alien passions, all acquired culture, and all external possessions be they good or evil" (*CL* 741–44).

Similarly, Wilde hoped to arrive at a more perfect articulation of himself by accepting everything, even the loss of position, happiness, freedom, wealth, and the permanent removal of his children's affection. It was a high ideal, perhaps driven partly by Wilde's knowledge that the "Christ-like" Nelson would be the manuscript's first reader, and if the years that followed would fully test Wilde's ability to live up to it, it was nonetheless vital to hold that ideal in mind if he were to approach his release without fear and loss of hope. A continual assertion of the imagination is the basis of all spiritual and material life, Wilde wrote, just as for Christ "imagination was simply a form of Love, and . . . Love was Lord in the fullest meaning of the phrase" (*CL* 749). With Christ as his example, he would emerge from prison with Love not hatred in his heart, recognizing that humanity had been in the prison alongside him in spite of his own personal suffering. "Things in themselves are of little importance," and in a Platonic sense, they have "no real existence," Wilde wrote in conclusion: "the spirit alone is of importance" (*CL* 754). His personal suffering in the last two years reflected a corrupt and inhumane system that he intended to try his best to alter upon his release. But "there is nothing in the world so wrong but that the spirit of Humanity, which is the spirit of Love . . . of the Christ who is not in Churches, may make it, if not right, at least possible to be borne without too much bitterness of heart" (*CL* 754–55).

Correspondingly, *De Profundis* ends movingly, with Wilde envisioning his release from prison into a world of peace or "Spirit," as well as a fateful reconciliation with the man who had been the subject of so much invective. "I tremble with pleasure," he writes, "when I think that on the very day of my leaving prison both the laburnum and the lilac will be blooming in the gardens, and that I shall see the wind stir into restless beauty the swaying gold of the one, and make the other toss the pale purple of its plumes so that all the air shall be Arabia for me" (*CL* 777). Merely to live in the presence of nature would assuage some fundamental element in his character: "there is not a single colour hidden away in the chalice of a flower," he writes evocatively, with renewed faith in his own linguistic powers, "or the curve of a shell, to which, by some subtle sympathy with the very soul of things, my nature does not answer" (*CL* 777). Still, he remained "conscious . . . that behind all this Beauty, satisfying though it be, there is some Spirit hidden of which the painted forms and shapes are but modes of manifestation, and it is with this Spirit that I desire to become in harmony" (*CL* 777). Society, he understood, "will have no place for me." But Nature "will have clefts in the rocks where I may hide, and secret valleys in whose silence I may weep undisturbed. She will hang the night with stars so that I may walk abroad in the darkness without stumbling, and send the wind over my footprints so that none may track me to my hurt: she will cleanse me in great waters, and with bitter herbs make me whole" (*CL* 777–78). It was a superb Romantic vision, and doubtless one that enabled Wilde to step outside his prison with courage and conviction. The years to follow would prove only too accurately that Society would have no place for him. But Nature would ultimately prove less hospitable than Wilde could imagine, and the darkness more intractable.

PART TWO

OSCAR WILDE IN EXILE
1897–1900

3

Release

$\mathcal{D}$*e Profundis* WAS finished by April 1, 1897, just over six weeks before Wilde's release, when he wrote to Robert Ross explaining that he would be sending the manuscript to him under separate cover and that it dealt with his own "mental development in prison, and the inevitable evolution of character and intellectual attitude towards life that has taken place" (*CL* 780–81). He wanted Ross and others who were prepared to stand by him to know in what mood and manner he hoped to face the world. But he also wanted Ross to send the original manuscript to Douglas, after first making copies of it, saying that he hoped it would do Douglas some good. Curiously perhaps, given the notes of longing and reconciliation that Wilde strikes toward the end of *De Profundis,* he returned to a tone of anger and recrimination in his comments to Ross anticipating how Douglas would react upon reading the manuscript: "it is the first time anyone has ever told him the truth about himself . . . the letter is one he thoroughly deserves, and . . . if it is unjust, he thoroughly deserves injustice. Who indeed deserves it more?" (*CL* 782). He was clearly still conflicted and changeable in his feelings regarding Douglas, and it is understandable that he should be so. He had inherited from his parents a name of high distinction in literature and art, he explained, and he would not, for all eternity, allow that name to be "the shield and catspaw of the Queensberrys" (*CL* 780).

On April 2, Nelson asked his superiors whether Wilde might be allowed to send the manuscript by mail.[1] Four days later Nelson was told that the manuscript could not go out, but that it might be kept and handed over to the prisoner upon release. As the date of release drew nearer, with the adder now removed from his breast, Wilde's mind turned to other things entirely, and Douglas no longer preoccupied his every thought. He began to obsess over where he would go upon leaving prison, over who would meet and accompany him, how he would afford to live, and how soon he might emerge from bankruptcy. His financial affairs were in disarray, but more troubling still was his marriage, which had broken down irretrievably. The hope for a reconciliation, which both husband and wife had expressed in the wake of Constance's prison visits, had quickly evaporated.

Over the course of the year before Wilde's release, a bitter dispute had erupted between Constance and Wilde's representatives over provisions for the couple's two sons in the event of Constance's death as well as the fate of Wilde's "life-interest" in Constance's marriage-settlement.[2] (Interest-bearing investments had been settled upon Constance by her family when she married Wilde in 1884, so as to provide her with an assured source of independent income.)[3] To be sure, Constance's principal motivation was the welfare of her children: she knew from experience (and from her own lighter purse) that Wilde was profligate, even untrustworthy, with money; with good reason she therefore believed that Wilde could not be entrusted with the boys' financial well-being in the event of her death. In March 1897, she had obtained a formal dissolution of Wilde's legal responsibility for his children, under the terms of the Guardianship of Children's Act (1886), on the grounds of his unfitness.[4] One month later, around the time he finished composing *De Profundis,* Wilde was gravely anxious that she would soon petition him for divorce too.[5] In the event, Constance had no desire to put the family through further painful courtroom proceedings. But she insisted on a legal separation, as well as upon the revocation of any remaining rights that Wilde possessed as father of their two children. She recognized that he had a pressing need for (and arguably a legal claim to) some of the property she had brought into the marriage. For this reason, she was prepared to make Wilde an annual allowance of £150, to be continued in the event of her own death, but only on condition that he agreed to communicate with her neither against her will nor without her leave, nor attempted to communicate with his children, and also on condition that he not associate in future with any person deemed disreputable in the eyes of his own lawyer, Arthur D. Hansell, who, in addition to his responsibilities as Wilde's personal lawyer, would henceforth act independently as a trustee of any separation agreement. Wilde signed a formal deed of separation agreeing to these terms on May 17, 1897.[6] When he left Reading Prison for good the next day, as he was transferred to Pentonville Prison in London, he was dressed in his own clothes and accompanied by two warders. "As he left his cell, Mr. Wilde turned and took a last look, then bent his head and followed down the steps," a warder later recalled: "There were tears shed in Reading Gaol that night."[7] On the morning of May 19, Wilde was released from Pentonville into the waiting hands of More Adey and Stewart Headlam.

It was fitting that Wilde began his new freedom in Headlam's company. A man of great principle and the model for the crusading Rev. James Morrell in Bernard Shaw's play *Candida,* Headlam had long been a champion of the downtrodden and the victimized. He later wrote that, despite not knowing Wilde at the time, he had stood bail for Wilde in 1895 "on public grounds: I felt that the action of a large section of the press, of the theatrical managers at whose houses his plays were running, and of his publisher, was calculated to prejudice his case before his trial had even begun."[8] Over the years, Headlam had developed a fierce reputation as a campaigner against puritanism, especially where the theater was concerned. Bloomsbury, where he lived, bordered by the British Museum and University College, had long been associated with free thinkers, artists, scholars, and immigrants. Headlam's living-room epitomized the kinds of "aesthetic" interiors that Wilde loved and had once championed in his lectures "The House Beautiful" and "The Decorative Arts." The designer Selwyn Image and the architect Arthur Mackmurdo, two pillars of the Arts and Crafts Movement (they had co-founded the influential Century Guild of Artists in 1882), had been consulted about the room's decoration, and it was filled with Century Guild furniture, pictures by Edward Burne-Jones and Dante Gabriel Rossetti, and William Morris wallpaper and curtains. Here, in 1906, Headlam founded the short-lived Anti-Puritan League, which included Selwyn Image and G. K. Chesterton among its members.

Once Wilde arrived at Headlam's, he bathed and shaved, changed into a new suit of clothes bought for him by Frank Harris, breakfasted, and gratefully received the first cup of coffee he had had in two years: "I would like coffee for breakfast," he had written to Reginald Turner, "as I have been living on cocoa, and don't think I could taste tea" (*CL 832*). He had not meant to stay long in London: "being in London, the place I wished to avoid, is terrible," he had written (*CL* 832). Arrangements had been made for him to travel immediately by train to Newhaven and take the morning boat to Dieppe, in Normandy, where Ross and Turner had engaged rooms at the Hôtel Sandwich and were waiting. But he was eager to talk about his recent treatment in prison and even keener to talk about Dante, insisting upon writing down for Headlam the titles and authors of books on Dante that he had read in prison. Before long, visitors started arriving, and, as Ross later wrote, "Wilde talked so much and insisted on seeing so many people that he missed the train," so not till afternoon did he journey to Newhaven in order to cross to Dieppe by the night-boat.[9]

The earliest visitors to Headlam's included Ernest Leverson and his wife, Ada, the comic writer, whom Wilde had wittily dubbed "The Sphinx" in 1893. The Leversons remained among the bravest and most loyal of Wilde's friends: in May 1895, they had accommodated Wilde in their house when he was out on bail, when no other house or hotel in London would accept him, and Ernest continued to lend Wilde money. As they waited for Wilde to make his entrance, they felt "intensely nervous and embarrassed," Ada Leverson wrote later, at once fearful "of showing our feelings and . . . of not showing our feelings." But when he entered, Wilde at once "put us at our ease": "He came in with the dignity of a king returning from exile. He came in talking, laughing, smoking a cigarette, with waved hair and a flower in his buttonhole, and he looked markedly better, slighter, and younger than he had two years previously. His first words were 'Sphinx, how marvellous of you to know exactly the right hat to wear at seven o'clock in the morning to meet a friend who has been away!' "[10]

The pressing question was where he was to go. Frank Harris had proposed taking Wilde on a driving tour of the Pyrenees, but Wilde was against this, saying "it would be like a perpetual football match" to be with the combative Harris for so long.[11] "Your demands on life are enormous," Wilde explained to Harris a few weeks later: "you require response, or you annihilate. The pleasure of being with you is in the clash of personality . . . the war of ideas. . . . In your luncheon-parties, in old days, the remains of the guests were taken away with the debris of the feast. I have often lunched with you . . . and found myself the only survivor" (*CL* 895). Wilde required less taxing companionship now. When the talk turned to religion, Wilde remarked that while he looked on all the different religions as "colleges in a great university," Roman Catholicism was "the greatest and most romantic," and according to Headlam's account a note was then dispatched to the Jesuit Church in Farm Street asking for a priest to be sent, so that Wilde might receive spiritual guidance from a Roman Catholic.[12]

While they waited for a response, Wilde chatted happily away. He spoke of Reading Prison as if he had simply been paying a social visit there: "The dear Governor, such a delightful man, and his wife is charming. I spent happy hours in their garden, and they asked me to spend the summer with them. They thought I was the gardener."[13] He joked that "one of the punishments that happen to people who have been " 'away' [is] they are not allowed to read the *Daily Chronicle*." During his transfer to Pentonville, he said, "I begged to be allowed to read it in the train. 'No!' Then I suggested I might be allowed to read it upside down. This they consented to allow, and I read all the way the *Daily Chronicle* upside down, and never enjoyed it so much. It's really the only way to read newspapers."[14]

The messenger returned, but the priests at Farm Street would have nothing to do with him.[15] Although everybody looked away as Wilde read the reply, he broke down and sobbed bitterly. The Leversons left shortly after this, although in her published recollections Ada Leverson testifies to Wilde's "wonderful powers of recuperation" and states that he "soon recovered his spirits."[16] Wilde stayed at Headlam's until lunch-time, then took a cab, accompanied by Adey, to West Croydon, where they took the afternoon train to Newhaven. (Wilde feared a big London station, so West Croydon, in London's southern suburbs, was chosen because it lessened the chances of his being recognized.) Headlam later wrote, "I like to think of him as I knew him for those six hours on that spring morning, and to hope that somewhere and somehow the beauty of his character may be garnered and the follies and weaknesses burnt-up."[17]

———

From Newhaven, Wilde cabled Ross in Dieppe, informing him that they would be arriving by the night boat, telling him not to dream of waiting up and that words could not express his gratitude. Ross and Turner were waiting when the boat docked at half past four in the morning—a magnificent spring morning, Ross later recalled, such as Wilde had anticipated in the closing words of *De Profundis,* where he had written that "merely to look at the world will be always lovely" and that "I tremble with pleasure when I think that on the very day of my leaving prison both the laburnum and the lilac will be blooming in the gardens, and that I shall see the wind stir into restless beauty the swaying gold of the one, and make the other toss the pale purple of its plumes so that all the air shall be Arabia for me." Ross has left a memorable account of Wilde's arrival: "As the steamer glided into the harbour Wilde's tall figure, dominating the other passengers, was easily recognized from the great crucifix on the jetty where we stood. That striking beacon was full of significance for us. Then we began running to the landing stage and Wilde recognised us and waved his hand and his lips curled into a smile. His face had lost all its coarseness and he looked as he must have looked at Oxford in the early days before I knew him and as he only looked again after death. . . . There was the usual irritating delay and then Wilde with that odd elephantine gait which I have never seen in anyone else stalked off the boat."[18]

While Turner sorted out the customs inspection of Wilde's luggage, Wilde entertained his fellow travelers, "sitting at the head of the buffet table, drinking his coffee and dominating the whole seasick company."[19] Two of the items that Wilde carried with him as he disembarked were of special importance. As Ross relates, "He was holding in his hand a large sealed envelope. 'This, my dear Bobbie, is the great manuscript about which you know.' . . . The manuscript was of course *De Profundis*." The other item was an expensive dressing bag, given to Wilde by Reggie Turner as a gift, embroidered with the initials of Sebastian Melmoth, the pseudonym by which Wilde wished to go henceforth. Wilde had been told of Turner's gift a fortnight before, and he had already thanked Turner by letter from prison, but he cannot have fully appreciated the gift's splendor until Adey handed it to him at Headlam's house. The bag, to which Wilde seems to have become sentimentally attached as if it were a physical objectification of his own identity, much as a monogrammed handbag or an initialed cigarette case is for characters in *The Importance of Being Earnest,* was the subject of affectionate jokes for weeks thereafter, and he chaffed Turner a great deal about it. Adey "was anxious to deprive me of the blessed bag" on the boat over, Wilde quipped to Ross.[20] It "has been blessed by the *curé*," he joked to Turner on June 3 (*CL* 878). Following Turner's departure, Wilde wrote that "the population came at dawn to look at my dressing-case. I showed it to them, piece of silver by piece of silver. Some of the old men wept for joy. Robbie detected me at Dieppe in the market-place of the sellers of perfumes, spending all my money on orris-root and the tears of the narcissus and the dust of red roses. He was very stern and led me away. I have already spent my entire income for two years. I see now that this lovely dressing-case with its silver vials thirsty for distilled odours will gradually lead me to the perfection of poverty. But it seemed to me to be cruel not to fill with rose-petals the little caskets shaped so cunningly in the form of a rose" (*CL* 855). As he had written years earlier, "The only thing that can console one for being poor is extravagance."[21]

Wilde had said in *De Profundis* that he hoped upon release "to go at once to some little seaside village abroad with Robbie and More Adey," since the sea "washes away the stains and wounds of the world" (*CL* 776). He had only reluctantly accepted the idea of retreating to the Normandy coast. Originally he had proposed "to live, if I live anywhere, in Brussels," and when More Adey suggested in late January 1897 that he "might like to go to some quiet seaside place in Brittany for the first few weeks," Wilde "would not hear of it," saying, "I shall have to face the world sometime, and I intend to do it immediately" (*CL* 675).[22] By early April he had come around to the idea of an obscure seaside retreat: he now craved "really bracing air" and "freedom from English people," but he proposed "places like Morlais or Quimper" in the western reaches of Brittany, writing that "all the watering places on the Channel, from Calais to Dinan, would be impossible for me" (*CL* 800). When the Brittany idea fell through, he suggested Boulogne or Le Havre, further along the Normandy coast, because "Dieppe is relaxing, fashionable, and I am too well known there . . . and of course my arrival will be telegraphed to London." Perhaps his aversion had to do with the fact that he had been in Dieppe with Douglas in the late summer of 1894 (Douglas stood "between me and the sun," he had written a few days earlier [*CL* 815]). Wilde and Constance had also spent a week of their honeymoon in Dieppe in 1884. But Ross was adamant, so Wilde reluctantly agreed to go to Dieppe, saying "I can move on I suppose," and instructed Ross to "find a little place ten miles off by rail where we could go—a little quiet place" (*CL* 835–36).

Fashionable and artistic considerations might have played a role in Ross's decision. By the 1890s, the attractions of Dieppe appealed to a broad cross-section of English tourists so that, for the summer months at least, a microcosm of English society could be found there. As many as twelve thousand English men and women descended upon Dieppe each summer, and another six hundred lived in the *Quartier Anglais,* just below the castle ramparts. In Dieppe, says the Wilde scholar John Stokes, Wilde "could look the English in the face again"—although, as it turned out, the English were not always prepared to look back.[23] Both French and English elites had long appreciated the town's natural advantages: visits by the Duchesse de Berri in the 1820s had made Dieppe fashionable among the French, just as Lord Salisbury's annual holidays there with his family in the 1860s had made it respectable among the English. "Dieppe was and was not French, was and was not English, a border town, a liminal place," says Stokes, and as importantly, it had become the resort favored by artists, musicians, and writers, a number of whom—Jacques-Emile Blanche, Frits Thaulow, Walter Sickert, the novelist Henrietta Palmer, Alexandre Dumas *fils*—made it their home.[24] Roughly equidistant from London and Paris, and easily reachable from both, it had witnessed an extraordinary interchange of ideas. Aesthetes of vastly different stripes came to Dieppe believing that they could combat respectability with refinement. "Dieppe is a reduced Florence, every type of a character for a novelist seems to gather there," wrote Henry James.[25] It was a theatrical town, at once working port, resort, and artist's colony, and simultaneously "a 'stage' for ostentatious self-fashioning."[26] One "cannot take things seriously at Dieppe," wrote Arthur Symons: in Dieppe, "life, if you will but abandon yourself to the natural current of things, passes in a dream."[27]

Upon arrival, Wilde was ebullient, though when he got to his hotel—where Ross and Turner had filled his room with flowers, prepared a feast of sandwiches, and arranged on the mantelpiece all of the books that Wilde had been given as gifts, with Max Beerbohm's recently published *Works* and *The Happy Hypocrite* in the center to catch the eye—he briefly broke down.[28] He recovered quickly and talked until nine, when Ross insisted upon going to lie down. Later the four friends drove to the castle at Arques-la-Bataille, where Wilde enjoyed the trees, grass, and country scents and sounds in a way that Ross had never known him to before. "I am . . . dazed with the wonder of the wonderful world," Wilde would write a couple of days later: "I feel as if I had been raised from the dead" (*CL* 846). For days following his arrival, he talked of nothing but Reading Prison, says Ross, "and it had already become for him a sort of enchanted castle of which Major Nelson was the presiding fairy. The hideous machicolated turrets were already turned into minarets, the very warders into benevolent Mamelukes and we ourselves into Paladins welcoming Coeur de Lion after his captivity."[29]

Stokes writes that for Wilde "Dieppe was a brave and optimistic place to go, part joke, part confrontation," but in fact Wilde was apprehensive.[30] "If you write to me please do so under cover to R. B. Ross, who is here with me," he wrote to Frank Harris (*CL* 845). "Pray let my name and place of sojourn be quite a secret to all," he wrote to another correspondent (*CL* 857). "I am staying here as Sebastian Melmoth—not Esquire but Monsieur Sebastien Melmoth," he wrote to Ada Leverson: "I have thought it better that Robbie should stay here under the name of Reginald Turner, and Reggie under the name of R. B. Ross. It is better that they should not have their own names" (*CL* 845).[31] Wilde had taken his elaborate pseudonym in order to "avoid the prying eye and the foolish tongue" (*CL* 864). That such circumspection was well founded soon became evident: The proprietor of a restaurant, seeing him about to sit down with three friends, said he only had food for three, not four. When a deputation of young French poets came from Montmartre to pay their respects, the resulting dinner at the Café des Tribuneaux became so raucous that an official letter arrived, warning Wilde that any public misconduct would lead to his expulsion from France. "He's sure to make trouble here. . . . He'll use the Café Suisse as his platform and he'll make an exhibition of himself," feared the

Hôtel de la Plage, Berneval. Wood-engraving by Ethelbert White, from *After Reading: Letters of Oscar Wilde to Robert Ross* (Westminster: Beaumont Press, 1921).

resident painters Charles Conder and Walter Sickert, who had received news of Wilde's impending arrival in Dieppe "without enthusiasm."[32] Despite the pseudonym, his presence in Dieppe was noted in the French papers. When Wilde one day beckoned to Blanche from the terrace of the Café Suisse, Blanche (to his later regret) pretended not to see and Wilde was wounded to the quick. Within a matter of days Wilde had decamped to the Hôtel de la Plage ("a little inn by the sea) in Berneval-sur-mer, a village five miles along the coast, where "the name Sebastian Melmoth was a disguise which had a chance of working" (*CL* 875).[33]

Before he left for Berneval, he undertook two important pieces of unfinished business. In entirely different ways, each spoke to his renewed sense of belief as a writer and each pointed a meaningful way ahead. A year earlier, on February 11, 1896, the French actor-manager Aurélien-Marie Lugné-Poe had produced Wilde's play *Salomé* at the Théâtre de l'Œuvre in Paris—the play's first-ever theatrical production—and other French intellectuals had exerted themselves by bravely writing newspaper articles in support of Wilde during his sentence. On hearing about them in jail, Wilde had been greatly affected by these tributes to his artistry, and he felt that Lugné-Poe's *Salomé* production in particular had done much to bring about a more humane and respectful treatment on the part of the English authorities. On May 24, therefore, he invited Lugné-Poe to do him the honor of dining with him. When Lugné-Poe took up Wilde's invitation the very next day, he evidently told Wilde of his intention to report the meeting in the Paris papers, where he knew the news would be warmly greeted by Wilde's French sympathizers. In response, Wilde impressed upon Lugné-Poe "the importance of writing no interview, and giving no details of my strange name, my place of sojourn, my altered appearance, and the like" (*CL* 847). All the same, he knew that Lugné-Poe was an important conduit to the French intelligentsia, and he wanted Lugné-Poe to publicize broadly "how grateful I was and am to France for their recognition of me as an artist in the day of my humiliation, and how my better treatment in an English prison was due to the French men of letters" (*CL* 847).[34] At the same time, he discussed with Lugné-Poe the possibility of staging a new, as yet unwritten play, based like *Salomé* on a Biblical incident. "Being religious in surroundings and treatment of subject," he said, this would be "not a play for a *run,* at all. Three performances are the most I think I could expect. All I want is to have my artistic reappearance, and my own rehabilitation through art, in *Paris,* not in London" (*CL* 873).

The other piece of unfinished business concerned imprisonment. In April Wilde had promised Thomas Martin, the kindest of his warders at Reading, that he hoped upon release to write about prison life and to try to change it for others. The prison system "is absolutely and entirely wrong," he had written in *De Profundis:* "I would give anything to be able to alter it when I go out. I intend to try" (*CL* 754). On May 24, one day before Lugné-Poe's visit, the *Daily Chronicle,* long interested in prison reform, printed a letter from Martin recounting how he was just dismissed from his job for giving a biscuit to a small, crying, hungry child—one of a group of three children who, unable to pay a fine, had been imprisoned for snaring rabbits. Wilde must have read this letter with alarm. Four days later, on the twenty-eighth, the *Chronicle* printed a long letter from Wilde in which he carefully exposed the injustices to which all British prisoners, adult and children, were subject as a result of the system's inherent cruelty. The letter began personally, though Wilde took pains to avoid referring to his own suffering. He had seen the children himself the Monday prior to his release, he recounted, and the child to whom Warder Martin had given a biscuit was "a tiny little chap," too small even for the regulation prison clothing in which the authorities had attempted to dress him (*CL* 848). Factually but nonetheless movingly, Wilde described the children's fear and isolation—although Wilde did not inform the paper's readers that he later paid the children's fine himself, saying to Martin "I must get them out," thereby securing their release the very next day (*CL* 831).

Wilde documented the brutality of the current British prison system and the terrible cruelty that it inflicted on child prisoners especially. The first and most prominent emotion produced by prison life, he said, was terror, which "seizes and dominates the child, as it seizes the grown man also, [and] is of course intensified beyond power of expression by the solitary cellular system of our prisons" (*CL* 847). Of another child prisoner whom he had personally seen, incarcerated on remand and as yet unconvicted, he wrote, "the child's face was like a white wedge of sheer terror. There was in his eyes the terror of a hunted animal. The next morning I heard him . . . crying, and calling to be let out. His cry was for his parents" (*CL* 847). The letter also detailed the sufferings of an unusually "half-witted" prisoner, with the prison number A.2.11, who, unable to sit peacefully or to control erratic mannerisms, and suspected by the prison authorities of shamming, was repeatedly flogged and punished, with the result that he was slowly "becoming insane" and his "wretched face bloated by tears and hysteria almost beyond recognition" (*CL* 853). Although A.2.11 was halfway through a six-month sentence, Wilde said, "something should be done at once for him," and Wilde pleaded with the paper to use its influence "to have this case examined into, and to see that the lunatic prisoner is properly treated" (*CL* 854). Both the flogged lunatic and the terrified children would later reappear briefly in the haunting *Ballad of Reading Gaol:*

> The vilest deeds like poison weeds,
>   Bloom well in prison-air;
> It is only what is good in Man
>   That wastes and withers there. . . .
>
> For they starve the little frightened child
>   Till it weeps both night and day:
> And they scourge the weak, and flog the fool,
>   And gibe the old and grey,
> And some grow mad, and all grow bad,
>   And none a word may say.

The only really humanizing influence in prison, Wilde's letter went on to say, is the influence of other prisoners, whose "cheerfulness under terrible circumstances, their sympathy for each other, their humility, their gentleness, their pleasant smile of greeting . . . their complete acquiescence in their punishments, are all quite wonderful" (*CL* 851). By contrast, the prison authorities, obliged to execute the most inhumane regulations, were the source of mindless cruelty. Wilde took care to exempt from his indictment the present governor of Reading, Major James Nelson, "a man of gentle and humane character, greatly liked and respected by all the prisoners. . . . [But] the system is of course beyond his reach so far as altering its rules are concerned. . . . His hands are tied" (*CL* 854). "Suffering and the community of suffering makes people kind. . . . It is not the prisoners who need reformation," he concluded, "it is the prisons" (*CL* 851–52).

Wilde's letter is a masterpiece of plain rhetoric, all the more powerful because it bore his personal signature at a time when he was carefully effacing his real identity in Dieppe and employing the signature "C. 3. 3.," his prison cell-number, in communications with his ex-fellow-inmates, as he would also do in early editions of *The Ballad of Reading Gaol*. That he published the letter using his own name at all, contrary to the advice of Ross and other friends, shows that he was acutely aware of his power to command an audience. The letter's effect on the debate that led to the 1898 Prisons Act, as well as on attitudes toward the imprisonment of children, is clear.[35] Wilde's letter appeared one day after the Irish member of Parliament Michael Davitt had questioned the home secretary on the floor of Parliament about Martin's dismissal, and it elicited leading articles in the *Daily Chronicle* (May 28) and the *Catholic Times* (June 4). A translation, along with an article about the letter, appeared in *Le Soir*, a Brussels paper. "The D. C. letter has produced . . . the best effect," Wilde wrote a few days later (*CL* 890). "Please send a *Chronicle* to my wife," he instructed Ross on May 31, knowing that it would go some way to rehabilitating him in her eyes, not least because of its sympathy with children (*CL* 869). The letter was subsequently issued as a penny pamphlet in England, titled *Children in Prison and Other Cruelties of Prison Life*.

Martin's dismissal was the catalyst for expressing the deep sense of injustice that had been simmering in Wilde for some time, and prison—and particularly his fellow inmates, or the officials who had shown him personal kindness—preyed much on his mind in these early weeks of his release. He was briefly flush with money—by some accounts, Ross had raised as much as £800 from friends, and Wilde's wife Constance supplied money too—so he sent small sums and letters to several inmates and warders at Reading whom he had known. Ross, who had returned to London on May 27 or 28, was his agent in this, in part because he carefully controlled Wilde's purse strings. The money represented "debts of honour" Wilde explained somewhat dubiously to the cautious Ross, "and I must pay them" (*CL* 860). "Please be careful not to mix the letters. They are all *nuanced*," he instructed Ross, telling him to explain to his housekeeper that any replies that came back "addressed to C. 3. 3., 24 Hornton Street [Ross's address] are for you" (*CL* 860). "I send you a line to show you that I haven't forgotten you," he wrote to one ex-fellow-inmate: "We were old friends in gallery C. 3, were we not? I hope you are getting on well and in employment. . . . I am in France by the sea, and I suppose I am getting happy again. I hope so. It was a bad time for me, but there were many good fellows in Reading. . . . Your friend, C. 3. 3." (*CL* 861–62). This letter subsequently appeared in the *Newbury Express,* on July 1, 1897, under the heading "Mr. Oscar Wilde Writes to a Former Prisoner at Reading Gaol." For all his efforts to remain C. 3. 3., in the eyes of the world he would always be Oscar Wilde.

Now that Ross had departed, Wilde's days were filled with solitary letter writing. The same day he wrote to his former fellow inmates and jailers as C. 3. 3., Wilde wrote another important letter concerning Reading Prison. "Of course I side with the prisoners. . . . I belong to their class now. I am not a scrap ashamed of having been in prison," he wrote to Major Nelson, the governor of Reading Prison, expressing his "affectionate gratitude . . . for your kindness and gentleness . . . and for the real care that you took of me at the end" (*CL* 862–63). He had delayed writing till the *Chronicle* letter appeared, and now that it had done so, he felt obliged to explain its contents to Nelson. On the night before leaving Reading, he said, he had wanted to speak to Nelson about the treatment of the young children, but doing so "might have put you in a difficult position" (*CL* 862). Nonetheless he knew that Nelson would be sympathetic with the letter's spirit and, somewhat flatteringly, he told Nelson that "the man who could change the system—if any one man can do so—is yourself" (*CL* 863). Tellingly, Wilde ended this letter not with his prison identification number but "your sincere and grateful friend, Oscar Wilde." Nelson, the first reader of *De Profundis,* would later also be one of the first readers of *The Ballad of Reading Gaol.*

Another significant correspondent at this time was the Irish socialist member of Parliament Michael Davitt, who had himself suffered frequent and lengthy imprisonment as a result of his Fenian activities and whose *Leaves From A Prison Diary* (1885) possibly served as a model for Wilde as he contemplated writing his own prison memoirs. "No one knows better than yourself how terrible life in an English prison is," wrote Wilde, "and what cruelties result from the stupidity of officialism, and the immobile ignorance of centralisation" (*CL* 870). He had heard that, prompted by his own letter to the *Chronicle,* Davitt intended questioning the home secretary in Parliament about the treatment of A.2.11 in Reading, just as he done about the dismissal of Warder Martin. He wanted to assure Davitt that everything he had stated about the treatment of A.2.11 was true and that, in writing the letter, he had not been motivated by personal bitterness: "with my own punishment I have nothing to do, except so far as it is the type of what is inflicted on much better, nicer fellows than myself" (*CL* 870). He had written "merely . . . as any other of the prisoners might have written, who had pen he could use, and found a paper sufficiently large-minded to publish his letter" (*CL* 870–71). But with the letter "I am forced to stop" and "powerless to do any more." Indeed such powerlessness "is part of my punishment—the new part that I have to face, and am facing very cheerfully and without despair or . . . complaint" (*CL* 871). Wilde accepted a measure of responsibility for his own incrimination: his "life of senseless pleasure and . . . mode of existence," he told Davitt, had been "unworthy of an artist" and still more "unworthy of my mother's son." Wilde knew that Davitt would view his mother—still known among the Irish by the pen-name *Speranza,* with which she had found fame in her youth—as an iconic figure by virtue of her poetic support for the Young Irelanders of 1848. "I have no bitterness at all," he concluded: "I have learnt pity; and that is worth learning, if one has to tramp a yard for two years to learn it" (*CL* 870).

The *Chronicle* letter had instantly renewed Wilde's self-belief. "I now think I shall write my prison article for the *Chronicle*," he remarked upon hearing of the letter's publication (*CL* 859). "I hope to be able to write again," he announced the next day (*CL* 863). "I have . . . begun to live as a man of letters should live," he declared a few days later (*CL* 873). Around May 29 or 30, he sent the *Chronicle* a postscript "of some importance" (*CL* 865), while also asking the paper's editor if he would be interested in a syndicated publication of his own prison experiences: "I think now, as the length of my letter is so great, that I could do *three* articles on Prison Life. Of course much will be psychological and introspective: and one will be on Christ as a Precursor of the Romantic Movement in Life, that lovely subject which was revealed to me when I found myself in the company of the same sort of people Christ liked, outcasts and beggars" (*CL* 865). It was around this time too that he began composing the poem that would eventually become *The Ballad of Reading Gaol*, telling Ross on May 31 that he was "forced to write poetry" and that he had "begun something that I think will be very good" (*CL* 869).[36]

———

This new fit of creativity and introspection had something to do with Ross's departure and Wilde's move to Berneval, from where Wilde wrote to Ross on the twenty-eighth: "This is my first day alone, and of course a very unhappy one. I begin to realise my terrible position of isolation, and I have been rebellious and bitter of heart all day . . . moods of rage passing over my nature, like gusts of bitter wind or storm" (*CL* 858). "I am living quietly . . . by the sea, and for the moment am quite alone," he told another correspondent, "pray let my name and place of sojourn be a secret to all" (*CL* 857). Something of Wilde's bitterness was the result of isolation as well as a concern that by cultivating a strong dependency on Ross, he was "spoiling another's life" and harming Ross in the eyes of others (*CL* 859). He was haunted by the idea that "those who love you will and do think it selfish of me to allow you and wish you to be with me from time to time," he told Ross

(*CL* 858). But there were other, even more powerful reasons for Wilde's sudden introspection.

Within a day or two of arriving in Dieppe, Wilde had written to Constance, begging for a reconciliation of some kind. He was tortured by the idea that he had caused injury and pain to Constance and their children, and despite the recently signed separation agreement, part of him still yearned to turn back the years. He especially longed to see his children and to be remembered by them with love and respect. Shortly after Constance had successfully nullified his parental rights, he had written dejectedly from prison that being deprived of his children "is and always will remain to me a source of infinite distress, of infinite pain, of grief without end or limit. That the law should decide, and take upon itself to decide, that I am one unfit to be with my own children is something quite horrible to me. The disgrace of prison is as nothing compared to it. I envy the other men who tread the yard along with me. I am sure that their children wait for them, look for their coming, will be sweet to them" (*CL* 728). The loss of his parental rights was "a tragedy" and "a blow appalling," he wrote again just days before his release, "so terrible that to expunge it from the scroll of History and Life I would gladly remain in this lonely cell for . . . ten years if needs be" (*CL* 821).[37] Wilde was never to recover from the loss of his children. A year or two later, during a visit by the journalist Claire de Pratz to his Paris hotel room, Wilde asked de Pratz: "Is there on earth a crime so terrible that in punishment of it a father can be prevented from seeing his children?"[38] There is no doubt that Wilde was a loving father and that arguably the most tragic element of his final years was his inability ever to see his sons again.[39]

On May 24, Constance wrote to her brother Otho saying that Oscar had written her a letter "full of penitence" and requesting that she bring the children to Dieppe (*CL* 865 n.2). "No one should be judged entirely by their past," pleads the guilty Sir Robert Chiltern in *An Ideal Husband:* "It is not the perfect, but the imperfect, who have need of love."[40] Constance, who two months earlier had told her brother that it would be "impossible" for her to go back to Oscar, had written back immediately, although cautiously, saying that she would see him twice a year on certain conditions, but making no promise to allow Wilde to see the boys, photographs of whom—"lovely little fellows in Eton collars" as Wilde told Ross—she enclosed with her letter (*CL* 783 n.2, 865). Her reply made Wilde distraught: "I want my boys. It is a terrible punishment," he told Ross, "and oh! how well I deserve it. But it makes me feel disgraced and evil" (*CL* 865). Constance has been much blamed in retrospect for her reluctance to see Wilde again immediately. Lord Alfred Douglas later wrote that Wilde found Constance's letter "insulting," that Wilde "turned pale and trembled" when speaking about it, and that it "finished all chance of reconciliation and finally killed all that was left" of Wilde's love for Constance.[41] Even Constance's recent biographers have faulted her: "It was time for a grand gesture," writes Franny Moyle: "that Constance failed to grasp this proved a decisive mistake."[42] "Unfortunately Constance now listened to her family and her legal advisers," says Ann Amor: "The decision was fatal to the marriage, and to any real possibility of the re-establishment of family life."[43] But marriage to Wilde had been a source of unhappiness to Constance for as many as eight years before his arrest, and she had recently told her brother, "though I think he is affectionate, I see no reason for believing that I should be able now to perform miracles" (*CL* 783–84 n.2).[44] She was unconvinced of Wilde's commitment to restarting married life, and she probably suspected, with some justice, that Wilde wished to see her again principally because this would bring him back into a relationship with their two sons. As Wilde himself later acknowledged, "what I want is the love of my children" (*CL* 952).

Wilde cannot have known at this point—as he was to find out from his old friend Carlos Blacker at the end of July—that Constance was suffering from creeping paralysis, which made even simple movements painful and would contribute to her death the following year.[45] She was now lame, and even the act of writing was very difficult. It is also likely that she was more ambivalent than Wilde realized, for by early

July she was writing to him every week. But despite the frequency of her letters, "she continually gave some reason for postponing seeing him."[46] She did not rule out the possibility of resuming married life, contends one of her biographers, but she allowed herself to be persuaded by her family and her legal advisers that a trial period must first elapse, during which Oscar must demonstrate his remorse and his determination to lead a new life.[47] Perhaps Ross too hoped to bring about a reconciliation, since he sent Wilde a photograph of Constance in early July. A few weeks later Wilde received with shock the news of his wife's deteriorating physical condition. "I had no idea it was so serious" he told Blacker, and he could now see that "Of course she could not come here . . . the journey would be too much" (*CL* 920). Should he go and see her in about three weeks' time, he asked Blacker? "I really think it would be better for her to see me, and have it over. I would only stay a couple of days," he told Blacker on July 29 (*CL* 920). "I don't mind *my life* being wrecked," he informed Blacker a few days later: "that is as it should be—but when I think of poor Constance I simply want to kill myself" (*CL* 921).

Blacker, to whom Wilde had dedicated *The Happy Prince* in 1888 and whom Wilde at this point considered a close family friend, was perhaps more instrumental in thwarting any rapprochement, however unlikely, than Wilde realized. Constance and the children were at this period vacationing with Blacker and his family in Freiburg, Germany, where he lived, and he cannot have been unaware of the depth or complexity of Constance's feelings. Moreover there was a strain of homophobia in Blacker's makeup, which meant that he could never reconcile himself to what he had learnt about Wilde as a result of his trials and conviction. Blacker's biographer, J. Robert Maguire, says that "Blacker could only have been dumbstruck by the prospect of Wilde's coming to Freiburg, where his presence would be bound to attract unwelcome attention and involve impossible complications."[48] In reply to Wilde's question, Blacker advised Wilde against visiting Constance and the children, at least until the boys had returned to boarding school and

Constance had moved to her new home near Nervi, Italy, as she intended to do once the summer was over: "Mr. Blacker has persuaded him to wait and come to me at Nervi when I am settled," wrote Constance to her brother on August 5 (*CL* 865, note 2). "I am greatly disappointed that Constance has not asked me to come and see the children," Wilde wrote to Blacker in early September: "I don't suppose now I shall ever see them" (*CL* 935). "Not a sign of Oscar or a word from him," Constance wrote to Blacker from Nervi on September 25, "but I have an idea that he will turn up some day without writing."[49] But by this point it was too late. "I have never been so unhappy," declared Wilde to Blacker on September 6: "I am trying to get some money to go to Italy, and hope to be able to find my way to Sicily" (*CL* 935). Had Constance allowed him to see his boys, he wrote Blacker sixteen days later, "my life would, I think, have been quite different. But this she would not do. I don't in any way venture to blame her for her action, but every action has its consequence" (*CL* 947).

—————

It was not simply Constance's obduracy that had changed Wilde's attitude. By June 2 or possibly even earlier, Wilde was writing "beautiful letters" to Lord Alfred Douglas, who was clearly unaware of all that Wilde had said against him in *De Profundis*. By June 4, he was telling Douglas: "Don't think I don't love you. Of course I love you more than anyone else" (*CL* 872, 880). This apparent change of heart, if that's what it was, is amazing. Shortly before leaving prison, Wilde had stated that "on no account" was Lord Alfred Douglas to be told of the arrangements made for Wilde's release: "for him to appear . . . would be horrible. I could not stand it" (*CL* 810). From prison, Wilde had instructed Ross to write Douglas saying "that I will receive any letter from him through you, but that he is not to attempt to see me, till I allow him." (*CL* 824). To be with him again would be "to return to the hell from which . . . I have been released," he had told Ross as recently as May 28, either forgetting what he had written near the end of *De Profundis* about reuniting with Douglas in some quiet foreign town, or else hoping that Ross had not yet read the manuscript: "I hope never to see him again" (*CL* 858). But by this date, Adey had forwarded to Wilde "a poem from Bosie—a love lyric!" (*CL* 861). And the previous night, Wilde had lost sleep over a "revolting" letter from Douglas, which "foolishly" he had read twice over and left by his bedside (*CL* 858). Wilde now had a "real terror" of Douglas, he confessed, and felt him as "an evil influence." Bosie "can almost ruin me," he stated to Ross at the end of May: "I earnestly beg that some entreaty be made to him not to do so a second time. His letters to me are infamous" (*CL* 865).

But by June 6, Wilde was writing to Douglas every day, experiencing "the strange new joy of talking to you daily" as he put it to Douglas, and by this point Douglas was in constant communication with Wilde by letter and telegram (*CL* 885). By June 7 or 8, Wilde was exploring possible "conditions" for a meeting with Douglas and asking Lady Queensberry, Douglas's doting mother, for her consent to such a meeting. Lady Queensberry, who had divorced Douglas's father, the Marquess of Queensberry, ten years earlier on the grounds of his adultery, had always been sympathetic to Wilde, it seemed, and Wilde saw no reason for thinking she would be averse. On June 9, Lady Queensberry replied via More Adey that "nothing would ever induce me to interfere now in any matter between [Wilde] and Alfred" and that "Mr. Wilde must decide all matters connected with seeing or not seeing Alfred entirely for himself."[50] By the middle of June, Wilde had issued an invitation to his "honey-sweet boy" to "come on Saturday. . . . I have a bathing costume for you, but you had better get one in Paris. Also bring me lots of books, and cigarettes. I cannot get good cigarettes here or at Dieppe" (*CL* 898–99). "I am going to let him come and see me in a few days," Wilde wrote of Douglas to another correspondent on the fifteenth: "Our lives are divided, but we love each other deeply and our souls touch in myriad ways through the estranging air" (*CL* 898).

What had brought about Wilde's change of attitude to Douglas in the space of barely two weeks? Possibly Wilde's change of heart owes something to Constance's refusal of him. The letter in which Constance had set conditions upon seeing him had coincided with Wilde's receipt of the "revolting" letter in which Douglas said in effect "I am told that you now hate me and do not wish to see me or have anything to do with me, but all the same I write to tell you that I have not changed to you, in spite of all the efforts that have been made to put me against you, that I have remembered and kept my solemn promise to stick to you through thick and thin, and that I long to see you again."[51] Douglas offered him love, whereas Constance seemed to offer a cold, disapproving shoulder. As Wilde was to write later in justification of his decision to go with Bosie to Naples, "I cannot live without the atmosphere of Love: I must love and be loved, whatever price I pay for it" (CL 942).

But there is at least one other possibility. Wilde's expressions of horror in the face of Douglas's letters are almost exclusively voiced in letters to the more upstanding and respectable Robbie Ross. Ross clearly disapproved of Douglas, but his distaste was also driven by jealousy at the depth of feeling Douglas was capable of arousing in his friend. Wilde may have been sensitive to this jealousy, especially since he wanted to retain Ross's love as well. Moreover, Ross controlled Wilde's purse strings and was thus keenly aware that Wilde's association with Douglas would nullify the terms of the separation agreement between Oscar and Constance. Ross was eager to restore something of Wilde's standing in the eyes of society, and keen also to bring about a rapprochement between Wilde and his family. Ross felt that for Wilde to get back together with Douglas would be a disastrous misstep. Just as importantly, Wilde, who playfully called Ross his "financier" and his "banker," was aware and possibly fearful of the power Ross held over him: the entirely business-like tone of a recent letter, he tells Ross, "makes me nervous . . . that it is merely a form of the calm that hides a storm." (CL 883, 877). The marked contrast in tone between Wilde's affectionate and playful letters to Douglas in the first weeks of June and the sometimes stiff and business-like tone of his letters to Ross, who was demurring at the price Wilde proposed to pay to rent a house and "scolded"

Wilde for distributing small amounts to his fellow-inmates, suggests that Wilde was playing a double-game, concealing from Ross the real depth and nature of his feelings for Bosie (*CL* 888). As Douglas himself later put it, "it was easy for me to see that Oscar was very far from having arrived at the state of mind so much desiderated by his 'faithful friends'. . . . To put it plainly, I guessed at once that he was longing to see me, but that other people were putting obstacles in his way."[52]

Wilde must have known, at least in a general way, the risks he ran in courting Douglas's friendship and love. "I love you more than anyone else," he wrote to Douglas on June 4, but "our lives are irreparably severed, as far as meeting goes. What is left to us is the knowledge that we love each other, and every day I think of you" (*CL* 880). We cannot know if Wilde believed that he was under surveillance, but there is little doubt that Ross and Adey suspected he was: days earlier, Adey had been told by his lawyer Holman, who was also Queensberry's lawyer, that the Marquess of Queensberry had "made arrangements for being informed if his son joins Mr. Wilde and . . . expressed his intention of shooting one or both."[53] It seems certain that it was Ross who, having by now got wind of Wilde's invitation to Bosie to come to Berneval, informed Wilde's own solicitor, Arthur Hansell, thereby prompting the latter to write to Wilde directly, in the middle of the month, resigning his position with immediate effect and refusing to act for Wilde personally henceforth (although Hansell agreed to remain a trustee of Wilde's deed of separation).[54] "It is impossible for us to meet," Wilde painfully told Douglas, as a result, on June 17: "I am so upset and distressed in nerve by my solicitor's letter, and the apprehension of serious danger, that simply I must be alone. . . . I have to find out what grounds my solicitor has for his sudden action, and of course if your father . . . came over and made a scene and scandal it would utterly destroy my possible future and alienate all my friends" (*CL* 901). Wilde was terrified by the solicitor's letter: "chasms of moonless night divide us," he told Douglas, but "we cannot cross it without hideous and nameless peril" (*CL* 902). "The beast [Queensberry] has been sending detectives to Dieppe and annoying the poor chap again," Douglas told his brother on August 5.[55]

––––––––

The solicitor's admonishing letter brought a temporary halt to Wilde's determination to see Douglas, but it also greatly affected his mood generally. "It would be no joy for me to let you see me as I am now," he tells Douglas straight away (*CL* 902). "I have been so worried—Bosie wiring all day long, and Hansell throwing up my interests—that I am not well. I simply cannot stand worry," he writes on June 19 (*CL* 903). For the time being, Wilde could distract himself by throwing himself into what little social and spiritual life his existence in Berneval as "Sebastian Melmoth" allowed. He bathed daily in the sea, he regularly attended mass and vespers, and he became a regular devotee at a small chapel or shrine, "as tiny as an undergraduate's room at Oxford," a few steps from the hotel where he had been staying (*CL* 869). He became particularly close friends with the local priest, M. Constant Trop-Hardy, an old curé who "influenced [him] very much" and who thought him "*volontaire* [self-willed] but extremely *good*" (*CL* 885).[56] This presented Wilde with a dilemma: should he confess his "great disgrace" to Trop-Hardy? (*CL* 885). We have no way of knowing what, if anything, Wilde confessed to his new friend, but Wilde was very nearly received into the Catholic Church at Berneval, and according to Father Cuthbert Dunne, the priest who would later receive Wilde into the Catholic Church on his deathbed, he was only deterred at this point by Ross, who feared that Wilde "might perhaps be in 'one of his varying moods' and that, if received, he might not persevere" (*CL* 1226).[57]

On or shortly after June 21, Wilde moved into a small villa or chalet, the Chalet Bourgeat, in the grounds of the hotel. He had described it excitedly to his English friends at the beginning of the month—it had a writing room, a small garden, a balcony, and several guestrooms—but the necessary down payment was slow in coming from Ross, so Wilde had been forced to wait to move in. A "simple and peaceful . . . life may be waiting for me in this little garden by the sea," he wrote near the end of the first week of June (*CL* 882). Bosie was to have been one of the first guests to stay, and although this became impossible, Wilde continued to speak excitedly about the chalet and its decoration for much of June and July. Upon moving in, one of the first things he did was to place on the chalet's walls a print of William Nicholson's famous portrait of Queen Victoria, published in the June 1897 number of *New Review*. "Every poet should gaze at the portrait of his Queen," he remarked (*CL* 897).

June 22, 1897, was the Diamond Jubilee of Queen Victoria, and Wilde—for whom Queen Victoria was, along with Napoleon and Victor Hugo, one of the three great personalities of the nineteenth century—was determined to celebrate the Jubilee in style.[58] Doubtless pining for his sons, he invited twelve local boys to a celebratory feast in the garden of his chalet, whose walls were being freshly papered. The list of guests "was strictly limited to twelve," he joked: "as the garden only holds *six* at most, I felt that *twelve* would be sufficient: I hate crowds" (*CL* 906). "My *fête* was a huge success," he told Douglas in a letter the following day:

> Fifteen *gamins* were entertained on strawberries and cream, apricots, chocolates, cakes, and *sirop de grenadine*. I had a huge iced cake with *Jubilé de la Reine Victoria* in pink sugar just rosetted with green, and a great wreath of red roses round it all. Every child was asked beforehand to choose his present: they all chose instruments of music!!!
>
> 6 accordions
>
> 5 trompettes
>
> 4 clairons.
>
> They sang the Marseillaise and other songs, and danced a *ronde,* and also played "God save the Queen:" they said it was "God save the Queen," and I did not like to differ from them. They also all had flags which I gave them. They were most gay and sweet. I gave the health of *La Reine*

d'Angleterre, and they cried "*Vive la Reine d'Angleterre*"!!!! Then I gave "*La France, mère de tous les artistes,*" and finally I gave *Le Président de la République:* I thought I had better do so. They cried out with one accord "*Vivent le Président de la République et Monsieur Melmoth*"!!! So I found my name coupled with that of the President. It was an amusing experience as I am hardly more than a month out of gaol.

They stayed from 4.30 to seven o'clock and played games: on leaving I gave them each a basket with a jubilee cake frosted pink and inscribed, and *bonbons.* (*CL* 906–7)

Coinciding with his move into the Chalet Bourgeat, the feast might unconsciously have constituted a celebration of Wilde's own newfound independence as well as a form of compensation for the painful loss of his own children. But whatever its motivations, the party, rather than spreading joy as Wilde had intended, had unfortunate consequences, said one of the invited children years later, when recalling the party's effects on Wilde's standing in Berneval. "People began to gossip. First of all, why had he only invited the boys and not the girls and their schoolmistress? Why this ostracism? . . . Then, one day—it's unclear how—we learned that our Mr. Sebastian Melmoth was not at all Sebastian Melmoth but, in fact, Oscar Wilde, whose prison sentence was still fresh in people's minds. The villagers began to be worried. . . . Parents forbade their children . . . to have anything to do with a man hiding under an alias and attempting to smother a recent scandal. . . . If Sebastian Melmoth honoured Berneval by his presence when we were unaware of his true identity, Oscar Wilde shamed us. We steered clear of him now that he was unmasked."[59]

The day following the feast, Wilde dined with the Norwegian painter Frits Thaulow and his wife, who had gone out of their way to make Wilde feel welcome in their house. "Mr. Wilde, my wife and I would feel honoured to have you dine with us *en famille* this evening," Thaulow

had loudly proclaimed upon witnessing Wilde being publicly humili-
ated in a Dieppe cafe.[60] Wilde became a frequent guest at the Thaulows',
and at one point the Thaulows planned a reception in his honor. They
sent invitations to the sub-prefect, the mayor, and other citizens of note,
French and English, but it is not known which of them, if any, attended
the party. The Thaulows' fellow-Norwegian, the painter Christian
Krogh, has left a memorable account of one dinner at their house in
the course of which Wilde announced to his shocked fellow guests that
he was writing an essay titled "A Defence of Drunkenness." "London
must be shocked at least twice a year," he explained.[61] When asked
whether he was being serious, Wilde replied, "Oh, yes; the soul is never
liberated except by drunkenness. Here in a small place like Dieppe your
soul can listen to the words and harmonies and behold the colours of
the Great Silence. And that intoxicates. But one is not always in Dieppe.
And it is difficult to find the Great Silence. But a waiter with a tray will
always find it for you. Knock, and the door will always open, the door
of *le paradis artificiel.*"[62]

Accompanying him to the Thaulows on June 23 was the dissolute
poet Ernest Dowson, now one of his closest confidantes, whom Wilde
had known back in London and who resided near Dieppe, at Arques-
la-Bataille, until his departure for London in mid-July. Dowson had
dined with Wilde at Berneval on June 3, along with the musician Dalhousie Young and the painter Charles Conder, staying over till the
fourth or the fifth. During this visit the wealthy Young—one of just a
handful of British intellectuals to have publicly defended Wilde in
1895—offered to have a house built at Berneval for Wilde "so that I
shall have a home" (*CL* 1089).[63] Wilde declined Young's offer, calling
it "a piece of generous but Quixotic enthusiasm," on the grounds that
he "hardly knew" Young and "did not think it right to accept such an
offer" (*CL* 1089). He remained ever-grateful for Dowson's frank and
unguarded friendship in these difficult days, at one point thanking
Dowson for "the many gentle ways by which you recalled to me that,
once at any rate, I was a Lord of Language, and had myself the soul of

a poet" (CL 883). Dowson's premature death in 1900, just nine months before his own, was to affect him greatly. For his part, Dowson was impressed by Wilde's "enormous joy in life just at this moment" and "had some difficulty in suppressing my own sourness" as a result.[64] His first impression was that Wilde had changed a great deal for the better: "he seems of much broader sympathies, much more human and simple. . . . His delight in the country, in walking, in the simplicities of life is enchanting."[65]

Within days of their first meeting, the two men were seeing each other regularly, and if rumor is to be believed, Dowson tried to interest Wilde in having sexual relations with women by taking him to a brothel: "It was like chewing cold mutton," Wilde is reputed to have said on leaving, "but tell it in England, where it will entirely restore my reputation."[66] He told Dowson: "There is a fatality about our being together that is astounding—or rather quite probable" (CL 901). The "fatality" is partly attributable to a shared love of poetry and alcohol, particularly Pernod and other brands of absinthe. "I decided this morning to take a Pernod," Wilde told Dowson of one early morning tipple: "The result was marvellous. At 8.30 I was dead. Now I am alive, and all is perfect, except your absence" (CL 901). When Christian Krogh complained privately that Dowson drank too much absinthe, Wilde replied "if he didn't drink he would be somebody else. *Il faut accepter la personnalité comme elle est. Il ne faut jamais regretter qu'un poète est soûl, il faut regretter que les soûls ne soient pas toujours poètes.*"[67] "Come with vine-leaves in your hair," Wilde wrote to Dowson from the Café Suisse, one of their favorite Dieppe haunts (CL 901). "His gorgeous spirits cheered me mightily," Dowson wrote of Wilde at this time: "I was amused by the unconscious contrast between his present talk about his changed position & his notions of economy & his practise, which is perversely extravagant."[68]

————————

Other visitors at this time included the artist William Rothenstein, who brought a cigarette box (Wilde's cigarettes were being destroyed by the damp sea air) as well as lithographs and a clever pastel he had created in Paris in late 1891, showing Wilde wearing the red waistcoat he always wore in the city, in homage to the writer Théophile Gautier.[69] Other visitors included Smithers's companionable assistant, Edward Strangman, who brought much-needed books; Arthur Cruttenden, a recently released fellow convict whom Wilde wished to set on his feet; and the writer André Gide, who arrived unheralded from Paris on a cold ugly day in June and was discovered waiting at the hotel when Wilde returned late at night from Dieppe. Gide found Wilde in pensive mood, careful to subdue any obvious display of emotion in front of the hotel staff, as well as apprehensive that a peacock feather that his servant had brought him the previous evening presaged a misfortune. When Gide asked him if he had foreseen the dangers attending his scandalous life in the years before prison and if he had "rushed into" them, Wilde replied: "Of course! Of course I knew that there would be a catastrophe—that one or another, I was expecting it. It had to end that way. Just imagine: it wasn't possible to go any further, and it couldn't last. That's why, you see, it has to be ended. Prison has completely changed me. I counted on it for that. [Bosie] is terrible; he can't understand it; he can't understand my not going back to the same existence; he accuses others of having changed me. But one should never go back to the same existence. . . . My life is like a work of art; an artist never starts the same thing twice . . . or if he does, it's that he isn't successful. My life before prison was as successful as possible. Now it's something that's over."[70]

Wilde recounted much about his prison life, telling Gide that he had learned the value of pity and that only pity had kept him from killing himself in prison. He complained that Douglas "writes me terrible letters" and "doesn't understand—can't understand—me any more."[71] He told Gide that he reiterated in each new letter to Douglas that "we cannot follow the same path," that "he has his [and] I have mine." He also told Gide about plans for two new plays, both biblical dramas— the first about Pharaoh, the second about Ahab and Jezebel—as well as an "ingenious" story about Judas.[72] Gide noticed the abundance of books in Wilde's rooms, including his own recently published autobiographical prose poem *Le Nourritures Terrestres* [The Fruits of the Earth], about which Wilde was more discreet than he had been days earlier in a letter to Douglas.[73] "Gide's book fails to fascinate me," Wilde had told Douglas: "The egoistic note is, of course, and always has been to me, the primal and ultimate note of modern art, but *to be an Egoist, one must have an Ego.* It is not everyone who says 'I, I' who can enter into the Kingdom of Art" (*CL* 874). The visit ended with Wilde making Gide promise never to use the word *I* in his writing again: "in art, don't you see, there is no first person."[74]

Many of these visits brought Wilde joyful respites from loneliness. He looked "surprisingly well, thinner and healthier than heretofore," wrote Rothenstein: he had "lost none of his old wit and gaiety" and was "full of plans for the future."[75] This corresponds with Wilde's own description of himself, to Frank Harris, as "cheerful, happy, and . . . full [of] that passionate interest in life and art that was the dominant chord of my nature" (*CL* 895). But this was in the period when Wilde harbored hopes of seeing Douglas again. And when any conflict or unpleasantness threatened, Wilde cut these friendly visits short. "I have been obliged to ask my friends to leave," he tells Douglas upon receiving the solicitor's resignation letter: "I find that any worry utterly destroys my health, and makes me horrid and irritable and unkind, though I hate to be so" (*CL* 901). "I want to have a poet to talk to, as I have had lots of bad news since you left me," he wrote to Dowson on June 28, "I want to be consoled" (*CL* 908).

The bad news was not merely the fact of his solicitor's resignation, the fears raised by the solicitor's letter, or the cancellation of Douglas's visit: just as troubling was the fallout from the solicitor's letter. Perhaps remembering Wilde's request of late May that some entreaty be made to Douglas not to ruin him for a second time, Ross had written to Douglas taking responsibility for the solicitor's action and reminding Bosie of the risks his friendship posed to Wilde. Bosie had replied angrily, chastising Ross for his "interference," "intrigue," and "backstairs wire-pulling,"[76] leading Ross in turn to write—with anger, sarcasm, and a note of unconcealed triumph—that since Bosie was better off than any of them, why did he not provide the £150 per year that Wilde would lose through associating with him: "With your £150 he will have the added pleasure of your perpetual society and your inspiring temper."[77] "You overlook the fact that I am passionately devoted to him," Douglas replied once again, "and that my longing to see him simply eats my heart away day and night."[78] The fiasco led to a permanent, ultimately fatal breach between the two men Wilde most loved, and it evidently caused him considerable pain. "Bosie has sent me a long indictment of you," he wrote to Ross on June 28, "you can understand in what tone I shall answer him" (*CL* 908). "I have written a long letter—of twelve foolscap pages—to Bosie," he told Ross on July 6, "to point out to him that I owe everything to you and your friends, and that whatever life I have as an artist in the future will be due to you. . . . I hope *you* will be firm with Bosie" (*CL* 909). "I have no words in which to express my contempt for his lack of imaginative insight," he wrote again two weeks later, "and his dullness of sensitive nature" (*CL* 915). But Wilde was looking to Ross to exhibit a "firmness with Bosie" of which he himself was incapable, or else simply misleading Ross, for on July 7 he wrote to Douglas in a tone that was anything but admonishing: "My darling Boy, I received your letters all right. . . . I write now on nicer things just to know how you are, and why you stay at a place that bores you. . . . I hate to know that you are lonely. . . . Tell me about your days. Is Gaston waiting? Are you writing anything? Whom have you met? Tomorrow I am going to write my poem. I will send it to you. With my love, dearest boy, ever your Oscar" (*CL* 910).

Given the absence of any surviving letters from Wilde to Douglas between July 7 and August 31, and giving the loving nature of the letters to Bosie that frame this gap, there seems no reason to doubt Bosie's claims, in his *Autobiography,* that Wilde now sent him letters containing more and more affection and that Bosie later destroyed "many of those which contained the most exaggerated expressions of affection and devotion." According to Douglas, Wilde "made no secret of the fact that he was longing to see me again and that it was only the necessity of 'keeping in' with certain people, including, of course, Ross . . . that prevented him."[79]

As this clandestine correspondence hurtled toward its inevitable conclusion, Wilde continued to amuse himself in Dieppe cafes or dining with the few Dieppe residents willing to be seen publically with him. "He spent money with the recklessness of sailors on shore—and prisoners free of gaol," Robert Sherard later wrote, and he continued to issue invitations to friends to visit.[80] The actor-manager Charles Wyndham came in July with the object of getting Wilde interested in either writing a new play or else adapting Scribe's *Le Verre D'Eau.* Robert Sherard and Robert Ross visited in August, and during this visit the heterosexual Sherard—who had always adamantly and foolishly disbelieved in Wilde's homosexuality—caught sight of Wilde in a sexual embrace with Ross, the first and perhaps the most loyal of his male lovers. Years later, Sherard wrote "there is no doubt—and I am speaking from absolute knowledge—that it was [Ross] who . . . dragged Oscar back into the delights of homosexuality,"[81] although Neil McKenna says that Ross only answered Wilde's need for "comfort," providing "sex as consolation, sex born out of long and deep affection . . . loving, but . . . not love."[82] Back in England, Wilde's friend Max Beerbohm gossiped that "I hear that Oscar is under surveillance by the French police. I am afraid he may be playing the fool."[83]

At some point in late July or August, Wilde was also visited by a young architect, John Rowland Fothergill, a friend of Ross's, whom Wilde had already dubbed (without meeting him) "the Architect of the Moon." Fothergill brought with him, as a gift for Wilde, a copy of Adolf Erman's recently translated *Life of Ancient Egypt,* which Wilde had joked he wanted "only to find out how Pharaoh said to his chief butler 'pass the cucumbers.' "[84] Fothergill stayed for what Wilde called "a sextette of suns" (*CL* 942) and later recorded the impression left upon him by Wilde immediately upon his arrival:

Dance of the Seven Veils is, and can see that invisible dance."[88] Beardsley was accompanied by the publisher Leonard Smithers, whom Wilde had never met before and whom he found "very intoxicated but amusing" (*CL* 919). Smithers has been called the "publisher to the decadents," and he had once vowed "I'll publish anything that the others are afraid of."[89] By this date, he had published important volumes by the decadent poets Ernest Dowson, Theodore Wratislaw, and Arthur Symons, as well as John Addington Symonds's *A Problem in Modern Ethics,* the pornographic novel *Teleny,* and the avant-garde periodical *The Savoy.* He also had exclusive rights to publish new work by Beardsley, who had designed his publisher's logo and to whom he paid a weekly retainer, prompting Wilde to call him facetiously the "owner of Aubrey" (*CL* 924). Wilde's relations with Smithers would deepen considerably over the coming months: on August 4, thanking Smithers for sending a gift of books, Wilde wrote "I hope very much that some day soon I shall have something that you will like well enough to publish," and on August 18, he told Ernest Dowson that "Smithers is devoted, and breakfasts here every Monday. I like him immensely" (*CL* 922, 926). Fothergill, in his unpublished memoirs, mentions that Smithers was briefly a fellow guest during his own stay in Wilde's chalet. On August 22, Wilde wrote to Smithers: "there is a moral atmosphere about Dieppe that you should come over and dissipate." Wilde had by now come to appreciate Smithers's "most interesting and . . . charming personality" (*CL* 926), as is clear from the memorable portrait of Smithers he etched in a letter to Turner dated August 10: "He is usually in a large straw hat, has a blue tie fastened with a diamond brooch of the impurest water—or perhaps wine, as he never touches water: it goes to his head at once. His face, clean-shaven as befits a priest who serves at the altar whose God is Literature, is wasted and pale—not with poetry, but with poets, who, he says, have wrecked his life by insisting on publishing with him. He loves first editions, especially of women: little girls are his passion. He is the most learned erotomaniac in Europe. He is also a delightful companion, and a dear fellow, very kind to me" (*CL* 924). By mid-September, Wilde and Smithers had "struck up an alliance."[90]

Relations with the illustrator Aubrey Beardsley, by contrast, were frostier. On seeing Beardsley with Smithers in Dieppe on July 24, Wilde had issued an invitation to Beardsley to come dine with him in Berneval, and relations were evidently still friendly when Wilde saw Beardsley again a few days later in Dieppe, in the company of Conder and Young, and "made Aubrey buy a hat more silver than silver" (*CL* 921). But Beardsley kept apart from Wilde, and when Wilde attempted to call on Beardsley, "Beardsley received him with cold embarrassment . . . and then wrote asking him not to call again."[91] "It was *lâche* of Aubrey," Wilde reportedly remarked later: "a boy like that, whom I made! No, it was too *lâche* of Aubrey," and when Smithers proposed the creation of a new magazine in December, Beardsley agreed to contribute a cover design and be the Art Editor only "if it is quite agreed that Oscar Wilde contributes nothing to the magazine anonymously, pseudonymously, or otherwise."[92]

Wilde's relationship with Smithers would turn out to be of the utmost importance to what remained of his literary career. "I don't dream of social rehabilitation," he told W. R. Paton, "nor do I want it, but I *do* want to do artistic work again" (*CL* 922). Perhaps spurred by his sudden friendship with Dowson, as well as by his reading around this time of A. E. Housman's *A Shropshire Lad,* he made serious advances in the composition of *The Ballad of Reading Gaol* once he moved into the Chalet Bourgeat in late June, and by mid-July, he was telling Adey and Ross, "I like most of what I have done," "the poem is nearly finished," and "some of the verses are awfully good" (*CL* 914, 915).[93] The poem is usually discussed as the fruit of Wilde's imprisonment and of his unwilling witness to the execution at Reading on July 7, 1896, of the murderer Charles Wooldridge. But its central refrain—that "all men kill the thing they love, / . . . Some with a flattering word. / The coward does it with a kiss, / The brave man with a sword"—draws upon Wilde's recent tribulations with Constance and Bosie as much as it reflects

Wilde's attitude to Wooldridge's murder of his wife. Had Constance unwittingly "killed" the man she loved, or vice versa, as Douglas later suggested? Was Wilde aware that the epistolary courtship dance he was now performing with Douglas was an extension of the fatal course along which he had started five years earlier? "Why is it that one runs to one's ruin?" he asked Blacker in early August, with regard to his relationship with Constance: "Why has destruction such fascination?" (*CL* 921).

When Smithers entered Wilde's life in late July, Wilde had by his own account nearly finished the poem and begun to think about its publication.[94] "I hope the *Chronicle*—reckless in art—will publish [it]," he declared only half-jokingly on July 20 (*CL* 916). He knew that the poem was written to a high standard and would find a receptive, ready-made audience in the *Chronicle*. "I am out-Henleying Kipling!" he wrote to Strangman (*CL* 916). By combining the grim realism of the poet William Ernest Henley—who had a real passion for what is horrible, ugly, or grotesque, Wilde had once said—with the subject matter and form of Rudyard Kipling's "Danny Deever," from *Barrack-Room Ballads,* he was surpassing them both. "It is a new style for me," he explained, "full of actuality and life in its directness of message and meaning," more realistic than anything he had previously written and "drawn from actual experience, a sort of denial of my own philosophy of art" (*CL* 922, 928).

Wilde was occupied on the poem for much of July and during Ross's visit in August, although by his own account he could only work for about an hour and a half at a time, and after that was utterly prostrate. By the third week of August, he was struggling to finish the poem and getting "sick of my manuscript," though he knew that some stanzas were "splendid" and he had now been persuaded that Smithers should publish the poem in book form in England (*CL* 926). He had not given up on the idea of newspaper publication as well, in either England or America, and he harbored hopes of publishing the poem in either Joseph Pulitzer's *New York World* or William Randolph Hearst's *New York*

Journal for a hefty fee. On August 25, he sent the unfinished poem off to Smithers, saying, "I want to see it type-written" (*CL* 931).[95]

Although much of *The Ballad* had evidently been written by the final week of August, when Wilde sent it to be typewritten, Wilde had by this date reached a hiatus in the poem's composition. "I am not in the mood to do the work I want," he wrote to Rothenstein on August 24, "and I fear I never shall be. The intense energy of creation has been kicked out of me. I don't care now to struggle to get back what, when I had it, gave me little pleasure" (*CL* 930). In part this hiatus is attributable to Robbie Ross's departure for England on August 19; Ross had offered much useful advice in the course of his visit, and his literary instinct and judgment, Wilde later said, had always influenced him (*CL* 971). Ross's departure the previous May had prompted Wilde to begin writing the poem, but his absence now had the opposite effect. "I miss you dreadfully, dear boy," Wilde wrote Ross on the twenty-fourth, enclosing a newly written verse for Ross's comment: "I fear it is out of harmony, but wish you were here to talk about it" (*CL* 929). But by this date it was Wilde himself who was "out of harmony," and there were other reasons for the hiatus in the poem's composition.

"Since Bosie wrote that he could not afford forty francs to come to Rouen to see me, he has never written. Nor have I. I am greatly hurt by his meanness and lack of imagination," ends Wilde's letter to Ross of August 24 (*CL* 930). These disenchanted sentences are the prelude to one of the most momentous decisions of Wilde's life—to what Richard Ellmann has called Wilde's "second fall."[96] Wilde had proposed meeting Douglas in Rouen, fifty miles south—he "could not face Paris yet," he had told Douglas—and the nonchalance with which he reveals this fact to Ross suggests that Wilde had at least partially reconciled Ross to the inevitability of such a meeting.[97] That Wilde complains of the manner in which Douglas has rejected his proposal, moreover, only makes it more striking that within a matter of days Wilde had run into Douglas's welcoming arms.

"Do you really think that it is weakness that yields to temptation?" Sir Robert Chiltern asks Lord Goring in *An Ideal Husband:* "There are terrible temptations that it requires strength, strength and courage, to yield to. To stake all one's life on a single moment, to risk everything on one throw . . . there is no weakness in that." On August 28 or 29, Wilde finally met up with Douglas, in Rouen, where they stayed overnight at the Hôtel de la Poste under their own names. Douglas provides a moving account of their reunion in his 1929 *Autobiography:* "I have often thought since that if he or I had died directly after [our reunion], our friendship would have ended in a beautiful and romantic way. Poor Oscar cried when I met him at the station, and I did the same. We walked about all day, arm in arm, or hand in hand, and were perfectly happy. Next day he went back to Berneval and I returned to Paris, but we had settled that when I went to Naples about six weeks later he was to join me there."[98]

Love is "better than wisdom, and more precious than riches," declares the hero of Wilde's story "The Fisherman and His Soul," in one of most moving and powerful paeans to the spirit of love in all of Wilde's works: "fires cannot destroy it, nor can the waters quench it."[99] "My only hope of again doing beautiful work in art is being with you," Wilde wrote to Douglas upon his return to Berneval: "Everyone is furious with me for going back to you, but they don't understand us. I feel that it is only with you that I can do anything at all. Do remake my ruined life for me, and then our friendship and love will have a different meaning to the world. I wish that when we met at Rouen we had not parted at all. There are such wide abysses now of space and land between us. But we love each other" (*CL* 933).

4

The Pursuit of Love

EVEN WILDE'S CLOSEST friends were shocked by his return to Douglas, when they found out about it some weeks later, but in hindsight, the reunion was predictable. "My going back to Bosie was psychologically inevitable," Wilde wrote to a reproachful Robbie Ross a month later: "setting aside the interior life of the soul with its passion for self-realisation at all costs, the world forced it on me. . . . The world shuts its gateway against me, and the door of Love lies open" (*CL* 942). "You leave out of consideration the great love I have for Bosie," he remarked to a shocked Reginald Turner, "I love him, and have always loved him" (*CL* 948). "I must remake my maimed life on my own lines," he told Blacker (*CL* 947).

Whatever the exact nature of the agreement made by Wilde at Rouen to meet up with Douglas again later in Naples, Wilde kept it secret from even his closest friends.[1] But he was clearly restless when he returned to Berneval. "I think of going south," he told Rothenstein on September 2, without mentioning his travelling companion (*CL* 933). "I simply cannot stand Berneval. I nearly committed suicide there last Thursday," he told Ross on the fourth (*CL* 934). "Yes, I saw Bosie," he added with little fanfare, "and of course I love him as I always did, with a sense of tragedy and ruin." "My last fortnight at Berneval has been black and dreadful, and quite suicidal," he told Blacker on the sixth: "I have never been so unhappy. I am trying to get some money to go to Italy" (*CL* 935).

Berneval had become intolerable, but it was back to Rouen, less than a week after he and Douglas had departed from there, that Wilde initially fled. Ostensibly Wilde planned to finish *A Florentine Tragedy,* but he was lonely and craved love and company—if not Douglas's, then some other close friend's. Turner, who had been in Rouen when Wilde met Douglas the previous week, was still there, and in swift succession Wilde invited Smithers, Ross, and Rothenstein to join him there also. In the event, none of them came, and according to the novelist Gertrude Atherton, who was staying at the same Rouen boarding house as Turner, Turner had felt seriously compromised by Wilde's earlier visit. As Lord Alfred Douglas later observed, "in those days . . . it required a certain amount of courage to be seen about in Wilde's company."[2] Turner was trying to live as if he had never known Wilde, according to Atherton: Wilde was "an evil influence" and "distorted one's outlook on life," she reports Turner as saying, and when Wilde insisted that it was Turner's duty to stand by him, and that he must have companionship or he would go mad, Turner's response was to turn tail and flee to London on the pretext that he had received a telegram calling him there on business.[3] Wilde "certainly couldn't follow me to England," Turner purportedly told Atherton, "but—it does seem like an act of desertion." Turner "wished to be a friend and not a *copain,*" writes Richard Ellmann, who thinks that Wilde wanted the independently wealthy Turner to live with him.[4] It seems equally likely that Wilde was unconsciously pleading with Turner and the rest to be saved from his desire to return to Douglas.

By September 12, Wilde was back in Dieppe, trying to drum up enough money to travel to Italy. "I hope to go to Naples in three days, but I must try and get some more money," he wrote Douglas on the twelfth (*CL* 935). "The expenses of travelling are frightening," he told Blacker, again taking care not to reveal that Douglas would be his companion (*CL* 935). "Could you advance me £20 on my poem?" he asked

Smithers: "I want to get away to Italy, but must have money" (*CL* 937).
A potentially more serious problem was that Douglas proposed spending
longer at Aix-Les-Bains, where he had gone with his mother, ostensibly in search of a rheumatic cure, and from there going directly to
Venice—without Wilde. "Of course, wait until your cure is finished,"
Wilde told him on the twelfth, and "as regards Venice, of course do
just as you will, but the sooner you come to Naples the happier I shall
be" (*CL* 935).

Was Douglas getting cold feet? In the event, Douglas joined Wilde's
train at Aix a couple of days later, though not before leaving a for-
warding address in Venice, and the two arrived in Naples on September 19 after first spending a day in Genoa, where Guido Reni's
painting in the Palazzo Rosso depicting the martyrdom of St. Sebastian had made such a profound impression on Wilde twenty years
earlier. Vincent O'Sullivan had been prevailed upon to give Wilde the
travelling costs, after Wilde had sheepishly told him "I am in an absurd
position. I have no money." Giving Wilde the sum he wanted "is one
of the few things I look back on with satisfaction," O'Sullivan later
wrote: "It is not every day that one has the chance of relieving the anxiety of a genius and a hero."[5] "I have thought it all out and I would not
take advice from anyone," Wilde told O'Sullivan over lunch in a seedy
Montmartre restaurant, en route to meet Douglas, as he detailed the
plans he was making.[6]

Naples, it has been said, more than anywhere else, "opens windows
on the meaning of the homosexual journey."[7] To outsiders, especially
those in search of sexual liberation, it possesses a persistent magic of
place. By the late nineteenth century, the scholar John Pemble writes,
"Naples had become the foremost Italian city of fun: a warm and wicked
place which was, to quote *Macmillan's Guide to the Western Mediterranean,* 'a delightful winter residence for those fond of pleasure and
gaiety.' "[8] In Wilde's day and for long after, it was a city to which
Northern European homosexuals naturally gravitated. (Norman Douglas,
Somerset Maugham, and E. F. Benson all spent significant amounts of

Wilde and Douglas in Naples, Italy, late 1897.

time there). "In Naples," one nineteenth-century sex tourist remarked, "love between men is so common that one cannot choose to refuse the most daring demands."[9] Homosexuality was not a crime in Italy: Italian police, politicians, and prosecutors made little attempt to ban homosexual behavior, expel homosexual expatriates, or otherwise harass them, and as the scholar Robert Aldrich has shown, Southern Italy provided an especially appealing destination for Northern homosexuals in flight from strict homophobic laws in their home countries.[10] "In Naples, Sicily or Capri," one fin-de-siècle writer observed, "one has only to show an interest in a half-grown youth, to remark on his curly hair or his almond-shaped eyes, and the young man begins to flirt . . . and with unmistakable intentions begins to sidle up to the foreigner."[11] Wilde himself described the city as "evil and luxurious" (*CL* 1185).

It was Douglas who chose their destination, although Wilde, ready to escape the dreadful Northern European climate, was eager to be "where there is sunlight, and a *joie de vivre* all about me" (*CL* 935). "I dare say Paris would have been better," Wilde later wrote, "but Bosie said he could not winter there" (*CL* 980). Douglas had spent several months in Naples in 1895 and 1896, and he longed to take Wilde there.[12] "Are you aware of the reputation of Naples?" the presiding judge asked one of the counsels when Douglas—in an uncanny repetition of the disastrous libel suit that had precipitated Wilde's demise— misguidedly prosecuted Arthur Ransome for libel in 1913.[13] The judge implied that Naples "meant the very lowest depths of wickedness and profligacy," but Douglas was adamant that Naples was "a resort of the most exclusive set of the Italian aristocracy," where there was a large and permanent English colony, and that there was "nothing at all about the reputation of Naples to differentiate it from Rome or Genoa or Florence or Venice or any other Italian city."[14] Many people of distinction went there every season, Douglas pointed out—indeed his own grandmother had lived there for twenty years, up to her death in 1893—and "there was not a person of position in the place . . . with whom [he] was not on calling terms if [he] cared to follow up [his] social duties."[15]

The ill-fated reunion of Oscar Wilde and Lord Alfred Douglas in Naples is one of the most misunderstood and misrepresented events in the history of literature. Reported in all the papers, it scandalized the French and the Italians no less than the English. Wilde had kept his plans secret from his closest friends, and Ross, Blacker, and Turner were all outraged. "I have not answered your letters," Wilde wrote to Ross on October 1, "because they distressed me and angered me, and I did not wish to write to *you* of all people in the world in an angry mood" (*CL* 949). As Ross made clear, Wilde's reunion with Douglas put paid to whatever hopes of respectability and a decent livelihood Wilde nurtured. But the ideas that Douglas was callously indifferent to Wilde, that he agreed to stay with Wilde in order to exploit him, or that their parting nearly three months later was emotionally predictable, while oft-repeated, are heavily colored by the acrimony of *De Profundis,* and they do not bear up under close inspection. Douglas evidently knew nothing at this period of the accusations that Wilde had leveled against him in writing, and he later wrote that, in seeking a reconciliation with himself, Wilde must have "purged his bosom of his rancour and unreasonable fury . . . [and] put the thing out of his mind and thought no more about it."[16] Even from within the hell of his prison cell, Wilde had looked forward to meeting Douglas "in some foreign town" as early as mid-June. "I hope that our meeting will be what a meeting between you and me should be," he had written, and though wider "chasms" than ever before now separated them, "to Love all things are easy" (*CL* 778).

From Wilde's standpoint, the primary context for understanding the reunion is his unquestionable and deep-seated love for Douglas. "I must see you soon—you are the divine thing I want—the thing of grace and genius," he had written in early 1893 (*CL* 560). "I can't live without you," he had written in July 1894, "I think of you all day long, and miss your grace, your boyish beauty, the bright sword-play of your wit, the delicate fancy of your genius. . . . Your lovely life goes always hand in hand with mine" (*CL* 594). Douglas meant more to him than anybody had ever realized, he wrote from Worthing a month later—at a time, Wilde falsely wrote later in *De Profundis,* when he was supposedly trying to concentrate all his attention on writing *The Importance of Being Earnest*—"you are the atmosphere of beauty through which I see life: you are the incarnation of all lovely things. . . . I think of you day and night" (*CL* 602). Ten months later, when Wilde was imprisoned in Holloway on remand awaiting trial, Douglas had visited Wilde daily in his cell: "every day someone whose name is Love comes to see me," Wilde wrote at the time, "and weeps so much through prison-bars that it is I who have to comfort him" (*CL* 644). Douglas's daily visits "quicken me into life," Wilde wrote, and though Wilde felt caught in a terrible net and did not know where to turn, "I care less when I think that he is thinking of me. I think of nothing else" (*CL* 644–45).

Wilde's expressions of love for Douglas had been sustained throughout his criminal trials, by which time Wilde and his lawyers had persuaded Douglas to flee England for fear of prosecution, and only intensified further when conviction and a lengthy prison term seemed imminent. "If prison and dishonour be my destiny," Wilde wrote Douglas toward the end of the first criminal trial, "think that my love for you and this idea, this still more divine belief, that you love me in return will sustain me in my unhappiness and will make me capable . . . of bearing my grief most patiently" (*CL* 646). Only the hope, "nay rather the certainty, of meeting you again," he said, gave him strength to "continue to live in this world" (*CL* 646). In lines written from Holloway Prison in late April 1895, clearly predicting the two men's cohabitation in Naples two-and-a-half years later, Wilde had said: "If one day, at Corfu, or in some enchanted isle, there were a little house where we could live together, oh! life would be sweeter than it has ever been. Your love has broad wings and is strong, your love comes to me through my prison bars and comforts me, your love is the light of all my hours. Those who know not what love is will write, I know, if fate is against us, that I have had a bad influence upon your life. . . . Our love was always beautiful and noble, and if I have been the butt of a terrible tragedy, it is because the nature of that love has not been understood. . . . I stretch out my hands towards you. Oh may I live to touch your hair and your hands. I think that your love will watch over my life" (*CL* 646–47). In prison, "I am going to test the power of love," Wilde had written to Douglas shortly before his conviction: "my heart is a rose which your love has brought to bloom, my life is a desert fanned by the delicious breeze of your breath, and whose cool springs are your eyes; the imprint of your little feet makes valleys of shade for me, the odour of your hair is like myrrh, and wherever you go you exhale the perfumes of the cassia tree. . . . My soul clings to your soul, my life is your life, and in all the worlds of pain and pleasure you are my ideal of admiration of joy" (*CL* 651–52).

For his part, Douglas was aware that Wilde was given to exaggeration and verbal seduction: "the most remarkable and arresting thing about Wilde," he later wrote, "was that without any apparent effort he exerted a sort of enchantment which transmuted the ordinary things of life and invested them with strangeness and glamour. . . . He saw things in a strange and illuminative way."[17] Douglas himself later made poetry out of this tendency in his sonnet "The Dead Poet," written shortly after Wilde's death:

> I dreamed of him last night, I saw his face
> All radiant and unshadowed of distress,
> And as of old, in music measureless,
> I heard his golden voice and marked him trace
> Under the common thing the hidden grace,
> And conjure wonder out of emptiness,
> Till mean things put on beauty like a dress,
> And all the world was an enchanted place.

And then methought outside a fast locked gate
I mourned the loss of unrecorded words,
Forgotten tales and mysteries half said,
Wonders that might have been articulate,
And voiceless thoughts like murdered singing birds.
And so I woke and knew that he was dead.[18]

But there is no question that Douglas loved Wilde in return, as his sonnet tacitly recognizes, notwithstanding—or perhaps because of—Wilde's "golden voice." "Do keep up your spirits, my dearest darling," Douglas had written from France when Wilde was out on bail: "I am always your own loving and devoted boy."[19] "I love him . . . for the constant gentleness of his character, his extraordinary kindness, and his eternal and inexhaustible tenderness for me, as for his verve, his magnificent intelligence and his genius," Douglas wrote in the passionate unpublished defense of Wilde that he had been prevented from publishing in the *Mercure de France* through Wilde's own intervention.[20] "I shall kill myself if Oscar throws me over," he had written later that year, upon discovering that Wilde had started to turn against him: "If he doesn't love me I can't live."[21] "My longing to see him simply eats my heart away night and day," Douglas told Ross in July 1897, shortly after he had been prevented from visiting Wilde in Berneval.[22] "More than two years ago," Douglas told Adey around the same time, "I was parted from the person I love best in the world and . . . ever since I have waited and hoped and longed to see him again. . . . At last the light broke. I knew that my friend still loved and wished to see me. He wrote to me to say 'come on Saturday' and I thought to myself 'all the misery is over and everything is going to be right at last after so long waiting and so much sorrow.'"[23] "I wanted to go back to him, I longed for it and for him," he later wrote his mother, "because I love him and admire him and think him great."[24] "When people speak against me for going back to Bosie," Wilde explained to Ross, "tell them that he offered me love, and that in my loneliness and disgrace I, after three months' struggle against a hideous Philistine world, turned naturally to him" (*CL* 943).

Douglas's letters to Wilde in the run-up to their reunion in Naples have not survived, although Wilde said as early as July that Douglas was "bombarding from a distance" (*CL* 910) and later wrote that "Bosie for four months, by endless letters, offered me a 'home.' He offered me love, affection and care, and promised me that I should never want for anything" (*CL* 1029). "When people say how dreadful of me to return to Bosie," Wilde told Turner shortly after their arrival, "do say *no*—say that I love him, that . . . Bosie is my romance . . . and he loves me very dearly, more than he loves or can love anyone else" (*CL* 948). "I dare say that what I have done is fatal," Wilde explained to Ross, "but it had to be done. It was necessary that Bosie and I should come together again; I saw no other life for myself. For himself he saw no other" (*CL* 950). "The mere fact that he wrecked my life makes me love him," Wilde told Ross, unconsciously echoing the central refrain of *The Ballad of Reading Gaol,* that "each man kills the thing he loves" (*CL* 943).[25]

Douglas would have been distraught at the idea that he had "wrecked" Wilde's life. For much of the previous two years, Douglas had been making his love and loyalty to his friend evident in his writing, although not always in the most politic of ways. In the immediate wake of his friend's conviction, he had written boldly to W. T. Stead and Henry Labouchere, the editors of *The Review of Reviews* and *Truth* respectively, defending Wilde's conduct and the "vices" for which he had been imprisoned.[26] He had petitioned Queen Victoria to stay Wilde's sentence, calling attention to the falsity of his father's claim to have been motivated by love for his youngest son, as well as to how maliciously Queensberry had persecuted Wilde and himself in the run-up to the disastrous libel trial. He had vainly tried to organize petitions on Wilde's behalf, to be signed by the most eminent men of letters in both France and England. In late 1895, as we have seen, he had written a defense of Wilde for the *Mercure de France,* in which he had included lengthy quotations from the letters that Wilde had written him from Holloway in order to demonstrate, as he put it, that "our friendship was love, real love . . . completely pure but extremely passionate . . . perfect love, more spiritual than sensual, a truly Platonic love."[27] Douglas's first book of poems, published in France in 1896, was to have been dedicated to the imprisoned Wilde, and in a controversial article defending the volume, written for *La Revue Blanche,* Douglas had defiantly proclaimed "I could not be more proud to have been loved by a great poet."[28]

While in jail, Wilde had taken umbrage at these (to him) reckless and self-indulgent measures. Far from appearing loyal, the immense publicity that Douglas cultivated seemed to him insensitive and self-advertising—and from prison, as we have seen, Wilde managed to prevent publication of both the *Mercure de France* article and the dedication to Douglas's first volume. Nonetheless, when he emerged from prison, Wilde had a stunning change of heart. Douglas was now "far the first of all the poets of England," and Wilde cannot have been unaware of both the personal and artistic compliment that Douglas had intended, the previous year, by wanting to dedicate his first book of poems to him (*CL* 948). Indeed several poems in Douglas's first volume speak eloquently of Douglas's love for Wilde. In "Rejected," for instance, written shortly after Wilde's incarceration, Douglas had encapsulated his deep sense of loss at Wilde's imprisonment:

Alas! I have lost my God,
My beautiful God Apollo.
Wherever his footsteps trod
My feet were wont to follow.

But Oh! it fell out one day
My soul was so heavy with weeping,
That I laid me down by the way;
And he left me while I was sleeping.

And my soul awoke in the night,
And I bowed my ear for his fluting,
And I heard but the breath of the flight
Of wings and the night-birds hooting.

And night drank all her cup,
And I went to the shrine in the hollow,
And the voice of my cry went up:
"Apollo! Apollo! Apollo!"[29]

The conceit here, behind which Douglas thinly veils his sadness at the loss of Wilde, is one Wilde would have approved: it echoes that of Lord Henry Wotton, in *The Picture of Dorian Gray,* who tells the ever-youthful Dorian, "It seems to me that you are the young Apollo, and that I am Marsyas listening to you."[30]

In "Amoris Vincula," also published in Douglas's first volume, Douglas likened his heart, "linked to thine with triple links of love," to "a white dove that, in a cage of gold, / Is prisoned from the air, and yet more bound / By love than bars, and will not wings unfold / To fly away."[31] No less "prisoned" than Wilde himself, Douglas surrenders to the "links" that "chain" him to his absent love. Although Douglas had first published "Amoris Vincula" as early as 1893 in the Oxford under-graduate magazine *The Spirit Lamp,* the poem must have taken on new meaning to both its author and Wilde as a result of the latter's impris-onment. In Wilde's physical absence, Douglas says, he had briefly en-deavored to become "a dove grown wanton [that] false . . . sought / To break its chain, and faithless quite to rove / Where thou woulds't not." But within the space of a month, he had "grown sick with longing for a voice unheard / And lips unkissed" and so "spread wings and home flew fast." Physical freedom, which "seemed a sword to cleave its chain, / Was but a link to rivet it again."[32]

In "The Travelling Companion," first published in 1899, Douglas makes clear that his reasons for returning to Wilde were love and sorrow:

Douglas following their night in Rouen, "my only hope of again doing beautiful work in art is being with you." He had read Douglas's poems "with great pleasure and interest," he told Douglas barely two weeks after emerging from prison, in the first of his letters to Douglas that survive from that summer, while urging Douglas to write him about "your art and the art of others" and saying he wanted "to meet on the double peak of Parnassus" (*CL* 873). He told his friends Blacker and Young that he planned to travel to Naples for literary reasons—"If I cannot write in Italy, where can I write?" he asked Blacker in a fit of pique; "I am on my way to Italy, where I hope to give myself entirely to literature," he told Young (*CL* 936). "At Naples I intend to finish my poem, and begin my play," he told Smithers (*CL* 937). Given that he did not tell anybody that Douglas was to be his companion in Italy, it is easy to see these justifications for the move south as disingenuous. But this would be to miss the real note of frustration that had crept into Wilde's reports of his literary activities by late August as well as the fact that he had reached a hiatus in the composition of *The Ballad of Reading Gaol.* Indeed, the poem had arguably been conceived in a letter to Douglas, in which, after remarking on Douglas's "real sympathy" as a poet with the ballad form and enjoining Douglas to "pray again return" to the writing of ballads, Wilde proclaimed, "the Ballad is the true origin of the Romantic drama." (*CL* 874).[34] In Wilde's praise of Douglas as a writer of ballads, one can see the foundation being set for Wilde's own important contribution to the ballad tradition.

"It is to a poet that I am going back," Wilde told Turner near the end of September (*CL* 948). "My only hope of life or literary activity was in going back to the young man whom I loved before with such tragic issue," Wilde explained to the reproachful Ross: "I hope to do work with him. I think I shall be able to do so" (*CL* 943). Only Douglas, he maintained, could "recreate in me that energy and sense of joyous power on which art depends" (*CL* 933). "He understands me and my art, and loves both," Wilde explained to Smithers: "I hope never to be separated from him" (*CL* 952). Upon their arrival in Naples on September 19, they quickly ran up a bill of £68 at the Hôtel Royal des Etrangers in the Via Chiatamone ("a hotel of absurd prices, which I am anxious to leave at once" [CL 949]). Within days they were seeking "a little villa or apartment somewhere," and by the twenty-fifth they had taken the Villa Giudice at Posillipo, a beautiful, quiet residential neighborhood by the shore, south-west of Naples, named by the Greeks *Pausylipon,* meaning "place where unhappiness ends" (CL 943). Here they were to remain for two months. They hoped to stay for far longer. Italy was "the land for which my life had yearned," Wilde had written twenty years earlier.[35] "I intend to winter here. Perhaps live here," Wilde wrote shortly after their arrival, though "much depends of course on my ability to write again" (CL 947). "All we want now is to be left alone," he wrote at the beginning of October, "but the Neapolitan papers are tedious and wish to interview me, etc. . . . I don't want to be written about. I want peace—that is all. Perhaps I shall find it" (CL 950).

They settled quickly into their villa, leading a life that was "perfectly harmless," according to Douglas's later account, consisting "mainly of fairly strenuous literary toil."[36] Their villa, which still stands today and which was then in a fashionable part of town, had a terrace with marble steps leading down to the sea, as well as a good piano. "The place was very beautiful," a curious local journalist observed: "All around, flower beds kept with the utmost care; farther on shadowy alleys, and beyond the trees, the vastness of a calm sea, of a livid hue [and] a deep silence."[37] Wilde took lessons in Italian conversation three times a week from a young poet, Giuseppe Rocco, who would later produce the first Italian translation of *Salomé.* A month after arriving, Wilde playfully bragged, "I am getting rather astonishing in my Italian conversation. I believe I talk a mixture of Dante and the worst modern slang" (CL 967). For little more than the price of their keep, they employed a cook named Carmine, a maid named Maria, and two boys, Peppino and Michele, to wait on them. When they discovered that the villa was overrun with rats, Douglas, mortified, hired a room in the house opposite to sleep in. But after a time, Douglas later recalled, they got rid of the rats, partly by means of a professional and orthodox rat-catcher, "but also (and chiefly, according to Oscar's opinion) owing to the ministrations . . . of a potent witch who was recommended as infallible by Michele, and who came and 'burned odours' and muttered incantations."[38] The "witch" also told both their fortunes, although unfortunately Douglas does not say what she prophesied, "and Oscar professed to regard her as a wonderful and powerful sorceress."

Within a day or two of their arrival, both Wilde and Douglas turned their minds to writing, and Wilde hoped to complete *The Ballad of Reading Gaol* quickly. "The intense energy of creation has been kicked out of me," he had written a month previously. But now, in Naples, he felt all his old power coming back. On September 21, he announced that he was beginning to work. But Wilde and Douglas initially turned to the libretto for a proposed opera by Dalhousie Young, of Longus's pastoral romance *Daphnis and Chloe*.[39] The proposed libretto, which never came to anything, was partly a money-making scheme: before leaving Berneval, Wilde had asked Young for £100 down and another £50 on production, adding that he could go to work on the libretto at once. Once in Naples, and wondering whether this request had fallen on deaf ears, he added that "the £100 will solve the difficulty and give me the chance to work" (*CL* 945). Young was only too happy to oblige with the requested down payment, which Wilde asked to be telegraphed to him in Naples, since "I would not like to go to a strange banker with my own name on a cheque" (*CL* 948–49). The libretto was to consist of "recitative prose" interspersed with lyrics, although Wilde was unclear about what kind of prose would work best with music, and Douglas was to write at least some of the lyrics. Wilde asked Young for guidance on the number and kind of voices: as well as a general chorus, he envisaged "a chorus of treble voices—shepherd lads, who would come on about half through . . . when Chloe is deserted by Daphnis [and] they beg her to return to the sheepfold" (*CL* 944). Anticipating Ravel and Diaghilev, he also envisaged "at least one ballet—a shepherd dance," instructing Young to "work at that . . . as soon as you have set the lyric to music" (*CL* 945–46). But although Wilde told Young that Douglas was "doing a really lovely thing for the opera" and that neither Douglas's name nor his own was to appear on the playbill or the printed libretto, nothing further came of either the libretto or Young's score, save for one lyric by Douglas, now lost, that Wilde sent Young two days after their arrival (*CL* 949).

Besides the opera, Wilde was also thinking about returning to the drama. On September 25, he told Ross that he hoped to arrange a Naples production of *Salomé,* translated into Italian, and less than a week later he informed Ross "tomorrow I begin the *Florentine Tragedy*" and "after that I must tackle *Pharaoh*" (*CL* 950). After finishing *The Ballad* he would return to the drama, he informed the writer and editor Stanley Makower, but the *Ballad* was proving difficult to complete, and it weighed heavily on his mind. "I find it difficult to recapture the mood and manner of its inception," he told Makower: "It seems alien to me now—real passions so soon become unreal—and the actual facts of one's life take different shape and remould themselves strangely. Still, it must be finished" (*CL* 947).

At first Douglas was the more productive of the two. Within days of arriving at Naples, he had written the "three lovely sonnets" published in 1899 under the collective title that Wilde gave them, "A Triad of the Moon," as well as "The City of the Soul," a "Sonnet on the Sonnet," and a sonnet on Mozart that he submitted to Makower for publication in *The Musician.* The third sonnet in "A Triad of the Moon" nicely captures the fragility of their shared happiness:

My soul is like a silent nightingale
Devising sorrow in a summer night.
Closed eyes in blazing noon put out the light,
And Hell lies in the thickness of a veil.
In every voiceless moment sleeps a wail,
And all the lonely darknesses are bright,
And every dawning of the day is white
With shapes of sorrow fugitive and frail.[40]

Douglas later wrote that both men were busy with literary work and that "we had not an idle week during the whole time we were together."[41] In fact, the two visited Capri in mid-October, and when inviting Dowson to visit, Wilde wrote that the "only bother" about the lovely Greek bronzes on display at the Museum of Antiquities in Naples was that "they all walk about the town at night"—although "one gets delicately accustomed to that—and there are compensations" (*CL* 958). They also saw a great deal of a homosexual friend named Ashton, who was in Naples for much of October and November and whom Wilde would later describe as "astounding . . . in his capacity for pleasure, grand in his cups, and with a heart of gold" (*CL* 1118). The following year in Paris, they would again see much of Ashton, whom they nicknamed "Sir John," and Wilde would describe with great amusement Ashton's often-inebriated escapades with boys and with an irate hotel keeper.[42] But distractions aside, and allowing for Douglas's habitual exaggerations, there can be no question that Wilde finished *The Ballad of Reading Gaol* in Douglas's company.[43]

Although he had not advanced its composition in nearly a month when he arrived, Wilde had been thinking about the manner of the poem's publication for much of this time. In early September, Smithers had shown Wilde's working draft to Beardsley (Beardsley was "much struck with it," Smithers had said, and "promised at once to do a frontispiece to it—in a manner which immediately convinced me that he will never do it"), whereupon Wilde had replied that "there is no use his hedging. If he will do it, it will be a great thing."[44] Wilde wanted "something curious—a design of Death and Sin walking hand in hand, very severe, and medieval," and if Beardsley would not do it, "why not try some of the *jeunes Belges*—Khnoppf for example" (*CL* 933).[45] Ten days later, on the point of leaving Berneval permanently, Wilde had told Smithers that he intended to finish the poem at Naples, that he had only three new stanzas to add, and that he intended to offer it to the *New York Journal* for £200. Two or three days later still, in Paris en route to Naples, Wilde met the German artist Paul Herrmann, who told him about a novel process for etching in four colors and was "very anxious to do a cover and frontispiece design" for the *Ballad* (*CL* 944). From Naples Wilde now wrote to Smithers excitedly about Herrmann's drawings, urging Smithers to go see Herrmann in Paris, and suggesting that the type used to print the poem ("the strongest, blackest, finest type you have") should be as large and strong as the "great masses of black, and strong curves and contrasts" of Herrmann's work (*CL* 945).[46] "I now feel that the poem should be published in a very artistic form, with a wonderful cover . . . frontispiece, initial letters, *culs-de-lampes,* etc," he told Smithers, though he had not given up hope of getting a large sum of money from simultaneous publication in an English or American paper (*CL* 944–45).[47]

If he was not as quick as Douglas in setting about literary work, by early October Wilde was nonetheless working hard on *The Ballad* again. He labored over the poem at Naples, Douglas later observed, "in a manner which I had never known him to labour before. Every word had to be considered; every rhyme and every cadence carefully pondered. I had 'The Ballad of Reading Gaol' for breakfast, dinner and tea, and for many weeks it was almost our sole topic of conversation."[48] Douglas later said that he would never for a moment claim that he helped Wilde to write *The Ballad of Reading Gaol.*[49] However, Wilde certainly admired Douglas's "Ballad of St. Vitus," which Douglas had composed just days earlier while staying with his mother at Aix. Wilde viewed his companion as "an exquisite artist in lyric and ballad," as we have seen, and A. E. Housman for one later suspected that parts of Wilde's ballad were in fact written by Douglas.[50]

But Wilde appears to have at first turned to Ross—"still a literary friend," as Wilde pointedly remarked to Smithers—for help.[51] Having arranged for Smithers to send Ross a typewritten draft, he asked Ross on October 1 to send him suggestions and criticisms, adding that "I think bits of the poem very good now, but I will never again out-Kipling Henley" (*CL* 950). By October 8, Ross, who had in the interim told Smithers, the poem's eventual publisher, that he did not think Wilde's poem had "any market value" (*CL* 955 n.2), had replied with detailed criticisms, prompting Wilde to put on paper some of the most pointed self-criticism of the poem that we possess:

> With much of your criticism I agree. The poem suffers under the difficulty of a divided aim in style. Some is realistic, some is romantic: some poetry, some propaganda. I feel it keenly, but as a whole I think the production interesting: that it is interesting from more points of view than one is artistically to be regretted.
>
> With regard to the adjectives, I admit there are far too many "dreadfuls" and "fearfuls." The difficulty is that the objects in prison have no shape or form. To take an example: the shed in which people are hanged is a little shed with a glass roof, like a photographer's studio on the sands at Margate. For eighteen months I thought it *was* the studio for photographing prisoners. There is no adjective to describe it. I call it "hideous" because it became so to me after I knew its use. In itself it is a wooden, oblong, narrow shed with a glass roof.[52]
>
> A cell again may be described *psychologically*, with reference to its effect on the soul: in itself it can only be described as "whitewashed" or "dimly-lit." It has no shape, no contents. It does not exist from the point of view of form or colour.
>
> In point of fact, describing a prison is as difficult artistically as describing a water-closet would be. . . .
>
> I am going to retain the opening of Part IV, but to cut out three stanzas at the opening of Part III.
>
> As regards the spirits, I think the *grotesqueness* of the scene to a certain degree makes their speech possible, but Bosie agrees with you. (*CL* 956–57)

Three days later, Wilde told Ernest Dowson "My poem is finished at last. . . . I have added a good deal to it," and three days later still, he told Turner "I have finished the great poem—six hundred lines now" (*CL* 957, 959). He hoped the poem would produce a good effect, he told Turner, and he liked it greatly himself, although "much is, I feel, for a harsher instrument than the languorous flute I love" (*CL* 959). Five days after this, on October 19, in response to further criticism from Ross, Wilde wrote "you are quite right in saying that the poem should end at 'outcasts always mourn,' but the propaganda, which I desire to make, starts there. I think I shall call the whole thing *Poésie et Propagande* or *Dichtung und Wahrheit*" (*CL* 964).[53]

By October 27, the poem was "now as good as I can make it" (*CL* 972). But two days later he sent Smithers an itemized list of small verbal changes, saying that he was anxious to have as few changes as possible in the printed proofs; and as late as November 8, Wilde was still tinkering with points of wording or inflection and agonizing over the beginning of Canto III. By his own calculation, Wilde had now added about one hundred lines to the poem in the space of a month, as well as making numerous small verbal changes—giving the lie to his claims in *De Profundis* that he "never wrote a single line" in Douglas's company and that his life, as long as Douglas was by his side, was "entirely sterile and uncreative." By mid-November he was anxiously awaiting page proofs "to correct . . . before retiring from a world of injustice and wrong and annoyance" (*CL* 982). He would not like to die without seeing the poem as good as he could make a poem, he told Smithers, although he still wondered whether the subject was all wrong and the treatment too personal.

————

As well as completing the composition and revision of *The Ballad* at Naples, Wilde also concerned himself with arrangements for the poem's publication. To some degree, this was a matter of sheer necessity: Wilde and Douglas were in dire need of money, and Wilde was keen to profit from the poem, as well as to extract a significant advance from Smithers as soon as possible. "Our sole hope of food is . . . *The Ballad of Reading Gaol,*" he told Turner (*CL* 961). I "cannot buy note-paper. This is *your* foolscap," he told Ross; "at present I am quite penniless" he informed Dowson; "Beg you to wire money today. Really serious difficulties," he telegraphed Smithers, explaining in a letter that "the crisis is of a grave and usual character—were it unique, I would not feel so agitated" (*CL* 957, 951). For nearly three weeks after arriving in Naples, Wilde tried repeatedly to obtain an advance of £20 from Smithers, eventually extracting £10 from the cash-strapped publisher, who would go bankrupt two years later; Smithers also assisted Wilde in obtaining the partial repayment of a debt from Ernest Dowson. At times, these efforts led Wilde to great heights of bawdy humor. Since he had abandoned earlier plans to publish *The Ballad* simultaneously in an English paper, he told Smithers, "you have now the perfect virginity of my poem for the satyrs of the British public to ravish. . . . I don't think I am really asking a great favour in saying that I wish you to advance me £20 on account [since] . . . I give you a clear market and offer you a virgin who has never been engaged to Arthur Symons— harmless though such a thing would have been in the eyes of all sensible people" (*CL* 953). But at others, these efforts were desperate and sad: "Smithers has not behaved well to me at all," he told Dowson: "I wanted a paltry £20 in advance on my poem—secured on its sale and the American rights—and for three weeks he has put me off with silly promises" (*CL* 958). As the self-centered miller in Wilde's children's tale "The Devoted Friend" remarks, with little empathy for his impoverished friend Little Hans, "I will certainly take care not to give away anything again. One certainly suffers for being generous."[54]

Perhaps unsurprisingly, Wilde was making plans for the poem's publication even before leaving for Naples. He was determined to make money from the poem, and Smithers had told him that he had no objection to the poem appearing in a paper or journal simultaneously with its publication in book form. By mid-September, Wilde had employed that" (*CL* 972).[57] Since Smithers was proposing an edition of just five-hundred inexpensively priced copies, generating little income for Wilde himself, Wilde now thought he "had better publish in an English newspaper" (*CL* 964). Smithers "knows all about bad wine and bad women," Wilde explained to Ross, "but on books he is sadly to seek" (*CL* 956).

Over the course of October, as he revised the poem with Ross's and Douglas's assistance, Wilde continued to involve himself closely in plans for the poem's publication, at one point eliciting from Smithers the remark that Wilde knew as much about the publishing business as a chrysanthemum (*CL* 974). As early as October 3, he was discussing with Smithers a possible illustrated *second* edition of the poem: he had been excited by Beardsley's and Herrmann's reactions to the poem, and he had "a longing for visible symbols to reinterpret my realism in the spirit with which I think it is informed" (*CL* 959). By the third week of October, he was composing his book's dedication, reviewing type specimens—he wanted type "as black as one can get"—and deciding who would receive signed presentation copies of the first edition (*CL* 969, 966). He was now proposing that the poem be published simultaneously in Hearst's *New York Journal,* the Sunday Paris edition of the *New York Herald,* and in a London Sunday newspaper such as the *Sunday Sun* just prior to its appearance in book form (*CL* 970). But Wilde had begun to have doubts about the effectiveness of Pinker as his agent—"Pinker seems an absurdity," he wrote: "it was simply the fatal attraction of his name that made me pin my faith to him"—and by the end of the month, Wilde was suggesting the names of other agents to represent him in negotiations with American papers: Elisabeth Marbury, who had represented him previously as a playwright and who "is in touch with everything of journalistic position in New York"; and one "Murphy, the accredited representative of the *New York Journal*" (*CL* 976, 970, 968). Marbury later wrote a vivid account of how, upon receiving Wilde's manuscript, along with Wilde's request that she "be his good angel and get him a few pounds for it," she read it with tears rolling down her cheeks, as though in the presence of "a voice from the dead."[58]

The Ballad of Reading Gaol had now become "my American poem," and Wilde even briefly contemplated offering the poem to an American newspaper syndicate (*CL* 976). "If *they* won't publish, you must publish simultaneously in New York," Wilde informed Smithers (*CL* 973). He now thought that "after Christmas would be better for publication," especially if he were to secure an American newspaper for simultaneous publication, given that "I am hardly a Christmas present" (*CL* 993). Sales and reviews of any book edition of *The Ballad* were less likely before Christmas, Wilde well knew, since book buyers and reviewers alike were preoccupied at that time of year with finding or recommending books as appropriate gifts, and *The Ballad* would inevitably get overlooked. "If one gives away a book, it should be a charming book," Wilde had once remarked, in answer to his own question "What are the best books to give as Christmas presents?"[59] But by mid-November he acknowledged, "I cannot get my poem . . . accepted by even the most revolting New York paper." It was for Wilde "a dreadful shock . . . to find that there is such a barrier between me and the public," and Wilde promised Smithers that he would not write any further about America (*CL* 978). Nonetheless he enjoined Smithers to establish copyright in the United States since "there is a *chance*—just a chance—of a big sale" (*CL* 982). It was at this point too that Wilde first proposed the binding—of "cinnamon cloth, with a white back gold-lettered"—in which the book was to appear the following year (*CL* 984).

For all his attention to *The Ballad*, Wilde still harbored hopes of asserting himself through other kinds of literary activity. "Whatever future may be in store for me," he wrote O'Sullivan from Naples, "depends entirely on my art, and the possibility of my art coming again into touch with life" (*CL* 964). He was full of ideas for new projects. He planned on writing the aforementioned romantic dramas about Pharaoh and Jezebel, as well as rewriting and completing the never finished *A Florentine Tragedy;* he thought briefly of writing a new comedy for George Alexander, who had produced and starred in *Lady Windermere's Fan* and *The Importance of Being Earnest;* and he told Smithers that a bust of the decadent Roman Emperor Heliogabalus, which he had seen in the local museum, had filled him with a desire to write his life. Heliogabalus's marriage with the moon, to which Wilde referred very briefly in *The Picture of Dorian Gray,* would make "a beautiful chapter of coloured words" (*CL* 973). But he could not see himself writing comedy—"my sense of humour is now concentrated on the grotesqueness of tragedy," he remarked—and nothing came of these other ideas (*CL* 962).

A more serious prospect of bringing his art "again into touch with life" lay in his efforts to have *Salomé* staged locally and published in an Italian translation. Wilde was heartened that his Italian instructor, Rocco, had expressed an interest in translating it. Rocco had previously enjoyed a modest success as editor of the Neapolitan magazine *Strenna Margarita,* and he would later be the author of a gay novel, *L'uomo femmina* (The Female Man), set in Naples. Since neither Wilde nor Douglas possessed a copy of *Salomé* in either the original 1893 French edition or the 1894 English translation, Wilde wrote repeatedly to friends in England requesting the loan of one, eventually securing one from Ada Leverson.[60] Wilde anticipated the arrival, near the end of October, of "the best Italian company of actors there is" (*CL* 959). Since they had recently played Giovanni Bovio's *Cristo alla festa di Purim* with great success, Wilde explained to Turner, they "would like to do *Salomé,*" another religious drama, and "it would help me here greatly to have it done, as the papers have been rather offensive, and I want to assert myself here as an artist. Once I do that, they will leave me alone" (*CL* 959). On October 21, he announced that he was supervising the translation and that he hoped "to produce it on the stage here, if I can find an actress of troubling beauty and flute-like voice" (*CL* 967). Unfortunately "most of the tragic actresses of Italy—with the exception of Duse—are stout ladies," he added, "and I don't think I could bear a stout Salomé." Six days later, Wilde formalized his agreement with Rocco in a notarized memo, a copy of which is preserved in the archives of the translation's eventual publisher, Ferdinando

Wilde's correspondence speaks eloquently and often amusingly of the strain produced on the pair by their dire finances. "I suppose you think that mental anxiety is good for poets," Wilde told Smithers, complaining that the expenses incurred in waiting for Smithers's £20 advance were greater than the advance itself (*CL* 977). But the situation was made more dire, and ultimately unbearable, by the scandal that erupted when it became widely known that Wilde was living with Douglas. Within days of their arrival, the local papers got wind of Wilde's presence in the city and were seeking interviews with him (*CL* 950). On October 7, *Il Mattino,* still the leading Neapolitan daily, opined that Wilde's presence in Naples was "a calamity" and "has put several people . . . in a certain anxiety bordering with panic."[64] Two days later a rival paper, *Il Pungolo parlamentare,* corroborated the news and faked an interview with the exiled aesthete, leading Wilde to remark "The Neapolitan papers have turned out to be the worst form of American journalism" (*CL* 958).[65] The French papers soon weighed in as well, describing Wilde, much to his amused disgust, "as living, broken down in health, in the lovely villa of the son of Lord Douglas!" (*CL* 966).

But long before this, news of Wilde's fresh association with Douglas had reached the ears of his wife and friends in England, creating a furor ultimately more forceful and destructive than anything appearing in the press. "People who have nothing to do with my life write long tedious letters to me informing me that I have wrecked my life a second time," he complained to Turner (*CL* 961). In mid-October, he received reports that his old friend Robert Sherard had condemned his actions in the smoking-room of London's Authors' Club. This led Wilde to write angrily to Sherard, on or around October 16, "When you wish to talk morality—always an amusement—and to attack me behind my back, don't like a good fellow, talk so loud, as the reverberation reaches from the Club to Naples; also it is easy—far too easy—for you to find an audience that does not contain any friends of mine; before them, play Tartuffe in the style of Termagent to your heart's content; but when you do it in the presence of friends of mine, you expose yourself to rebuke and contempt, and of course I hear all about it" (*CL* 963). It was, to the lasting sadness of both men, the end of a noble and longstanding friendship.[66] Within days of arriving in Naples, Wilde acknowledged that "my being here . . . gives pain to most of my friends" and Robert Ross was writing Wilde "unkind and detestable letters" that Wilde was refusing to answer at first (*CL* 947). Ross, along with others of Wilde's English friends, adopted "the attitude of the world in its relations with me," Wilde said, and at one point Ross even refused to have anything to do with the development of *The Ballad of Reading Gaol* (*CL* 1004).

To make matters worse, the English colony at Naples was ostracizing the couple, and during their visit to Capri in late October, Wilde and Douglas were ejected from the Quisiana Hotel, Capri's leading hotel, after the hotel's English clientele rose from their seats in the dining-room in disgust at the couple's entrance (*CL* 955).[67] Shortly afterward, Wilde announced, "I have retaken my own name, as my incognito was absurd" (*CL* 971). A few days later still, Denis Browne, an attaché from the British Embassy in Rome, came, ostensibly for a friendly chat, to warn Douglas discreetly that his cohabitation with Wilde was causing a scandal, and to pressure him to eject Wilde from the house. "I told him that I cared nothing for gossip and scandal," Douglas later maintained, "and that it was unthinkable that . . . I should turn [Wilde] out of my house simply because evil-minded people chose to concern themselves with what was no affair of theirs."[68] Although Wilde found Browne "very witty and talkative," Browne told Douglas privately that he was "a quixotic fool" and left the house in anger (*CL* 976).[69]

The most serious reactions came from Constance and from Douglas's mother. After months of stonewalling, Constance had finally written to Oscar in September saying that he might visit her in her new villa at Nervi, near Genoa, now that the children were back in school. But as Wilde explained to Smithers, her letter "came too late. I had waited four months in vain, and it was only when the children had gone back to school that she asked me to come to her—whereas what I want is the love of my children" (*CL* 952). Constance's invitation, sent to Berneval, was forwarded to Wilde in Naples, from where Wilde replied around the third week of September that he must delay his visit for at least a month. According to More Adey, Wilde was so irritated by his wife's "extraordinary want of tact that, contrary to the advice of his friends, he refused to go to her, and apparently wrote to the effect that he was . . . worn out with her perpetual procrastination, and was therefore going to live with the only person ready to give him companionship, Alfred Douglas."[70] "Had Constance allowed me to see my boys," Wilde told Blacker, while promising him that he would go and see Constance in October, "my life would, I think, have been quite different. But this she would not do. I don't in any way venture to blame her for her action, but every action has its consequence" (*CL* 947). Whatever the exact nature of Wilde's reply to her invitation, Constance's suspicions were aroused by the Naples postmark, leading her to write back immediately asking whether he "had been to Capri or . . . had met anywhere that appalling individual [i.e. Douglas]."[71] Three days later, without waiting for his reply, she wrote her husband "a very violent letter, saying 'I forbid you to see Lord Alfred Douglas. I forbid you to return to your filthy, insane life. I forbid you to live at Naples. I will not allow you to come to Genoa.'"[72] Barely able to restrain his emotions, Wilde replied saying that he would never dream of coming to see her against her will, that the only reason that would induce him to come and see her was "the prospect of a greeting of sympathy with me in my misfortunes, and affection, and pity," and that, for the rest, he only desired peace, to live his own life as best he could, and "certainly hoped to winter in Naples" (*CL* 994–95). To this he received no answer. Oscar was "as weak as water," Constance reflected privately to the sympathetic Carlos Blacker.[73]

Wilde knew immediately that he was jeopardizing his allowance under the terms of the deed of separation, and within days he was "awaiting a thunderbolt from my wife's solicitor" (*CL* 954). "How can she really imagine that she can influence or control my life?" he angrily complained to Ross: "she might just as well try to influence and control my art. I could not live such an absurd life—it makes one laugh. . . . I wish to goodness she would leave me alone. I don't meddle with her life. I accept the separation from the children: I acquiesce" (*CL* 955). But if Wilde anticipated his wife's legal reaction, he was blindsided when he discovered that Ross and Adey, his representatives in his dealings with Constance's lawyers, acquiesced in the decision to revoke his allowance, thereby tacitly endorsing the notion that Douglas was a "disreputable person" in the eyes of the law. At first, Wilde was ignorant of their role in the affair. Upon receipt of a lawyer's letter announcing that he was to be deprived of his income, Wilde forcefully complained to Ross as follows:

> I felt it due to myself and to Bosie to write [the lawyer] a letter of protest, on the ground that I do not think it just or socially-speaking accurate to describe Bosie as a "disreputable person." After all, no charge was made against him at any of my trials, nor anything proved, or attempted to be proved.
>
> Nor do I think it is fair to say that I have created a "public scandal" by being with him. If newspapers chronicle the fact, that is their business. I can't help that. If I were living here with you they would chronicle my being here with equal venom and vulgarity: or if I were living with someone of unblemished reputation and unassailable position. I think I should only be held accountable for any scandal caused by my getting in trouble with the law. My existence is a scandal. But I do not think I should be charged with creating a scandal by continuing to live: though I am conscious that I do so. I cannot live alone, and Bosie is the only one of my friends who is either able or willing to give me his companionship. If I were living with a Naples renter I would I suppose be all right. As I

> live with a young man who is well bred and well born, and
> who has been charged with no offence, I am deprived of
> all possibility of existence. (*CL* 979)

To Wilde it seemed that his having been convicted as a homosexual
was the real issue ("my existence is a scandal"), not whether or not he
was consorting with a disreputable person. The legalistic phrases used
by Constance and the lawyer were simply a smokescreen, just as the
aristocratic and well-bred Douglas was simply a pretext enabling the
class-obsessed English to make a complete and final break. Wilde would
not be pressed into repudiating how or whom he loved.

But a few days later, Wilde discovered to his anger that Ross and
Adey, far from being innocent bystanders to the lawyers' decision, were
complicit in it. With feelings of "utter amazement and indignation"
(*CL* 989), he wrote to Adey, who had passed on this news with little
feeling for the effect it would have, as follows:

> You tell me that you, and Bobbie, on being asked whether
> Bosie was "a disreputable person" felt bound at once to
> say yes; and that you declared that my wife was acting
> "strictly within her legal rights according to the agree-
> ment" in depriving me of my allowance, because I have
> the pleasure of Bosie's companionship, the only compan-
> ionship in the world open to me.
>
> In what way, my dear More, is Bosie more disreputable
> than either you or Robbie? . . .
>
> Hansell is bound to decide according to the legal agree-
> ment: it is his duty . . . [although] he utterly ignores the
> wording of the agreement, and gives a decision entirely
> illegal. . . .
>
> As for you and Robbie calmly acquiescing in this mon-
> strous injustice, I do not know what to think about either
> of you. I simply cannot comprehend it. (*CL* 989–90)

Adey and Ross had done an "unfair, stupid, and utterly unjust" thing, Wilde said, by "calmly throwing me and my legal rights overboard" (*CL* 991). But more than this, Wilde was appalled at the hypocrisy and cowardice of Adey and Ross, both of whom shared Wilde's sexual orientation, and the latter of whom had once been Wilde's own lover and was no less "disreputable" than Douglas. "If Robbie had lived with me, would you have taken the same course?" he pointedly asked Adey (*CL* 989). Indeed, Adey himself had been described as an "infamous companion" by Wilde's wife, who had reacted in horror when she first discovered that Adey had visited him in prison and had insisted that Wilde should never see Adey again.[74] Wilde strongly complained about his friends' misguided action, protesting in vain to Adrian Hope, his children's guardian, that "those who held my interests in their hands had not my interest in their hearts" (*CL* 991). "I don't mind being a Don Quixote," he complained to Reggie Turner, "but it is rather hard that my life should depend on two Sancho Panzas" (*CL* 991). But the legal decision was irrevocable—his allowance would be cut off henceforth—and within a matter of days Wilde was seeking a compromise, writing to Adey and Ross to ask whether his wife and her lawyers might be placated "if I engaged not to *live* with Bosie—in the same house" (*CL* 991). However, he neither would nor could promise never to see or speak with Douglas again. Douglas was "the only friend with whom I can be in contact, and to live without some companion is impossible": he had endured two long years of silence and solitude while imprisoned, and for his wife "to condemn me now to silence and solitude would be barbarous" (*CL* 994).

Constance remained obdurate, leaving Wilde in stunned wonderment: "This scheme is put forward on moral grounds! It is proposed to leave me to die of starvation or to blow my brains out in a Naples urinal. . . . Moral people, as they are termed, are simply beasts. I would sooner have fifty unnatural vices than one unnatural virtue. It is unnatural virtue that makes the world, for those who suffer, such a premature Hell" (*CL* 996).

At first, Wilde and Douglas were defiant. "I shouldn't dream of leaving Oscar against his will to please ridiculous asses and meddling busybodies," Douglas remarked on November 20: "as we are far from being starved yet, we can and shall certainly wait till that catastrophe is more imminent before surrendering the plain right of any two single human beings to hold intercourse with each other."[75] But in a letter speculatively dated 30 November 1897 by Merlin Holland and Rupert Hart-Davis, editors of Wilde's *Complete Letters,* Wilde announced that "as I have lost my entire income, of course I cannot live with Alfred Douglas any more" and revealed that Douglas is on the point of departing for Paris (*CL* 998). As we shall see, Wilde later construed Douglas's departure, falsely, as a betrayal and a desertion.[76] But Vincent O'Sullivan, who spent time with Wilde in Naples after Douglas's departure, says that Wilde "never blamed" Douglas for leaving their *ménage,* believed "there was nothing else for [Douglas] to do [but leave]," and "formed no implacable grudge against Douglas."[77] Douglas too had finally been placed under insupportable pressure by his family to end his relationship with Wilde. Lady Queensberry, Douglas's mother, had delivered an ultimatum: unless Douglas left Wilde and immediately departed from Naples, pledging never to live in the same house or sleep under the same roof with him again, she would discontinue his own allowance.[78] The two men were "still great friends," Douglas later wrote, "and when my mother's ultimatum came as a bombshell to break up our association we were both very distressed."[79]

Even still, Douglas's defiance persisted at first. Did Lady Queensberry seriously expect Douglas to desert the friend with whom he had lived at the height of his fame, he wrote to her, now that Wilde was bankrupted, penniless, and friendless? All his love and gratitude for her "could not make me a cad and a snob and a low filthy hypocrite."[80] Her ultimatum was "cruel," "unjust," and "utterly disappointing," not least because it associated one who had "suffered enough" in her own right with "the pack of those who hound down the wretched."[81] Nonetheless, as Douglas later wrote, "there was nothing for it but for me to leave him . . . much against my will."[82] He felt he was forced to give in. The two men were now "actually in view of positive starvation," and neither of them was in a position to raise a penny.[83]

But Douglas did not capitulate without a struggle or without making provision for the man who had suddenly become dependent upon him. He insisted that his mother should send Wilde £200 at once, as well as settle all their unpaid bills in Naples, including rent on the Villa Giudice through till the end of January, so that Wilde might live in some comfort. "Pledge yourself to pay £200 more in six months time," he insisted vainly, "and £100 six months after that."[84] Perhaps incredibly, Lady Queensberry agreed to pay the first £200 so long as Wilde would issue a written pledge not to live with Bosie henceforth.[85] This Wilde agreed to do, and Bosie was thus forced to concede. But "you mustn't misunderstand me," he wrote in a heartbreaking letter to his mother, shortly after he left: "Don't think I have changed about him or that I think him bad. . . . I still love and admire him, and I think he has been infamously treated by ignorant and cruel brutes. I look on him as a martyr to progress. I associate myself with him in everything. I long to hear of his success and artistic rehabilitation in the post which is his by right at the very summit of English literature, nor do I intend to cease corresponding with him or not to see him from time to time in Paris and elsewhere. I give up nothing and admit no point against him or myself separately or jointly. Do not think either that he has been unkind to me or shown himself to me in an unfavourable light. On the contrary, he has been sweet and gentle and will always remain to me as a type of what a gentleman and a friend should be."[86]

As Wilde had written, he was "a problem for which there was no solution" (CL 995). He only desired peace and to live his own life as best he could, but the world still exercised a "social tyranny" over him and forced him, by starvation, to live in silence and solitude again (CL 994–95). Toward the end of De Profundis, he had described the fresh spirit with which he expected to meet the world as well as his hope for a narrowing of the "wide chasm" between himself and Douglas by their coming together in "some quiet foreign town." But the world had proved unamenable to Wilde's grand intentions. With some justice, Douglas wrote toward the end of his own life that the cruelty of other people was in Wilde's day what it always is and will be, "and the world, having driven [Wilde] out of every other refuge, proceeded to smoke him out of this last asylum also."[87]

5

The Ballad of Reading Gaol

B Y DECEMBER 6, 1897, Douglas was on his way to Paris via Rome. Wilde had known what he risked by living with Douglas—he had been warned on all sides, he said, and his eyes were not blinded—but he was nonetheless a good deal shattered by how things had turned out. One may go to the dentist of one's own free will, he remarked, but the moment of tooth-extraction is nonetheless painful (*CL* 1000). He had begun to question whether it was worthwhile "fighting on against the hideous forces of the world" as soon as he had received news of the cessation of his allowance (*CL* 983). But now that Douglas had departed, and Wilde had alienated all his friends (he thought), a new note of dejection crept into his affairs. "I have not much hope. . . . Things have come to a crash of a terrible character," he told Ross in the last surviving letter that he would write him for over two months (*CL* 1000). "I don't eat, or sleep: I live on cigarettes" and "am a wreck of nerves," he told Smithers (*CL* 999).

On top of the loss of Douglas, he felt "quite broken-hearted" about the sudden cooling in his friendship with Ross and the way the latter had written of him behind his back, the previous summer, in his angry letters to Alfred Douglas (*CL* 1002). Ross, it seemed, was behaving very unkindly. Ross was angry at how Wilde portrayed his role in the forfeiture of Wilde's allowance—as angry as he was at Wilde's course of action that precipitated it. Ross told Smithers that he no longer wished to be connected with Wilde's affairs and even refused to interest himself in *The Ballad of Reading Gaol* as it neared publication (*CL* 997, 1004). "How useless it all is!" Wilde lamented to Smithers: "My life cannot be patched up. There is a doom in it. Neither to myself, nor others, am I any longer a joy" (*CL* 1006). He was utterly ruined, unhappy, lonely, and disgraced, he told Smithers, now virtually his only correspondent: "All pity, or the sense of its beauty, seems to me dead in the world" (*CL* 1004).

It was in this mood that two notable visitors to Naples encountered Wilde shortly after Douglas's departure. The explorer Harry de Windt, brother of Constance's good friend Margaret Brooke, the Ranee of Sarawak, ran into Wilde seated alone outside the Cafe Gambrinus, nursing a beer, on the corner of Piazza Plebiscito: "The change in him was terrible, and his weary eyes had the furtive, hunted look with which a long association with prisons has made me only too familiar. The exile had, he told me, just been offered a large sum to lecture in America (a scheme inspired by his exquisite *Ballad of Reading Gaol*), but had refused it, as he now only needed peace and rest, which, poor fellow, came to him, and in their fullest sense, not long afterwards."[1] To the poet Vincent O'Sullivan, who visited Wilde in Naples shortly after Douglas's departure, Wilde said that he was so downcast that he had thought of suicide, that he had come "to wish that he was back in my prisoner's cell picking oakum," and that he frequented "a garden where those who have determined to kill themselves go."[2] Only the thought that his soul might not ascend to heaven and would instead be trapped in Naples forever, he told O'Sullivan, prevented him.[3] To O'Sullivan, who would see Wilde again repeatedly in Paris, it seemed that Wilde's very existence was a calamity. As they sat late in a restaurant one night, the fashionable first-night crowd turned out of a nearby theatre and entered the restaurant:

Those who knew him by sight began pointing him out to others. . . . Wilde was profoundly disturbed. He seemed to strangle. "Let us go," he said, in a thick voice.

Outside, the city lay quiet and strange under the moon. We went a little way in silence. Then one of those tragic beggars of Naples arose in a doorway where he had been crouching and held out his hand. Wilde gave him money, and I heard him murmur in English "You wretched man, why do you beg when pity is dead?"[4]

Thankfully there was *The Ballad of Reading Gaol* to see to, with publication growing ever nearer. "There's life in Art, take refuge there," he told Smithers, quoting Goethe (*CL* 1005). So far as marketing the book was concerned, he thought a paper cover and a price of 2s. 6d. would do, because "no one, except a damned and chosen few" would pay any more for a "meagre pamphlet" (*CL* 999). On December 6, he informed Smithers, "I await the revises, and promise not to 'make my quietus with a bare bodkin' till I have returned them. After that I think of retiring" (*CL* 1003). Such casual references to suicide should not be taken too literally and contain a measure of theatrical effect: it had crossed his mind to take his own life, he smilingly told his sybaritic publisher, but "first I would like to dine with you here, since to leave life as one leaves a feast is not merely philosophy but romance" (*CL* 1003). He was delighted with the size of the book, he went on to tell Smithers after seeing the revises, and he now thought they might charge three shillings for it, as well as have a limited number of large-paper copies at say 10s. 6d., to give the book a cachet (*CL* 1003–5). Would Smithers please check the poem's dedication against the newspapers to be sure that Wooldridge, the guardsman whom the poem commemorates and whose execution it dramatizes, was in the *Horse* Guards and not the *Dragoons?* The last page was "dreadfully placed," in need of resetting, and the poem ought to conclude with "C. 3. 3.," so as to "emphasize the fact that the pseudonym is not a mere literary caprice, but the actual name for eighteen months of the man who wrote the poem" (*CL* 1004). The signature should be printed in the same size as or one size larger than the capital "R" of "Reading Gaol" (*CL* 1004). "C. 3. 3." was not well printed on the title-page—it was too thin and "should be as black and thick as the title"—and moreover Smithers's name was too large: "there is no balance, and it looks as if the poem was by Leonard Smithers" (*CL* 1006). On December 11, he finally relinquished control of his text: "I think you had better send me no more proofs of the poem," he told Smithers: "I have the *maladie de perfection* and keep on correcting. I know I have got it now to a fairly high standard, but I don't want to polish for ever" (*CL* 1007).

Notwithstanding his expressions of self-pity, Wilde managed to sustain a sharp interest in life after Douglas's departure, asking Smithers if he would kindly see that he be sent the *Daily Chronicle* for four weeks, laughing at the names of those who had been proposed for a possible English Academy of Letters, and reading with pleasure Vincent O'Sullivan's new book *The Houses of Sin*, marveling at how finely bound and printed it was, and at "what maladies he draws from the moon" (*CL* 1002).[5] In mid-December, £5 arrived from Smithers "like manna from heaven" to alleviate immediate difficulties, and shortly after this More Adey telegraphed £100, representing the first of two installments of Lady Queensberry's promised payout. On December 18, she received in return his written pledge that he would never again live under the same roof as Douglas.[6]

Lady Queensberry's money enabled Wilde to escape his immediate woes and to fulfill a long-held ambition: on December 15, he announced his plan to go to Taormina in Sicily for a few days, as the guest of a "very cultivated" Russian (never since identified) of "advanced years" whom he had recently met (*CL* 1008). He told Blacker as early as September 6 that he hoped to go to Sicily, and the island, which to Victorians represented a living remnant of ancient Greece on Italian soil, featured in a number of his works. In *The Duchess of Padua*, for instance, Wilde's eponymous heroine nostalgically recalls her childhood in Sicily, where she "took the scarlet poppy from the corn," while in "The Critic As Artist," the music of Matthew Arnold's "pipe" is said to have "lured Proserpina from her Sicilian fields."[7] Sicilian wine and brocades are mentioned briefly in *Salomé,* "Charmides," and *The Picture of Dorian Gray;* and in his early poem "Theocritus. A Villanelle," with its repeated refrain "O Singer of Persephone!/Dost thou remember Sicily?," Wilde represents Sicily as the foundational site of the idyllic or pastoral tradition in poetry.[8] Sicily was for Victorians, in the words of critic Stefania Arcara, "the emblem of a longed-for mythical, sensual past," a pastoral Arcadia that evoked images of abundance and sensuous splendor.[9] It implied a return to the innocent life of the senses in a natural, timeless environment and, more broadly, an idealized "Hellenic" vision of male homoeroticism that stood in direct contrast to both the pathologization of male same-sex love in contemporary medical literature and its criminalization in British law.

That Wilde's first trip to Sicily (he was to visit the island again in 1900) can be seen as an expression of an emerging understanding of himself as a homosexual man can be gleaned from the few facts known about it. While there, he sought the company of two of Sicily's most accomplished and unapologetic homosexual inhabitants. From the fact that Wilde later sent one of the first copies of *The Ballad of Reading Gaol* to "Illustrio Signor Alberto Stopford, Taormina, Sicily," it seems highly likely that while in Sicily Wilde met with Albert Stopford, a disgraced English art connoisseur and homosexual who maintained a pretty home with a well cultivated garden at Taormina (*CL* 1032). Wilde must have known Stopford previously through their mutual close friend Gladys de Grey, the dedicatee of Wilde's *A Woman of No Importance.* There are eerie parallels between the lives of the two men. Like Wilde, Stopford had been forced into exile to avoid homosexual scandal. In 1894, a warrant had been issued for Stopford's arrest in England on charges of gross indecency, although it was later allowed to lapse unexecuted, and again like Wilde, a brilliant career would come down around Stopford's ears in 1918, when Stopford was imprisoned with hard labor for gross indecency.[10] During his trip to Taormina, Wilde also visited the studio of the photographer Wilhelm Von Gloeden, one of the founders of modern homosexual iconography, who specialized in the photography of nude or nearly nude Sicilian peasant boys, dressed in togas or loincloths, with garlands in their hair or laced-up sandals on their feet, posing as Ancient Greeks in Arcadian settings. Von Gloeden was the creator of "a theatrical idyll . . . a faux-Greek paradise . . . a place of pastoral grace, eternal youth and budding masculinity," and his photographs "interlaced . . . Hellenism, aestheticism, 'Greek love' and Mediterranean travel."[11] Wilde's signature is recorded in Von Gloeden's guest book alongside those of Eleanor Duse, J. P. Morgan, Richard Strauss, Kaiser Wilhelm II, King Edward VII, and numerous other prominent Northern Europeans and Americans. Von Gloeden's photographs, while widely popular with an educated Victorian audience, were especially appealing to fellow homosexuals such as Wilde (who owned two of them, according to Neil McKenna), for they espoused " 'the fundamental ideal of a homosexual utopia,' where Sicily is a new-found Arcadia, a sunlit paradise populated by beautiful youths."[12] There was nothing undeliberate or coincidental about Wilde's choice of Taormina as his destination. Von Gloeden also would be sent one of the first copies of *The Ballad* two months later.

When he returned to Naples, Wilde, no less depressed than before in spite of acquiring a mysterious and beautiful new lover, moved into cheaper lodgings in the Via Santa Lucia.[13] Shortly before this, the British consul at Naples, E. Neville Rolfe, apparently lacking a complete picture of Wilde's life, wrote to the ex–prime minister, Lord Rosebery (who had recently bought a villa at Posillipo), to assure him that Wilde was "fully two miles from you," "lives a completely secluded life," and "looks thoroughly abashed, much like a whipped hound."[14] "I have had many misfortunes since I wrote to you," Wilde told Smithers: influenza, ill health, loneliness, "the robbery, during my absence in Sicily, of *all* my clothes, etc., by a servant whom I left at the villa . . . and general *ennui* with a tragi-comedy of an existence, but I want to see my poem out before I take steps" (*CL* 1011). In the absence of an agreement to publish *The Ballad of Reading Gaol in* America, Wilde now realized that "it is my *name* that terrifies," that it would be better to publish in America without it, and that "the withdrawal of my name is essential in America as elsewhere" (*CL* 1011). Smithers accordingly wrote on January 12, 1898 to Wilde's American agent Elisabeth Marbury, telling her to take any reasonable sum of money which she could get for the poem, to secure its publication with or without Wilde's name, to secure American copyright, and to fix the date on which she wished to publish. Smithers would publish the English edition—which he expected to have printed in the next eight or ten days—on the same date, so as to ensure no pirated editions could be printed. She replied disappointingly on January 25, saying that "nobody here seems to feel any interest in the poem" and that no newspaper syndicate would handle it. The *New York World* "refuses to give us anything" and the *New York Journal* would only pay $100.[15] If Smithers accepted this offer, she wrote, the *Journal* would publish the poem in its Sunday edition on February 13. Smithers in turn replied that should Marbury fail to place the poem, he would himself have the book set up in the United States and its copyright registered at his own expense.

In the meantime, Smithers continued to consult Wilde about every aspect of the English book edition's production, right down to samples of the cloth in which the book might be bound. In order to satisfy Wilde's request for blackness and thickness of type, Smithers had gone to the trouble of having a zinc block of the signature "C. 3. 3." drawn and specially made, while at the same time reducing the size of his own name ("to satisfactorily show that I am not the author of the poem, but only that humble person, its introducer to the public").[16] On January 26, with four hundred copies of the book now printed and ready for binding, Smithers told Wilde that he would the next day be sent twenty copies of the unstitched title-sheet, to inscribe to particular friends. Twelve days later Wilde returned the inscribed sheets to Smithers, saying that he was charmed by the book as a production, that the title page was a masterpiece, and that Robert Ross would supply the addresses of all those whom he wished to receive inscribed copies, except for Alfred Douglas, who was staying at the Hôtel Bellevue in Mentone, France. Two days later, he sent Smithers a letter containing the addresses of the artist Frits Thaulow, who had been so bravely hospitable in Dieppe, and other recipients whose addresses Ross might not know, including Governor Nelson at Reading Prison and a well-disposed warder named George Groves. "I don't know Robbie's address," he added sadly as a postscript to his letter, and "it is three months since he last wrote to me. . . . My life has gone to great ruin here and I have no brains now, or energy. . . . I shall be in Paris on Sunday next. It is my only chance of working, [though] my chief object in going to Paris is to dine with you, I need hardly say" (*CL* 1013).

Smithers published *The Ballad* in England on February 13, 1898, the date the *New York Journal* had proposed. Three days later Marbury sent him the *New York Journal*'s meager payment, less her commission and associated fees.[17] But the poem had not appeared in the *Journal* on the thirteenth; instead the *Journal's* pages on that day carried news of the sinking of a transatlantic steamship and details of Emile Zola's trial for exposing high-level corruption and miscarriages of justice in the Dreyfus case, while simultaneously echoing loudly with the saber-rattling that would result in the Spanish-American War two months later. Nor would *The Ballad* appear on any subsequent date in the *Journal*.[18] In the event, it is probably lucky that Wilde's poem was not tainted by any association with the Hearst-owned *Journal*—the embodiment of sensational yellow journalism. Had it appeared in Hearst's paper, the format too would have reflected poorly upon Wilde's poem, especially when contrasted with Smithers's English first-edition of eight hundred copies, finely printed at the Chiswick Press on Dutch hand-made paper, bound in cinnamon cloth with a white linen back.[19] For a

The Ballad of Reading Gaol (London: Leonard Smithers, 1898). Title page.

The

Ballad of Reading Gaol

By

C. 3. 3.

Leonard Smithers
Royal Arcade London W
Mdcccxcviii

"meagre pamphlet" priced cheaply at 2s. 6d., the poem arrived in the most exquisite dress.

The Ballad of Reading Gaol is arguably the best and most important of Wilde's poems. It is at once a coruscating political poem—an indictment not merely of the late-Victorian prison system but of the society that convicted and imprisoned Wilde—a visionary literary ballad, and more indirectly a moving and unapologetic reassertion of Wilde's sexual orientation. It "aims at eternity." Wilde said when drafting the poem, and as soon as it was published it was acclaimed as "a remarkable addition to contemporary poetry" and "a very beautiful, very powerful, perhaps a great poem" (*CL* 918).[20] He had first conceived the poem in prison, Alfred Douglas later said, but its composition had cost him more time and effort than just about any of his other literary works. A few weeks after its publication, Wilde called it his literary swansong or "chant de cygne" (*CL* 1035). With his death still two and a half years away, he feared that something vital had died in him: the poem was indeed to prove the last of his works, but it was his best-selling work in his lifetime. The first edition of eight hundred copies sold out within days, and within four months the poem had gone through six editions, representing five thousand copies. "I feel like Lipton's tea," Wilde remarked in response to a publisher's advertisement announcing that the poem had sold three thousand copies in just three weeks (*CL* 1043).

The poem opens dramatically by describing the physical appearance and demeanor of its central symbolic figure, a condemned guardsman—certainly a prisoner though not yet legally a "convict" when the poem opens, since he is in prison on remand, dressed in his own clothes—as he tramps the exercise yard. Wilde's detailed dedication to the poem ("In Memoriam C. T. W., Sometime Trooper of the Royal Horse Guards, Obiit. H.M. Prison, Reading, Berkshire, July 7th, 1896") makes clear that, although embellished by Wilde's imagination, the poem's central figure is based closely on the actual guardsman, Charles Thomas Wooldridge, who had been a fellow prisoner of Wilde's at Reading prior to his execution there on July 7, 1896.[21] "The man's face will haunt me till I die," Wilde remarked of Wooldridge to the journalist Chris Healy.[22] In the first stanza, Wilde tells us that the guardsman has killed the woman he loved, with "blood and wine . . . on his hands," in a fit that has perhaps as much of ritual sacrament or Dionysian frenzy about it as sexual passion and drunkenness.[23] Crucially, this prisoner has not yet been judged and sentenced in any legal sense, but is rather condemned in his own eyes and in those of his fellow prisoners by the equanimity with which he greets his terrible end. Although he awaits his day in the "black dock's dreadful pen," this event will confirm rather than establish his guilt, after which he will no more be seen by his fellow prisoners.[24]

But although it opens with a figure who has killed and awaits execution according to the penal code of his day, the poem quickly dispenses with the usual easy and comfortable moral frameworks by establishing, in the very first stanza, the guardsman's childlike innocence and humanity: he was "with the dead, / The poor dead woman whom he loved" when "they found him."[25] As the narrator observes the guardsman tramp the exercise yard, he is struck by how oblivious and indifferent the condemned man seems to the harsh world of the prison:

> A cricket cap was on his head,
>   And his step seemed light and gay;
> But I never saw a man who looked
>   So wistfully at the day.
>
> I never saw a man who looked
>   With such a wistful eye
> Upon that little tent of blue
>   Which prisoners call the sky,
> And at every drifting cloud that went
>   With sails of silver by.[26]

Unlike his fellow prisoners, he stares wistfully and unremorsefully at the sky, his cricket cap emphasizing the lightness and gaiety of his step. To his fellow prisoners, tortured by guilt and by their walled-in surroundings, he is an enigma, perhaps even a hero:

He did not wring his hands, as do
    Those witless men who dare
To try to rear the changeling Hope
    In the cave of black Despair:
He only looked upon the sun,
    And drank the morning air.

He did not wring his hands nor weep,
    Nor did he peek or pine,
But he drank the air as though it held
    Some healthful anodyne;
With open mouth he drank the sun
    As though it had been wine!

And I and all the souls in pain,
    Who tramped the other ring,
Forgot if we ourselves had done
    A great or little thing,
And watched with gaze of dull amaze
    The man who had to swing.

For strange it was to see him pass
    With a step so light and gay,
And strange it was to see him look
    So wistfully at the day,
And strange it was to think that he
    Had such a debt to pay.[27]

While the guardsman carries his punishment lightly, "the very prison walls / Suddenly seemed to reel" when the narrator hears a fellow prisoner whisper "*That fellow's got to swing*," and the "little tent of sky" becomes "a casque of scorching steel."[28]

From this point onward, our attention shifts to the narrator in his distress and suffering. He is a "feeling" man who senses an immediate bond of kinship with the condemned guardsman. Wilde's first readers would have had little difficulty identifying this man as Wilde himself: the poem's authorship "is not difficult to detect," the *Daily Chronicle* remarked upon reviewing the poem.[29] Wilde had invoked his own prison cell number on the poem's title page, together with the location of his own highly publicized imprisonment (Reading Prison or "Gaol"); and in case any doubt were left, he had insisted to Smithers upon the poem ending with the signature "C. 3. 3." to underscore "that the pseudonym is not a mere literary caprice, but the actual name for eighteen months of the man who wrote the poem." Wilde's prison-signature underscored more than merely his authorship of the poem, however: by citing his cell number at the poem's end, Wilde effectively identifies himself as the poem's narrator no less than its author, placing himself "inside" the poem as a direct witness to Wooldridge's execution.

Our identification of Wilde as the narrator of his own poem has profound implications for what comes next, for the narrator understands perfectly why the guardsman rushes to his death: "The man had killed the thing he loved / And so he had to die."[30] Implicitly Wilde too had killed the thing he loved, and like the guardsman he has already judged himself, whatever the legal merits and demerits of his case. "Each man kills the thing he loves," Wilde tells us in the poem's famous central refrain, "yet each man does not die."[31] We "kill" each other in a thousand different ways, Wilde goes on to say, "Some with a bitter look, / Some with a flattering word," some with "hands of Lust, / Some with the hands of Gold."[32] These lines, which Wilde echoes forcefully at the poem's conclusion, are the most vital in the entire poem, for they raise far-reaching questions about justice and speak to the violence wrought upon and by Wilde as a result of his affair with Douglas.

Just as Wilde felt he had unwittingly "killed" his staunchly loyal mother—who, after urging him to stand trial and refusing to believe in his guilt, had died impoverished and heartbroken while he was in jail—Wilde must have felt that, through his actions both before and after his conviction, he had effectively destroyed or "killed" his wife and children.[33] "My life has all been cut to pieces" and "my husband [has] ruined the lives of my darling boys," Constance wrote the day Wilde was committed for trial.[34] After their father's arrest, the children never again saw their father, and Cyril, the couple's older child, who at nine years old made it his mission to find out the nature of the offences committed by his father, "never smiled again" according to his brother.[35] In an effort to put the scandal behind them, Constance took the boys to live on the continent, where she put them in separate boarding schools, and thereafter she saw them only intermittently before her own sudden death in the spring of 1898. Despite changing the family surname to "Holland," she lived the rest of her brief life in fear that the boys would always afterward be tainted as Wilde's offspring. It was a fear shared by Cyril, who turned "while yet a child, into a taciturn pessimist."[36]

Constance never lived in Britain again. After her death, the children returned to Britain as wards of their mother's cousin, Adrian Hope. Hope, however, "did not take [the] duties he had towards us very seriously," Vyvyan Holland later wrote, and the children scarcely ever saw their legal guardian.[37] Instead they were raised from 1898 onward by their mother's aunt, Mary Napier, and her daughter Eliza, who taught them to believe that their father too was dead. To be sure, Wilde did not know when composing *The Ballad of Reading Gaol* just how unkind fate would prove to his wife and children. But he wept bitter tears when he pondered how he had failed them, and he certainly knew the terrible destruction he brought upon the family.[38] "I don't mind *my life* being wrecked . . . but when I think of poor Constance I simply want to kill myself," he had written to Blacker in early August 1897 (*CL* 921).

But the poem generalizes from Wilde's own experiences and suggests the ubiquity of pain as well as the thoughtless, sadistic capacity within each of us. The murder of love is worse than the murder of flesh and blood, Wilde suggests, because "the dead so soon grow cold."[39] Where the coward does it with a kiss, the "brave man" kills "with a sword" and "the kindest use a knife."[40] Real cruelty resides in the bitter look and the flattering word, whereby we inflict a hundred deaths on a daily basis. No crime is worse than the thoughtless slighting or "killing" of love, Wilde implies, and a life without love is perhaps the worst life of all.

Yet if "each man kills the thing he loves," each man "does not die." Common forms of cruelty are left unpunished, Wilde implies, while the kind man "dies" in prison. Wilde speaks here of the hypocrisy and rush to judgment that often carry innocent, loving, or penitent men to the execution chamber, but he is also speaking indirectly of his own "death" at the hands of British justice. In passing sentence on Wilde in May 1895, Justice Wills, the presiding judge at Wilde's second criminal trial, had determined upon meting out "the severest sentence that the law allows," two years of imprisonment with hard labor, while announcing his personal view that it was "totally inadequate for such a case as this."[41] To Wilde, the sentence was a form of death, and as we have seen, press commentators and government officials feared that Wilde would not survive his term. In his own mind, Wilde is one with the killer condemned to die in prison, notwithstanding that the latter is imprisoned for a greater crime and facing a greater punishment. They pass in the prison's yards and corridors "like two doomed ships that pass in storm," making no sign and saying no word to each other, in accordance with the silent and separate systems of punishment.[42] But they are both "outcast men" who share a common fate:

> A prison wall was round us both,
>   Two outcast men we were:
> The world had thrust us from its heart,
>   And God from out His care:
> And the iron gin that waits for Sin
>   Had caught us in its snare.[43]

This kinship between "outcast men" lies at the heart of the poem, which is at once a defiant expression of Wilde's solidarity with his fellow prisoners and an affirmation of male community and camaraderie in the face of a culture that had declared Wilde's previous relations with men to be grossly indecent. Both Wooldridge and Wilde are the helpless, despised victims of a pitiless, hypocritical justice system through which the state mechanically and impersonally inflicts a "death of shame" upon the body of the prisoner, while the majority are left free:

> For each man kills the thing he loves,
>   Yet each man does not die.
>
> He does not die a death of shame
>   On a day of dark disgrace,
> Nor have a noose about his neck,
>   Nor a cloth upon his face,
> Nor drop feet foremost through the floor
>   Into an empty place
>
> He does not sit with silent men
>   Who watch him night and day;
> Who watch him when he tries to weep,
>   And when he tries to pray;
> Who watch him lest himself should rob
>   The prison of its prey.
>
> He does not wake at dawn to see
>   Dread figures throng his room,
> The shivering Chaplain robed in white,
>   The Sheriff stern with gloom,
> And the Governor all in shiny black,
>   With the yellow face of Doom.

He does not rise in piteous haste
    To put on convict-clothes,
While some coarse-mouthed Doctor gloats, and notes
    Each new and nerve-twitched pose,
Fingering a watch whose little ticks
    Are like horrible hammer-blows.

He does not feel that sickening thirst
    That sands one's throat, before
The hangman with his gardener's gloves
    Comes through the padded door,
And binds one with three leathern thongs,
    That the throat may thirst no more.[44]

To be sure, these lines directly represent Wilde's imaginative recreation of Wooldridge's terrible last hours. But they are driven by Wilde's empathy with the condemned man, and Wilde is indirectly describing his own torment in prison. They are among the first of many imaginative "displacements" whereby Wilde projects his own suffering and fear onto the condemned man.

Wilde's empathy with Wooldridge transforms *The Ballad of Reading Gaol* into something far greater than the narrative account of a real man's execution, the stuff of popular ballads—about Captain Kidd, Jack Shepherd, Dick Turpin, and Sam Hall—for nearly two centuries. By the middle of canto 3, the poem has become not merely a reflection on the nature of justice and the implacability of a cruel legal system, but also a cry of personal suffering from a nameless man, C. 3. 3., stripped of his real identity, whose wide imaginative and emotional sensibility stands in sharp contrast to his unfeeling and life-denying surroundings. The symbolic guardsman's equanimity in the face of an implacable doom is certainly remarkable as well: despite a number of clemency petitions, the real-life Charles Wooldridge petitioned the home secretary so that his execution be allowed to proceed immediately, with no possibility of reprieve. But equally remarkable is the sense of kinship with the condemned man Wilde and Wooldridge's fellow prisoners feel generally, as if Wilde were determined to prove, as he had written to the *Daily Chronicle,* that "prisoners are, as a class, extremely kind and sympathetic," that "the only really humanising influence in prison is the influence of the prisoners," and that "suffering and the community of suffering makes people kind" (*CL* 851). Wilde later told a warder that the moment when, alone in his cell, he heard the bell tolling for Wooldridge's execution was "the most awful of a time rich in horrors."[45]

Robert Ross told Wilde that properly speaking the poem should end with Wilde's moving description, in canto 4, of Wooldridge's ignominious burial in unconsecrated ground, within the prison walls:

> They hanged him as a beast is hanged:
>   They did not even toll
> A requiem that might have brought
>   Rest to his startled soul,
> But hurriedly they took him out,
>   And hid him in a hole.
>
>   . . . .
>
> Yet all is well, he has but passed
>   To Life's appointed bourne:
> And alien tears will fill for him
>   Pity's long-broken urn,
> For his mourners will be outcast men,
>   And outcasts always mourn.

In Ross's view, Wilde's implied kinship with Wooldridge formed the crux of the poem. Nine years after Wilde's death, in 1909, Ross underscored this kinship by inscribing the final four of these lines (from

"And alien tears" to "outcasts always mourn") upon Wilde's grave at Père Lachaise Cemetery, after first transferring Wilde's corpse from the pauper's grave at Bagneux where it was buried in 1900. For Ross, "outcast men" meant homosexuals and others forced to live beyond the pale, not merely prisoners and ex-convicts. Ross clearly felt that the poem allegorized the sacrifice of its author to Britain's harsh, homophobic laws, and it is hardly surprising that Wilde's grave has, in the years ever since, become a site of secular pilgrimage for homosexuals and non-homosexuals alike.

But instead of ending the poem with Wooldridge's burial in unconsecrated ground and the mourning of outcast men, Wilde wanted to end the poem on a more politically incisive note: "the propaganda, which I desire to make" begins at this point, he told Ross (*CL* 964). Consequently Wilde steps boldly forward in canto 5, under the thin veil of anonymity that the pseudonym C. 3. 3. affords him, to pronounce his personal views on the justice system and its antithetical character to Christianity:

> I know not whether Laws be right,
>   Or whether Laws be wrong;
> All that we know who lie in gaol
>   Is that the wall is strong;
> And that each day is like a year,
>   A year whose days are long.
>
> But this I know, that every Law
>   That men have made for Man,
> Since first Man took his brother's life,
>   And the sad world began,
> But straws the wheat and saves the chaff
>   With a most evil fan.
>
> This too I know—and wise it were
>   If each could know the same—

That every prison that men build
　　Is built with bricks of shame,
And bound with bars lest Christ should see
　　How men their brothers maim.

With bars they blur the gracious moon,
　　And blind the goodly sun:
And they do well to hide their Hell,
　　For in it things are done
That Son of God nor son of Man
　　Ever should look upon!

　　　　. . . . .

Each narrow cell in which we dwell
　　Is a foul and dark latrine,
And the fetid breath of living Death
　　Chokes up each grated screen,
And all, but Lust, is turned to dust
　　In Humanity's machine.

The brackish water that we drink
　　Creeps with a loathsome slime,
And the bitter bread they weigh in scales
　　Is full of chalk and lime,
And Sleep will not lie down, but walks
　　Wild-eyed, and cries to Time.

　　　　. . . . .

With midnight always in one's heart,
　　And twilight in one's cell,

We turn the crank, or tear the rope,
　　Each in his separate Hell,
And the silence is more awful far
　　Than the sound of a brazen bell.

And never a human voice comes near
　　To speak a gentle word:
And the eye that watches through the door
　　Is pitiless and hard:
And by all forgot, we rot and rot,
　　With soul and body marred.

And thus we rust Life's iron chain
　　Degraded and alone:
And some men curse, and some men weep,
　　And some men make no moan:
But God's eternal Laws are kind
　　And break the heart of stone.[46]

The pronouns "I" and "we" are especially important in these lines: Wilde *in propia persona* declares his kinship with all prisoners and protests the "fetid breath of living Death," "the "brackish water," the "bitter bread . . . full of chalk and lime," and the soul-destroying system of silent, solitary confinement that renders each cell a "separate Hell." While he knew that "there is much more in the poem than a pamphlet on prison reform" (*CL* 1019), he was determined to end by emphasizing the poem's continuities with his letter to the *Daily Chronicle*, thereby lending justice to Seamus Heaney's comments from 1993 that the poem properly belongs, along with John Mitchell's prison diaries and Brendan Behan's *Borstal Boy*, in "that most disaffected of Irish genres, the gaol journal," and that by writing it "Wilde converted himself into the kind of propagandist poet his mother (the fiery Speranza) had been fifty years before, the kind of poet that he had gone to England to avoid becoming."[47]

———————

The Ballad of Reading Gaol was the most successful of Wilde's published writings in his lifetime, and it has never been out of print since. But it is a hybrid production, the work of "a romantic artist . . . working on realistic material," as Arthur Symons once put it.[48] When including Wilde's poem in *The Oxford Book of Modern Verse, 1892–1935,* the poet W. B. Yeats later felt obliged to exclude some seventy of the poem's original 109 stanzas, including all of the poem's final two cantos, in order to "bring into the light a great, or almost great poem."[49] For Yeats, the chief strength of the poem was its "stark realism," and he was determined to strip the poem of its most romantic and sentimental elements in order to reveal its essence as a singular work of art.[50] Similarly, the poet W. E. Henley commented upon reviewing the poem in 1898 that "there are not a few passages in the ballad" which seem "instinct and vigorous with veracity."[51] Yet to Henley, a pioneer of free verse, the poem was also replete with "traditional phrases and effects," a self-consciously literary work, deplorable in its artifice, and no less redolent of "aesthetic Chelsea" than many of the works Wilde wrote before he went to jail.[52]

The hybridity Henley, Yeats, and Symons detected in the poem owes much to the circumstances in which it was written. Heaney observes rightly that the poem was conceived and largely composed when its author was "still, psychologically, very much a prisoner," determined to write about prison life and to try and change it for others.[53] Wilde's earliest inclination was to publish the poem in the *Daily Chronicle* ("reckless in art"), as we have already seen, and a large part of the poem's fascination to its earliest readership lay in its identity as a sequel to what readers already knew of Wilde and the terrible conditions he had faced in prison. The immense publicity given him at the time of his trials and during the early months of his imprisonment had been unwanted, but in the case of the *Ballad,* Wilde and his publisher actively courted such publicity, notwithstanding the deliberate and, to most readers, transparent effort to obscure Wilde's personal identity behind the signature "C. 3. 3." As the journal *The Critic* archly remarked shortly after the poem's release, "the publishers of this volume have evidently counted upon" an "element of personal interest."[54] If Smith's bookstalls have not yet "taken the poem," Wilde told Smithers at one point, "do work it—and supply them with a placard" (*CL* 1043). Perhaps Smithers could "have a leaflet, with criticisms, put into the leaves of a good magazine? Like Pears' soap, and other more useful things?" It would not merely be profitable, but would also "irritate the reader" (*CL* 1043).

Wilde's dedication commemorating the date and fact of Wooldridge's execution is central to the poem's protest against the justice system. The dedication is sometimes omitted from modern editions, presumably on the basis that it is a dedication to the first edition rather than to the poem as such. But it is a critical element of Wilde's text, explicitly designed to "suit the title," as Wilde said, for it predisposes the reader to see the poem as the record of an actual execution at an actual place ("H.M. Prison, Reading, Berkshire") and its central figure an actual person ("C. T. W., Sometime Trooper of the Royal Horse Guard") rather than a purely symbolic one (*CL* 986). Wilde's earliest readers would have inferred quickly that many of the poem's descriptive details were based on Wilde's own prison experiences, and the poem's basis in actuality would have been especially clear to Governor Nelson and Warder Groves, the officers at Reading to whom Wilde sent copies of the first edition. Nelson and Groves would have known, as few others would, that the "little roof of glass" through which the condemned man stares at the moment of his execution is an exact description of the roof of the execution chamber at Reading, which, until the construction of a special "execution center" in 1900, doubled as the prison's photography studio and therefore needed good natural light. They would have known, too, that the "dripping wall" of Debtor's Yard alludes to the fifty-foot algae-covered east-facing wall in Reading Prison's "A" yard, a yard once used exclusively for debtors rather than for other categories of prisoner and, in Wilde's day, used for stone-breaking as a form of hard labor. Since the wall was east-facing, it was in almost permanent shadow and therefore constantly dripping with condensation and algae. Likewise C. 3. 3.'s statement "I saw the shadowed bars / Like a lattice wrought in lead, / Move right across the whitewashed wall"[55] correlates closely with Wilde's numerous prose descriptions of the poor light conditions in his cell, such as his statement that "the very sun and moon seem taken from us. Outside, the day may be blue and gold, but the light that creeps down the thickly-muffled glass of the small iron-barred window beneath which one sits is grey and niggard. It is always twilight in one's cell, as it is always midnight in one's heart" (*CL* 720). As Anthony Stokes has shown, to anybody who knows the prison's architecture and history, the "Reading Gaol" of Wilde's poem correlates closely with the actual Reading Prison.[56]

These actual and realistic elements constitute the basis for the poem's success as a work of prison reform. *The Ballad* is "good literature," one early reviewer remarked, because "the document is authentic" and the poem is "the faithful record of experiences through which the writer . . . has passed."[57] But the poem gives the sense of being an authentic document for more personal reasons as well. It was "wrung out of me, a cry of pain," Wilde writes, like the "cry of Marsyas, not the song of Apollo" (*CL* 1025). To the *Academy*, reviewing the poem on February 28, 1898, the author's "peculiar gift" was "to feel and chronicle sensations," and "so long as he honestly reproduces emotion he holds it."[58] In his May 1897 letter to the *Daily Chronicle*, Wilde had said that "the first and most prominent emotion produced by modern prison life [is] terror," which seizes the grown man no less than the child and is "intensified beyond power of expression by the solitary cellular system of our prisons" (*CL* 849). To a large degree, the poem is a moving literary demonstration of this terrible fact. It should not be judged by the standard of "lyrical beauty," Wilde observed at one point during its composition, "but of realistic presentation and actuality, at least by a sane critic, if there is one outside Bedlam" (*CL* 999). It was a realistic expression of personal suffering, born out of Wilde's own direct experience of prison under the Du Cane regime. "According to its sincerity," remarked one of its first reviewers, "so is it valuable."[59]

But Wilde's intentions for the poem were more complicated and even contradictory than this. If at times he saw the poem as a cry of pain "wrung out of me . . . like the cry of Marsyas," at others he felt that the poem was "too autobiographical" and its treatment "too personal" (*CL* 982). It is "a sort of denial of my own philosophy of art in many ways," he told Laurence Housman, "terribly realistic for me, and drawn from actual experience" (*CL* 928). Similarly, he felt that to emphasize the poem's relation to contemporary prison life was to mistake his main intent, since "there is more in the poem than a pamphlet on prison reform" (*CL* 1019). From the very start he had been conscious of the special challenge that prison writing presented to him *as an artist,* especially one who had always insisted on the distinctions between art and life. Prison life "is too terrible and ugly to make a work of art of," he had told the warder Thomas Martin in April 1897 (*CL* 798). "The difficulty is that objects in prison have no shape or form," he explained to Ross in October: the "horror of prison is . . . so degrading, and hideous, and revolting in its effect" that it makes "describing a prison . . . as difficult artistically as describing a water-closet would be" (*CL* 956–57).

In light of these doubts and Wilde's desire to produce a "work of art," the poem's inception in Wilde's reawakened love and admiration for Alfred Douglas comes to assume a singular importance. Douglas had many good reasons to express himself directly and sincerely in the years they had been apart, Wilde wrote in early June 1897. Nonetheless, Douglas was above all else a poet "of real sympathy with the Ballad," said Wilde, and his best work to date had been done before the calamitous events of 1895 (*CL* 874). For this reason, Wilde encouraged Douglas to abandon personal lyrics and to return to poetic forms "more remote from actual events and passions" (*CL* 873). As Wilde had written in "The Critic as Artist," "one can really . . . be far more subjective in an *objective* form than in any other way" (*CL* 873–74).[60] This "the ballad-writers of the Border" had understood no less well than Wilde himself, who had "taken the Drama, the most objective form known to art, and made it as personal a mode of expression as the Lyric or the Sonnet" (*CL* 874). The ballad "is the true origin of the Romantic Drama," Wilde told Douglas as he urged him to return to the form of poetry in which he had excelled previously; and the primeval ballad writers, even more than the tragedians of the Greek or Roman stage, were "the true predecessors of Shakespeare" (*CL* 874). As he begged Douglas to write more ballads, Wilde had unconsciously stumbled on his own solution to the problem of writing about prison in a way that reconciled artistry with personal experience.

Whatever else it is, *The Ballad of Reading Gaol* is first and foremost a ballad, with an in-built self-awareness of its debts to and continuities with a tradition that includes such literary ballads as Samuel Taylor Coleridge's "The Rime of the Ancient Mariner" and Keats's "La Belle Dame Sans Merci" and "The Eve of St. Agnes," as well as more popular ballads such as Kipling's "Danny Deever" and Thomas Hood's "The Dream of Eugene Aram." As with Coleridge's poem, which opened Wordsworth's and Coleridge's important 1798 volume *Lyrical Ballads, The Ballad of Reading Gaol* is a text designed to be *read,* aimed principally at a literate, educated readership to whom it nonetheless speaks (in the famous words with which Wordsworth had explained *Lyrical Ballads*) in the "real language of men in a state of vivid sensation."[61]

Yet Wilde's *Ballad* is conscious too of its debts to a popular and spoken tradition of oral balladry in which events of general, often sensational interest are narrated and made pleasurable by being fitted to an almost metronomic "voice" situated somewhere midway on the continuum between singing and speaking. At once bardic and anonymous, the ballad voice is nonetheless always human and compassionate. Wilde's correspondence is full of references to those authors of his own day—Henley, Kipling, A. E. Housman, George Sims—whose work weighed upon his mind during the composition of *The Ballad of Reading Gaol*. While this correspondence by no means yields a full list of the poem's many literary influences—Wilde is notably silent on his poem's debts to Thomas Hood and Samuel Taylor Coleridge, for instance—it comes as no surprise that three of the authors whom Wilde identifies as influences were self-conscious balladeers, determined to extend a venerable ancient tradition so that it spoke directly to a late-Victorian readership. When Wilde says that in writing the poem he is "out-Henleying Kipling" or aiming for language that is "G. R. Sims at best," he is confessing that *The Ballad* is in part an attempt to write himself into this tradition (*CL* 916, 992). For all its appearances to the contrary, *The Ballad of Reading Gaol* is no less a "literary" endeavor than were the sonnets, narrative idylls, and ballads with which Wilde had commenced his literary career twenty years earlier.

Heaney usefully calls our attention to the influence on Wilde's poem of a patriotic ballad by Wilde's own mother, "The Brothers: A Scene From '98." Published in 1864, "The Brothers" is about the trial and execution of the brothers Sheare, two Irish brothers judged as traitors by the English in 1798.[62] But in light of Wilde's love for Douglas as a poet of "real sympathy with the ballad," Douglas's 1894 "The Ballad of Perkin Warbeck" deserves our interest more. Douglas's ballad narrates the story of Perkin Warbeck, a young pretender to the Tudor throne—and in Douglas's rendering, a youth of extremely prepossessing appearance, with the "voice . . . and the face of the king"—executed by Henry VII in 1499.[63] Although in most historical accounts, Warbeck is a rebel or traitor to the throne, in Douglas's ballad he is decidedly a victim, a poor weaver's son, first plucked against his will from humble anonymity by the House of York as their anointed pretender to the throne of England and then abandoned in defeat to face the hangman's "hempen rope" and a "narrow ditch."[64] The subject matter has obvious parallels with Wilde's ballad, but just as important is Douglas's mastery of the traditional ballad stanza, with its alternately rhyming lines of iambic tetrameter and trimeter. The prosody of Douglas's poem is highly regular and traditional: it is the prosody of "The Rime of the Ancient Mariner" and countless other ballads. With one small exception, it is also the prosody that Wilde utilizes in *The Ballad of Reading Gaol*—and quite distinct from that used by Wilde's mother in "The Brothers" or by Wilde himself in his earlier ballads "Ballade de Marguerite" and "The Dole of the King's Daughter." The exception is Wilde's employment of the sestet or six-line stanza, a variation upon the traditional ballad quatrain borrowed, almost certainly, from Hood's "Dream of Eugene Aram." When Albert Friedman writes that "ballad discipline" shows itself "capable of chastening even the lush allusiveness and verbal exoticism of Wilde," he is thinking precisely of how effectively Wilde employed traditional ballad prosody in *The Ballad of Reading Gaol*.[65] And when Seamus Heaney writes of the "peculiar undermusic" whereby Wilde's poem transcends its "stylistic faults" and acquires "the gathering force of lamentation," he is similarly remarking upon the relative unobtrusiveness of the meter and rhyme-scheme that operate like a heartbeat at the core of the poem, even as they link it to a common cultural inheritance.[66]

In a sense then, Henley was correct to say upon reviewing the poem that its style "reminds you now of Mr. Kipling, now of [Thomas Hood's] 'Eugene Aram,' now of 'The Ancient Mariner,' now of the Border ballads."[67] Wilde had consciously endeavored to write a literary ballad. In Wilde's view, however, these echoes of his antecedents were virtues, not flaws, since they were what made his poem literary and "aesthetic" in the first place. For Wilde, the articulation of formal and technical elements was a key attribute of art: in the course of reviewing Henley's own *A Book of Verse* in 1888, Wilde had written that by embracing free verse and by "his constant rejection of rhyme, Mr. Henley seems to me to have abdicated half his power" as a poet.[68] For Henley, by contrast, such articulation spoke only of the work's origins in "aesthetic Chelsea,"

lines because of their self-consciously literary and Parnassian qualities. As Wilde wrote to Ross, "I can't always be 'banging the tins'" (*CL* 954). For Arthur Symons, these lines were an example of "beauty . . . claiming its own in a story meant to be so sordid, so veracious, so prosaically close to fact."[72] As Symons explained, "the glimmerings of romance which come into these pages, like the flowers which may not grow out of the dead man's body as he lies under the asphalte of the prison-yard, are significant because they show us the persistence with which temperament will assert itself."[73] The poem was not simply or wholly the cry of Marsyas, in other words: Wilde wanted it to be the song of Apollo too, and *The Ballad* is consequently no less an "aesthetic" work than the poems and plays Wilde had written before he went to jail. "Much is, I feel, for a harsher instrument than the languorous flute I love," Wilde said of it (*CL* 959). He recognized that *The Ballad* would be disparaged precisely for the reasons Henley and Heaney later gave, but he was nonetheless proud and emphatic about his love for the languorous flute.

In retrospect then, *The Ballad* is not quite the "denial of my own philosophy of art" that Wilde took it to be. As the haste with which Henley condemned the poem indicates, it contains elements that are consistent with his earlier writings, that sit uneasily with our propensity to read it as sincere or realistic, and that ultimately speak of the persistence of Wilde's view of art as a "made" or "beautiful thing." Wilde had written in "The Decay of Lying" that "the moment Art surrenders her imaginative medium it surrenders everything."[74] Far from surrendering its imaginative medium, *The Ballad* repeatedly makes its ballad medium self-conscious, insisting that before anything else it is a work of literary art. As importantly, it is irreducible and hybrid, and Yeats's attempt to banish its more intractable elements in the effort to make it adhere to preconceived notions of what poetry and "stark realism" should be misunderstands what is most distinctively Wildean about it. Arthur Symons wrote perceptively that the "curious interest" of Wilde's poem "comes from the struggle between form and utterance, between personal and dramatic feeling, between a genuine human emotion and a style formed on other lines, and startled at finding itself used for such new purposes."[75] "Some is realistic, some is romantic: some poetry, some propaganda," Wilde had himself written earlier: "I feel it keenly, but as a whole I think the production interesting" (*CL* 956). It was a fitting work with which to re-announce himself as an author and, it was to be hoped, rebuild his shattered career.

6

The Seduction of Paris

ILDE ARRIVED IN Paris by train from Naples on or around February 13, 1898, the date Smithers had chosen for the publication of *The Ballad of Reading Gaol*.[1] Using the pseudonym Sebastian Melmoth, he checked himself into the Hôtel de Nice in the Rue des Beaux Arts on the Left Bank, the first of several cheap hotels in which he would reside over the next few years.[2] He had once called Paris "the artistic capital of the world" and "the abode of artists . . . *la ville artiste*," and he been considering a permanent move there virtually from the moment of his release.[3] Although shortly after leaving prison he told Robert Ross of his determination to reside in the "simple and healthy" environment of Berneval, saying that he was "frightened" of Paris and that "if I live in Paris, I may be doomed to things I don't desire," just two days later he spoke of his wish to have his artistic reappearance and "rehabilitation through art" in the French capital (*CL* 869, 873). The publication of *The Ballad* was the chance he had been waiting for. The city had embraced him warmly in the past: while on an extended visit there in late 1891, he had been feted by *L'Echo de Paris* as "*le 'great event*'" of the season.[4] He now had good reason for thinking Paris would embrace him warmly once again. Many leading French intellectuals had come to his defense in the French press at the time of his trials, and Lugné-Poe's production of *Salomé*, which had drawn a glittering crowd at the Théâtre de L'Œuvre halfway through his prison sentence, represented an artistic compliment for which he would always be thankful.[5] "In Paris all my friends have welcomed me with the same eagerness they showed when I was at the height of my fame," he boasted somewhat exaggeratedly to his friend the writer Gustave Le Rouge shortly after he arrived in Paris in February 1898.[6] Except for brief sojourns in Italy, Switzerland, and on the French Riviera, Wilde would spend the next, and final, thirty-three months of his life in the city, until his death from meningoencephalitis on November 30, 1900. "In Paris!" exclaims the prim and proper Canon Chasuble, in *The Importance of Being Earnest,* when informed of the desire of the elusive, licentious "Ernest" to be buried in the city: "I fear that hardly points to any very serious state of mind at the last."[7]

One of Paris's attractions was that it offered a greater sense of personal and sexual freedom. The city had long possessed a reputation for openness and toleration, especially in the eyes of the British. "While in London one hides everything, [but] in Paris one reveals everything. One can go where one likes, and no-one dreams of criticizing one" Wilde had once told the journalist Jacques Daurelle.[8] With its bohemian bars, taverns, cabarets, and riotous Montmartre nightlife, Paris offered many seductions, not least unparalleled opportunities for "slumming": in 1891 he boasted to Daurelle that, when in Paris, he visited "all those spots where I might experience emotion" and that he frequented the Château Rouge, a notorious tavern in the Latin Quarter, as much as the Café Anglais.[9] The historian David Sweetman surmises that during his two-month visit in late 1891, Wilde trawled the nightclubs and cabarets of Montmartre, accompanied by Sherard, Rothenstein, and Henri de Toulouse-Lautrec, the semi-official artist of the Montmartre nightlife, whom Wilde probably met around this time and who would later make a number of portraits of Wilde.[10] Wilde biographer Neil McKenna writes that even when honeymooning in Paris with Constance in 1884, Wilde would go "slumming in the bars and brothels of Paris with Robert Sherard and one or two others, leaving Constance to her own devices."[11] Richard Ellmann too speculates that during his honeymoon in Paris, Wilde felt drawn to an illicit underground homosexual life as a result of reading Joris-Karl Huysman's scandalous novel *A Rebours* (Against Nature), a work that celebrates the satisfaction of "unnatural" desire and that hints broadly at the homosexuality of its groundbreaking protagonist Jean Des Esseintes. (Six years later, Huysmans's novel would do much to shape Wilde's own novel *The Picture of Dorian Gray.*) Homosexual acts were not prohibited per se under French law, and like many foreigners, Wilde—who had been urged to flee to France shortly before his arrest—perceived the French capital to be one of Europe's most sexually liberated cities. While it cannot be said with certainty that he had taken any French male lovers before his imprisonment, the male friendships that he had formed in Paris in the past were often homoerotic in nature, and he was to take many Frenchmen as lovers during his residency there over the final years of his life.[12]

Wilde experienced more than just greater personal and sexual freedom in Paris. The City of Light represented for Wilde, as it has for so many writers before and since, the glittering capital of the World Republic of Letters, and he had always enjoyed a greater sense of intellectual freedom and recognition in the city.[13] "Parmi les poètes de France je trouverai de véritables amis" (*among the poets of France I shall find my true friends*), he had once remarked to the French poet and writer Pierre Louÿs (*CL* 497). Even before Wilde had reached the height of his fame, he had been warmly welcomed at the weekly salons the great French poet Stéphane Mallarmé gave, which he had always made a point of attending whenever he had made a trip to Paris.[14] Following the publication of *The Picture of Dorian Gray,* Wilde was lionized in Parisian literary circles: Mallarmé admired his novel highly, and during Wilde's extended visit to Paris in late 1891 (his second extended visit of that year), he befriended a number of other leading French literary figures including Pierre Louÿs, Stuart Merrill, André Gide, Ernest Raynaud, Jean Moréas, and Paul Bourget, as well as the artists Jacques-

Emile Blanche, Henri de Toulouse-Lautrec, and the cabaret singer Aristide Bruant. "There is no modern literature outside France," Wilde had told another French literary friend, Catulle Mendes, in 1884.[15] By 1893, when he published his symbolist drama *Salomé* in Paris with Librairie de l'Art Indépendant, one of the leading publishers of symbolist poetry and music, Wilde was himself regarded by many French intellectuals as one of the key practitioners of such "modern" literature. He had composed a number of important English-language works during visits to the city, including "The Harlot's House," "The Sphinx," and his early play *The Duchess of Padua;* and as early as 1891, he was making plans for his play *Lady Windermere's Fan* and his essay collection *Intentions* to be translated into French.[16] In the eyes of many Frenchmen, however, Wilde's most significant modern work was *Salomé* itself, which he had composed entirely in French, with assistance on points of language from the French writers Adolphe Retté, Marcel Schwob, Pierre Louÿs, and Stuart Merrill.[17] Not only was *Salomé* written almost entirely in Paris over two months in 1891, it also had its first publication (1893) and stage debut (1896) in the French capital. "To me there are only two languages in the world," Wilde proclaimed a year after composing the play, two years before its translation into English: "French and Greek."[18]

But it was above all the contrast between English public condemnation and French acceptance of his most controversial works that led Wilde to feel more at home among the French. Whereas *The Picture of Dorian Gray* was vilified in the English press, French writers, critics, and artists took warmly to the novel, with Mallarmé describing it as "one of the few books with the power to move me" (*le livre, un des seuls qui puissent émouvoir*) and praising Wilde for "a miracle in which you employ all the writer's arts" (*un miracle que vous accomplissez et selon quel emploi de tous les arts de l'écrivain*).[19] In 1912, one critic would call *Dorian Gray* "one of the first French novels to be written in English," and the first French translation appeared even as Wilde languished in an English prison.[20] It was a similar story with *Salomé:*

banned from performance in 1892 by the English censor and condemned by the London *Times* as "morbid, *bizarre,* repulsive and very offensive," the play was immediately welcomed by Parisian intellectuals such as Mallarmé, the novelist Pierre Loti, and the Belgian symbolist playwright Maurice Maeterlinck.[21] Indeed, when the play was banned by the English censor, Wilde announced in an interview given jointly to the *Pall Mall Budget* and *Le Gaulois* that in England people were "essentially anti-artistic and narrow-minded," that he was unable to tolerate "a country that shows such narrowness in its artistic judgment," and that he would shortly leave England and settle in France.[22]

It is a matter of considerable regret that it took five years and a lengthy prison sentence for Wilde to deliver on that announcement. But as Wilde was well aware from his English jail cell, where he was kept abreast of developments by the Francophile Robert Sherard, French writers and intellectuals continued to embrace his work publicly well into his prison years. "It is astonishing how different the feeling about him is in Paris to what it is in London," observed Ernest Dowson roughly midway through Wilde's prison sentence.[23] This difference in feeling owed much to those prominent French writers, including Henri Bauër, Octave Mirbeau, Paul Adam, Henri de Régnier, Hughes Rebell, Stuart Merrill, and Laurent Tailhade, who had rallied around Wilde publicly in the wake of his conviction.[24] Dowson was referring more directly, however, to the world premiere of Wilde's play *Salomé* at the Théâtre de L'Œuvre in February 1896, when the playwright was still serving his prison sentence. The production was directed by Aurélien Marie Lugné-Poe, who would visit Wilde at Berneval just over a year later, after his release. The opening night was sold out and the house packed with prominent artistic figures, including Alfred Jarry, Aubrey Beardsley, and Ernest Dowson. Founded in 1893, the Théâtre de l'Œuvre, which would mount Jarry's revolutionary play *Ubu Roi* in December 1896, was Paris's leading avant-garde theatre. It constituted a home for symbolist drama rich in mystery and poetry, and its opening nights have been called "the principal meeting place for the city's creative elite, where famous figures like Emile Zola, Puvis de Chavannes, Pierre and Marie Curie rubbed shoulders with the scruffiest unpublished poets."[25] The painters Edouard Vuillard, Pierre Bonnard, Odilon Redon, and Henri de Toulouse-Lautrec were all closely associated with Lugné-Poe's theater—each designed either costumes, sets, or programs for it—and it seems likely that some or all of them attended the opening night of *Salomé*. Toulouse-Lautrec operated on the sidelines of all Lugné-Poe's productions, says the historian David Sweetman, and was eager to take part whenever possible. Equally important, Toulouse-Lautrec, who had painted or drawn several portraits of Wilde by this point, designed the program for Lugné-Poe's *Salomé* production, with a portrait of Wilde incorporated into it.[26] Wilde subsequently regarded Lugné-Poe's staging of *Salomé* not merely as an indication of the high regard the French intelligentsia held for him, but also as instrumental in bringing about his more humane treatment during the final fifteen months of his imprisonment. And if, in the immediate aftermath of his release from prison, he feared Paris lest it "doom" him to "things I don't desire," nine months later he relished the prospect of returning to the city. On the point of departing from Naples, he remarked to Smithers, "I miss an intellectual atmosphere," explaining why Paris offered "my only chance of working" (*CL* 1013). "You don't realize . . . how stimulating the air of Paris is," he told the Parisian writers Ernest La Jeunesse, Maurice Du Plessys, and Gustave le Rouge shortly after arriving: "Here in this frantic atmosphere it's as if one were breathing liberty and tolerance."[27]

———————

The timing of Wilde's arrival in Paris, simultaneous with the publication of *The Ballad of Reading Gaol*, was clearly not coincidental: Wilde expected that the poem would consolidate his personal and intellectual relationships, both in England and in Paris, and his correspondence in the weeks following his arrival is filled with excitement about his poem's publication. Just before leaving Naples, after returning the signed

Program for *Salomé* (staged jointly with Roman Coolus's *Raphaël*), Théâtre de l'Œuvre, February 11, 1896, featuring lithographic portraits of Coolus and Wilde by Henri de Toulouse-Lautrec.

unstitched title-page sheets, he had instructed Smithers to send signed copies of the first edition to some twenty-five English friends and acquaintances, including Robert Ross, Alfred Douglas, Reggie Turner, More Adey, Ada Leverson, William Archer (England's leading drama critic), and Max Beerbohm, as well as Stewart Headlam, Governor Nelson and George Groves (a warder) at Reading Prison, and Hugh Massingham, editor of the *Daily Chronicle*. Within days of his arrival in Paris, he was asking Smithers if a few additional copies might be printed "on some special paper" for distribution in Paris among French friends as well (*CL* 1018). Over the next week or two, he expanded the list of those to whom personalized copies of the first edition were to be sent. Included in this expanded list were Frank Harris, Oscar Browning, Lionel Johnson, Arthur Clifton, Dal Young, the actor-managers George Alexander, Lewis Waller, and Charles Wyndham, the designer-poet Selwyn Image (who had publicly written in Wilde's defense in 1895, in Headlam's magazine the *Church Reformer*), the English playwrights Stephen Phillips and Sydney Grundy, W. D. Morrison, the reforming chaplain at Wandsworth Prison, and—almost as an afterthought—his wife Constance.[28]

At first he complained that "none of the people to whom I sent copies have written to me" and that "the lack of imagination in people is astonishing," but Wilde seems nonetheless to have felt sure that the poem would make a sensation (*CL* 1022). In a letter speculatively dated 18 February by the editors of his correspondence, Wilde chastised Smithers (who had initially printed only four-hundred copies) for his want of faith in the poem, remarking to a friend that Smithers was "so fond of 'suppressed' books that he suppresses his own," and he instructed Smithers to advertise the book lest the press ignore it (*CL* 1019). But in fact Smithers had already doubled the first edition's print run and advertised the book prominently in *The Athenaeum,* leading Wilde to remark on February 19 that "the *Athenaeum* advertisement is capital: it *looks* like a success" (*CL* 1021). Around this time, Wilde told the journalist Chris Healy that he trusted "the generosity of the English people to judge [the poem] on its merits, and apart from their Philistine prejudices against myself."[29] Within days Wilde was proudly telling friends that the poem had already proved a great success and that the first edition had been exhausted on the day of issue, while also eagerly making arrangements for a second edition. The list of those to receive personalized copies was now extended yet further to include Baron von Gloeden and Albert Stopford, recently his hosts at Taormina in Sicily, Robert Sherard (whose personal copy Wilde inscribed "in memory of an old and noble friendship"), and Laurence Housman. A total of six editions, representing some 5,100 copies, was issued in the first four months following publication, with a seventh edition—the first to bear Wilde's own name on the title page—of 2,000 copies appearing the following year.

As well as hoping that the poem would resurrect his literary and personal fortunes in England, Wilde hoped the poem would bring about much-needed change in the British criminal justice system, as we have seen. He was gratified when, on April 4, 1898, during parliamentary debate of the Prisons Bill, the radical Irish member of Parliament T. P. O'Connor observed that "Everybody in this House has read the startling and striking poem, written by a prisoner recently liberated, entitled 'The Ballad of Reading Gaol.'"[30] The poem "has been twice quoted in the House," Wilde proudly announced early in April 1898 (on March 28, MP John Redmond had quoted a full stanza of the poem during parliamentary debate of the Prisons Bill); and at the end of May, following passage of the bill, Wilde proclaimed that "I have been able to deal a heavy and fatal blow at the monstrous prison-system of English justice" (*CL* 1053, 1080). Wilde knew that he could hardly claim sole responsibility for the Prisons Act's reforms—that as he put it, "I put the fly in motion, but I cannot drive the wheels" (*CL* 1080). The radical MPs Michael Davitt, John Burns, and T. P. O'Connor had all played major roles, too, and early in May Wilde proposed (unsuccessfully) that Smithers should issue a cheap edition of the poem, priced at 6d. or 1s., with a preface largely on prison reform by one of these politicians, adding that that "the provinces must be made to rise like one man" (*CL* 1063). Smithers might even "give away a cake of Maypole soap with each copy," Wilde quipped, "as I want the poem to reach the poorer classes" (*CL* 1063).[31]

One month after arriving in Paris, Wilde capitalized on the *Ballad*'s success to make his final and perhaps most lasting contribution to the prison-reform movement. On March 23, in the run-up to the second reading of the Prisons Bill, Wilde wrote a second lengthy letter to the *Daily Chronicle* outlining where the bill fell short. Unlike his letter of the previous May, prompted by Warder Martin's dismissal for passing biscuits to imprisoned children, this letter was designed to affect parliamentary debate and legislation. Wilde's proposals were specific and to the point. He had read that the home secretary proposed only to increase the number of prison inspectors and official visitors. Such a reform, he observed, was entirely useless, since official visitors' only power and concern was to ensure that prison regulations were being carried out. It was the regulations themselves that needed changing, he insisted, since as presently constituted they seemed to have the destruction of both the prisoner's physical and mental capacities as their object.

The necessary reforms were very simple, he said, concerning either "the needs of the body" or "the needs of the mind of each unfortunate prisoner" (*CL* 1045). As presently constituted, the English law authorized and exacted three permanent and savage punishments upon prisoners: hunger, insomnia, and disease. The food supplied to prisoners, which "in most cases consist[s] of weak gruel, badly-baked bread, suet, and water," was entirely inadequate, Wilde argued, leading to pain, sickness and incessant diarrhea (*CL* 1046). Neither the prison's medical facilities nor its sanitary arrangements were equipped to cope with the diseases that resulted from the unhealthy prison diet. But the mental depredations of prison life were perhaps more severe than the physical ones. The hard plank bed produced only insomnia, he writes, while the system of solitary or "separate" confinement, along with the deprivation of books and human contact, "seems almost to have for its aim the wrecking and the destruction of the mental faculties" (*CL* 1047). He concluded his letter with a list of specific changes that would improve things: adequate and wholesome food, improved cell ventilation, and access to lavatories when necessary. So far as the mind was concerned, prisoners should have an adequate supply of good books; should be permitted visits from friends once a month and for a reasonable time, rather than merely four times a year for no more than twenty minutes each time; and should be allowed to write and receive letters at least once a month, rather than just four times per year. While not all of these reforms were incorporated into the 1898 Prisons Act, they were eventually incorporated into reforms of the prison system early in the twentieth century. That Wilde signed this second *Daily Chronicle* letter "The Author of *The Ballad of Reading Gaol*" indicates that letter and poem were closely associated in his mind, just as they must have been in the minds of the letter's original readers. Even before the poem was mentioned or quoted in Parliament, Wilde was determined that *The Ballad of Reading Gaol* should help shape the debate leading up to the passage of the 1898 Prisons Act.

Wilde's second *Daily Chronicle* letter both presupposed and built upon the poem's success as a publishing phenomenon in England, and it testifies to Wilde's broadly political hopes for *The Ballad* in England. His intentions for the poem in France, by contrast, were rather different. Not long after his arrival in Paris, he told Ross that he has "hardly seen anyone" because "I am waiting to distribute twelve copies to my friends here, Henri Bauër, Mirbeau, and others" (*CL* 1022). A poem "gives one *droit de cité,*" he explained, "and shows that one is still an artist" (*CL* 1022). Le Rouge, later one of France's leading science-fiction writers, says that when he found Wilde in the company of La Jeunesse and du Plessys at the Calisaya Bar shortly after the poem's publication, Wilde possessed the air of an idol and "had recovered . . . all his equanimity and serenity."[32] Given the personal despair expressed in the poem, which they considered his masterpiece, the young French writers were somewhat surprised by Wilde's good spirits and laughter. Le Rouge adds that within a matter of days, Wilde was "familiar with the literary cafes" as well as with "the wine-cellars frequented by amateur songwriters and even the dens of ill repute."[33]

The publication of *The Ballad of Reading Gaol* briefly increased Wilde's literary standing in France. The writer Henri Mazel, who had been both fascinated and repelled by Wilde upon first meeting him in 1892, writes primly of his profound satisfaction, when first reading *The Ballad,* at seeing "that the soul of Wilde had indeed benefited, like that of Paul Verlaine, from the severe but well-merited experience which they were both condemned to undergo."[34] Within days of the poem's publication, Wilde received news that there would soon be "a recitation in a French translation of some of my poems in prose, at the Odéon—at a literary matinée" (*CL* 1030). In mid-April a laudatory notice of the poem appeared in the avant-garde journal *Le Revue Blanche,* and within days its editor, Felix Fénéon, now recognized as "the most gifted of the critics who devoted themselves to new art in Paris in the last years of the nineteenth century," had written Wilde "a charming letter begging me to go and see them all" (*CL* 1057).[35] At the end of May, after a performance of a miracle play at the annual *Fêtes des Fous* (Feast of Fools) in the Latin Quarter, Wilde dined with his old friend the symbolist poet Stuart Merrill, who had invited most of the actors and actresses to meet him. There were four other poets in attendance, Wilde proudly told Robert Ross: they were "most nice and sympathetic, and we were all very gay on *vin ordinaire*" (*CL* 1078). The next day Wilde attended a performance of the controversial German play *Les Tisserands:* he sat in a private box sent to him by the play's translator-director, André Antoine, founder of the pioneering Théâtre Libre, at this time renamed the Théâtre Antoine.[36] Around this time, Wilde also dined with the Vicomte Robert d'Humières, director of the Théâtre des Arts, with Charles Ducoté, editor of the artistic review *L'Ermitage,* and with the Belgian playwright Maurice Maeterlinck and his mistress, the actress Georgette Leblanc.[37] Leblanc has left a detailed record of her impressions of Wilde's visit to the apartment she shared with Maeterlinck in the Bois de Boulogne. Wilde possessed "that kind of freshness of soul which emanates from those who have suffered too much," she wrote.[38] When he entered the low-ceilinged apartment, "he seemed gigantic," his walk "balanced and assured . . . his wide torso admirably erect," his "magnificent body" denoting "an intact dominant force."[39] But Leblanc quickly realized this entrance was a "little play," and when Wilde sat down by the fireplace, she observes, "an irresistible lassitude had returned to him, a weight like a yoke was on his neck."[40] "The cruelty of a prison sentence starts when you come out," Wilde told his hosts: "I drank the sweet, I drank the bitter, and I found bitterness in the sweet and sweetness in the bitter."[41]

The most consequential French upshot of *The Ballad*'s English publication was an appreciation, sent privately to Wilde around the end of February, by the French Anglophile man-of-letters Henry Davray, who would soon go on to translate Wilde's poem into French and later

become a close friend of Wilde—and, later still, a mourner at his funeral, as well as Wilde's first French biographer. Davray, a friend of the
artist Paul Herrmann, whom Wilde had considered to illustrate *The
Ballad,* was in charge of reviewing and translating foreign literature for
the *Mercure de France,* Paris's leading literary monthly review. Wilde
first met him when passing through Paris in September 1897 en route
to Naples, and shortly afterward proclaimed Davray to be a "charming
fellow" and a good English scholar (*CL* 946). Wilde was touched and
gratified to receive Davray's appreciation of his poem, prompting him
to tell Davray that he would greatly like to have *The Ballad* published
in a translation by the Frenchman in a literary review or as a freestanding book publication. No French man-of-letters could render
English so well, Wilde told Davray flatteringly. Perhaps Davray could
ask Alfred Vallette, the editor and founder of the *Mercure de France,*
about it?

This is the first mention of what was to become the first and most
influential French translation of *The Ballad,* on which Wilde worked
alongside Davray over the coming weeks. Davray's translation appeared
in the May 1898 issue of *Mercure de France,* followed in the autumn by
the freestanding book edition that Wilde had envisaged, with the poem
in the original English on facing pages, bearing the *Mercure de France*
imprint. Davray also reviewed the poem in the April 1898 issue of
Mercure de France, and the following year he would publish the first
French translation of Wilde's *Poems in Prose.* Davray's translation not
only created a French readership for *The Ballad,* but also promised to
pave the way for Wilde to gain a wider measure of personal acceptance
among French readers. Reviewing Davray's translation in *La Plume* in
February 1899, the critic Léon Sougenet commented that whereas
Wilde had in the past been known for exasperating paradoxes, "a man
shows himself here to be simply human: a soul reveals itself in its
beauty."[42] Through Davray, Wilde met with Alfred Valette, editor and
publisher of the *Mercure de France,* the novelist Rachilde (who was married to Valette), and the brilliant playwright and novelist Alfred Jarry,

the rising light of the Latin Quarter, who one week later sent Wilde a complete collection of his works (*CL* 1075).[43]

The success of *The Ballad* in the weeks after his arrival in Paris led Wilde to hope briefly that his artistic resurrection might follow. The "intellectual atmosphere of Paris has done me good," he remarked to More Adey in late February: "I now have ideas, not merely passions" (*CL* 1023). "As soon as I get rooms, I am going to begin a new play, which I hope you will like," he told Davray at the beginning of March; "I am starting on a play, so perhaps there will be something for me in the future," he informed Harris around the same time (*CL* 1028, 1033). Possibly this play was *Pharaoh,* one of the two prospective dramas he had mentioned to Gide and Lugné-Poe the previous summer.[44] Yet the new play was never to materialize, and in spite of the critical and commercial success of *The Ballad,* by the early spring of 1898 Wilde had started to realize that he would never again recover the social and literary standing he had lost. As a result, he once again began to succumb to those fits of lassitude and self-pity to which he had been periodically subject since the last "suicidal" days in Berneval. "I have lost the main-spring of life and art, *la joie de vivre,*" he informed Harris as early as the end of February: "I am going under: the morgue yawns for me" (*CL* 1025). Doubtless it was moments such as these to which Lord Alfred Douglas referred when, five years after Wilde's death, he said that "of course, he had his bad moments, moments of depression, and sense of loss and defeat."[45] However, these moments "were not of long duration," Douglas said, and it "was part of his pose to luxuriate a little in his tragic circumstances."[46]

⸻

In late March, Wilde moved from the Hôtel de Nice to the cheaper Hôtel d'Alsace down the street—"a poor little Bohemian hotel, only suited for those Sybarites who are exiled from Sybaris"—where he would die just under three years later (*CL* 1107). Officially, the d'Alsace was tenth category, although its proprietor was convinced that it ought to be fifth.[47] "Poverty with its degrading preoccupation with money, the loss of many friends, the deprivation of my children . . . [and] the terrible effects of two years of silence, solitude, and ill-treatment—all these have . . . to a large extent, killed if not entirely that great joy in living that I once had," he mournfully told Georgina Weldon in May (*CL* 1080). "His will had been broken," André Gide later wrote, somewhat exaggeratedly: "the first months he could still delude himself, but he very soon gave way. It was like an abdication. Nothing remained in his shattered life but the mournful musty odour of what he had once been."[48] In the middle of May, Wilde wrote confidentially to Ross that "I cannot bear being alone, and while the literary people are charming to me when they meet me, we meet rarely. My companions are such as I can get, and I of course have to pay for such friendships" (*CL* 1068). The reflection was extremely telling. The high hopes he possessed three months earlier for even a partial "rehabilitation through art" were now crumbling into ashes. Literary Paris, it turned out, was not much more willing than London to look him in the eye. Despite the complimentary attention of radicals such as Jarry and Fénéon or the generous friendship of Davray, Wilde was in fact being avoided by many of the literary figures he had arrived in Paris hoping to court, while others would turn on him over the coming months and years. "O[scar] W[ilde] whom I have defended so ardently inspires me now only with contempt. . . . I turn away from his foul odour; he no longer exists for me," Henri Bauër, who had bravely defended Wilde in the pages of *L'Echo de Paris* in June 1895, wrote privately in August 1898.[49] "People had shut their doors to him," remarked André Gide; "they would look the other way if they saw him coming," observes Vincent O'Sullivan; and even among those who had remained faithful the longest, some were now saying that Wilde was no longer fit to be seen.[50]

The reasons for this ostracism are complex, although Wilde himself alludes to the primary reason when he says that he pays for "such [companions] as I can get." Even more than London in the years before Wilde's criminal conviction, Paris in 1898 possessed a thriving and extensive homosexual subculture, often centered on cafés and bars near

(*CL* 1073, 1083); with "Edmond"—presumably a ragamuffin or petty thief—who "is very smart, and directs his little band of brigands on the Boulevard with great success" (*CL* 1058); with "Leon," with whom "when the moon is full" Wilde often returned to his hotel at night "to smoke a cigarette or to weave words about life" (*CL* 1074); and with Eugene, "that harvest moon," who "looked like a prize melon" when he "loomed on me on the Boulevard the other day" and to whom Wilde sent his love despite thinking "it is very unkind his not writing to me" (*CL* 1095, 1075). A young Corsican named Giorgio, who worked at the Restaurant Jouffroy, was "a most passionate faun": his position was menial, Wilde observed, but his "eyes like the night and a scarlet flower of a mouth made one forget that" (*CL* 1104). Another unnamed young man "always wanted to behave badly" and was "quite an imp, though attractive in love-scenes" (*CL* 1107). As the historian William Peniston has described, sexual exhibitionism was a marked trait among young men active in Paris's homosexual subculture, and such men frequently created "a peculiar form of popular entertainment that made their sexual acts into spectacles."[54] Wilde picked up such young men as Giorgio and Eugene in the bars and cafés, and was not shy of being seen with them on the street or when inviting them back to his hotel. "You think that I have boys to tea every day, and shower gold on them," Wilde jokingly accused Robert Ross, but "I have not been visited by a single boy since the day Edmond came—in the *daytime* I mean" (*CL* 1074).

Although an active and polygamous homosexual himself, Ross had always urged Wilde to be more cautious, and when, at the end of May, Wilde expressed an interest in moving into a small unfurnished apartment in a street near the lower end of the Champs Elysées, Ross immediately suspected that Wilde's motive was to "have boys" (*CL* 1078). But "boys can be had everywhere," Wilde protested, and while it was true that if he moved into a more expensive furnished apartment with a concierge on site, he might be turned out at a moment's notice, "the difficulty I am under is my name, my personality. . . . In unfurnished I am my own master" (*CL* 1078). In fact, the lower end of the Champs Elysées was the most popular homosexual meeting place in Paris, and Wilde's reason for wanting an unfurnished apartment was precisely so that he might remain undisturbed should Edmond or some other young man come to see him.[55] Wilde was never to succeed in moving into a rented apartment, either furnished or unfurnished, where he could be his own master, but within weeks of arriving in Paris he was living openly as a homosexual, and he took many young men back to his hotel, whose proprietor did not place any restrictions on his guest's movements or companions. "When you talk morals to me," Wilde quipped to Ross, casting himself as Pan, "I always pipe on a reed and a faun comes running out of the thicket" (CL 1105–6). Wilde rejoiced in precisely that sexual freedom and unrestraint to which the more cautious Ross objected. Recalling this period many years later, Lord Alfred Douglas would write that Wilde "was hand in glove with all the little boys on the Boulevard. He never attempted to deny or conceal it. . . . Oscar believed, as many other eminent people do, that he had a perfect right to indulge his own tastes. . . . In fact nothing irritated him more than to meet (as he occasionally did) admirers who refused to believe that he was addicted to the vices for which he was condemned. This used to infuriate him."[56]

One of the "fauns" who came running at the sound of Wilde's pipe was a young man named Maurice Gilbert, a one-time marine infantryman, the son of a French mother and an English father—Wilde called him "all French lily and English rose"—about whom very little is known except what can be gleaned from Wilde's surviving letters (CL 1077). Two years later, Gilbert would prove himself to be one of Wilde's closest, most loyal friends, nursing him through sickness, attending Wilde as he lay dying, and then days later following Wilde's corpse to its grave before placing his own wreath upon it. Gilbert also was to take the famous, oft-reproduced photograph of Wilde's corpse on his deathbed, just prior to the closing of the coffin. Wilde had first met Gilbert "by chance" twelve days after his arrival in Paris in 1898, and within days the two were intimate friends: they played bezique on a daily basis and, if Wilde is to be believed, Gilbert even wrote nearly all the signatures on the "signed" title pages of the expensive Author's Edition of The *Ballad* prior to its publication in March 1898 (*CL* 1025, 1032). The early months of their friendship had a strong sexual component, as we can infer from Wilde's recorded comments about Gilbert's "beautiful mouth" ("the curves of his mouth are a source of endless fascination and wonder to me," Wilde was to remark of Maurice in July: "Out of such a mouth I would drink Lethe in this world and in the next ambrosia" [*CL* 1090]). But there was genuine affection, even love, between the two men: "He grows dearer to me daily," said Wilde in March, and "he is always sweet and nice," Wilde remarked in July (*CL* 1031, 1090).

At some point in the spring of 1898, Wilde's old friend Robert Sherard refused to visit Wilde on the grounds that Gilbert was actually staying in Wilde's rooms,[57] and Robert Ross remarked in early April, when visiting Wilde for a few days, "When I arrived the Mauritius was not here but has since turned up," suggesting that Gilbert lived briefly with Wilde and that Ross understood the closeness between Wilde and his young lover.[58] Wilde is known to have bought Gilbert an expensive nickel-plated bicycle in 1898, and, while Frank Harris is by no means always a reliable reporter of the truth, there is an air of veracity to the account, subsequently verified by Henry Davray, that Harris gives in his 1916 biography of the painful, months-long parting between Gilbert and Wilde in December 1898, when Wilde accompanied Harris to the French Riviera.[59] Wilde and Gilbert had spent many evenings together, a sad and depressed Wilde purportedly told Harris as the two men travelled south by train: Wilde had lent Gilbert books "and he read them, and his mind opened from week to week like a flower, till in a short time, a few months, he became an exquisite companion and disciple."[60] On the day of Wilde's departure, Gilbert accompanied Wilde to the Gare de Lyon: "[Maurice] knew I was going away for six months. His heart was like lead, tears gathered in his eyes again and again in spite of himself, and yet he tried to be gay and bright for my sake; he wanted to show me how glad he was that I should be happy, how thankful he was for all I had done for him, and the new mental life I had created in him. He did his best to keep my courage up. I cried, but he shook his tears away. 'Six months will soon be over,' he said, 'and perhaps you will come back to me, and I shall be glad again.'"[61]

But "my golden Maurice" was not Wilde's faun alone. In May 1898 Gilbert visited London, possibly with the object of entering journalism, where he was "wildly loved" by a number of Wilde's close English friends as well (*CL* 1066). While Gilbert was in London, Wilde repeatedly wrote to Ross asking whether he loved Gilbert, clearly rejoicing in the thought that they shared the same lover, and when Gilbert stayed with Reggie Turner in his rooms in Clement's Inn, Wilde joked "I am thinking of writing a novel called *The Boy-Catcher of Clement's Inn*" (*CL* 1058, 1061, 1073). The independently wealthy Turner was at this time a successful journalist, and Wilde joked that Gilbert would by no means make him a good assistant: "his upper-lip is more like a rose-leaf than any rose-leaf I ever saw [but] he would not be a good secretary [because] his writing is not clear enough, and his eyelashes are too long" [*CL* 1066].[62] Late in May "our dear Maurice" arrived back in Paris, "looking tired and beautiful" (*CL* 1072). He appeared "jonquil-like in aspect," Wilde rhapsodized to Turner, "a sweet narcissus from an English meadow . . . and was as sweet and loving and loveable as ever . . . quite cut up at his parting with you and Robbie" (*CL* 1074).

———

The timing of Gilbert's trip to London was opportune, because in April Douglas arrived in Paris—if not attracted by the sound of Wilde's own pipe, then drawn by the same lights that had brought Wilde himself to Paris. Wilde and Douglas had made a big show of separating from one another in Naples in December, and in order that their allowances might be restored by their families, they had vowed to Douglas's mother that they would not live under the same roof ever again. But they had only very reluctantly parted in Naples and had stayed in touch by letter.[63] After a decent interval, which Douglas spent largely with his mother on the French Riviera and in Venice, Paris provided opportunities for seeing one another and for chasing young men together without attracting the disapproving attentions of English journalists. Douglas arrived in Paris sometime in early April 1898 and immediately set about seeing Wilde as well as finding rooms to rent. Wilde had assured Ross, just days after his own arrival in February, that he was irrevocably parted from Douglas, that they could never be together again, and a few days later still he assured Ross that Douglas "fills me with horror" (*CL* 1023, 1029). In a widely quoted letter that has been instrumental in twentieth-century representations of Wilde as Douglas's unwitting victim, Wilde explained to Ross that "the facts of Naples are very bald and brief":

> Bosie, for four months, by endless letters, offered me a "home." He offered me love, affection, and care, and promised that I should never want for anything. After four months I accepted his offer, but when we met at Aix on our way to Naples I found that he had no money, no plans, and had forgotten all his promises. His one idea was that I should raise money for us both. I did so, to the extent of £120. On this Bosie lived, quite happy. When it came to his having, of course, to repay his own share, he became terrible, unkind, mean, and penurious, except where his own pleasures were concerned, and when my allowance ceased, he left.
>
> ... [T]he bald fact is that I accepted the offer of a "home," and found that I was expected to provide the money, and that when I could no longer do so, I was left to my own devices. It is, of course, the most bitter experience of a bitter life; it is a blow quite awful and paralysing, but it had to come, and I know it is better that I should never see him again. I don't want to. He fills me with horror. (*CL* 1029)

However, there are good reasons for questioning the veracity of Wilde's account. Relations with Ross had been tense at best where Douglas was concerned. More to the point, having separated from Douglas in Naples, Wilde was in February trying to obtain the restitution of his allowance from Constance, and, as Wilde was fully aware, Ross was a party to these negotiations.[64] Wilde's "bald and brief" statement was thus likely meant for Constance's eyes as much as Ross's. But the most compelling reason for doubting the truth of Wilde's statement is that upon Douglas's arrival in Paris in April, Wilde quickly resumed his friendship with Douglas. They had met at least once by April 17, and thereafter they met and dined together frequently.[65] "Bosie . . . has been very nice to me indeed," Wilde was to tell Ross some weeks after Douglas's arrival, "very hospitable and generous in paying for things" (*CL* 1067). Douglas seems to have quickly succumbed to Gilbert's charm as well, because in late April Wilde told Ross that "Bosie is very angelic and quiet. It did him a great deal of good being trampled on by Maurice" (*CL* 1057). When Douglas was furnishing a new apartment in the Avenue Kléber around this time, Wilde chose the furniture (*CL* 1057, 1065). Shortly afterward, the two vacationed together, escaping the summer heat with Gilbert and the journalist Rowland Strong at Nogent Sur Marne, east of the city. Until Douglas's departure from Paris in August 1898 (Douglas would spend two months with his mother, in Trouville and in Aix les Bains, before returning to England, in November, for the first time in over three years), Wilde saw a great deal of Douglas: they attended the Salon together in May, and in July Wilde made Frank Harris invite Douglas to dinner (the bill "was terrific" and "Bosie was childlike and sweet" [*CL* 1090]). Douglas says that Wilde used his apartment as if it were his own, invariably turning up at meal times, and that he "might just as well have lived [there] for [all] the use he made of his hotel except to sleep in."[66] Doubtless an anecdote Wilde related to the American journalist Clare de Pratz dates from around this time: one day Wilde got into the Montparnasse-Etoile tram to go to Douglas's apartment on the Avenue Kléber. Suddenly realizing that he had forgotten his wallet (or more likely spent his last penny), he boldly asked his fellow passengers "Is there anybody who will kindly lend me thirty centimes?" Total silence ensued, whereupon he made the driver stop, got down, hailed a cab and, after settling himself comfortably, waved delightedly to the stunned tram passengers, knowing that Douglas's porter would pay the cab driver.[67]

Biographer Rupert Croft-Cooke says that Wilde's relationship with Douglas at this time was "on . . . light and easygoing terms," and there is reason to believe that, while the two maintained a close interest in one another's sex lives, the strictly sexual element in their love for each other had disappeared in the early years of their relationship.[68] Douglas, attracted to men younger than himself, had never been comfortable with the older Wilde's sexual fascination with him. In a revealing confidential letter to Frank Harris, written in 1925, Douglas said that, with the exception of Wilde, he had never had sexual relations with a man older than himself.[69] In a second letter to Harris, written two days later, he says that sexual relations between Wilde and himself ("simply what is euphemistically called 'the sort of nonsense that goes on between schoolboys'") entirely ceased about six months before Wilde went to prison, never resumed after Wilde's release, "nor did [Wilde] ever make the slightest attempt to resume them."[70] The biographer Neil McKenna, who has made a close study of Wilde's sex life, agrees that "sex was never the most important element of their relationship," and that in its later stages, and certainly after Wilde's release from prison, their relationship was "ideal and idealised."[71] But the two men still loved each other, and their continued friendship and affection was a public scandal. More privately, if sexual relations had long ago ceased between them, they nonetheless remained interested in one another's sex lives, and even pursued the same sexual partners. Bosie "is devoted to a dreadful little ruffian aged fourteen, whom he loves at night . . . [and who] every time he goes home with Bosie he tries to rent him," Wilde salaciously told Turner in May (*CL* 1066). Days later Douglas incurred Wilde's wrath when he interrupted the only recorded meeting between Wilde and

Alfred Jarry by turning up uninvited with a questionable companion (*CL* 1070). Wilde's own "sweet Maurice" appears to have finally succumbed to Douglas's longing for him too, because on May 24, with Maurice still in London, Wilde told Ross mischievously that when Douglas had resided on the Rue Tronchet, "Bosie had great trouble because Maurice used to stay with him . . . [and] passed the night in the house" (*CL* 1071). By June Bosie was inseparable from and almost certainly sexually involved with Gilbert, even though two months earlier he had been "trampled on" by the latter (*CL* 1081).

Wilde was quite frank, public, and unapologetic about his own relationships with young men such as Maurice: if he made little concealment in London "he made none at all in Paris," remarked Vincent O'Sullivan; "he made no secret of the fact that he had once more given himself over to his old habits" confirms Douglas.[72] Within days of arriving in Paris, Wilde privately defended his cohabitation with Douglas in Naples by saying that "a patriot put into prison for defending his country loves his country, and a poet in prison for loving boys loves boys. To have altered my life would have been to have admitted that Uranian love is ignoble. I hold it to be noble—more noble than other forms" (*CL* 1019).[73] "Who *are* the people who object to my having been with Bosie at Naples, and spent my days with Heliogabalus and my nights with Antinous?" he wrote to Ross: "I mean are they people who were *ever* my friends? Or are they simply those to whom Uranian love is horrible? If the latter, I cannot care" (*CL* 1022).

It was precisely this frank and unapologetic attitude to his own homosexuality that explains the opprobrium with which Wilde was frequently greeted in Paris, within weeks of his arrival and in spite of the acclaim afforded *The Ballad of Reading Gaol*. His one-time friend the journalist Jacques Daurelle accused him of having "*retourné à son vomissement*" (returned to his vomit) upon witnessing Wilde embracing Gilbert in public. ("*Il est si beau,*" Wilde calmly replied to the shocked and disapproving Daurelle: "*Il a le profil de Bonaparte*" ["He is so good-looking. . . . He has the profile of Bonaparte"].)[74] There were few even

7

A Confraternity of the Damned

I N THE SPRING of 1898, Wilde's relations with Maurice Gilbert and other young men led to a notable falling out with his old friend Carlos Blacker, to whom he had dedicated *The Happy Prince* ten years prior. This in turn affected the small part Wilde played in the Dreyfus scandal, which rocked Paris for much of 1898, just as his own scandal had caused uproar in London three years earlier. When Wilde arrived in Paris in mid-February, the scandal was reaching its height: one month before, Emile Zola had published his famous letter "J'Accuse," in which he sensationally accused the French government and military establishment of conspiring to frame the innocent midlevel Jewish military officer Alfred Dreyfus for passing military secrets to Alessandro Panizzardi and Maximilian von Schwartzkoppen, the Italian and French military attachés, and further colluding to suppress evidence of Major Ferdinand Walsin Esterhazy's culpability for the crimes, which had come to light in 1896, a year after Dreyfus's conviction. As a result of publishing "J'Accuse," Zola was immediately prosecuted for criminal libel at the instigation of the Ministry of War. Zola's trial was underway the day Wilde arrived in the French capital, and some days later, on February 23, against all justice, and as a result of collusion between the French judiciary and the military establishment, Zola was found guilty. Among those who knew that both Zola and Dreyfus were innocent, and that their convictions were the result of an anti-Semitic conspiracy that went to the very highest levels of the French government, was Wilde's one-time friend Blacker, who was an intimate friend of Panizzardi and thus knew the truth firsthand.

When Wilde arrived in Paris in mid-February, Blacker had been living in the city with his wife and two children for about a week.[1] Since the past summer, the Blackers had maintained close, friendly relations with Wilde's estranged wife, Constance, who had written regularly from her new home in Nervi. At the beginning of March, shortly after reading *The Ballad of Reading Gaol* and knowing that her husband was also now also living in Paris, Constance asked Blacker to visit Wilde: "Would it be at all possible for you to go and see him?" she asked Blacker. She had lately received the copy of *The Ballad* that Wilde had instructed Smithers to send, but since it was unsigned she was unsure whether Oscar was directly responsible. "Can you find this out for me," she asked Blacker, "and if you do see him tell him that I think the Ballad exquisite, and I hope that the great success it has had in London . . . will urge him to write more." Blacker, as we have seen, had sided with Constance the previous year when she had postponed visiting Wilde at Berneval. Subsequently Blacker had been among the many to be shocked, but perhaps not surprised, when Wilde took up with Alfred Douglas again in the fall of 1897. Another of Constance's motives, in asking Blacker to visit Wilde at his hotel, was to find out if he had indeed separated from Lord Alfred Douglas: "I hear that he does nothing now but drink," she informed Blacker, "and I heard that he had left Lord A. and had received £200 from Lady Q. on condition that he did not see him again, but of course this may be untrue. Is Lord A. in Paris? Do what seems right to you. . . . But I write to you on the chance of your seeing Oscar."[2]

Blacker was less willing than Constance to overlook all that had transpired over the previous six months: "wrote letter to Oscar," he confided to his diary, "telling him . . . how sorry I was that I could not see him as he had chosen his way of life."[3] Possibly Blacker was under the impression that Wilde was still living with Douglas. Both Constance and Wilde himself were quick to clarify. "I naturally would not have asked you to see Oscar if I had thought there was any chance of your meeting that person whom I know that very naturally you loathe. I heard long ago that Oscar was not with him," she told Blacker on March 10.[4] "I am living here quite alone," Wilde wrote Blacker from the Hôtel de Nice on March 9, "in one room, I need hardly say, but there is an armchair for you. I have not seen Alfred Douglas for three months: he is I believe on the Riviera. I don't think it probable that we shall ever see each other again" (*CL* 1035).

Not suspecting the depth of Blacker's resistance to him or Blacker's role in keeping Constance and himself apart the previous July, Wilde felt genuine affection for his old friend and was overjoyed to hear from him. "My dear Carlos, I cannot express to you how thrilled and touched by emotion I was when I saw your handwriting last night," he wrote upon receipt of Blacker's letter. "I want particularly to see you, and long to shake you by the hand again, and to thank you for all the sweet and wonderful kindness you and your wife have shown to Constance and the boys" (*CL* 1035). Reassured, Blacker visited Wilde at his hotel on March 13, where the two men discussed the suspension of Wilde's allowance and Wilde presented Blacker with a signed, inscribed copy of *The Ballad of Reading Gaol.* At this meeting, Blacker confided to Wilde what he knew about Esterhazy and Dreyfus, as well as a plan that he was himself involved in, with Panizzardi's blessing, to expose Esterhazy publicly in the English press.[5]

The reunion ended badly, however, with Blacker suddenly becoming aware that Wilde was not in fact living "quite alone," as Wilde had told him by letter, but that he had a young male companion—most likely Maurice Gilbert—in attendance. Blacker was deeply shaken by the revelation, which he shared with his wife, with Constance, and with his close friend the Oxford don Frederick Conybeare. "Spoke with Carrie [Blacker's wife] about Oscar's not having been made better by his experience," Blacker confided to his diary. Blacker's wife evidently advised him to have nothing further to do with Wilde, but Constance's response was more generous: "Your account of Oscar is a very sad one," Constance told Blacker. "Still I am glad that he is in Paris, for I know that he does require intellectual stimulus always. He would have been bored to death with family life, though he does not seem at present to realize this. What could either the children or I have given him?"[6] The reaction of Conybeare, who was later to tell Blacker that Wilde was "lower than the animals," was severest: "I am really not sure your wife's judgment is not sound. . . . He is clearly without any sense of respon-sibility or self-respect. . . . I should, were I in your place, write to him & say that you *were* fully prepared to preserve relations with him after he came out, if he seriously set himself to alleviate the pain & shame he had inflicted on his wife & children; but that, as he is doing just the opposite, your relations with him *must* cease. . . . In view of his *jeune homme blond,* I should, if I were you, certainly take your wife's advice. . . . Probably the best thing he can do is to drink himself to death, or better yet—shoot himself right off."[7]

Blacker was clearly in a quandary. On the one hand, he felt bound to his old friend, who cried out for affection and support. On March 15 he lent the penniless Wilde 150 francs—although the loan left him in a "very bad temper," Blacker confided in his diary—and at first he planned to meet Wilde again the following day.[8] On the other hand, he was genuinely repulsed by what he knew of Wilde's sexuality, as well as under pressure from his wife and from Conybeare to break all ties with Wilde. He wrote postponing further meetings, though evidently so tactfully that Wilde only replied, "My dear Friend, a thousand thanks for your good kindly letter. I do hope to see you soon" (*CL* 1039). Blacker nonetheless lent Wilde a further 150 francs when Wilde complained that he was "in dreadful straits," that he had been "forced to pay my hotel bill with the money you kindly lent me," and that he didn't "know what to do" having now "pawned everything I had" (*CL* 1039).

Blacker also interceded with Constance on Wilde's behalf when Wilde complained that, whilst agreeing to let Wilde have £10 a month following his separation from Douglas, she had as yet sent nothing and would pay no portion of the sum that Wilde had forfeited by living with Douglas. "I have a sort of idea she really wants me to be dead," Wilde informed Blacker, "and I daresay she would be relieved to hear you had recognized me at the Morgue" (*CL* 1039). Blacker's intercession elicited a furious response from Constance, in which she informed him that she had already sent Wilde £40—via Ross, who "would not, and I expect rightly did not, send more than £10 at a time to him"—and that "the actual sum I owe him, if you call it owing, is . . . little more than £20."9 She concluded: "Oscar is so pathetic and such a born actor, and I am hardened when I am away from him. . . . I do not wish him dead, but . . . I think he might leave his wife and children alone. . . . He knew perfectly well that he was forfeiting his income, small as it was, in going back to Lord A., and . . . it is absurd of him to say now that I acted without his knowledge" (*CL* 1041).

As a result of Blacker's intercession, Constance instructed Ross to send Wilde immediately the remaining £30 from the £40 that she had earlier sent him. Unaware that Constance had sent this money previously to Ross, or that Ross for his part had intended eking it out over a period of months, Wilde understood the sudden appearance of the £30 to mean that Constance had relented somewhat: "Whether this is meant as my income for the next three months, or as a restitution of my forfeited income, Robbie Ross does not know," Wilde informed Blacker (*CL* 1044). But regardless of what the money meant, Wilde felt he now possessed "something on which I can take a couple of rooms, and I hope to begin to write" and he was deeply grateful to Blacker (*CL* 1044). Within days he had moved from his cramped single room at the Hôtel de Nice into more spacious although far cheaper accommodation at the nearby Hôtel D'Alsace, having told Robert Ross days prior that "I want to take an apartment with two rooms—one for writing, one for insomnia (both in fact for insomnia)" (*CL* 1049). "A thousand thanks for your great kindness," he wrote to Blacker on March 25: "really you have saved my life for me, for a little at any rate, and your friendship and interest give me hope. I do hope to see you soon. Could we dine together at some little restaurant . . . just you and I together, and talk about divine and beautiful things?" (*CL* 1050).

On the same day he thanked Blacker for saving his life, Wilde had a bad accident when the cab in which he was travelling crashed after the horse stumbled and fell. Wilde was thrown almost through the front window. He later said that he "cut my lower lip almost in two," that it was "quite dreadful . . . a hideous shock," and that "it is so horrible to have no one to look after one" (*CL* 1051). Three days after the accident, he telegraphed Blacker in panic asking "could you come and see me this afternoon, any time you like—at *three,* if that will suit you?" (*CL* 1050). But unbeknownst to Wilde, Blacker had by this point decided to break with Wilde. His wife strenuously objected to his involvement, and moreover Constance had written giving her blessing to the breach.[10] "You are perfectly right to want your husband to be independent of Oscar," she had written to Blacker's wife on March 26: Wilde "would be a drag on anybody, from his apparently hopeless ineptitude to grasp money matters at all . . . If he had plenty of money he would drink himself to death and do no work."[11] In "The Happy Prince," the title story of the collection Wilde had magnanimously dedicated to Blacker in 1888, a little swallow comes to the aid of a tearful "happy prince," a statue standing high above the city on his pedestal. The prince, covered in gilt and with sapphires for his eyes, is an impressive figure of art to those who behold him from below, for they cannot see his tears. But the prince is in fact lonely and misunderstood, silently despairing at the suffering that he sees all around him. For this reason, he elicits the swallow's compassion, dedication, and fellow-feeling, to the point that the swallow abandons all social and personal ties in order to be the prince's loyal servant. But Wilde's story had evidently lost all its charm for its dedicatee, for within hours of Wilde's telegram asking Blacker to come and see him, three days after his accident, Blacker replied that he could not come.

Wilde in turn replied by letter, on March 28, with information that he knew would be of interest to Blacker:

> My dear Carlos . . .
>
> I am sorry you can't come to see me, as I have not been out since Friday, except one night when I was dragged out to meet *Esterhazy* at dinner! The Commandant was astonishing. I will tell you all he said some day. Of course he talked of nothing but Dreyfus *et Cie.* . . . I hope to go out tomorrow.
>
> I had a very nice letter from Constance yesterday.
>
> Ever yours,
>
> O. W.   (*CL* 1051)

In light of subsequent events, this letter has been understood as a threat of retribution, or at least as the deliberate and calculated revelation of "ominous information that was certain to cause Blacker alarm."[12] Within days Blacker had reason for thinking that Wilde had betrayed his confidence and sided with the Esterhazy camp. On March 29, Rowland Strong, the Paris-based correspondent of the *New York Times,* a friend of Esterhazy and a drinking companion of Wilde's, posted off an article headed "A Probability of New Revelations in the Dreyfus Case," in which he informed the *Times's* readers: "an English gentleman . . . named Blacker has obtained from Col. von Schwartzkoppen's own lips a statement to the effect that Major Esterhazy [had sold documents to the German military attaché]. . . . The Englishman . . . has secured through the good offices of Major Panizzardi copies of a certain number of these documents, and these are to be published shortly in *The Daily News* or *The Daily Chronicle.*"[13]

Panizzardi, not von Schwartzkoppen, was Blacker's true informant, but Strong's scoop may have come from Wilde. Supposing Wilde was Strong's source, had Wilde deliberately betrayed his friend's confidence in Esterhazy's presence with the intention that Strong would use the information to damage his friend?

According to J. Robert Maguire, whose 2013 book *Ceremonies of Bravery* tells the story of Blacker's doomed friendship with Wilde, Wilde's account of being "dragged out" to dinner with Esterhazy represents a "bitter response to the rebuff of his pitiful appeal . . . spelling disaster for Blacker and the end of their once cherished friendship."[14] Maguire is correct that Strong's report proved devastating to Blacker personally, and absolutely fatal to his and Panizzardi's plan to reveal Esterhazy's culpability in the English press. But if, as is likely, Strong's revelation was based on information that Wilde passed on in his cups, to suggest that Wilde was motivated by malice or bitterness is to discount the notes of affection—"My dear Carlos," "I had a very nice letter from Constance," "Ever yours"—with which Wilde framed his mention of his dinner with Esterhazy, and also to discount Wilde's promise to tell Blacker all that Esterhazy had said. Wilde might well have been indiscreet with Strong, as he often was in conversation, especially when he was drinking, but to suggest more malicious intentions stretches the evidence.

In the event, Strong's scoop was not published till April 10, owing to the time lag between New York and Paris. But Strong—an "anti-Dreyfusard" sympathetic to Esterhazy's cause—was not the only person to whom Wilde revealed Blacker's intentions. Chris Healy, Strong's assistant and a "Dreyfusard" sympathetic to Dreyfus's cause, was also present at the revelation, and he took the news directly to Zola. As Healy subsequently wrote, "Oscar Wilde was one of the direct instruments in freeing Alfred Dreyfus," for he "suggested the clue which enabled Zola to successfully defend Dreyfus."[15] On April 4, six days before the publication of Strong's report, a letter signed by "Un Diplomate" appeared in the Dreyfusard newsletter *Le Siècle,* detailing the information that Blacker had received from Panizzardi—information unavailable to Zola at the time of his trial—thereby "enabling the Dreyfusard cause overnight to regain the initiative that had been lost with Zola's conviction several weeks earlier."[16] The letter was probably written by Zola's close associates Yves Guyot and Francis de Pressensé, Maguire says, but at the time Blacker was widely suspected of being the author. From this moment onward, Blacker's position, as well as Panizzardi's, became increasingly untenable in anti-Dreyfusard Paris. As Blacker himself later put it, "I was attacked by the low and infamous press, & for days my family and I were insulted & dragged through the most filthy dirt. Anonymous and foul letters were addressed to me threatening me with assaults and death to myself & my family. I was followed and tracked without a moment's intermission for months . . . [until] I left France."[17]

———

Blacker had no doubt as to the source of the newly published information, although he did not immediately confront Wilde with his suspicions, instead merely attributing the perceived betrayal to Wilde's "having again become a drunkard [who] repeated everything [Blacker] had told him to Strong, another drunkard."[18] Blacker's suspicions rankled, but suddenly Blacker's and Wilde's relationship altered again when, on April 12, Wilde received news from his brother-in-law, Otho Lloyd, that Constance had unexpectedly passed away in Genoa five days earlier, on April 7, as the result of complications from an operation. The surgery was an effort to correct a longstanding and serious medical problem, ostensibly with her spine, which had meant years of pain, lameness, and creeping paralysis in her legs and right side. Despite a previous operation to remedy the condition, her health had continued to deteriorate, and on April 2, 1898 she checked herself into the Genoa clinic of a gynecologist named Bossi, who had operated on her unsuccessfully in 1895. Her family and friends subsequently let it be known that the operation was to relieve pressure on nerves along her spine.[19] Bossi removed a uterine tumor that he believed explained the painful genitourinary disorders of which Constance had lately complained. In fact these disorders were very likely symptomatic of the degenerative multiple sclerosis, undiagnosed in her own lifetime, from which Constance had long suffered.[20]

———

Regardless of Bossi's misunderstanding of the underlying problem, the operation proved fatal: within days Constance was dehydrating and vomiting constantly, and she never recovered.[21] Two days after her death, she was buried in the Protestant section of the *Cimiterio Monumantale* in the pretty foothills just outside Genoa, with her brother Otho as chief mourner. No mention of her marriage to Wilde was made on her gravestone, upon which was carved "Constance Mary, Daughter of Horace Lloyd, Q. C.," surmounted with a simple cross inlaid with ivy leaves. Only in 1963 would Otho's family allow the phrase "Wife of Oscar Wilde" to be inscribed on the stone. Her children, who were informed of her death by their respective schools, were not present at the funeral. She was just thirty-nine years old.

"Am overwhelmed with grief," Wilde telegraphed Lloyd: "It is the most terrible tragedy" (*CL* 1055). On the night Constance died, Wilde later told Douglas, he was tormented by sad dreams of her and awoke crying "Go away, go away, leave me in peace."[22] Blacker is one of just two individuals besides Lloyd—the other was Robbie Ross—to whom Wilde is known to have telegraphed seeking comfort immediately after he received the news. "I suppose you have heard the terrible news. Constance is dead," he telegraphed Blacker: "I would like to see you tomorrow at any hour you like" (*CL* 1055). "How good you were to come at once," he wrote Blacker the next day: "It is really awful. I don't know what to do. If we had only met once, and kissed each other. It is too late. How awful life is. . . . I have gone out as I don't care to be by myself" (*CL* 1055).

Wilde's youngest son, Vyvyan Holland, later questioned the sincerity and depth of feeling underpinning his father's response to his mother's death, by writing acerbically that Wilde had shed "telegraphic tears of Hibernian sorrow."[23] Moreover, Robert Ross, who like Blacker also came at Wilde's urgent appeal, wrote to Smithers from Paris in the wake of Constance's death that "Oscar of course did not feel it at all. . . . He is in very good spirits and does not consume too many."[24] But Ross—who after Wilde's death acted as something like a surrogate father to

Wilde's youngest son until his own death in 1918—had not seen his friend since the previous August, and a strong note of disapproval had since entered into many of his judgments about Wilde. According to Ada Leverson, who visited Wilde in Paris some time after his move there, Constance's death was "the greatest blow," and Wilde felt it more sharply even than the deaths of his mother and brother.[25] In 1899, Wilde would make a special journey to Genoa to place flowers on his wife's grave, at which time he would pronounce himself "deeply affected," and say that he found it "deeply tragic" (*CL* 1128). It is likely that Ross, and much later Vyvyan Holland as well, underrated Wilde's depth of feeling in the immediate wake of Constance's death.

Constance's death caused a temporary narrowing of the split between Blacker and Wilde. Over the next few weeks, Blacker helped Wilde obtain a permanent continuation of his wife's allowance, to be sent to Robbie Ross in trust and paid every quarter. He also provided a fifty-franc loan when Wilde told him that he "had been three days without any money at all" (*CL* 1062). But the split widened once again at the end of May, when Robbie Ross told Wilde that he had been informed, almost certainly by Blacker, that Wilde was living a disreputable life and would possibly be expelled from France as a result. "Do not listen to stories about my being expelled from Paris," Wilde reassured Ross: "I live a very ordinary life. I go to cafés like Pousset's where I meet artists and writers. . . . I dine in modest restaurants for two or three francs. My life is rather dull. I cannot flaunt or dash about. I have not got the money, nor the clothes. When I can I go to the Quartier Latin under the wing of a poet, and talk about art. I suppose Carlos is the author of the *canard?* It is unkind of him" (*CL* 1072).

Wilde was now keenly aware of Blacker's disapproval, and suspicious too that Blacker was casting aspersions upon him. Two months later the break was complete. "I never quarrelled with him," Wilde was quick to assure Ross, "you must not think I quarrelled with him" (*CL* 1086). For months Blacker had "treated [Wilde] with utter indifference," Wilde explained, and "never invited me to have bit [*sic*] or sup with him at a café or elsewhere, and in the course of five months only came four times to see me" (*CL* 1086). In June, Blacker wrote to Wilde breaking off the friendship once and for all, saying "I have no further interest in you or your affairs."[26] Although Wilde felt hurt and betrayed as a result, he realized "one cannot demand friendship as a right" and so made no reply to Blacker's letter (*CL* 1087). A week later, however, Blacker wrote a much worse letter in which he accused Wilde of attacking his personal life in a French newspaper. "This was a very different matter," Wilde felt, especially since the paper in question was one "that I had never seen" and "I never write anonymous attacks on people anywhere" (*CL* 1087, 1085).

Whereas the first letter concerned merely Blacker's "own attitude to me," the second "brought a disgraceful accusation," so Wilde wrote back insisting upon an apology (*CL* 1087). He probably realized that an apology would not be forthcoming—as we have seen, Blacker had been seeking a pretext for breaking with Wilde since February, and moreover he genuinely believed that Wilde had betrayed him—so Wilde took the opportunity to tell Blacker "a few truths about himself, which he can ponder on in exile" (*CL* 1087). For Blacker was by this point "quite over in Paris," Wilde was "glad to say" (*CL* 1087). The anti-Dreyfusard press had published details not merely of Blacker's behind-the-scenes involvement with Panizzardi, Schwartzkoppen, and the Dreyfusards: they also published older, more personal details, which few in Paris besides Wilde would have known, concerning Blacker's having been suspected of nefarious financial dealings and cheating at cards in London six years earlier. "His whole *dossier* is paraded," Wilde gloated, "and he has tumbled into the mud in Paris as completely as he did in London. . . . He treats me, his oldest and most faithful friend, with contempt because I am friends with Bosie and says that 'no one should know such an infamous friend' as Bosie. A fortnight later he has to bolt to Boulogne because from a little corner—a very little corner of his own life—a veil is raised" (*CL* 1087).

Blacker accused Wilde of revealing these compromising details about his private life to the press, as we have seen, and just as strenuously

Wilde countered these suspicions. Maguire speculates that Wilde attempted to blackmail Blacker by letter around this time, but no such letter survives and there exists no objective evidence to corroborate the position taken by either man.[27] At least initially, the pretext for Blacker's break with Wilde was the latter's continued association with Douglas, not his suspicions of Wilde's involvement in his personal downfall in Paris. "As he did not approve of my knowing Bosie, he thought it would be morally wrong of him to help me in any way except by advice," Wilde explained to Ross, and "so Tartuffe goes out of my life" (*CL* 1086). But there can be no question that Wilde took considerable pleasure in witnessing Blacker's personal downfall: "Blacker has behaved like a hypocritical ass to me," he explained to Ross, and "the comic thing about him is the moral attitude he takes up. To be either a Puritan, a prig, or a preacher is a bad thing. To be all three at once reminds one of the worst excesses of the French Revolution. . . . It amuses me to see Tartuffe in the pillory. I have the most terrible of all pleasures, the pleasure of the spectator, a pleasure without which Art would be dead, and Life would be humane" (*CL* 1085–88).

———

As Blacker was probably aware, Wilde continued to associate with Esterhazy and the anti-Dreyfusard Strong for several more months. The date and place at which Wilde first met Esterhazy is unclear, but the two men immediately hit it off and saw each other repeatedly over the summer of 1898, often in Strong's company.[28] "He is such a friend that he has honored me by giving me the pen with which he wrote the *bordereau*," Wilde is reported to have said.[29] "Esterhazy was lean and gaunt and haggard," recalled Vance Thompson: "he looked as though he had been cut down from some gallows of the Middle Ages," whereas Wilde was "a monstrous, fat, soft man, looking like something white, unwholesome, bloated, that had floated and been washed ashore in a storm."[30] In spite of—or perhaps because of—his obvious villainy, Esterhazy, with his lively intelligence, scathing humor, and "a physical appearance to match his villainy," was a compelling figure even to his adversaries.[31] To his employer, Schwartzkoppen, Esterhazy was "the most marvellous, audacious and wonderful *canaille* that it was possible to imagine, in fiction or history," while even Blacker found Esterhazy "superb and magnificent" in his incredible audacity.[32]

In 1900, Ernest La Jeunesse observed that "it would take the pen of Voltaire to recount the dinners and symposia that took place between Wilde and the man who, with tender irony and not a little admiration, Wilde termed 'The Commandant.'" La Jeunesse recalled one particular snatch of "dialogue from hell" at one such dinner in the late spring of 1898, when the net was closing around Esterhazy, in which Esterhazy remarked to Wilde that "we are the two greatest martyrs of humanity," before gloomily adding "but I have suffered most."[33] It was greater than something out of Dante, observed La Jeunesse, and more remote in time. Frank Harris recalled another such dinner, at Durand's, in which Esterhazy "for a long time bored us by insisting that Dreyfus was a traitor, a Jew, and a German—to him a trinity of faults—whereas he, Esterhazy, was perfectly innocent."[34] At length, says Harris, "Oscar leant across the table and said to him in French . . . 'The innocent . . . always suffer, M. *Le Commandant,* it is their *métier.* Besides, we are all innocent until we are found out; it is a poor, common part to play and within the compass of the meanest. The interesting thing is surely to be guilty and so wear as a halo the seduction of sin.' "[35] Esterhazy appeared put out by this for a moment, says Harris, but his vanity would not allow him to remain long in a secondary role, "and so . . . he suddenly broke out 'Why should I not make my confession to you? . . . It is I, Esterhazy, who alone am guilty. I wrote the *bordereau.* I put Dreyfus in prison, and all France cannot liberate him. I am the maker of the plot, and the chief part of it is mine."[36] When Henry Davray reprimanded Wilde for his friendship with such a "crapule," Wilde, the true antinomian that he was, replied that since his release he had been obliged to frequent the society of thieves and assassins, and that "if Esterhazy had been innocent I should have had nothing to do with him."[37] Esterhazy was more interesting than Dreyfus, Wilde maintained, since innocence required only being wronged, whereas it required imagination and courage to be a criminal.[38]

Wilde's friendship with Esterhazy has over the years elicited severe moral disapproval, but it is perfectly consistent with much that Wilde had written and done at the height of his social and literary success. Esterhazy was another of the panthers with whom Wilde enjoyed feasting. "One can imagine an intense personality being created out of sin," Wilde had written in "Pen, Pencil, and Poison," his tongue-in-cheek celebration of the writer-forger and purported poisoner Thomas Griffiths Wainewright, and "the fact of a man being a poisoner is nothing against his prose."[39] Similarly, the fact of a man being a traitor and liar was nothing against his conversation. One of the qualifications of a good talker, Wilde had written in 1887, was that he should not possess "any disproportionate excess of virtue," for even a consummate liar, recognizing that "recreation, not instruction, is the aim of conversation," was better company than a scrupulously truthful man.[40] Esterhazy was the living embodiment of the "true liar" whom Wilde had celebrated in his witty dialogue "The Decay of Lying," with his "frank, fearless statements, his superb irresponsibility, his healthy, natural disdain of proof of any kind."[41]

Wilde dined frequently with Esterhazy in the summer of 1898, often in the company of Lord Alfred Douglas and Strong, and in mid-August they were accompanied by Esterhazy's mistress, the prostitute Marie Pays, also known as "four-fingered Margaret," whom Wilde found "a most charming woman . . . very clever and handsome" (*CL* 1094). But the friendship terminated suddenly in September 1898, when Esterhazy fled France for permanent exile in England once the case against him became irrefutable. Two months previously, Wilde had told Wilfrid Chesson that "that remarkable man had said that at the age of thirteen he had a profound conviction that he would never be happy again as long as he lived. 'And it was true; he never was.' "[42]

8

The Solace of Spectatorship

T HE SUMMER OF 1898 witnessed a blinding heat wave. Paris "is a fiery furnace," Wilde complained to Ross: "I walk in streets of brass. And even the bad boys have left for *les bains de mer*" (*CL* 1094). Wilde spent much of his time on the banks of the Seine or the Marne, at a distant remove from the city center, sometimes in the company of Strong, Douglas, and Gilbert. In May, the artist Charles Conder asked him to stay as his guest, together with William Rothenstein, in the small town of Chantemerle, near La Roche Guyon, on the banks of the Seine, fifty miles northwest of Paris, where Conder had worked all that spring. "Rothenstein and Conder . . . have both been very nice to me," Wilde remarked after he had taken up Conder's invitation that August: "the Seine is lovely, and there are wonderful backwaters, with willows and poplars, with water-lilies and turquoise kingfishers. I bathed twice a day and spent most of my time rowing about" (*CL* 1095). "Some people were rather annoyed at my bringing him," Conder privately observed afterwards, "but he turned Chantemerle into a charming little state, made himself king and possessed himself of Blunt's boat—for his barge—and got little boys to row him from Chantemerle to La Roche every day, [where] he took his aperitif and returned laden with duck-ham and wine."[1]

In mid-June, he stayed with Douglas at Nogent-sur-Marne, to the east of Paris, at l'Idée, "a little inn where poor poets go, like *L'Ermitage* in literature," from where he telegraphed Maurice Gilbert inviting him to come too, proudly adding that he had taught the inn's chef to make *œufs a l'aurore* (*CL* 1084). He stayed well into July, telling Ross that Nogent was a lovely place and that "we have some charming days" (*CL* 1085). Such places as Nogent, although "fallen now, owing to the outspread of Paris," were in the late 1890s "at the height of their glory," Strong recalled in 1912. "Oh, the joys of the little riverside *pavillon,* or cottage, with its big garden filled with flowers and vegetables and fruit-trees. . . . It was but a cab-drive to get there! No need of railways. Boating, fishing, and bathing were the day-long amusements. . . . And the bathing in the river—hundreds of pretty *Parisiennes* jumping in and out of the water from the vast bathing pontoons. Their laughter could be heard almost as far as Paris."[2] But Wilde had an ulterior motive for staying at Nogent: he dared not go back to his hotel in Paris, where his bill was outstanding, and at l'Idée he had credit.

While he was staying at l'Idée, he was visited by Wilfrid Chesson, an Englishman who had rescued some of Wilde's manuscripts and books at the bailiff's sale in 1895, and who now wished to return them to Wilde personally. Chesson has left a memorable account of July 5, 1898, the bright summer day he spent with Wilde as the two men conversed, dined, and walked by the banks of the Marne. To his visitor, who had admired Wilde from afar for years, picturing him in his mind as a creature of "Postlethwaitian excess," Wilde now appeared "an unaffected Englishman, stalwart in homespun." Snatcher, a lively dog that Wilde was looking after for Rowland Strong, was present too, "and eagerly snapped up a morsel which Wilde rendered more appetising by christening it *Dreyfus.*" The conversation was wide-ranging: "I have lost the joy of writing," Wilde told Chesson. He spoke fondly of his fellow prisoners at Reading, saying "Have you ever noticed a thief's hands? How beautiful they are? How fine and delicate at the tips?"

When he had visited a palmist to have his own hands read shortly after his release, he told Chesson, she had confessed, "I am puzzled. By your line of life you died two years ago." Upon hearing this, Chesson himself scrutinized Wilde's hand and observed the line of Wilde's marriage, only for Wilde to reply, "That too was a fatality."[3]

When the two men went for a walk along the river bank, passing by a tall gate that allowed a tantalizing glimpse of something that lay just beyond, Wilde observed, "That is what I like, just to stand and peep through the bars. It would be better than being in paradise to stand like this, catch a glimpse as now, and want to go in." They conversed about literature and about Wilde's friends, and as the daylight faded into dusk, "the eyes of Oscar Wilde grew very bright and he gazed with devotional rapture into his own day." "My work was a joy to me," Wilde told Chesson: "when my plays were on, I drew a hundred pounds a week! I delighted in every minute of the day."[4]

While they were out walking, Chesson witnessed Wilde talking to a pretty French child whom Wilde had previously befriended. This led his visitor to realize instantly that Wilde was cut off from his own children. Attempting reassurance, Chesson suggested that work might make up for the absence of his children, to which Wilde replied only that "his work was in his head, he did not write it down."[5] Prompted by his visitor to reflect on Christianity, Wilde recalled Christ's words "What shall it profit a man if he gain the whole world and lose his own soul?" Chesson replied by speaking of "life in spirit." At this Wilde became indignant, echoing the words of the protagonist in his prose-poem "The House of Judgment" ("in hell have I always lived") by telling Chesson "there is no hell but this . . . a body without a soul, or a soul without a body."[6] When Chesson observed, as the visit drew to a close, that Wilde's life was "a harmony of two extremes," Wilde replied "Yes, artistically it is perfect; socially most inconvenient." They parted at the railway station, with Wilde quipping "It does not matter what class you go up to Paris."[7]

It was clear to Chesson, as to many of Wilde's devoted followers, that Wilde would never produce new work again. Wilde had told friends in May that he wished to do new work in the course of the coming year, and at one point in May he even had an idea as well as a title for a new novel.[8] But he found it increasingly hard to detach himself from the quotidian problems of a largely improvised existence or to recapture the imaginative freedom necessary for his work, and by August he had come to feel that he would never write again. "Something is killed in me," he explained to Ross. "I feel no desire to write. I am unconscious of power [and prison has] destroyed me body and soul. It could not have been otherwise" (*CL* 1095). "When I take up my pen, all the past comes back," he explained to Frank Harris: "regret and remorse, like twin dogs, wait to seize me. . . . I am face to face with my own soul: the Oscar of five years ago, with his beautiful secure life and his glorious easy triumphs, comes up before me, and . . . my eyes burn with tears."[9] He was born to "sing the joy and pride of life," he told Harris, "the pleasure of living, the delight in everything beautiful in this most beautiful world[, but] they took and tortured me till I learned sorrow and pity [and] now I cannot sing the joy."[10] All that was left was the pleasure of spectatorship. He could only go out and watch life, amuse and interest himself in the moment, otherwise he would go mad. "I don't think I am equal to the intellectual architecture of thought," he explained to Ross. "I have moods and moments; and Love, or Passion with the mask of Love, is my only consolation" (*CL* 1105).

And yet this wasn't an entirely accurate self-estimate, for if Wilde was incapable of producing entirely fresh work, he was excited at the prospect of preparing his final two plays for publication. Capitalizing on the success of *The Ballad*, Smithers had agreed as early as May to publish *The Importance of Being Earnest*, which had been running at the time of Wilde's arrest, in a format uniform with the exquisite first editions of *Lady Windermere's Fan* and *A Woman of No Importance*. Wilde later wrote that Smithers showed "great pluck in bringing it out," but Wilde felt rightly that his greatest comedy would have nothing like the publishing success of *The Ballad*: "it is so trivial, so irresponsible a comedy; and while the public liked to hear of my pain," he observed, he was "not sure that they will welcome me again in airy mood and spirit, mocking at morals, and [in] defiance of social rules" (*CL* 1127, 1124). Nonetheless Wilde went about revising the play with relish and great wit once he received from Smithers a typed copy of the script used in the first production, and he was busy revising the play when Chesson visited him at l'Idée.[11]

Wilde's revisions add considerable sparkle and polish to an already brilliant text, and some of the play's most memorable lines date from this time. Not till 1898, for instance, does Jack greet the sight of Algernon's cucumber sandwiches by asking "Why such reckless extravagance in one so young?" Similarly, not till 1898 does Lady Bracknell ring Algernon's doorbell in a "Wagnerian" manner, or is Gwendolen's invalid father under the impression that "she is attending a more than usually lengthy lecture by the University Extension Scheme on the Influence of a permanent income on Thought." (Perhaps not coincidentally, in November 1898 Wilde wittily described Robert Ross to Reggie Turner as "a combination of the University Extension Scheme and The Reformation" [*CL* 1103].)[12] It was with considerable pride that, upon its publication in February 1899, Wilde dedicated the play to Ross and sent signed copies to friends. "It was extraordinary reading the play over again," he observed to Reggie Turner: "How I used to toy with that tiger Life!" (*CL* 1122).

———

"That Tiger Life" continued to show its claws during the latter half of 1898, as preparations for the publication of *The Importance* came to fruition. In late September, his old friends Robert Ross and Reggie Turner deliberately bypassed Paris as they headed to Florence, Rome, and Naples for an autumn vacation. Turner's biographer Stanley Weintraub generously suggests that they probably feared that Wilde, depressed and lonely for English companionship, "would soften them into not going any further."[13] But Wilde was hurt and disappointed, and he begged them to stop for a night in Paris on their return. He was used to being shunned by strangers, but suddenly he was being avoided by those with whom he had previously been intimate, including fellow homosexuals like Turner and Ross, the latter of whom at one point wrote that he wished to "lecture" and "talk morals" to Wilde (*CL* 1105). In August he was cut in public by two old lovers, the actors Cosmo Gordon-Lennox and Harry Melvill, the former now married to the actress Marie Tempest. "I felt as if I had been cut by two Piccadilly renters," he observed at the time, and "was very much hurt" (*CL* 1095).

His hurt was probably compounded by the fact that Lord Alfred Douglas, after more than three years abroad, was now pining for a permanent return to London, where he hoped to develop an already promising literary career. But Douglas did not return to London immediately: he spent August and September with his mother, first in Trouville, and then in Aix-les-Bains, from whence he had returned to Paris penniless by October 3.[14] For three years Douglas had feared arrest if he risked returning to England, and in late September he had written that he had been semi-officially advised, through his family's connections in the government, that returning would be "very inadvisable." But he soon received assurances that he would be left untroubled upon his return, and by late November, Douglas was back in London, eagerly anticipating the imminent publication of a book of nonsense, titled *Tales With a Twist,* and making arrangements for the publication of two further books, including *The City of the Soul,* his first and most important book of poems to be published in England.[15] Although Wilde remarked bitterly shortly after Douglas's return to England that "I suppose that London takes no notice at all: that is the supreme punishment," it is clear that Wilde sympathized with Douglas's reasons for returning and that he was missing him: within a few days, he craved news of his friend, asking "Is he happy to be back? And are people kind to him? How is he behaving?" (*CL* 1102, 1104). Paris in late November was cold and wet, and "so like London that it was unnecessary for Bosie to return to England" (*CL* 1106). With Douglas now in London on the brink of literary success, a terrible reminder of all that Wilde had lost, Paris was rapidly becoming intolerable.

To make matters worse, money troubles continued to press upon him: in June he owed the Hôtel d'Alsace £14 for two months' lodging and as a result could not "either leave it or remain in it" (*CL* 1082). In August he claimed to have gone an entire week with nothing at all and begged £20 from Smithers on the grounds that "my hotel is clamorous for payment. . . . I really am without food . . . and have no money for even French cigarettes" (*CL* 1092). "I have no clothes but those you so generously supplied me with [in] May last year," he told Frank Harris in September, pleading for a continuation of the monthly allowance of £10 that Harris had begun sending him in July (*CL* 1097). In November he asked Ross if he might be sent his December allowance early, as "a wretched inn-keeper at Nogent to whom I owe 100 francs . . . threatens to sell Reggie's dressing-case, my overcoat, and two suits if I don't pay him by Saturday" (*CL* 1101). When Ross replied that Wilde had used the same excuse as a pretext for obtaining money once before, Wilde responded unabashed "I am so sorry about my excuse. I had forgotten I had used Nogent before. It shows the utter collapse of my imagination, and rather distresses me" (*CL* 1102).

In truth, Wilde was not so impoverished as he maintained. He received regular allowances from Ross, Harris, and Smithers, while many others gave him money when he asked. According to Vincent O'Sullivan, Wilde had more money at his disposal than many of the young writers and painters living in Paris at that time, and according to Lord Alfred Douglas, Harris alone gave Wilde more than enough for him to live comfortably.[16] The problem was the familiar one: that Wilde was careless and hopelessly inept in money matters. He loathed cheap restaurants and cheap lodgings, and he spent freely on others, especially drinking companions and young male companions.[17] Constance had told Blacker in March, shortly before her sudden passing, that "if he had plenty of money he would drink himself to death and do no work," and while she may have been exaggerating, it is certainly the case that Wilde spent a great deal on alcohol. His hotelier, the loyal Jean Dupoirier, later said that "he drank a tremendous amount" and fact already sold to the American actress Cora Brown-Potter the previous year (although Wilde did not reveal this to Sedger).[21] According to the scenario he gave Alexander in 1894, the play was to have been a modern romance of adulterous love, set among the English upper-classes, in which a neglected wife falls passionately in love with—and becomes impregnated by—an old friend of her husband's from his bachelor days, whom her husband has invited as a houseguest in the knowledge that his wife was once the object of his friend's desire. It was to be a play in which the "sheer passion of love [was] to dominate everything": there was to be "no morbid self-sacrifice [or] renunciation," just a "sheer flame of love" (*CL* 600). The contract with Sedger stipulated further remunerations for Wilde upon completion and production, but Wilde had no intention of writing the play. This was to become a bitter bone of contention in 1900, when Frank Harris, with whom Wilde proposed to collaborate in writing the play and sharing the profits from it, wrote up the scenario under his own name and staged it in the West End in late 1900 under the title *Mr. and Mrs. Daventry* (see pp. 274–76 below). The sale of the stage rights was simply a money-making scheme.

Nonetheless, if "that tiger Life" showed its claws, Wilde still toyed with it, and his correspondence in the fall of 1898 is filled with laughter, wit, and good spirits, sometimes at the very moment when he is pleading his straitened lot. In the same letter in which he asks Ross for an early advance of his December allowance, he thanks Ross for a gift of clothes, saying that he found them "quite charming—suitable for my advanced age" and adding that "Smithers I received in the same parcel"(*CL* 1100). The trousers were too tight around the waist, he confessed, but that "is the result of my rarely having good dinners; nothing fattens so much as a dinner at 1 fr. 50, but the blue waistcoat is a dream" (*CL* 1100). In another letter from this time, he finds great amusement in the difficulties of his homosexual friend Ashton, whom he nicknamed "Sir John" and of whom he and Douglas had seen a great deal in Naples. Ashton had just gone "through a romance with an absurd Boulevard boy," Wilde gossiped in November (*CL* 1101). He had given the young man a suit of clothes, but the latter had nonetheless cheated him and treated him badly. Ashton had thus proven himself to be "the last great sentimentalist," one who "clothes everybody except the naked" (*CL* 1104). "To undress is romance, to dress, philanthropy," Wilde concluded, when relating the story with great relish to Robert Ross and Reginald Turner (*CL* 1101).[22] He would shortly say that "Laughter is the primaeval attitude towards life—a mode of approach that survives only in artists and criminals" (*CL* 1106). Where one laughs, "there is no immorality: immorality and seriousness begin together" (*CL* 1073).

In Douglas's absence, Wilde continued unapologetically to laugh, beg, and carouse his way through the late summer and autumn of 1898, often in the company of the young poet Ernest La Jeunesse, who was to leave one of the most moving and personal written accounts of Wilde's final years. They met chiefly at the Calisaya, a plush American-style bar, near the Crédit Lyonnais, next door to the offices of the *Revue Blanche*. The bar served as the rendezvous for writers of widely differing stripes and nationalities. On occasion they were accompanied by the Guatemalan writer Enrique Gomez Carrillo, who later called the Calisaya "the 'ultimate' literary center in Paris."[23] Other companions at the Calisaya included the Greek Symbolist poet Ioannis Papadiamantopoulos (who wrote and published in French under the name *Jean Moréas*), the French writers Paul Adam, Jean de Mitty, and Jean de Bonnefon, the Spanish poet Manuel Machado, and (after his move to Paris in 1900) the Nicaraguan modernist Rubén Darío, as well as "one beautiful boy of bad character," as Wilde put it, who was not a poet but "so like Antinous, and so smart, that he is allowed to talk to poets" (*CL* 1108). Machado has left a memorable picture of the bar: "containing a huge countertop of shiny mahogany, with a copper rail for resting the arms, the *bar,* properly-speaking, was filled with drinkers, yankee-style, half of them standing, half of them seated on high wicker stools, who sipped their concoctions and then quietly slipped away, while the bartenders mixed the 132 cocktails that were on offer. More sybaritic, we Parisians slowly consumed our absinthes—this lasted all evening—lounging on

Within days of arriving in the South of France, it became clear to Harris that "the effort, the hard work, of writing was altogether beyond" Wilde.[28] Wilde found La Napoule pleasant but dull.[29] They stayed in the Hôtel des Bains, La Napoule's only hotel. Wilde quickly fell into a pattern of taking long indolent walks in the surrounding pine woods or amusing himself with the local fishermen, whom he soon discovered had "the same freedom from morals as the Neapolitans have" (*CL* 1112). By December 28 he had two boyfriends, one called Raphael, the other Fortuné. "Even at Napoule there is romance," he remarked: "It comes in boats and takes the form of fisher-lads, who draw great nets, and are bare-limbed" (*CL* 1119). He seemed to be content killing time talking to the young fishermen, or taking carriage rides into Cannes, where he would amuse himself at some café, but at bottom he was restless and sadly conscious that literary inspiration, which had once come so easily, had now dissipated, to be supplanted by the dubious pleasures of spectatorship. "I should be quite happy if I did not know how to read and write," he remarked revealingly (*CL* 1120). When Harris asked him where he went every afternoon, he replied "I go to Cannes, Frank, and sit in a café and look across the sea to Capri, where Tiberius used to sit like a spider watching, and I think of myself as an exile, the victim of one of his inscrutable suspicions."[30] Occasionally he went into Nice, where he was to move for the final two weeks of February, when he could stomach La Napoule no longer. But he knew that Cannes and Nice were popular winter vacation destinations with the English and that by going there he risked recognition. On one trip into Nice, he ran into a "renter" whom he knew from Paris, who borrowed five francs from him. The young man—"dark and bronze-like, with splendidly chiselled nose and mouth, and the tents of midnight . . . folded in his eyes"—was "visiting Nice on speculative business," he said, and Wilde promised to come and see him again (*CL* 1117). On another occasion the actor-manager George Alexander, who had produced and starred in *Lady Windermere's Fan* and *The Importance of Being Earnest*, appeared on a bicycle, only to cycle past hurriedly without stopping, with me. There is a sad lack of Fauns in the pinewoods at Napoule" (*CL* 1117). "I am still sitting on porphyry rocks, or roaming through pine-woods," he reported to Turner, "and twice a week I look at the shop-windows in Cannes" (*CL* 1119). He pleaded with Ross to come visit. The only solace was to be found in searching, in the cafés and tourist-spots of Nice or Cannes, for a small taste of the life he had once known. Trips into Nice became more frequent. During one three-day trip there as Mellor's guest, in January 1899, he became enamored of two young men named André and Pietro, the former "with wonderful eyes," and the latter "like a young St. John" whom Wilde "would have followed . . . into the desert" (*CL* 1118). Around this time, Ross evidently suggested that Wilde should try making himself respectable by marrying again, to which Wilde replied with amusement "As regards my marrying again, I am quite sure that you will want me to marry this time some sensible, practical, plain, middle-aged boy, and I don't like the idea at all. Besides I am practically engaged to a fisherman of extraordinary beauty, age eighteen" (*CL* 1116).

When Harris returned to La Napoule, he "found everything . . . altered for the worse." Mellor had now moved into the Hôtel des Bains, but Harris found him a sycophantic "insignificant, foolish creature" and was troubled by Wilde's friendship with him, especially when Wilde wanted Harris to meet Mellor's boyfriend, whom Mellor "called his servant." Harris was disturbed too by Wilde's lack of productivity, and he began urging Wilde more forcefully to "pull yourself out of the mud," at one point tactlessly remarking that "everyone grows tired of holding up an empty sack."[34] For his part, Wilde found Harris exhausting, reporting to Turner that "after our literary talk in the evening I stagger to my room, bathed in perspiration" (*CL* 1121). As Harris overheard Wilde telling Mellor, "talking literature with Frank must be very like playing rugby, where you end by being kicked violently through your own goal."[35]

It is little surprise, then, that the arrangement with Harris came to a premature end: in February 1899, when Harris was again away in

Monte Carlo, Wilde moved into the Hôtel Terminus at Nice. It was a cheap hotel near the station, and once again he checked in using the pseudonym Sebastian Melmoth. He stayed in friendly communication with Harris, however, who frequently travelled the short distance from Monte Carlo to dine Wilde in style at his own expense and to help him foot his bills. But Nice too failed to calm Wilde's restlessness. The Terminus's English inhabitants quickly saw through his pseudonym and objected to his presence. On or around February 22, 1899, Wilde was presented with his bill and asked to leave the same day. This humiliation led Harris to suggest that Wilde should stay at his own hotel, the Cesari Palace, in nearby Monte Carlo. But Wilde told Harris that he would not come "because it would not be good for your hotel for me to be seen there" (*CL* 1126).

Again using the pseudonym Sebastian Melmoth, he checked himself instead into the tiny Hôtel des Alpes-Maritimes, where his frazzled nerves were finally soothed and he slept in peace. But he had had enough of Nice: coming on top of the snub by George Alexander, the incident at the Terminus had frightened him. "There are too many English on this coast," he told Harris, "and they are all brutal to me. I think I should like to go to Italy if you would not mind."[36] His treatment at Nice calls to mind the words that he had once put into the mouth of Mrs. Erlynne, the sexual renegade at the center of *Lady Windermere's Fan:* "You don't know what it is to fall into the pit, to be despised, mocked, abandoned, sneered at—to be an outcast! to find the door shut against one, to have to creep in by hideous byways, afraid every moment lest the mask should be stripped from one's face, and all the while to hear the laughter, the horrible laughter of the world, a thing more tragic than all the tears the world has ever shed. You don't know what it is. One pays for one's sins, and then one pays again, and all one's life one pays."[37]

———

He was now living a peripatetic, day-to-day, hand-to-mouth existence, with no direction or plans. Some relief was offered by the kindly Harold

Mellor, who near the end of February invited Wilde to his home in Gland, Switzerland, as his guest. Wilde quickly accepted Mellor's offer, but he confessed to Harris that he was rather depressed at the prospect and felt a little ungrateful in consequence, for he dreaded the cold "and the lack of coloured, moving, beautiful life" (*CL* 1126). Even still, he hoped to be happy in Switzerland, and there would at least be free meals and champagne. But Wilde headed first to Genoa, 110 miles to the east, where Constance had died nearly a year earlier. It was an eight-hour journey by train, and he wished to lay flowers on his wife's grave before heading to the tranquility of Gland.

Wilde left for Genoa on February 25 and spent three days there. He had once described Genoa as "a beautiful marble city of palaces over the sea" (*CL* 45). Constance was buried in the beautiful *Cimitero monumentale,* in the foothills just to the north of the city, and Wilde drove there from the city in a little green ramshackle fly.[38] One of the most magnificent cemeteries in Europe, Genoa's *Cimitero monumentale* has over the years elicited the praise of many great writers, including Mark Twain, Friedrich Nietzsche, Ernest Hemingway, and Evelyn Waugh, who once called it "one of the wonders of the modern world" and commented that "if Père la Chaise and the Albert Memorial were obliterated, the loss would be negligible as long as this great repository survives."[39] Wilde too was much touched by the cemetery's beauty, describing it as "a garden at the foot of the lovely hills that climb into the mountains that girdle Genoa" (*CL* 1128). But as he placed his crimson roses on Constance's grave, he was haunted by a sense of tragedy: he later told Ada Leverson that he had broken down, sobbed and prayed, overcome by "a passion of grief, repentance, and bitter remorse," although not without a sense too of the uselessness of all regret.[40] Perhaps he remembered a story he had told André Gide years previously, about a man who had once made a bronze statue, representing "the sadness which dwells in life," which he had placed on the grave of his wife, the only woman he had ever loved, only years later to smash and melt it down so that he might make instead a statue of "the joy which dwells only in the moment."[41] Life "is a very terrible thing," Wilde reflected over Constance's grave, but "nothing could have been otherwise" (*CL* 1128).

The visit to Genoa was not without its consolations, however. He had intended to stay just one day, but in Genoa he met a good-looking young actor named Didaco, whom he "wildly loved" and "who had the look of Romeo, without Romeo's sadness: a face chiselled for high romance" (*CL* 1132). They spent three days together. He also met a fair-haired young man named Edoardo Rolla, possibly a sailor or fisherman ("one of the sea-farers"), who was always dressed in dark blue and to whom Wilde would write from Switzerland (*CL* 1140). As Mrs. Erlynne remarks magnificently in *Lady Windermere's Fan,* "what consoles one nowadays is not repentance, but pleasure. Repentance is quite out of date."[42]

By March 1, he had arrived at Gland on the edge of Lake Geneva for his visit with Mellor. It proved no less dispiriting than his last few weeks in France. There was "much beauty of an obvious old fashioned kind," but he quickly grew to dislike his host, and the Swiss were "so ugly to look at that it conveys melancholy into all my days" (*CL* 1129). The young men of Nice had been like bronzes, and young Englishmen were "chryselephantine," but the Swiss were "carved out of wood with a rough knife, most of them, [or else] carved out of turnips" (*CL* 1129). Within a day of arriving, he had invited Ross to come over and join him. He tried learning to ride a bicycle. But it was apparent that here, too, he was dissatisfied and restive: he took long walks by the lakeshore, delighting in the knowledge that this meant trespassing on private property ("I am a born trespasser" he quipped), and every day he visited Nyon, a little village three miles off, where he bought himself a bock and the French papers (*CL* 1129). Even Smithers's publication of *The Importance of Being Earnest* at the end of February failed to bring any excitement. He complained, rightly, that the play had been boycotted by the press and that none of his friends had written acknowledging receipt of the personalized copies he had signed.[43] He hoped that "some of the faithful, and all the elect, will buy copies," but he was not sanguine: "if you hear anything nice said about the play," he asked Ross, "write it to me; if not, invent it" (*CL* 1127). It had given him great pleasure to write Ross's name in the printed dedication, but he "wish[ed] it were a more wonderful work of art—of higher seriousness of intent" (*CL* 1128). "There are two ways of disliking my plays," he is reputed to have remarked: "one is to dislike them, the other is to like *Earnest.*"[44]

Within a fortnight of arriving, Wilde had had enough of Mellor and Gland. "I don't like Mellor very much, and would like to get away," he told Ross in the middle of March. He longed to return to Italy or England, "where beauty walks in the sun" (*CL* 1130, 1132). Doubtless he missed Didaco and Rolla, but he had also been much shaken by the contrast between the color of the South and what he called the Swiss "lack of physical beauty." In Switzerland "life is robbed of its first great element," he wrote, and "the people are formless, colourless" (*CL* 1132). "Their cattle have more expression," he told Louis Wilkinson (*CL* 1133). "I suffer very much," he told Harris; "[e]nnui is the enemy" (*CL* 1131). He wanted badly to get away, but escape was impossible for the time being: he was short of money and dependent on his host's largesse until the arrival of his next monthly allowance from Ross.[45] "I wait on Fortune like a discarded lover," he told Turner (*CL* 1133).

Without the funds to leave Switzerland, Wilde consoled himself by reading a great deal and revising the text of *An Ideal Husband* for publication. He rated the play more highly than *The Importance of Being Earnest* and, undaunted by the commercial failure of the earlier publication, Smithers now planned to publish the play in a format uniform with Wilde's other social comedies.[46] "It reads the best of all my plays," Wilde said (*CL* 1135). Among the changes Wilde now undertook was the insertion of the witty characterizations of the play's *dramatis personae* that are prominent among its stage directions. But he was uncertain about the additions, since he disliked "giving physical details about the bodies whose souls, or minds, or passions, I deal with," feeling that "I build up so much out of *words* that the colour of people's hair seems unimportant" (*CL* 1135–36). He asked Ross to review these and other changes, and also to check that he had successfully eliminated any traces of lingering Irishness and that his characters spoke in perfectly polished English.[47] Finally he wrote to Frank Harris seeking permission to dedicate the play to him, explaining that "the charming winter which you so generously and kindly gave me . . . can never be forgotten by me" (*CL* 1131). When the play was eventually published in July 1899, its dedication read "To Frank Harris, A Slight Tribute to His Power and Distinction as an Artist, His Chivalry and Nobility as a Friend." It was with genuine sincerity that Wilde told Harris "it is a real pleasure to me to see your name on the portal of a book of mine" (*CL* 1159).

As his visit to Mellor dragged on through the month of March 1899, Wilde experienced a nagging restlessness. He was conscious of the loss of his literary powers and desperate for money and new companions. He yearned to return to Paris, and he missed Douglas, Gilbert, and Strong, as well as the boulevard boys and the companionship to be found in the Calisaya bar. But Douglas was no longer in Paris, and Wilde owed the Hôtel d'Alsace money. On March 26, he reiterated his invitation to Ross to join him at Gland, but by the following day he had decided to leave for Genoa once his allowance arrived, since Paris was too expensive and Genoa "is better than the Boulevards" (*CL* 1137). He knew that in Paris he would spend all his money in no time, and he couldn't live there for under £1 a day. In some quiet village on the coast near Genoa, by contrast, he could live for ten francs a day, "boy *compris,*" and moreover "sunlight counts as half of one's income" (*CL* 1139, 1138). After the Swiss Alps' "chill virginity," he longed for "the red flowers of life that stain the feet of Italy" (*CL* 1140). Just as importantly, he hoped to find Edoardo Rolla waiting for him.

But things were no better once Wilde reached Genoa.[48] Within a few days of arriving, he announced that he now wanted to get back to Paris and that life in Genoa was too lonely. The much-anticipated re-union with Edoardo Rolla had been a disappointment, and once again he was out of money.[49] "Do you know anybody in the world who would advance me £100?" he asked Smithers: "I owe money at my hotel in Paris and elsewhere, and I really must get hold of some money" (*CL* 1141). "I am wretched," he told Ross shortly after moving to the tiny fishing village of Santa Margherita, twenty miles south of Genoa: "Whatever I do is wrong, because my life is not on a right basis. In Paris I am bad: here I am bored; the last state is the worse" (*CL* 1142).

———

Relief finally arrived in late April 1899, nearly five months after Wilde had left Paris for the Riviera. In an effort to raise Wilde's spirits, the loyal Smithers paid him a brief visit in Santa Margherita, where the two men dined at the Concordia restaurant, discussed Wilde's future, and Wilde formally signed over his royalties in his last two plays in exchange for the sum of £30. At Santa Margherita, Wilde also mentioned to Smithers (as he had done previously to Harris and others) that he intended to write a new play, the rights to which he had already sold to Sedger. Upon his return to England, Smithers wrote that "it is absurd your living at Sta. Margherita; but it would be much more absurd if you came to Paris and drifted about playing *bezique* instead of working."[50] Smithers offered Wilde a lifeline: he promised to pay off Wilde's hotel bills, to provide Wilde's fare to Paris, and to put Wilde in a position to live in comfort in Paris, so long as Wilde applied himself to writing the as-yet unwritten play—and providing Wilde let him buy the rights for the play's stage production from Sedger. Wilde agreed to this proposition, and within a matter of days, Smithers had made the necessary arrangements for Wilde to leave the Riviera. It was Ross, not Smithers, who acted as chaperone. By mid-May Wilde was back in Paris, where, after a few days spent at the pricey Hôtel de la Neva, in the Rue Monsigny, he checked himself into the cheaper Hôtel Marsollier, just around the corner from the Calisaya bar. After Ross had seen him newly settled in his hotel, and had himself returned to London, Wilde wrote telling Ross that "it was really most sweet of you to come to Italy to save me from Santa Margherita" and that he was now at last "quite happy" (*CL* 1143).

But he was by no means as happy to be back in Paris as he would have had Ross believe. Before long a familiar note of dissatisfaction crept back into his affairs, born chiefly from a combination of money woes and creative frustration. "Life is rather dust now," he told Harris at the end of May 1899, while begging his friend for yet another handout, "and water-wells are rare in the desert" (*CL* 1146). Smithers kept his promise to sustain him in comfort throughout the summer of 1899, and Wilde tried briefly to keep his end of the bargain too. On or around June 3, he told Smithers that he had "written more than half of the Fourth Act . . . a serious tragic act," but that he was "frightened" of "the comedy of Acts I and II" since it was now "difficult for me to laugh at life, as I used to" (*CL* 1150). Possibly Wilde was still thinking of writing the same play he had outlined to Alexander in 1894, sold to Sedger in 1898, and outlined again as recently as the previous December to Frank Harris—a play centered on a modern marriage gone wrong, in which the "sheer flame of love" dominated everything and in which the cuckolded husband kills himself in Act IV, after discovering that his wife is pregnant by the man for whom she has left him. But if so, it is hard to see where comic elements might have featured. And if Wilde was telling Smithers the truth about writing more than half of act four, no manuscript has survived attesting to Wilde's fresh efforts at playwriting.

Relations between the two men became notably tense at the end of May, after which Wilde made no further progress on the promised play. Smithers had by this point secured the production rights from Sedger, he thought, in the process securing for Wilde an additional advance of £25 for each completed act[51]—but only after Wilde had declined to deal with a would-be theatrical producer named Roberts, who had offered far higher terms.[52] Now, at the end of May, Wilde learned by hearsay that Smithers had been employed by Roberts to secure his play at one-fourth the terms he had personally offered. Wilde immediately wrote to Smithers seeking an explanation and an entirely new agreement. Smithers replied absolving himself of Wilde's charges, and

Wilde quickly came to realize that the hearsay about Roberts had been entirely false. But despite the happy resolution of "*l'affaire Smithers,*" as Wilde called it, and despite Wilde's apology for all that he had said to Smithers concerning his purported treachery, Wilde was unable to make further progress on the play, and within a matter of days he was making plans to leave Paris afresh (*CL* 1151).

Once again, Wilde was becoming paralyzed by the restlessness, humiliation, and frustration that had characterized all his affairs since Douglas's departure the previous November. At the end of May he visited the village of Marlotte in the forest of Fontainebleu, where he intended to stay for some days under his pseudonym Sebastian Melmoth, ostensibly to write an article for the *North American Review,* which had promised him a princely £75 upon the article's submission. Marlotte was "a *colonie artistique,* and creation is in the air," he told the *North American*'s editor, "so the surroundings will be conducive to work" (*CL* 1147). But the article (whose subject is not known) was never written, possibly because Wilde had been recognized and asked to leave his hotel, and within a day or two he had returned to Paris.[53] Upon his return to Paris, he immediately started making plans to visit the port city of Le Havre instead, on the Normandy coast, on the grounds that he missed the sea and that Paris cost him too much money.[54] But he did not leave immediately for Le Havre as intended. In early June, Lord Alfred Douglas returned unexpectedly to Paris to celebrate the publication of his first and most acclaimed English book of poems, *The City of the Soul,* which had appeared a few days previously under the imprint of the British publisher Grant Richards.

Shortly after Douglas arrived, he invited Wilde to dine with him at the Café de la Paix, the magnificent café where twelve years earlier Wilde had set his short story "The Sphinx Without a Secret." At the café they ran by chance into Wilde's old friends Ada Rehan, the American actress, and Augustin Daly, the New York impresario. "Wilde came over and sat with us and talked so charmingly," Rehan later reported, "it was just like old times—we had a lovely evening."[55] But Daly was in fact mortally sick, and when he died suddenly a few days later, Wilde, after sending Rehan a moving letter of condolence, helped Rehan with the funeral arrangements (*CL* 1152–53). "Oscar came to me and was more good and helpful than I can tell you," she recalled, "just like a very kind brother."[56] Wilde continued seeing Douglas regularly in early June; he was dining with Douglas when they heard that Douglas's poems had just received warm and enthusiastic praise from an anonymous reviewer for *The Outlook,* whereupon they immediately decamped to the Horseshoe bar to celebrate in appropriate style. In the first of many positive reviews of Douglas's volume, the reviewer for *The Outlook* had proclaimed the arrival of a true poet among "crowds of clever versifiers."[57] It was already becoming clear, as Richard Ellmann puts it, that with *The City of the Soul,* Douglas had "made his official claim to be a poet."[58]

Once Douglas had returned to London, Wilde finally decamped for Le Havre at the end of June, where he stayed for some days at the grand Hôtel Tortoni in the Place Gambetta. Here he corrected proofs for *An Ideal Husband,* which Smithers would publish to a deafening silence at the end of July. Reviewers shunned the play as completely as they had shunned *The Importance of Being Earnest* in February, and even many of Wilde's old friends failed to acknowledge the signed copies that he sent them. From Le Havre, a major port city, Wilde visited the nearby seaside resort of Trouville, described by one Victorian observer as "one of the handsomest watering-places on the northern coast of France."[59] But despite the pretty beach, the promenade, and the attractions of fashionable Deauville nearby, Wilde was tired and dispirited, while Le Havre itself was "too awful for words" (*CL* 1156). He was short of money, and seaside resorts had little to offer him now. By the end of June, after Smithers had wired him the money to pay his hotel bill and railway fare, he had returned to Paris, where he once again checked himself into the Hôtel Marsollier.

———

Back in Paris, Wilde threw himself again into the life of the café and the boulevard, despite a persistent shortage of funds. He viewed Parisian cafés as social meeting-places, comparable to London clubs, where one could talk and converse without fear of criticism.[60] One evening in July, he dined with Stuart Merrill and the symbolist poet and novelist André-Ferdinand Hérold, who gave him a copy of his 1895 book *Le Livre de la naissance, de la vie et de la mort de la bienheureuse Vierge-Marie,* an apocryphal life of the Virgin Mary that Wilde found "charming." He also saw a great deal of an "astonishingly handsome" young poet named Michael Robas (*CL* 1157). In July 1899 he accompanied Robas to a cabaret in Montmartre, where the poet Jehan Rictus—who, sixteen months later, would visit the Hôtel d'Alsace mournfully in the hours after Wilde's death—nightly recited his popular "soliloquies of the poor" and where Rictus and his cohorts received Wilde with great honor: "everyone was presented to me. I was not allowed to pay for my *bocks,* and the *chasseur,* a lad of singular beauty, begged for my autograph" (*CL* 1157). When not visiting cabarets and cafés, he continued courting boulevard boys: "Casquette is well, and has a blue suit," he told Robert Ross, "Edmond de Goncourt has returned from prison and shows himself on the Boulevard in a straw hat [and] I am still devoted to Le Premier Consul, but I also love a young Russian called Maltchek Perovinski, aged eighteen . . . quite charming, and very educated" (*CL* 1157).

Around this time he appears to have abandoned all pretense of ever writing again, and a number of his old Parisian friends were becoming increasingly worried that he was spending too much time among the denizens of the Calisaya bar. The Calisaya was "a place he would never have dreamed of entering in his best days," Vincent O'Sullivan writes, and "Wilde's resorting to this place did him harm with the censorious."[61] Marcel Schwob, Stuart Merrill, and others had told O'Sullivan that Wilde "was ruining what sympathy was left for him by showing himself drunk on the Boulevards in such a place as 'The Calisaya Bar' with sodomist outcasts, who were sometimes dangerous in other ways."[62] O'Sullivan had mentioned this to Smithers, who had in turn mentioned it to Wilde. But when Smithers told Wilde that he had given his address to O'Sullivan, cautioning him "on no account let him know that I told you his slander about yourself and Calisaya," Wilde only replied "I shall be charmed to see O'Sullivan. I shall say nothing about Kalisaya [*sic*]" (*CL* 1158).[63] As O'Sullivan remarked when recalling the incident years later, "the young Frenchmen were rather priggish; but then they had their careers to make, & Wilde knew his career was over."[64] Moreover, where was he to go and what was he to do? Those who criticized him were reluctant to be seen with him, and still more to invite them into their homes. As O'Sullivan observes, "he went to places like 'Calisaya' driven by the instinct for self-preservation. He knew that he would go mad if he sat alone with his bitter thoughts. Besides, where was he to sit?"[65] According to Reginald Turner, it would be enough for Wilde to be seen simply walking along the boulevard in the company of La Jeunesse "with his odd costume, empire cane, masses of unkempt hair, and pale face patched with eczema, for it to be thought that he was keeping bad company."[66]

The fears of Merrill and Schwob were justified, for Wilde was now consuming large amounts of alcohol—chiefly absinthe, brandy, and whiskey-and-soda. Jean Dupoirier, the proprietor of the Hôtel d'Alsace says that Wilde "used to whip himself up with cognac."[67] Stuart Merrill says that Wilde "had never been exactly sober" but that "he now gave himself to drinking beyond measure" and became "so overcome that he could scarcely stagger from the Madeleine to the Opera."[68] In 1937 Lord Alfred Douglas claimed to have seen Wilde "*over* and *over again* in the last two years of his life (never before then) so drunk that he could not walk, and had to be helped by myself and a waiter or chasseur to get into his cab."[69] While a number of other witnesses refute any suggestion that Wilde was to be seen drunk at this time, describing them as calumnies upon Wilde's character or as constituting the last of his hard labors, evidence to the contrary can be found in the account that Wilde himself gave to his friend Ada Leverson of once sitting up drinking absinthe for three nights straight, all the time thinking that he was "singularly clear-headed and sane."[70] When the waiter came in and began watering the sawdust, he told Leverson, "the most wonderful flowers, tulips, lilies and roses sprang up and made a garden of the café." "Don't you see them?" Wilde asked the waiter. "Mais non, monsieur," replied the waiter, "il n'y a rien." Similar evidence can be found in the "defence of drunkenness" that in 1897 he had told the Thaulows' shocked dinner-guests that he intended to write, as well as in André Gide's retrospective account of his own discomfort when Wilde asked him to sit with him on the terrace of a café and then proceeded to order cocktails. As Gide relates with touching regret for his earlier prudishness, when Wilde began to sense the younger man's embarrassment, he pointedly told the Frenchman that when, in times gone by, he had met the poet Paul Verlaine, he "didn't blush for him" and instead "felt that to be near him did me honor, even when Verlaine was drunk."[71]

It was clear to many of his friends that a new desperation had started to weigh him down. In addition to sometimes—or perhaps often—drinking to excess, he remained addicted to gold-tipped cigarettes, despite a persistent shortage of cash. Wilde was now a physically altered person. He had put on weight, and his once luxurious hair was thinning and turning grey. He had grown distinctly deaf in the ear that had troubled him in prison, and he now often spoke with his hand in front of his mouth to hide his bad teeth.[72] Requests for money—from Smithers, Ross, Harris, and even from his old friend the Piccadilly bookseller Arthur Humphreys—became more frequent, habitual, and insistent. In mid-July 1899, on a visit to Paris, Smithers gave him chloral or possibly hashish and advanced him £10, on the strength of which Wilde spent a few days at a sleepy inn on the Ile d'Amour at Chennevières-sur-Marne, to the east of Paris (*CL* 1158). Before leaving for Chennevières, Wilde had had to leave all his clothes at the Hôtel Marsollier because of his inability to settle his bill there. Upon returning, he moved back into his old hotel in the Rue des Beaux Arts, the Hôtel d'Alsace, but the Marsollier's proprietor, a "tiger," continued to worry him, and his clothes still remained in hock at the end of August. Eventually Jean Dupoirier, the owner of the Hôtel d'Alsace, who was to prove a loyal friend in the final months of Wilde's life, happy to let him live in his hotel on credit, paid to have Wilde's clothes reclaimed.[73]

The change that had come over Wilde is palpable in his surviving correspondence from late 1899, which, with one or two notable exceptions, is notable for its brevity and the absence of the gossip and banter with which it had been filled a year previous. "I am in a dreadful state . . . really in the gutter," he informed Smithers in August 1899; "in dreadful want—no money at all," he told Arthur Humphreys at around the same time (*CL* 1161–62). "Your friendship is a blossom on the crown of thorns that my life has become," he told his friend Aimée Lowther (*CL* 1164). "I will take care not to die on the wrong date" he told Ross in late September (*CL* 1165). "Things are dreadful and ridiculous," he informed Smithers in December (*CL* 1169). A brief respite was provided by Louis Wilkinson, a Radley schoolboy with whom Wilde had struck up a fitful correspondence the previous year, after Wilkinson had bravely written pretending that he wished to mount a dramatic production of *The Picture of Dorian Gray.* (Wilkinson later confessed that this was a ploy to get Wilde to enter into correspondence with him.) Wilde was never to meet Wilkinson, despite warmly inviting him to visit some months before his death, but Wilkinson sent original poems and photo-portraits, some of which reminded Wilde of his own youth, and Wilde sent inscribed copies of his plays and wrote back affectionately and at length.[74] His dealings with Wilkinson put Wilde in touch with his past, and unconsciously perhaps also reminded him of his estranged oldest son Cyril, four years Wilkinson's junior, who was at this time also a Radley schoolboy—although it would be many years before Wilkinson discovered that his one-time schoolmate, Cyril Holland, was Wilde's son.[75]

As the winter of 1900 approached, it was becoming no longer possible for Wilde to step out of the wreckage his life had become: he could no longer write creatively, his health was declining, and he was rapidly losing the confidence of some of his most loyal friends and supporters, including Harris, Smithers, and Ross. Even Douglas had embarked down the path toward a successful literary career in London that formed a sharp contrast with his own. Wilde had once written that "whatever is realized is right": at the end of *De Profundis* he had spoken of the new spirit of acceptance that would characterize his future conduct, adding that he would find "clefts in the rocks where I may hide . . . secret valleys in whose silence I may weep undisturbed," and that nature would "hang the night with stars so that I may walk abroad in the darkness without stumbling." But nature had proven less hospitable than he had imagined, and any spirit of acceptance had long been supplanted by one of open defiance and defeat. He had walked far and wide in the two-and-a-half years since his release, but in the falling darkness he was beginning to stumble.

9

Decline and Death

WITH THE EXCEPTION of a two-month vacation spent with Harold Mellor in Italy, the depression and sadness of the final year of Wilde's life were unbroken by any significant interludes. Wilde rose late in the day, before heading slowly, on foot and alone, to some bar or café where he would talk for hours with all manner of people before heading on to another café in the late hours. "He seemed ill, and was shabby and down at heel," says William Rothenstein, who met him awkwardly by chance on the street in the summer of 1900, "and he plainly depended on drink to sustain his wit."[1] The rich dinners with Harris or Douglas at Durand's or the Café de la Paix were now far and few between. Yet his motive in going to bars and cafés was not primarily alcoholic: he had a deadly fear of solitude. Although he no longer inhabited a prison cell, his shabby hotel room was its own form of prison, its decrepit furniture a symbol of all that he had lost. Perhaps he was also searching in his cups for a previous, vanished existence, in which the drawing rooms and dining rooms of England's wealthy classes were his greatest stage and he was lionized as England's greatest raconteur. "He had to have the oblivion which alcohol denied him," remarked his friend La Jeunesse, shortly after his death, "for even in the bars it was London he sought."[2]

While still a boy, he had learnt at his parents' dinner table that alcohol could be the stimulant for brilliant talk and sociability. Although he knew French fluently, he spoke it with a heavy accent in which traces of his original Irish intonation would occasionally appear. "You cannot imagine how he could talk, even in this bad French of his," says his friend and translator Jean-Joseph Renaud: "One by one we would leave this coffee-house, Calisaya. Then Oscar Wilde would go to another place, searching for other people to talk to. Then to another—until very late in the night. In these different cafés, night restaurants, brasseries, he kept talking, talking all the time, and as prodigiously, for all people who cared to listen—waiters, coachmen, sellers of late papers, beggars, poor street girls. Fear of solitude, perhaps, or nervous longing for expressing his visions as soon as they arose in his mind. At last, when there was nobody left to talk with, he used to walk home slowly, heavily, in the empty Paris streets."[3] He walked slowly, says La Jeunesse, shuffling along with little steps in order to allow his memory a freer play: "His heavy eyelids drooped beneath the weight of cherished visions—the visions of his former triumphs. . . . [H]e loved the solitude to which the world abandoned him, for he found himself there in the company of the man he had once been."[4]

Perhaps the saddest element of Wilde's final year was that he could no longer write. For at least two years after his release, he had remained determined to prove that he still possessed literary genius and that prison had not killed his creative spirit. But *The Importance of Being Earnest* and *An Ideal Husband* were greeted with silence upon publication in 1899, despite the skill he had put into revising them, and thereafter he never wrote another line. All he could now do, says Renaud, was tell stories in beautiful words to the few who would sit and listen.[5] As his arrangements with Smithers and Sedger indicate, publishers and theater producers were willing to pay handsomely for new work, and at one point Fernand Xau, the editor of the Parisian daily *Le Journal,* offered him a large fee for a series of articles. But as Wilde was putting pen to paper, Xau stupidly added "After all the noise your trial has made, these articles of yours will surely be successful," whereupon Wilde put his fountain-pen back into his pocket and quietly answered "Then I cannot accept writing them. My former successes, leaving out my condemnation, are enough for me."[6]

And yet if he could no longer write, he could still talk with a brilliance and fertility of tongue and imagination that nobody could match. When recalling a long-deferred reunion with Wilde that took place one afternoon in Paris, in the autumn of 1899, the English writer Laurence Housman later wrote of Wilde's "smooth-flowing utterance, sedate and self-possessed, oracular in tone, whimsical in substance, carried on without halt, or hesitation, or change of word, with the quiet zest of a man perfect at the game, and conscious that, for the moment at least, he was back at his old form again: this, combined with the pleasure, infectious to his listeners, of finding himself once more in a group of friends whose view of his downfall was not the world's view."[7] La Jeunesse, another lucky recipient of Wilde's verbal largesse at this time, writes similarly of a man haunted by his own powers of speech and imagination: "Slowly, word for word, he would invent in his feverish, stumbling agony of art, curious fleeting parables. . . . He wasted himself in words. Perhaps he tried to lose himself in them. . . . Words cannot properly paint the chaos of hope, of words and laughter, the mad sequence of half-concluded sentences, into which this poet plunged, proving to himself his still inexhaustible fancy, his battling against surrender, his smiling at fate; or suggest the grim darkness into which he must always turn, daily, fearing death, in the narrow chamber of a sordid inn."[8]

As 1899 passed into 1900, things went from bad to worse. Upon seeing his old Oxford friend J. C. Bodley (who lived in Paris) on the street, Wilde at first pretended not to recognize him; and when Bodley insisted on recalling their friendship, and then took Wilde to his house, Wilde fled at the door upon finding that Bodley's family was waiting inside.[9] "You don't know me, sir" (meaning he did not deem himself worthy of being recognized by an old friend), he told the Irish M.P. John O'Connor, who, upon recognizing Wilde in a restaurant, had been moved to speak to him by the sight of his front teeth gone.[10] "I have had my hand on the moon," Wilde told his friend Vincent O'Sullivan: "what is the use of trying to rise a little way from the ground?"[11] Vividly remembering that a year prior he had been on the Riviera living luxuriously at Harris's expense, he spent his final winter in the "icy north," because "one can't get railway-tickets on credit" (*CL* 1168). By his own account he was as well known in Paris as in London, but he continued using the name *Sebastian Melmoth* as a precautionary measure. In early February, he unexpectedly encountered in the Café de la Paix his old friend the homosexual-rights activist George Ives, who when in Paris would seek him out without giving any advance notice. ("Do, when again, if ever, you come to Paris let me know," Wilde wrote warmly to Ives, "and also let me know your address. Don't have with *me* the silly mania for secrecy that makes you miss the value of things" [*CL* 1172]). They chatted till past midnight over whiskey and soda, although Ives, a teetotaler, drank only hot milk. But Ives, always paranoid about conversing in public places, was irritated when Wilde refused to let him accompany him to the door of his hotel or to allow him to visit Wilde there the following day. "I don't invite my friends to my hotel because my room is cold and uncomfortable and I dislike it," Wilde explained, insisting that he only met his friends in cafés (*CL* 1172).[12]

Wilde told numerous friends in the winter of 1900 that he was ill and unhappy—as he put it, that "my throat is a lime kiln, my brain a furnace, and my nerves a coil of angry adders" (*CL* 1175). By mid-February he was consulting a physician, who was trying to cure him (unsuccessfully) with arsenic and strychnine. Writing from his bed at the end of February, he told Smithers that he had "some disease with a hybrid-Greek name: it attacks the throat and the soul" (*CL* 1174). In March he told another correspondent that he had been "suffering from a sort of blood-poisoning" (*CL* 1176) and that he had been hospitalized for ten days, while other letters from around this time make it clear that he believed he had been poisoned as the result of eating mussels.[13] But Wilde's doctor had also told him that he manifested all the symptoms of *neurasthenia,* an ill-defined medical condition characterized by lassitude, fatigue, headache, and irritability. Today *neurasthenia* is no longer a recognized medical diagnosis and is understood to have its basis in depression, emotional disturbance, or some kind of psychosomatic disorder. That such was the case with Wilde is suggested by his comment to Ross in late February 1900 that he had been neurasthenic "for four months, quite unable to get out of bed till the afternoon, quite unable to write letters of any kind" (*CL* 1175). But even depressed and in bad health, Wilde was able to find some measure of good humor. Maurice Gilbert had attended him daily, proving himself to be a sweet and devoted friend, and Wilde had "shared all my medicines with him, shown him what little hospitality I can" (*CL* 1175). And as for having all the symptoms of *neurasthenia,* "it is comforting to have them *all,* it makes one a perfect type" (*CL* 1174).

Financial woes weighed heavily on the ailing aesthete, and in early 1900 Wilde continued to make money by unscrupulously selling the scenario to his unwritten play, without telling the buyers that he had already contracted with others. In February 1900 the actress Ada Rehan gave him £100 for the rights to perform the play, Wilde flattering her in the old style that "I am only too pleased to have my work presented by so brilliant an artist" (*CL* 1170). He also entered into a contract with the New York producer Charles Frohman, which produced an advance of $500, via the theatrical agent Elisabeth Marbury, who left a memorable account of these dealings: "When I presented the agreements to him for signature, his hand trembled and he wrote 'Sebastian Melmoth,' a fanciful name he had chosen to conceal his identity. I looked at him fixedly and said 'This contract is being made with Oscar Wilde, who alone has the talent to fulfill it. I will accept no understudy, my friend. This is to be your recall to honor and fame.' His tears blotted the page. The first name was erased, and with firmness his own was affixed to the contract, which, alas, was never productive, as he died shortly after its execution."[14]

———

One again, it was Harold Mellor who offered Wilde temporary relief from his troubles. In March, Mellor offered to take Wilde to Italy for the spring. A year previously, Wilde had left Mellor's home in Gland in frustration and relief, having found his host miserly, boring, and unsociable. But he had now mended fences with Mellor, telling Ross that they were "now friends (below zero of course)," and he eagerly accepted Mellor's offer, especially since he knew that Ross had been in Rome all winter and was still there with his mother (*CL* 1177).

He embarked for Italy with Mellor at the end of March, and there was an immediate, noticeable improvement in his health and spirits. He had always been drawn to Italy: it was "the land for which my life had yearned," he had written many years before.[15] "As one nears Italy physical beauty comes running to meet one," he had written in 1899, shortly after visiting his wife's grave at Genoa (*CL* 1129). Their first destination was the Sicilian town of Palermo, where Wilde marveled at the fruit-groves of the Conca d'Oro and the mosaics in the Capella Patella, saying that the latter made one feel "as if one was sitting in the heart of a great honeycomb *looking* at angels singing" (*CL* 1178). There they also visited the nearby cathedral at Monreale. But ecclesiastical architecture was not the only thing that impressed Wilde, because the *cocchieri* (coachmen) were "most dainty finely-carved boys" (*CL* 1178). Manuele, Francesco, and Salvatore were "the most favoured" of his drivers, says Wilde, and "I loved them all, but only remember Manuele" (*CL* 1179). Wilde made great friends with a fifteen-year-old seminarian named Guiseppe Loverdi, who lived in a small room in the cathedral at Palermo. At first they talked of Loverdi's reasons for becoming a priest, with Wilde reminding the seminarian that "God used poverty often as a means of bringing people to him" (*CL* 1179). But Loverdi's eyes were beautiful, Wilde said, and Wilde gave him money, telling the young seminarian that he would become a Cardinal if he remained good and never forgot him: "he said he never would, and indeed I don't think he will, for every day I kissed him behind the high altar" (*CL* 1179).

Wilde's presence in Palermo did not fail to attract the attention of the local press, and he later boasted that "my incognito vanished in three hours" (*CL* 1183).[16] Upon leaving Sicily, Mellor and Wilde passed through Naples, where Wilde was reunited with old friends and "fell in love with a Sea-God," before arriving in Rome on April 12, 1900 (*CL* 1179). Before becoming enraptured by the paganism of ancient Greece in the late 1870s, Wilde had seriously considered converting to Roman Catholicism, and his earliest surviving letters, while he was still an undergraduate, are peppered with references to Rome, where he had hoped to be received and blessed by the pope. In the summer of 1875, when traveling in Northern Italy with his Trinity College tutor John Pentland Mahaffy, the young Wilde had been forced through shortage of funds to abandon plans to visit the city, prompting him to memorialize his disappointment and to display his Catholic allegiances in the papistic poem "Rome Unvisited":

O Roma, Roma, at thy feet
   I lay this barren gift of song!
   For, ah! the way is steep and long
That leads unto thy sacred street.

. . . .

A pilgrim from the northern seas—
   What joy for me to seek alone
   The wondrous Temple, and the throne
Of Him who holds the awful keys!

When, bright with purple and with gold,
   Come priest and holy Cardinal,

And borne above the heads of all
The gentle Shepherd of the Fold.

O joy to see before I die
 The only God-anointed King,
 And hear the silver trumpets ring
A triumph as He passes by!

Or at the brazen-pillared shrine
 Holds high the mystic sacrifice,
 And shows his God to human eyes
Beneath the veil of bread and wine.[17]

In late March, 1877, Wilde had set forth once again in the hope of seeing St. Peter's. Mahaffy was to accompany him as far as Genoa, along with the young George Macmillan, who observed at the time that "being . . . just now rather fascinated by Roman Catholicism, [Wilde] is . . . on his way to Rome in order to see all the glories of the religion which seems to him the highest and the most sentimental."[18] But the Protestant Mahaffy, determined to prevent Wilde from converting to Catholicism, had managed to derail Wilde's plans once again and had persuaded the impressionable young Wilde to accompany him to Greece instead, saying "we cannot let you become a Catholic but we will make you a good pagan."[19] Although Wilde had passed briefly through Rome in 1877 on his return from Greece, even receiving a private audience with Pope Pius IX while there, Rome had henceforth ceased to exert the strong pull on his imagination that it had done previously.

When Wilde visited Rome in 1900, seven months before his death and twenty-three years after first visiting the city, he relished going to the Vatican repeatedly to be blessed by Pope Leo XIII—"I do nothing but see the Pope: I have been blessed many times," he wrote with amusement to More Adey—but this should not necessarily be understood to mean that he was once again dabbling with religious conversion (CL 1184).

"I am not a Catholic," he insisted to Adey, "I am simply a violent Papist" (*CL* 1184). The irony in Europe's most notorious sexual criminal being repeatedly blessed by the head of the Catholic Church was not lost on him, and it was with considerable relish that he described his presence among the pilgrims waiting for the pope's blessing on Easter Day: "To the terror of Grissell and all the Papal Court, I appeared in the front rank of the pilgrims in the Vatican, and got the blessing of the Holy Father—a blessing they would have denied me. . . . I was deeply impressed, and my walking-stick showed signs of budding—would have budded indeed, only at the door of the chapel it was taken from me by the Knave of Spades" (*CL* 1180).[20] Wilde loved the theater of the Papal Court: he called the pope "an artist as well as a saint," expressed delight that "each time he dresses differently," and wrote that "I have seen nothing like the extraordinary grace of his gesture, as he rose, from moment to moment, to bless—possibly the pilgrims, but certainly me." (*CL* 1180, 1186, 1180). But part of the pleasure came from knowing that his presence among the pilgrims produced a *frisson* in those who knew his true identity: excitedly telling Ross on April 22 that "I see the Holy Father again tomorrow . . . am thrilled with the prospect of an old pleasure, and I am promised a seat for the canonisation, or beatification, on the 24th," he wrote that he "would like to go. It would annoy the withered Grissell and fill me with holy joy" (*CL* 1183). When Grissell, the pope's chamberlain, whom Wilde had known long ago, subsequently wrote to Ross objecting to Wilde's presence, Wilde replied "he who seven times sought and seven times received the blessing of the Holy Father is not to be excommunicated on postcards by the withered eunuch of the Vatican Latrines" (*CL* 1191). "I cannot stand Christians," Wilde added, "because they are never Catholics, and I cannot stand Catholics because they are never Christians."

(*opposite*) Wilde at St. Peter's, Rome, April 1900, probably taken with his own camera.

Ross, a Catholic, says that while in Rome Wilde "wanted me . . . to introduce him to a priest with a view to being received into the Church, but I really did not think he was quite serious" (*CL* 1225). Ross had not seen Wilde in nearly a year, and he now noticed that a great change had come over Wilde's health, although he was in very good spirits. While in Rome, Wilde took up photography, using a recently acquired pocket camera and remarking at one point that "my photographs are now so good that in moments of mental depression (alas! not rare) I think that I was intended to be a photographer" (*CL* 1187). He admired Velasquez's portrait of Pope Innocent X in the Doria Palace ("the greatest portrait in the world") as well as a statue of a "beautiful voluptuous marble boy" at the Museo Nazionale (*CL* 1182). He also enjoyed the Borghese Gardens, where he took a photograph of cows "so marvellous that I destroyed it," and the Villa d'Este at Tivoli. But if he was a conventional tourist, Wilde was also a sex tourist (*CL* 1183). When Ross departed for London shortly after Wilde's arrival, he bequeathed Wilde "a legacy of a youthful guide, who knows nothing about Rome" as well as the companionship of a young man named Homer, who "talks much—a little too much—of you," he told Ross, and "slightly suspects you of treachery" (*CL* 1185, 1181). Within days Wilde had befriended a third young man, named Pietro Branca-d'Oro, telling Ross "he is dark, and gloomy, and I love him very much" (*CL* 1181). Other young men swiftly followed.[21] Recapitulating his Roman amours in a letter at this time, he tells Ross "in the mortal sphere I have fallen in and out of love, and fluttered hawks and doves alike. How evil it is to buy Love, and how evil to sell it! And yet what purple hours one can snatch from that grey slowly-moving thing we call Time! My mouth is twisted with kissing, and I feed on fevers" (*CL* 1187).

He returned to the French capital and to the Hôtel d'Alsace in May, after first spending ten days with Mellor at Gland, where he experienced riding in an automobile for the first time. Some of Wilde's friends have left detailed records of the seedy rooms at the Hôtel d'Alsace where

Wilde was to die six months later. Frank Harris says that "they were ordinary, mean little French rooms, furnished without taste . . . a preposterous bilious paper on the walls."[22] The furniture was ugly, plain, the bed covered with a hideous brown blanket, and there was not a creature comfort visible.[23] Wilde himself famously told his friend Claire de Pratz that he was fighting a duel to the death with the bilious wallpaper—chocolate-colored flowers on a blue background—and that "one of us has to go." (It was the wallpaper that won, quipped de Pratz, when recounting the incident years later: "It's the wall-paper that still lives, convulsed and curled up on itself owing to all the strychnine it has absorbed so as to avoid decaying completely.")[24] The bedroom was small and gloomy, but it opened onto a larger room where sunshine entered. "Behind a rickety table a maculated couch squatted like a toad," says Sherard, and on the table were littered papers as well as a bowl filled with cigarette ends and ash. Everything was disorderly: the personal neatness once so distinctive had now deserted Wilde. Clothes were scattered everywhere, and books were piled haphazardly on chairs or on the floor.[25] A bottle of Pernod absinthe stood on the washstand.

The writer Henri Mazel says that, after his return to Paris, Wilde "still enjoyed some happy days," especially at the *Exposition Universelle,* which ran from April 14 to November 12, 1900.[26] Wilde went to the *Exposition* two or three evenings a week and "amused himself like a big child."[27] Here he marveled at Charles Shannon's self-portrait, *A Man in a Black Shirt,* on display in the British fine art section, and he frequented the Egyptian pavilion, in whose café he was waited upon by "a slim brown Egyptian, rather like a handsome bamboo walking stick" (*CL* 1196). La Jeunesse says that Wilde loved the *Exposition,* that he "drank" it "in large measures, greedily, as one drinks blood on the battlefield," but that he "died of its passing, as he died of everything." In every pavilion of the *Exposition,* "he built again his own palace of fame, riches, and immortality."[28] He especially relished visiting Rodin's pavilion, in which was displayed a massive plastercast of Rodin's masterwork *The Gates of Hell.* One day, finding himself alone in the pavilion

Hôtel D'Alsace,
Paris, c. 1898.

with the sculptor, he received a personal tour from Rodin himself. Rodin "showed me anew all his great dreams in marble," he excitedly told Ross: "he is by far the greatest poet in France" (*CL* 1192).

Douglas was in the vicinity of Paris when Wilde returned to the city in May. He had arrived in February, together with his brother, both newly enriched from the death of their loathed father, the Marquess of Queensberry, who had left them large legacies upon his death at the end of January.[29] ("They are in deep mourning and the highest spirits," Wilde remarked with his customary wit [*CL* 1173].) But Douglas was busy establishing an expensive racing stable at Chantilly, the horse-racing center roughly fifty miles north of Paris. After acquiring the stable and ensconcing himself in the Hôtel Condé in Chantilly, Douglas lavished all his attention as well as his entire inheritance on horse racing and breeding. Sadly, Douglas now had far less time for Wilde than he once did.

In June the two men had a terrible falling out when, during a meal at the Café de la Paix and at Ross's urging, Wilde suggested that Douglas should settle a large sum of money on him. Douglas refused to recognize that Wilde had any financial claim upon him whatsoever and "went into paroxysms of rage . . . and said . . . that he would do nothing of the kind" (*CL* 1188). According to the younger man, Wilde insisted on his giving him as much as £2000 of his inheritance, notwithstanding that Douglas had given him more than £200 already that year, including £80 just moments before; and while Douglas was willing to continue helping his friend regularly within reason, and even believed that Wilde "would get far more than [£2,000] out of [him] in the long run," he recognized no duty or obligation to support Wilde permanently.[30] Whatever the precise facts of the case, Douglas certainly resented the demands that Wilde was making upon him, and by Harris's account, he felt that Wilde was now behaving "just like an old fat prostitute."[31] For his part, Wilde was disgusted and annoyed at Douglas's reaction. Frank Harris tried smoothing the waters between them, and within days Douglas had agreed, like Constance before him, to make some kind of regular, permanent financial provision, leading Wilde to remark that "the age of miracles is clearly not over" (*CL* 1189). Douglas was to give or send Wilde another £125 in checks alone before Wilde's death in November 1900, and he would also contribute £20 to the costs of Wilde's funeral. On top of what he had already given Wilde between February and May, this meant that Douglas had given Wilde over £325 in checks in 1900 alone by the time of Wilde's death, and it is likely that Douglas gave Wilde cash handouts from time to time as well.[32] In August they dined together for the final time, again at the Café de la Paix, when according to Douglas Wilde seemed "perfectly well and in the highest spirits," and "kept me delighted and amused."[33] But their argument over a permanent financial settlement was decisive, and they saw little of each other before Douglas's departure for London later that summer.

Within a day or two of Wilde's falling out with Douglas, says Harris, "the clouds lifted and the sun shone as brilliantly as ever."[34] Wilde quickly recovered his gaiety and good humor, and he was appreciative of Harris's hand in smoothing the waters between himself and Douglas. But within weeks Wilde was to fall out with Harris as well. Harris was obliged to leave Paris for London in June, but before he left, he made one last effort at motivating Wilde to write. As a result, Wilde agreed with him verbally to collaborate on the unwritten play that he first had spoken of at La Napoule. Wilde was to compose the first act, Harris the second and third, after which they were jointly to tackle the final and fourth act.[35] But Wilde hadn't mentioned to Harris that he had already sold the production rights to Sedger, Smithers, Brown-Potter and Rehan among others. In early September, after Harris had begun composing his share of the script and had spoken directly with Cora Brown-Potter, Wilde was forced to explain that "Mrs. Potter . . . holds the agreement for the play. I cannot . . . break with her" and that Kyrle Bellew also had a claim upon the play, having advanced Wilde money for the scenario in 1899 (*CL* 1195). Later that month, Harris returned to Paris with the play now finished. He had provisionally titled it *Her Second Chance,* and he was already making plans for its stage production in London, in October, with Mrs. Patrick Campbell in the leading role. (When staged in late October, the play would be newly titled *Mr. and Mrs. Daventry.*) But Wilde, who had contributed nothing to the script and claimed not to have seen a line of it previously, was furious.[36] On or around September 19, an altercation took place over dinner, after which Wilde realized that it was fruitless to pursue a genuine collaboration with Harris. So he now proposed instead that Harris should simply buy the plot and scenario outright, for £200 plus one quarter of all profits in the play, adding that he would personally pay off Bellew so that he had no claim upon Harris. On September 26, Wilde wrote Harris a formal memo acknowledging receipt of the sum of £175 and assigning Harris "full rights to deal with [the] said plot and scenario as you choose" (*CL* 1198).

But according to Wilde's later account, Harris had in fact given him only £25, explaining that he had left his checkbook in London and that the remainder of the £175 would be forthcoming within a week (*CL* 1200, 1203).[37] Shortly afterwards, Harris discovered that many others possessed rights in Wilde's scenario and that he was obliged to pay them all off before the play could be successfully produced. Viewing these obligations as Wilde's debts, he now decided to withhold the remainder. "Now you send me £25 instead of £175," Wilde angrily wrote Harris in mid-October: "you now calmly propose to hand over £125 of my money to Bellew. I don't, I can't, allow you to do that. . . . I insist on your carrying out your agreement with me" (*CL* 1200). It is a sad fact that the last five surviving letters that the great wit and aesthete ever wrote, dating from October 12 to November 21, 1900, nine days before his death from meningoencephalitis, are lengthy diatribes complaining of his treatment at the hands of Harris, who had long ago proven himself to be among the most generous and loyal of Wilde's friends. Quite irrationally and unreasonably, Wilde absolved himself of responsibility for the legal difficulties in which Harris now found himself. Indeed, Wilde's final written words seem to blame Harris for his own imminent death from illness: "I need not say how distressed I am that things should have turned out in this manner between us, but you must remember that the fault is in no sense mine. Had you kept your word to me, fulfilled the agreement and sent me the money that was due to me and for which I gave you a receipt which you still hold, all would have been well; and indeed I myself would have perfectly recovered two weeks ago, had it not been for the state of mental anxiety which your conduct kept me in all day long, with its accompanying sleeplessness at night, a sleeplessness over which none of the opiates the doctors dared to order me seemed to have any effect" (*CL* 1208).[38]

There can be no question that these final recriminatory letters to Harris were unfair. George Bernard Shaw perhaps goes too far in saying that Wilde ended his days "an unproductive drunkard and swindler."[39] But as Ross was to write shortly after Wilde's death, "Oscar, of course, had deceived Harris about the whole matter" (*CL* 1211).[40] Nonetheless, as Wilde became consumed with worry, anger, and increasing ill-health, his friends tried to reassure him that all would turn out for the best. He was in a much better position than formerly, Ross suggested in October, because Harris would pay off those individuals who had claims upon the play, and eventually Wilde would get more money from the play for himself. But Wilde only replied baldly that "Frank has deprived me of my only source of income by taking a play on which I could always have raised £100" (*CL* 1212). Three days before Wilde's death (in a letter that Wilde would never read) Ross repeated the attempt, saying "I hope with the new century Frank Harris is going to turn over at least a new cheque in your favour. . . . You must not get too depressed. Things are sure to come right, and remember violent letters, though justifiable in every way, are of no use in the present case."[41]

As Ross was well aware, Wilde's financial worries were exacerbated by ill-health and isolation. When the recently married William Rothenstein and his wife met Wilde by chance in the street, having previously decided not to let him know they were in Paris, "he knew we had meant to avoid him . . . [and] there was a stricken look in his eyes."[42] To Bernard Thornton, the Treasurer of New York's Grand Opera, who also met him accidentally around this time, he appeared "bent with a weight not of years," he had "an old man's obesity," his cheeks were flabby and sagging, his eyes dull, "his words came very slowly . . . his sentences were timorous, [and] he seemed grateful for the least consideration."[43] When his old friend the operatic soprano Nellie Melba met him by chance in the street, he appeared tall and shabby, with his collar turned up, and "a hunted look in his eyes."[44] She was about to pass by when Wilde identified himself, saying "I'm going to do a terrible thing. I'm going to ask you for money." Melba could hardly look at him for shame and pity, she says, and hastily gave him all she had in her purse—about ten louis—after which he muttered a word of thanks and departed.

The American journalist George Barr Baker saw him one day at the Deux Magots, sitting at a table by himself, waited upon by sullen waiters, under the "stony glare" of his fellow diners: his blue eyes seemed a trifle misty, declares Barr Baker, his fine shoulders seemed aged and bent, his mouth "twitched just a little, and the grey of age had spread over the usually pinkish cheeks."[45] Some months before Wilde's death, his old friend Anna de Brémont saw him in the Spanish café at the *Exposition Universelle:* his eyes were heavy, she says, he walked slowly, and his skin had a pallor that added to his look of ill-health. When she came across him again by chance the next morning, for the final time, he told her that he had "lived all there was to live" and rather than sorrowing for him, she should "watch and pray—it won't be long—watch and pray."[46]

Sickness and poverty compounded the loneliness and isolation. In yet another generous effort to fortify his friend, Harold Mellor invited Wilde to visit him in Gland once more. But when Wilde returned to Paris in August, he said that "the 'Mellor cure' was dull" and that the visit had given him "melancholia" (*CL* 1194, 1195). He briefly entertained a good-looking young Italian—possibly the "Sea-God" with whom he had first "fallen in love" when passing through Naples in April, and almost certainly the last of his many lovers—but by early September this "wanton sylvan boy of Italy" (*CL* 1196) had returned home, leaving Wilde sad at his loss (*CL* 1196).[47] Within days he was bedridden once again. "I am writing in bed," he told Harris on September 20, "in considerable pain," and this time the sickness was degenerative and fatal (*CL* 1198). Although there has been a great deal of confusion and misinformation surrounding Wilde's final illness, the physicians Ashley Robins and Sean Sellars have concluded that in early September 1900, Wilde suffered a fatal relapse of the middle-ear infection that had afflicted him so painfully in prison.[48] Wilde himself had stated in his unsuccessful petition of July 1896 to the home secretary that he suffered from an abscess in the ear, which prison doctors had refused or failed to recognize or to treat, and that his hearing had only gotten progressively worse in the first fourteen months of his imprisonment as a result. In August 1896, a local practitioner from Reading, brought in by Governor Nelson to examine Wilde independently of the prison doctor, had diagnosed a perforation of the tympanic membrane and had noted that the resulting discharge might be stemmed by daily syringing of the ear with diluted carbolic lotion. But while the local medic's remedy had proved effective in relieving the infection temporarily, the recurring discharge and infections were indicative of a deeper, underlying problem that possibly predated Wilde's imprisonment and that was never diagnosed by a medic in Wilde's lifetime: Wilde suffered from a *cholesteatoma,* a painful and potentially serious cyst in the middle ear, resulting from chronic suppurative otitis media, that was only correctible by surgery.[49]

———

Although Wilde's ear infection appears to have been in remission in the interval since Reading Prison, it had effectively progressed by the time it flared up fatally in September 1900. The disease now extended into the mastoid, and Wilde's attending physician quickly—and rightly—recognized that the situation was life-threatening. Left untreated, the infection might suddenly develop into something far worse. There is considerable irony in the fact that Wilde's own father, one of Victorian Britain's pre-eminent otologists and oculists, had written in his book *Practical Observations on Aural Surgery and the Nature and Treatment of Diseases of the Ear* that "so long as otorrhoea is present, we can never tell how, when or where it will end or what it may lead to."[50] As Robins and Sellars point out, this was a euphemistic way of stating that a discharging ear might be the harbinger of an early death. The only solution was a *mastoidectomy,* a radical operation to eradicate the underlying disease by exteriorizing the middle ear and the mastoid cavity. It was a destructive and dangerous procedure, which even if successful would result in permanent and complete hearing loss. But there was no alternative. As Wilde put it in the last recorded letter of his life, "the surgeon felt it his duty to inform me that unless I was operated on immediately it would be too late, and that the consequences of the delay would probably be fatal" (*CL* 1206).

On October 10, after his friends had raised the 1,500 francs necessary to meet the surgeon's fee, Wilde was operated on under chloroform in his hotel room. "The operation . . . was a most terrible one," he explained to Frank Harris, and the day afterward he telegraphed Ross twice, asking him to "please come" and saying that he was "terribly weak" (*CL* 1200, 1199). Subsequently he had both a hospital nurse and a doctor in constant attendance; after receiving Wilde's urgent telegrams, Ross arrived in mid-October and stayed for nearly a whole month.[51] The surgeon's fee, about £3,000 in today's currency, is a sign that the operation was major and extensive. The postoperative treatment was difficult, with open wounds, daily dressings, and cavity packing for weeks afterwards. Considerable pain required frequent administration of morphine injections, oral opium, and chloral.

When Wilde's sister-in-law passed through Paris about one month before his death, Wilde had reached a very low point. He was "dying above his means," he said; "he would never outlive the century. . . . [T]he English people would not stand him—he was responsible for the failure of the Exhibition, the English having gone away when they saw him there. . . . [A]ll the French people knew this, too, and would not stand him any more" (*CL* 1212). In fact there were signs of improvement in the days immediately following the surgery: when Ross arrived in mid-October, he found Wilde in surprisingly good spirits, and although Wilde assured him that his sufferings were dreadful, "he shouted with laughter and told many stories" (*CL* 1211).[52] On October 29 he got up for the first time in weeks, and he and Ross even ventured to a small café nearby, where Wilde insisted on drinking absinthe.[53] The next day, Wilde suffered great pain in his ear, but on October 31, he and Ross went for a drive in the Bois de Boulogne and Wilde appeared better, despite complaining of giddiness. Apart from some unsteadiness of gait (probably due to labyrinthine involvement from the middle-ear disease) he appeared relatively well and was able to venture out of his hotel. An unpaid invoice for toiletries, including eau de cologne and lotion in Wilde's possession at his death, suggests that he took pains over his appearance to the last.[54]

But at the beginning of November, Wilde told Ross that "he did not care if he had only a short time to live" and that he "had had a horrible dream [in which] he had been supping with the dead" (*CL* 1213). These dark sentiments were possibly inspired by Ross himself, who on All Soul's Day (November 2) had decided to pay his respects to the dead by visiting the famous Père Lachaise Cemetery, where Wilde himself would be re-interred nine years later. When Ross returned from the cemetery, Wilde asked him if he had chosen a spot for his tomb, and the two men "discussed epitaphs in a perfectly light-hearted way" (*CL* 1213). Shortly after this, Wilde suffered a fatal relapse, and from this point onward his condition went rapidly downhill. He now rarely slept, and he had taken so much morphine "that it has no more effect on me than water" (*CL* 1204). Chloral and opium were his only panaceas, he said, since the surgeon declined to allow any subcutaneous injections until the wounds had healed up. But the agony was so great that despite the surgeon's proscription, Wilde's hotelier Jean Dupoirier—who continued treating Wilde as an honored personal guest, notwithstanding Wilde's inability to pay his bills—administered up to eighty subcutaneous injections of morphine per day.[55] Two years later, the Pravaz syringe used by Dupoirier was on sale at Dupoirier's hotel, along with Wilde's gold-mounted dentures.[56]

On November 12, Wilde was forced to endure a final, painful, parting from Ross, the most loyal and affectionate of all his friends. After spending nearly a month attending to Wilde, Ross needed to return to his aging mother in the South of France. Like the devoted swallow in Wilde's story "The Happy Prince," who feels impelled to answer the call of his friends in the warm south in spite of the prince's entreaty to stay with him one night longer, Ross felt torn between his devotion to Wilde and his obligations to the world. He promised to write and assist in finding a solution to Wilde's impasse with Harris. Wilde tear-

refusing food and treatment. His head was now kept in ice, to reduce the inflammation, although Wilde was beyond realizing the danger he was now in. Once more Turner expressed his desperation to know what arrangements he needed to make in the event of Wilde's death.

On November 28, Turner wired Ross to come immediately, explaining that "I'm afraid it's all over with Oscar. He has been delirious for two or three days and gets worse . . . He talks nonsense the whole while in English and French . . . [and] is quite gone in the mind" (*CL* 1217). Turner recalled years later that "from time to time [Wilde] recited in delirium some piece of Greek or Latin or French, and I could not but notice that his French accent was marked by a sort of Irish brogue, never to be heard when he talked English."[58] According to Wilde's doctors, meningoencephalitis had now set in: the bacteria had spread to his brain, and nothing more could be done.[59] Ross arrived breathlessly on the twenty-ninth: Wilde's appearance was now "very painful," he writes, "he had become quite thin, the flesh was livid, [and] his breathing heavy" (*CL* 1219). The doctors informed Ross that his friend could live for two more days at most. Wilde now had difficulty speaking, says Ross, but he was conscious that people were in the room and raised his hand when Ross asked him whether he understood.

Ross says that he "had always promised to bring a priest to Oscar when he was dying" (*CL* 1220), and so believing the end was near he went in search of one. He returned some hours later on the twenty-ninth with Father Cuthbert Dunne of St. Joseph's Church in the Avenue Hoche. On entering Wilde's bedroom, Dunne administered the last rites of conditional Baptism and Extreme Unction to the dying man, while Ross himself articulated the necessary responses. Ross and Dunne had hoped that Wilde might be offered Holy Communion too, but Wilde was now in a semi-comatose condition, by Dunne's own admission, and he was unable to take the Eucharist wafer. Dunne later assured the Catholic Truth Society of Ireland that Wilde was "inwardly conscious" throughout these rites and that, although he could not utter actual words, he understood the priest when he told Wilde that he was being received into the Catholic Church (*CL* 1223). Reginald Turner, however, later wrote privately that "I was in the room with Ross when Father Cuthbert Dunne . . . 'received' Oscar, who was, I should have said, hardly conscious."[60] Ross himself later told Wilfrid Scawen Blunt that he had fetched Dunne for the sake of his own conscience and the promise he had made to Wilde, and that nobody could be entirely sure whether Wilde had been completely conscious.[61] Moreover Ross had feared that, in the absence of any formal obsequies, Wilde's corpse might be taken to the Paris Morgue, where it might lie unclaimed indefinitely as "Sebastian Melmoth," the name under which he was registered at the Hôtel d'Alsace. The performance of the Catholic death rites would help prevent such an outcome, he reasoned. As Ellmann aptly puts it, nobody can be sure whether the application of sacred oils to Wilde's hands and feet, just hours before his death, was truly "a ritualized pardon for his omissions and commissions," on the one hand, or "like putting a green carnation in his buttonhole" on the other.[62]

Following Dunne's departure, Ross telegraphed everybody he could think of—Frank Harris, the solicitor Holman (who was in contact with Adrian Hope, the legal guardian of Wilde's children), and Alfred Douglas—telling them that Wilde would live only for a day or two longer at most. That night he and Turner slept upstairs, in a separate room of the hotel, where they were awakened twice by Wilde's nurse, who thought that Wilde was on the point of dying. In fact Wilde lingered on painfully until the next afternoon. Ross himself has left a moving, detailed account of the day on which Wilde died, November 30, 1900:

> About 5.30 in the morning, a complete change came over him, the lines of the face altered, and I believe what is called the death rattle began but I had never heard anything like it before; it sounded like the horrible turning of a crank, and it never ceased until the end. His eyes did not respond to the light test any longer. Foam and blood came

from his mouth, and had to be wiped away by someone standing by him all the time. At 12 o'clock I went out to get some food, Reggie mounting guard. He went out at 12.30. From 1 o'clock we did not leave the room; the painful noise from the throat became louder and louder. Reggie and myself destroyed letters to keep ourselves from breaking down. The two nurses were out, and the proprietor of the hotel had come up to take their place; at 1.45 the time of his breathing had altered. I went to the bedside and held his hand, his pulse began to flutter. He heaved a deep sigh, the only natural one I had heard since I arrived, the limbs seemed to stretch involuntarily, the breathing came fainter; he passed at 10 minutes to 2 P.M. exactly. (*CL* 1220)[63]

Just six weeks had passed since Wilde's forty-sixth birthday. The great Irish playwright, novelist, and poet was dead. After washing the body and removing the "appalling débris," which had to be burnt, Ross and Turner, accompanied by Dupoirier, the hotel proprietor, went about the task of formally certifying Wilde's death and making funerary arrangements. With Dunne's assistance, they enlisted two nuns to watch over Wilde's body at night, but it was not till the following day that they succeeded in fetching the district doctor, as required by law, to make out a death certificate.[64] At first the doctor was suspicious and asked if Wilde had committed suicide or been murdered. Moreover Dupoirier was reluctant to admit that his guest had been residing under an assumed name (a criminal misdemeanor), giving rise to the possibility that Wilde's name at death would be certified as "Sebastian Melmoth." But after being plied with drinks, jokes, and a generous fee, the doctor eventually consented to sign the permission for Wilde's burial under his real name. In the meantime, Dupoirier and one of the nuns washed and laid out Wilde's body: Dupoirier clothed Wilde's corpse in "his nice maroon suit," caring for his dead tenant as if he were one of

Wilde laid out on his deathbed, December 1, 1900, probably taken with his own camera.

his own family.[65] After the doctor's departure, news of Wilde's death started to spread, with the result that various poets and literary people called to pay their respects, along with a few English people, under assumed names, and two mysterious veiled women. Among the known visitors on December 1 were Raymond de La Tailhède, Eugène Tardieu, Charles Sibleigh, Jehan Rictus, Robert d'Humières, George Sinclair, Ernest La Jeunesse, Leonard Sarluis, Carlos Blacker, Henry Davray, and (possibly) André Gide.[66] Ross says that, now that he was properly laid out, "Oscar looked calm and dignified, just as he did when he came out of prison," and "there was nothing at all horrible about the body after it had been washed. Around his neck was a blessed rosary . . . and on the breast a Franciscan medal given me by one of the nuns, a few flowers placed there by myself and an anonymous friend who had brought some on behalf of the children. . . . Of course there was the usual crucifix, candles and holy water" (*CL* 1221). At 8:30 in the evening of

December 1, after Maurice Gilbert had at Ross's request taken a photograph of Wilde lying on his deathbed, the coffin was sealed.

————

The funeral took place on Monday, December 3, a typical winter day in Paris—gray, chilly, and damp. Wilde's two children were not among the mourners.[67] Cyril and Vyvyan had been led to believe by their guardians that their father had died years before—and they were informed of neither his death nor his funeral. A distraught Lord Alfred Douglas, who had arrived from Scotland (where he had been shooting) the day before, was the chief mourner.[68] A small cortege consisting of Douglas, Ross, Turner, Maurice Gilbert, Dupoirier, and one or two others who had attended Wilde in his final hours accompanied the hearse on foot from the Hôtel d'Alsace to the nearby church of St. Germain de Prés, where a requiem mass was held in a small chapel behind the high altar. The hearse was shaky and plain, with shabby metal ornaments, and the coffin covered with a simple pall.[69] There were twenty-four wreaths— one of them a cheap garland of beads from the loyal Dupoirier, inscribed simply "*A mon locataire*" (to my tenant)—including wreaths from Douglas, Adey, Turner, Max Beerbohm, Adela Schuster, Arthur Clifton, the *Mercure de France,* Harold Mellor, Wilde's sister-in-law Lily, Maurice Gilbert, and Maurice Tucker, the physician who had attended Wilde in his final illness. At the head of Wilde's coffin, Ross placed a wreath of laurels inscribed "A tribute to his literary achievements and distinction," to which Ross attached the names of eighteen individuals, including Alfred Douglas, Frank Harris, Harold Mellor, and Carlos Blacker, who had shown kindness to Wilde during or after his imprisonment (*CL* 1222).

Ross had been anxious to keep the funeral quiet, and no bell tolled as Wilde's body was admitted by a side door of the church. The journalist Miriam Aldrich, who had once known Wilde and was present, says that the chapel was practically empty, with just a few men scattered about, and no women except for herself and two female friends she had asked to accompany her.[70] Along with the principal mourners, a small number of Parisian literary and artistic figures attended the funeral, including Paul Fort, Armand Point, Jean de Mitty, Charles Lucas, Marcel Bataillant, Charles Sibleigh, Marius Boisson, Ernest La Jeunesse, Michel Tavera, Henry Davray, Frederic Boutet, Leonard Sarluis, Henri Davenay, Raymond de La Tailhede, and Pierre Louÿs. Stuart Merrill, who was bed-bound with flu, was represented by his wife. A low mass was said, part of the burial office being read by Father Cuthbert Dunne: "it was a brief, sad, depressing low mass," says Aldrich, "cold and formal, especially so as . . . no one seemed to have any part in the service, and there was no solemnity about it."[71]

After the requiem mass, a small procession consisting of three carriages and a few mourners on foot accompanied the hearse on its journey to Wilde's grave in the paupers' cemetery at Bagneux, an hour and half's drive away in the south of Paris, outside the city limits.[72] In the first carriage were Father Dunne and his acolyte, in the second Douglas, Ross, Turner, and Dupoirier, while the third contained Madame Stuart Merrill, Paul Fort, Henry Davray, and Leonard Sarluis. According to Ross, "a cab containing strangers unknown to me" followed behind, and according to Miriam Aldrich, who left a moving unpublished account of her own journey to the cemetery on foot, Ernest La Jeunesse and two other men whom she did not know also followed on foot (*CL* 1222).[73] *Le Journal* reported that hardly a dozen friends accompanied Wilde's coffin on its journey and that at a turn in the road, the few poets among them vanished into thin air like a flight of crows.[74] The early Wilde scholar and children's author Arthur Ransome wrote (almost certainly upon the authority of his friend Robert Ross) that of those who filled the coaches, "several went about their business before reaching the cemetery," while Paul Fort confirms that of thirteen individuals who set out for the cemetery, only six or so arrived.[75]

Ross had leased the grave under his own name, in the knowledge that Wilde's remains might need to be housed permanently elsewhere at some later date.[76] Miriam Aldrich, who arrived at the graveside after Wilde had been buried and the mourners had departed, later heard that after "an unpleasant hysterical scene," the few mourners present at the burial were feint with hunger and quickly adjourned to a nearby restaurant.[77] Aldrich was not told who had caused the "scene," although Richard Ellmann speculates that it was Douglas, "perhaps jockeying for the role of principal mourner."[78] Years later, Paul Fort confirmed that Douglas had made a "ridiculous scene," screaming "Oscar! Oscar!" before throwing himself into the open grave, and that Douglas, besmeared with dirt, had had to be forcibly removed from the grave.[79]

For nine years, a simple stone with an iron railing around it marked Wilde's gravesite. On the stone was inscribed the following:

OSCAR WILDE
Oct 16th 1854–Nov 30th 1900
Verbis meis addere nihil audebant
et super illos stillebat eloquium meum.[80]
Job xxix, 22.
R.I.P.

In 1909 Wilde's remains were removed to their present location, in Paris's Père Lachaise Cemetery. Lord Alfred Douglas was not present on this occasion: seven years earlier, he had renounced his homosexuality and attempted to recreate himself as a conventional *pater familias*— Douglas had married and fathered a child in 1902, although the marriage dissolved in 1913—and within a few years, Douglas was to turn violently upon Wilde's memory and influence. It fell instead to Wilde's loyal friend and former lover Robert Ross to take charge of the disinterment. He had ordered a sumptuous coffin to be made specially for the occasion. However, owing to petty regulations, the coffin could not be used and was replaced instead by a locally made coffin of plain oak, with a silver plate on the lid on which was engraved "OSCARD WILDE 1854–1900," with "Oscar" misspelled.[81] The disinterment turned out to be at once remedial and distressingly grisly. The grave at Bagneux had always been a temporary concession, and when Wilde's corpse was being prepared for burial in 1900, doctors had advised Ross to put Wilde's body, like that of Charles Wooldridge, the executed guardsman in *The Ballad of Reading Gaol,* in quicklime. They had said that this would consume the flesh, leaving intact the bones, which could then be moved easily. But when Wilde's corpse was disinterred in 1909, with Wilde's youngest son Vyvyan now standing alongside, the onlookers found to their horror that the quicklime had preserved Wilde's flesh instead of destroying it. Wilde's face was distinctly recognizable, except that now his hair and beard appeared to have grown long after death.[82] Ross immediately asked Vyvyan Holland to step aside and, as the sextons were about to use their shovels, he ordered them to desist. Instead Ross himself, perhaps remembering Douglas's leap into the grave nine years earlier, climbed into the grave and carefully lifted out Wilde's body with his own hands, placing it lovingly in the new coffin.[83] It was an action at once touching, theatrical, and extremely literary. Like Shakespeare's Hamlet, who was not to be outdone by Laertes in his love for Ophelia, Ross would not be outdone by his own rival.

Five years later, the famous monument by Jacob Epstein was unveiled over Wilde's new and permanent grave, and in 1950, thirty-two years after his own death (and five years after the death of Douglas), the ashes of Robert Ross were placed in Wilde's tomb in accordance with Ross's will, in a small compartment that had been specially built into the monument at Ross's request. On the monument—which in 1995 was declared a French Historic Monument—are inscribed the following lines from the *Ballad of Reading Gaol:*

And alien tears will fill for him
 Pity's long-broken urn,
For his mourners will be outcast men,
 And outcasts always mourn.

Paris Metro also opened while the fair was underway, allowing visitors to traverse the city by underground trains, and then to emerge aboveground through the now-iconic *art nouveau* Metro entranceways to each of the eight stations that dotted the *Exposition* site. Electric walkways and escalators—historic antecedents of the moving walkways found today in airports and shopping malls—shepherded crowds over vast distances aboveground, revealing unexpected vistas as they went.

But it was the exhibition pavilions that constituted the heart of the fair. Designed by the exhibitor nations so as to reflect their own unique style, these housed the latest art, technologies, and consumer wares from around the globe. Among the exhibits on display were diesel engines, automobiles, bicycles, talking films, an early aeroplane, escalators, X-ray photographs, and the "telegraphone" (the first magnetic audio recorder). Along with Rodin, the progenitor of modern sculpture, the exhibitors included Thomas Edison and the Lumière Brothers, the pioneers of modern film (and in Edison's case, sound recording). In one pavilion, a *cinéorama* took visitors on an imaginary voyage in a balloon, while in another, called *le globe céleste,* visitors enjoyed a ride into outer space, seated in an easy chair, with the help of a rolling canvas.

The construction and appearance of the pavilions were as notable as their contents: designers spared no pains in creating elaborate architectural fantasies or in simulating far-flung geographic regions or historical periods. An ornate *Palais de l'Electricité* was constructed in the Champs de Mars, just in front of the *Galérie des Machines,* where visitors could marvel at the massive dynamos silently pumping electric life into the whole fair through a complicated network of wires and junction boxes. At night the Palace's façade was illuminated by thousands of multicolored lights, surmounted by a chariot drawn by hippogriffs and driven by the Spirit of Electricity, from which projected showers of multicolored flames. At the *Château d'Eau,* streams of water, powered by electricity, gushed down from hidden grottos. On the final night of the fair, every pavilion was flooded with electric light, while the entrance gate, arcades, and illuminated fountains drew all the electrical power

"Moving sidewalk panorama" of the *Exposition Universelle,* 1900, Paris.

they could tap, and the speed of changing colored lights increased. As one visitor remarked, the *Exposition* represented "a new and ephemeral city hidden in the center of the other, a whole quarter of Paris in fancy dress, a ball, where the buildings were the masqueraders. . . . It was a marvel, a coloured picture-book, a cave filled by strangers with treasure."[2]

For the American writer Henry Adams, the *Exposition* represented a historical revolution of the order of those brought about centuries earlier by Copernicus, Galileo, and Columbus: staring dumbfounded at the massive electrical dynamos on display in the Palace of Electricity, he felt that his "historical neck" had been "broken by the sudden irruption of forces totally new."[3] It was not simply technological and scientific exhibits that exemplified radical change. The seething crowds, the flash of electric light, and the near-silent surge of the electric walkways and dynamos embodied a new kind of physiology or felt experience. The fair encapsulated "an eruptive nonrational world" characterized by mobility, indeterminacy, and an unconscious fluidity.[4] This new sensibility was also reflected in much of the art on display. The sculpture of Rodin, which occupied a pavilion to itself, embodied a new understanding of humanity based on the primacy of the individual mind, including its most irrational components. Rodin's has been called a "psychiatric vision," emphasizing turmoil, pressure, and psychological turbulence—disturbing elements of industrial modernity that Rodin realized were unavoidable constituents of artistic creation, dreams, and modern thought too.[5] The fair was "the triumph of *art nouveau,*" it has been said, for it represented the greatest single expression to date of a new interiorized psychology in art, vividly displayed also in the American, German, Austrian, and Hungarian pavilions.[6] The most spectacular embodiment of *art nouveau,* however, was the private pavilion of the French dealer Siegfried Bing, who has been called "the impresario of the Art Nouveau movement."[7] Constructed as a model home consisting of six richly decorated and furnished rooms, Bing's pavilion was the culmination of new strains in the decorative arts that he had been nurturing at his architect-designed shop, the Maison de l'Art Nouveau, in the Rue de Provence, since 1895. Thanks in no small part to Bing's efforts, *art nouveau* embodied modernity of both form and meaning, and the *Exposition* was its apotheosis.

Wilde was a frequent and enthusiastic visitor to the *Exposition,* as we have seen. It is apt to imagine him at home in the setting of the *Exposition* in the final days of his life, for Wilde too was an artist of the *nouveau,* the harbinger of new attitudes that would eventually come to replace the repressive Victorian laws and morality surrounding matters of sex and gender. In the days when he could afford expensive clothing, rich buttonholes, and immaculate coiffure, he had sought to embody in his person a new kind of masculinity and what he called "the absolute modernity of Beauty."[8] In *The Picture of Dorian Gray,* he had written of the "harsh uncomely Puritanism that is having in our own day its curious revival."[9] His writings after the commencement of his affair with Ross in 1886 are, in one sense, an extended critique and dismantling of that "uncomely Puritanism." Along with the death of Queen Victoria herself, less than two months after Wilde's own, his demise marked the end of a Victorianism with which he had always been at odds.

At least a few of his supporters felt at the time that his death presaged a more liberal era. Vincent O'Sullivan, for instance, commented that "Wilde endured too much cruelty in the Paris of his time," while Stuart Merrill observed that Wilde died "a victim of . . . moralists" and of the "prudishness of public opinion."[10] As Wilde himself had remarked to the homosexual activist and pioneer George Ives in 1898, "I have no doubt we shall win, but the road is long, and red with monstrous martyrdoms. Nothing but the repeal of the Criminal Law Amendment Act would do." The day after Wilde's death, Ives recorded in shock in his diary that "Oscar Wilde, victim and martyr, died yesterday in Paris."[11] But O'Sullivan, Merrill, and Ives were in a small minority, and their reactions to Wilde's death are as notable for their viewing their friend as a victim as they are for suggesting that Wilde might someday be viewed in a more generous light. Just how sharply Wilde lived and died at odds with an age that refused to recognize the personal freedoms on which he insisted is clear in the wider reaction to his death. If, upon leaving prison, he had "begun a decent life, people would have forgiven him," the writer Wilfrid Scawen Blunt, his one-time friend, privately remarked, "but he returned to Paris and to his dog's vomit and this is the end."[12] "Oscar Wilde died as he should have died, in foul obscurity," observed the *North American* in one of many brief and unsympathetic press notices that appeared in the wake of Wilde's death: "That he should have been able to outlive exposure proves how utterly the manhood had been rotted out of him."[13]

While such brutal condemnation of Wilde thankfully no longer persists, the idea that in exile he was a tragic victim or martyr, with its accompanying suggestion that his death was a merciful release from suffering, lives on in modern scholarship and biography. Richard Ellmann, Wilde's pre-eminent biographer, says bluntly that the hardships of prison and exile "left Wilde a broken man" and that, during his final three-and-a-half years, Wilde lived like "a scapegoat . . . as conspicuous in defeat as in triumph."[14] The psychoanalytic critic Melissa Knox says, similarly, that these were years of "mental, physical, and economic decline."[15] Typically, whole-life biographies of Wilde describe a downward trajectory, from "success" or "exaltations" in the 1880s and early 1890s to "decline" in the post-prison period that Ellmann calls "the leftover years."[16] One recent biographer, determined to rescue Wilde from this narrative of decline, says unequivocally that Wilde was "a martyr in an epic struggle for the freedom of men to love men," while another writes that "death came as a release," without honor and dignity, and that Wilde's pitiful end "damaged" the place in history owed to his eminent oculist-otologist father.[17] Moments of grace "were rare, and brief," says Ellmann; Wilde's final decline was even more mental than physical, and his love for Douglas (and presumably for other young men too) was an example of "berserk passion." In this reading, which is heavily influenced by the distortions of *De Profundis,* Wilde was the victim of Douglas as much as of his own century: apart from his beauty, Douglas was notable only for "his greed, rage, and cruelty," says Ellmann, and it was Wilde's tragic misfortune to have allowed himself to be caught in Douglas's net.[18]

———

Certainly the final year of Wilde's life saw him brought low by terminal illness, need, and an inability to produce new literary work. Moreover, on occasion Wilde saw and indeed portrayed himself as a martyr to

Victorian sexual morality, as his remark to Ives about the need for "monstrous martyrdoms" and his embrace of the name *Sebastian* make clear. But decline and martyrdom distort the truth of these final years. Wilde was not a martyr to Victorian morality: he was its enemy, and he was hardly the passive victim of his contemporaries' prejudices, as these pages have tried to show. According to Lord Alfred Douglas, Wilde retained in his last years "an extraordinarily buoyant and happy temperament, a splendid sense of humour, and an unrivalled faculty for enjoyment of the moment."[19] Douglas has frequently been disparaged because of the self-aggrandizing strains to the numerous accounts of Wilde he published in the decades before his death in 1945, but he knew and loved Wilde more intimately than any other individual in the period with which we are concerned, and there is more than a hint of truth to his observations about Wilde's undiminished capacity for enjoyment. "Pleasure is the only thing one should live for," Wilde had written in 1894, and in a late revision Wilde made to *The Importance of Being Earnest* in Paris in 1898, as he was preparing the play for publication, the pleasure-loving Algernon Moncrieff tells us that his "duty as a gentleman has never interfered with [his] pleasures in the smallest degree."[20] Similarly, until laid waste by illness just months before his death, Wilde dedicated himself wholeheartedly to what in *The Picture of Dorian Gray* he called a "new Hedonism," or a refusal to "sacrifice any mode of passionate experience," with a single-mindedness and conviction that still astonish us today.[21] He was in his last years unapologetic about his love for other men; his amours were always conducted with joy, affection, and good humor; and he clearly inspired the devotion of young lovers such as Maurice Gilbert. In some respects he enjoyed a sexual freedom in exile that he had not experienced before prison, as we can infer from his remark to Ross, while in Rome, that his mouth was "twisted with kissing" and that he had "fluttered hawks and doves alike." In his life no less than in his art—and he was a great artist—he was a subversive. Until a year before his death, when sickness began to set in, he lived an uninhibited life as a homosexual, expressed desire to lengthen his stay at Aix-Les-Bains with his mother the following month, and in the urgency with which Wilde asked Douglas to "come to Naples"—that Wilde was more the pursuer than the pursued. The freedom to love whom one chooses, in the face of entrenched opposition, is the great theme of Wilde's writings, from his early poem "Charmides," through his short stories "The Birthday of the Infanta," "The Fisherman and His Soul," and "The Portrait of Mr. W. H.," to the great works of the early 1890s—*The Picture of Dorian Gray, Salomé, The Importance of Being Earnest*—on which his literary reputation largely rests today. "Love is better than wisdom, and more precious than riches," declares the besotted fisherman in "The Fisherman and His Soul."[24] "The mystery of Love is greater than the mystery of Death," proclaims the tragic heroine of *Salomé,* just before her execution by Herod's officers.[25] "My soul clings to your soul, my life is your life," Wilde had written to Douglas in the days just before his imprisonment (*CL* 652). If the letters and poems that Wilde and Douglas exchanged weren't already proof of it, nothing speaks louder of Wilde's continued love for Douglas, and of Douglas's for Wilde, than their attempt at a settled life together in Naples, before the actions of their families and the press undermined it.

———

We should not forget that Wilde's and Douglas's writings featured prominently in the scandalous trials in 1895 that forever altered Wilde's life and career. Perhaps the most indelible moment occurred during the first criminal trial, when prosecutor Charles Gill, after attempting to use Wilde's own love letters to Douglas as evidence against him, turned to Douglas's poem "The Two Loves" as further evidence of Wilde's gross indecency. Gill asked the defendant to explain "the Love that dare not speak its name." Wilde's reply was as follows:

> "The Love that dare not speak its name" in this century is such a great affection of an elder for a younger man as there was between David and Jonathan, such as Plato made

the very basis of his philosophy, and such as you find in the sonnets of Michelangelo and Shakespeare. It is that deep, spiritual affection that is as pure as it is perfect. It dictates and pervades great works of art like those of Shakespeare and Michelangelo, and those two letters of mine, such as they are. It is in this century misunderstood, so much misunderstood that it may be described as the "Love that dare not speak its name," and on account of it I am placed where I am now. It is beautiful, it is fine, it is the noblest form of affection. There is nothing unnatural about it. It is intellectual, and it repeatedly exists between an elder and a younger man, when the elder man has intellect, and the younger man has all the joy, hope and glamour of life before him. That it should be so the world does not understand. The world mocks at it and sometimes puts one in the pillory for it.[26]

The speech drew loud applause from those in the courtroom. Appealing to an ancient Platonic idea of love, Wilde had briefly succeeded in counteracting an older notion of male homosexuality as "sodomy," grounded in proscribed sex acts that had no essential connection to personality, with a powerful new conception of male same-sex love based on personal identity, mind, sensibility, and emotion, as well as intellectual and social relationships. While he hadn't *named* the modern concept of homosexuality, at a stroke he had brought into the public sphere, as the scholar Linda Dowling has argued, "a modern discourse of male love . . . a new language of moral legitimacy pointing forward to Anglo-American decriminalization and, ultimately, a fully developed assertion of homosexual rights."[27]

He was beginning to think of his erotic relations with other men as a matter of personal identity, not just of sexual preference. It was a process that was consolidated in the wake of his release from prison and his reconciliation with Douglas, as we can see in his defense of the nobility of Uranian love. In Wilde's unabashed self-descriptions as a lover of "boys" in his final years, we can perhaps see the emergence of homosexuality itself in its modern sense. But even in 1895, Wilde's courtroom speech in defense of "the love that dare not speak its name" was not an aberration. He had in fact made precisely the same defense of male same-sex love on being turned down for membership at the Crabbet Club four years earlier.[28] Wilde's "unspeakable" love stood at the center of his life and work, and something of the spirit Wilde showed in its defense is palpable too in his letters to the *Daily Chronicle*, in defense of Warder Martin and prison reform, in his reactions to the calls for prudence that issued from the mouths of Ross, Merrill, and Gide, and in the "propaganda" that he insisted on "making" in the final Cantos of *The Ballad of Reading Gaol*, where he writes that "every Law / That men hath made for Man, / Since first Man took his brother's life, / And the sad world began, / But straws the wheat and saves the chaff / With a most evil fan."

When meeting Wilde in the straitened circumstances of exile on an autumn afternoon in 1899, the writer and illustrator Laurence Housman was greatly struck by Wilde's dignity, "the quiet, uncomplaining courage with which he accepted an ostracism against which, in his lifetime, there could be no appeal. To a man of his habits and temperament—conscious that the incentive to produce was gone with the popular applause which had been its recurrent stimulus—the outlook was utterly dark: life had already become a tomb." Yet Wilde's conversation on the occasion was as sparkling as ever, his "smooth-flowing utterance, sedate and self-possessed, oracular in tone, whimsical in substance, carried on without halt, or hesitation, or change of word."[29] The delights of conversation had always stood at the center of Wilde's fiction, plays, and essays, and many of his friends later said that his works are but a distant echo of his speech. He had once written that "every civilized man and woman ought to feel it is their duty to say something, even when there is hardly anything to be said."[30] The remark might almost be a motto for Wilde's final years. Residing in the

Hôtel d'Alsace, he had been for some time "fighting a duel to the death with his wallpaper," he told Claire De Pratz. "The Cloister or the Café—there is my future," he told Robert Ross shortly before his death. If Wilde lost the art of writing plays in his final years, he nonetheless used the cafés and bars of Paris to perfect what he'd once called "the delightful art of brilliant chatter."[31] "He retained to the last his inimitable supremacy as a talker," recalled Lord Alfred Douglas a few years before the end of his own turbulent life: "I retain glowing memories of dinners at cafés and subsequent amazing 'talks,' when he held his audience spellbound as he discoursed in his exquisite voice of all things in heaven and earth, now making his hearers rock with laughter and now bringing tears into their eyes."[32] The fruits of his verbal artistry in this period were more evanescent than printed poems, stories, and staged plays, but they are traceable today in the memoirs of Wilde's friends and above all in Wilde's surviving correspondence, where the distinctive patterns and cadences of Wilde's mind and speech are still palpable.

"Though we may regret that he did not follow the ideals he set before himself in prison," wrote Robert Ross piously in the wake of Wilde's death, "it is some consolation to think that the world even in its less noble manifestations was still full of pleasant places and pleasant moments for him."[33] Like Douglas when speaking of Wilde's "extraordinarily buoyant and happy temperament," Ross attests to Wilde's undaunted spirit. If he was ostracized by the self-important and the narrow-minded, or at a loss when obliged to live peripatetically as an accidental tourist on the Riviera and in Switzerland in the first half of 1899, Wilde was at home among the bohemians of the Latin Quarter and the denizens of the Calisaya Bar, many of whom—La Jeunesse, Renaud, Machado, Gomez-Carrillo—have left us eloquent records of his impromptu stories, eloquence, wit, and laughter. "Laughter is the primaeval attitude towards life," Wilde had told Turner in 1898. Until his swift and fatal decline in 1900, the keynote of Wilde's exile was indeed laughter, which still ripples through his correspondence and echoes long after we have closed its pages. "One should either be a work of art," he had once written, "or wear a work of art."[34] He could no longer afford fine clothing and personal accoutrements in his final years.[35] But Wilde nonetheless carried himself with a threadbare majesty, and if he had little opportunity for wearing works of art, he had perfected the art of living, realizing a deeper version of the "aesthetic" life about which he had proselytized in his early lectures and essays and which he had wittily incarnated in his plays and epigrams. Imprisonment and exile, paradoxically, had liberated him to pursue an uninhibited life, and the pleasure he received in consequence could be enjoyed more fully, as a total experience of heart, mind, soul, and body, with conversation as its medium and laughter its index. "They have greatly oppressed me," says Israel in the tenth "Song of Ascents," "but they have not gained the victory over me." Similarly, Wilde had been cut free from the cords of the self-righteous and the wicked. In exile he published his most moving and popular poem, *The Ballad of Reading Gaol,* while refining his plays *The Importance of Being Earnest* and *An Ideal Husband* much as a jeweler cuts and polishes a fine diamond, so that it reflects and refracts light all the more brightly. But Wilde's greatest achievement in exile was himself. Ambling along the boulevard or seated on some café terrace, he pursued his own course with bemusement, irony, and self-conviction, unbowed and impervious to the harsh judgments of smaller natures. He continues to cast his laughter and light on our world nearly 120 years after his death.

Notes

Prologue

1. On May 25, 1895, Wilde was found guilty at London's Central Criminal Court, or "Old Bailey," on seven counts of gross indecency with another man. See H. Montgomery Hyde, *The Trials of Oscar Wilde* (1962; repr. Mineola, NY: Dover Publications, 1973), 269–70; also Joseph Bristow's forthcoming critical transcript and history of Wilde's criminal trials, *Oscar Wilde On Trial: The Criminal Proceedings* (Yale University Press, forthcoming). Wilde's sentence, two years in prison with hard labor, was the maximum permissible by law and among the harshest to date for a conviction of gross indecency. By contrast, the two male prostitutes convicted of gross indecency in the Cleveland Street Scandal of 1889 received sentences of four and nine months.

2. *Complete Letters of Oscar Wilde,* ed. Merlin Holland and Rupert Hart-Davis (New York: Henry Holt, 2000), 815, hereafter cited in text and in notes as *CL.*

3. Quoted in *CL* 836.

4. More Adey to Adele Schuster, 12 March 1898, The William Andrews Clark Memorial Library, University of California, Los Angeles.

5. Headlam, unfinished memoir, quoted in F. G. Bettany, *Stewart Headlam: An Autobiography* (London, 1926), 131–32.

6. Robert Ross, unpublished letter to Lord Alfred Douglas, 23 June 1897 (typed copy), The William Andrews Clark Memorial Library, University of California, Los Angeles.

7. Robert Ross stated on numerous occasions that Adey contributed financially to Wilde's defense, but he gave differing amounts: in a letter to Frank Harris dated September 6, 1913 (Frank Harris Collection, 4.9, Harry Ransom Center, University of Texas at Austin), he writes that Adey, although a poor man at the time, gave Wilde £400 shortly after his arrest in order to help defray the costs of his defense. In a later letter to Frank Harris (11 July 1914, Frank Harris Collection, 4.9, Harry Ransom Center, University of Texas at Austin), he says the amount given was £300, while in a much earlier letter to Alfred Douglas (23 June 1897, [typed copy], The William Andrews Clark

Memorial Library, University of California, Los Angeles), he says that it was merely £200.

8. Ross, unpublished letter to Lord Alfred Douglas, 23 June 1897 (typed copy), The William Andrews Clark Memorial Library, University of California, Los Angeles.

9. Wilde, "Lord Arthur Savile's Crime," in *Complete Shorter Fiction,* ed. Isobel Murray (New York: Oxford World's Classics, 1979), 30.

10. Wilde, *The Picture of Dorian Gray: An Annotated Uncensored Edition,* ed. Nicholas Frankel (Cambridge, MA: Harvard University Press, 2011), 146.

11. Headlam, unfinished memoir, quoted in Bettany, *Stewart Headlam,* 132.

12. Wilde, "Lord Arthur Savile's Crime," 30–31. See also Mrs. Cheveley's blackmailing threat, in *An Ideal Husband,* to reveal publicly Sir Robert Chiltern's character as a swindler, thereby exposing him to "the foulness of the public placard" (p. 31 above).

13. Baudelaire, "Further Notes on Edgar Poe," in *"The Painter of Modern Life" and Other Essays,* ed. and trans. J. Mayne, 2nd ed. (London: Phaidon, 1995), 99. Baudelaire is describing the figure of the dandy generically, not Wilde specifically.

14. Scholars disagree about when Wilde's intimacy with Douglas began, and Wilde's and Douglas's own recorded statements on the question can be contradictory. Biographer Richard Ellmann dates their first meeting to June 1891, and in July 1891, at their second meeting, Wilde inscribed to Douglas a deluxe "large-paper" copy of *The Picture of Dorian Gray.* But most scholars agree that the two men weren't sexually intimate immediately. In a letter to More Adey of April 7, 1897, Wilde himself says that "the friendship began in May 1892" (*CL* 795), which is consistent with Douglas's remark that "familiarities" between them began "about nine months after I first met Oscar"; see *The Autobiography of Alfred Douglas* (London: Secker 1929), 75.

15. Refused bail before his first criminal trial, Wilde was finally granted bail six days after the first criminal trial ended in a hung jury, roughly two weeks before the second, decisive criminal trial began on May 20, 1895. Upon being released on bail, Wilde found that every hotel had closed its doors to him.

16. Ian Small and Josephine Guy, *Oscar Wilde's Profession* (Oxford: Oxford University Press, 2000), 133.

17. Vyvyan Holland, *Son of Oscar Wilde* (1954; repr. Oxford: Oxford University Press, 1988), 76.

18. Richard A. Kaye, " 'Determined Raptures': St. Sebastian and the Victorian Discourse of Decadence," *Victorian Literature and Culture* 27 (1999): 271.

19. Wilde, "The Ballad of Reading Gaol," in *Poems and Poems in Prose,* ed. Bobby Fong and Karl Beckson, vol. 1 of *The Complete Works of Oscar Wilde* (Oxford: Oxford University Press, 2000), 196.

20. [Thomas Martin], "The Poet in Prison" (1906), repr. in *Oscar Wilde: Interviews and Recollections,* ed. E. H. Mikhail (London: Macmillan, 1979), 2:335.

21. Like many late-Victorian books, the first edition of *The Importance of Being Earnest* was published in several different formats: a standard edition of 1,000 copies; a limited edition of 100 "large paper" copies, signed by Wilde personally and printed on Dutch handmade paper; and an edition of twelve numbered large-paper copies, bound in

vellum, printed on Japanese vellum, and signed by Wilde personally. In 2012, copy no. 3 of the signed large-paper vellum edition, containing a handwritten inscription to Robert Ross and with a letter to Ross from 1895 tipped in, sold at auction for $362,500. In 2015 it was resold for £197,000. It is not known how many copies of the first edition of *The Importance of Being Earnest* remained unsold at Wilde's death in 1900. The play received only one known review, in *The Outlook,* on its appearance in book form, although Wilde's name was not mentioned.

22. "There are two ways of disliking my plays," he once remarked: "one is to dislike them, the other is to like *Earnest*" (quoted in Richard Ellmann, *Oscar Wilde* [New York: Knopf, 1988], 561–62).

23. [Martin], "The Poet in Prison," 335.

24. The term had first been utilized by the German sexologist Karl Heinrich Ulrichs in the 1860s and was later popularized in English in the writings of Edward Carpenter and John Addington Symonds. André Raffalovich's book *Uranisme et Unisexualité* (Lyon and Paris, 1896) devoted an entire chapter to Wilde.

25. See Jeffrey Weeks, *Sexuality,* 4th ed. (London: Routledge, 2017), esp. 11–68.

26. Robert Harborough Sherard, *The Life of Oscar Wilde* (New York: Mitchell Kennerley, 1906), 405.

27. Wilde, *The Picture of Dorian Gray,* ed. Frankel, 192.

28. In March 1895, Douglas had encouraged Wilde's ill-fated prosecution of Douglas's father for libel, which subsequently led to Wilde's own criminal conviction just two months later; and in September 1897 he eloped with Wilde to Naples, an event that one biographer calls Wilde's "second fall" on account of the opprobrium it brought upon Wilde even among many of his most loyal supporters (Ellmann, *Oscar Wilde,* 547). For Douglas's departure from Naples in December 1897, see pp. 158–61 above.

29. Lord Alfred Douglas to More Adey, 4 July 1897, TS copy, The William Andrews Clark Memorial Library, University of California, Los Angeles.

30. Lord Alfred Douglas, letter to his mother, 7 December 1897, printed in Douglas, *Without Apology* (London: Secker, 1938), 303.

31. "Appendix B: The 1891 Preface to *The Picture of Dorian Gray,*" in Wilde, *The Picture of Dorian Gray,* ed. Frankel, 273.

32. Wilde, "The Decay of Lying," in *Criticism: Historical Criticism, Intentions, and The Soul of Man,* ed. Josephine M. Guy, vol. 4 of *The Complete Works of Oscar Wilde* (Oxford: Oxford University Press, 2007), 82, 85.

33. A. B. Walkley, review of *Lady Windermere's Fan* (1892), repr. in *Oscar Wilde: The Critical Heritage,* ed. Karl Beckson (London: Routledge & Kegan Paul, 1970), 123; William Archer, review of Pinero, *The Second Mrs. Tanqueray* (1893), repr. as "William Archer, in defence of his praise of Wilde," in *Oscar Wilde: The Critical Heritage,* ed. Beckson, 149.

34. George Bernard Shaw, review of *An Ideal Husband* (1895), repr. in *Oscar Wilde: The Critical Heritage,* ed. Beckson, 177.

35. *Self-Portrait: Letters and Journals of Charles Ricketts,* comp. T. Sturge Moore, ed. C. Lewis (London: Peter Davies, 1939), 124; *CL* 1132.

36. Wilde, *The Annotated Importance of Being Earnest,* ed. Nicholas Frankel (Cambridge, MA: Harvard University Press, 2015), 73, 203.

37. Wilde, "The Soul of Man," in *Criticism,* ed. Guy, 242.

38. André Gide, *Oscar Wilde: In Memoriam; De Profundis,* trans. B. Frechtman (New York: Philosophical Library, 1949), 17.

39. H. Montgomery Hyde, *Oscar Wilde: The Aftermath* (New York: Farrar, Straus, 1963), xxi.

40. Ellmann, *Oscar Wilde,* 548.

41. Ibid.

42. Wilde, *The Annotated Importance of Being Earnest,* ed. Frankel, 147.

1. Fettered and Chained

1. This is the implication of the remark made by Constance's brother Otho, long after Wilde and Constance were dead, that there had been a "virtual divorce" between them in 1886, after Constance became pregnant with their youngest son Vyvyan. See Neil McKenna, *The Secret Life of Oscar Wilde* (2003; repr. New York: Basic Books, 2005), 86–87.

2. Ibid., 3–35 and 69–75; also Rupert Croft-Cooke, *The Unrecorded Life of Oscar Wilde* (New York: David McKay, 1972), 1–96.

3. Regenia Gagnier, *Idylls of the Marketplace: Oscar Wilde and the Victorian Public* (Palo Alto, CA: Stanford University Press, 1986), 45–46.

4. William Archer, signed review of *The Importance of Being Earnest, The World,* February 20, 1895, repr. in *Oscar Wilde: The Critical Heritage,* ed. Karl Beckson (London: Routledge & Kegan Paul, 1970), 190; "Mr. Oscar Wilde on Mr. Oscar Wilde," *St. James's Gazette,* January 18, 1895; repr. in *Oscar Wilde: Interviews and Recollections,* ed. E. H. Mikhail (London: Macmillan, 1979), 1:250. For an overview of the play's allusions to Wilde's own life, see Nicholas Frankel, introduction to Wilde, *The Annotated Importance of Being Earnest,* ed. Nicholas Frankel (Cambridge, MA: Harvard University Press, 2015), 1–47.

5. See Nicholas Frankel, general introduction to Wilde, *The Picture of Dorian Gray: An Annotated Uncensored Edition,* ed. Nicholas Frankel (Cambridge, MA: Harvard University Press, 2011), 1–37.

6. Appendix B: The 1891 Preface to *The Picture of Dorian Gray,* in Wilde, *The Picture of Dorian Gray,* ed. Frankel, 273.

7. Wilde, *The Picture of Dorian Gray,* ed. Frankel, 188.

8. The Criminal Law Amendment Act 1885 (48 & 49 Vict. c.69), Sec. 11.

9. See *The Real Trial of Oscar Wilde,* intro. and with commentary by Merlin Holland (New York: Harper Perennial, 2003), 31, 50–51, 120–24.

10. Matt Cook, *London and the Culture of Homosexuality, 1885–1914* (Cambridge: Cambridge University Press, 2003), 25.

11. Prince Albert Victor became implicated solely on the basis of rumors, not firm evidence. For this and other details about the Cleveland Street Scandal, see Colin Simpson, *The Cleveland Street Affair* (Boston: Little Brown, 1976) and H. Montgomery Hyde, *The Cleveland Street Scandal* (New York: Coward, McCann & Geoghegan, 1976).

12. Apart from two of the prostitutes, who were given light sentences, only a radical journalist, Ernest Parke of the *North London Press,* was successfully prosecuted in the scandal's fallout.

13. This is also the case with the young Cambridge undergraduate Harry Marillier, with whom Wilde conducted a lengthy, suggestive, and flirtatious correspondence from late 1885 to mid-1886 and whom Wilde visited in his college rooms in late 1885.

14. Wilde, *An Ideal Husband,* ed. Russell Jackson, in *Two Society Comedies,* ed. Ian Small and Russell Jackson (London: Ernest Benn, 1983), 162.

15. Marquess of Queensberry, letter to Lord Alfred Douglas, 3 April 1894, quoted in *The Real Trial of Oscar Wilde,* 215.

16. The 1861 Offences Against The Person Act proscribed "buggery," and Statute 11 of the Criminal Law Amendment Act of 1885 proscribed "gross indecency with another male person." While the sentence under the earlier legislation was harsher (life imprisonment), the burden of proof was higher, and from 1885 onward most male homosexuals were prosecuted under the later act, which required merely proof of "indecency," not sexual penetration.

17. Wilde, *An Ideal Husband,* ed. Jackson, 183.

18. *The Real Trial of Oscar Wilde,* xxvi; Michael Taylor, *Oscar Wilde: Trial and Punishment, 1895–1897* (London: Public Record Office / National Portrait Gallery, 1997), 6–7; Sachaverell Sitwell, TLS to H. Montgomery Hyde, 25 July 1948, Oscar Wilde Collection, 3.9, Harry Ransom Center, University of Texas at Austin.

19. *The Real Trial of Oscar Wilde,* 207–8.

20. Ibid., 282.

21. Merlin Holland, introduction to *The Real Trial of Oscar Wilde,* xxxi.

22. *The Evening News,* April 5, 1895, repr. in *The Oscar Wilde File,* compiled by Jonathan Goodman (London: Allison & Busby, 1988), 71.

23. Quoted in H. Montgomery Hyde, *The Trials of Oscar Wilde* (1962; repr. Mineola, NY: Dover Publications, 1973), 145.

24. *The Illustrated Police Budget,* April 13, 1895, repr. in *The Oscar Wilde File,* 84.

25. Robert H. Sherard, *Oscar Wilde: The Story of an Unhappy Friendship* (1905; repr. London: Greening, 1909), 185.

26. Wilde, "Poetry and Prison" (1888), in *The Artist as Critic: Critical Writings of Oscar Wilde,* ed. Richard Ellmann (1969; New York, Vintage, 1970), 118; Wilfrid Scawen Blunt, preface to *In Vinculis* (London: Kegan, Paul, & Trench, 1889), quoted in Wilde, "Poetry and Prison," 116. The Perpetual Crimes Act, or Coercion Act, of 1887 aimed at the prevention of boycotting, unlawful assembly, and the organization of conspiracies against the payment of agreed rents in Ireland. One of many coercive acts aimed at

suppressing dissent to English rule in Ireland, it resulted in the imprisonment of hundreds of people, including over twenty MPs.

27. The phrase "hard labour, hard board, and a hard bed" originated in the Carnarvon Committee prior to the 1865 Prison Act. See C. Harding et al., *Imprisonment in England and Wales: A Concise History* (London: Croom Helm, 1985), 158. The full implementation of such a regime was not carried out until Du Cane's appointment in 1877.

28. Philip Priestley, *Victorian Prison Lives* (London: Methuen, 1985), 30–31.

29. Stuart Wood, *Shades of the Prison House* (1932), quoted in Priestley, *Victorian Prison Lives,* 93.

30. To Du Cane, says the prison historian Sean McConville, the suffering of the prisoner was a warning to others, and it "painfully imprinted the results of crime on [the prisoner] himself." Du Cane recognized that prison involved the prisoner in considerable distress and pain, but his concern was only "whether the suffering was rationally conceived, officially sanctioned, at an appropriate stage of the sentence, and in accordance with the scientific regulations emanating from one of his committees." See McConville, *English Local Prisons 1860–1900* (London: Routledge, 1995), 181, 173.

31. For discussions of prison diet, see David Taylor, *Hooligans, Harlots, and Hangmen: Crime and Punishment in Victorian Britain* (Santa Barbara, CA: Praeger, 2010), 184–85 and Priestley, *Victorian Prison Lives,* 148–53.

32. Sean McConville, "The Victorian Prison: England 1865–1965," in *The Oxford History of the Prison,* ed. N. Morris and D. J. Rothman (New York: Oxford University Press, 1995), 147; also Edward Marston, *Prison: Five Hundred Years of Life Behind Bars* (Richmond, Surrey: The National Archives, 2009), 114. The crank was "a cylindrical metal drum fitted with a handle to be turned and resembling the old-fashioned type of patent knife-grinder. On one side was a clock-like face, which recorded the number of revolutions made. The requisite amount of resistance was obtained by a metal band applied on the axle inside, which retarded its motion by friction. The ordinary resistance was about 6 lb. Prisoners were expected to perform 10,000 revolutions a day, which occupied them for about six hours. It was a particularly futile operation since, unlike the treadmill which often pumped water or ground corn, the labour involved was absolutely unproductive" (H. Montgomery Hyde, *Oscar Wilde: The Aftermath* [New York: Farrar, Straus, 1963], 8–9).

33. Hyde, *Oscar Wilde: The Aftermath,* 3, 2.

34. McConville, "The Victorian Prison," 146–47.

35. See Michael Ignatieff, "Chapter One: Pentonville," in his *A Just Measure of Pain: The Penitentiary in the Industrial Revolution, 1750–1850* (New York: Pantheon, 1978), 3–14; also N. K. Teeters and J. D. Shearer, "The Emergence of the Penitentiary System," in *The Prison at Philadelphia, Cherry Hill: The Separate System of Penal Discipline 1829–1913* (New York: Temple University Press / Columbia University Press, 1957), 17–23.

36. *The Illustrated Police Budget,* June 1, 1895, repr. in *The Oscar Wilde File,* 131.

37. Details about Wilde's admission to Pentonville are drawn from *The Morning,* June 6, 1895, repr. in *The Oscar Wilde File,* 136.

38. *The Morning,* June 6, 1895.

39. Frank Harris, *Oscar Wilde: His Life and Confessions* (1916; repr. New York, Dorset, 1989), 194.

40. *The Morning,* June 6, 1895.

41. Quoted in Ashley Robins, *Oscar Wilde: The Great Drama of His Life* (Brighton: Sussex Academic, 2011), 25.

42. Quoted in Robins, *Oscar Wilde,* 25.

43. Richard Burton Haldane, *An Autobiography* (London: Hodder & Staughton, 1929), 177; reprinted as "Oscar Wilde in Prison," in *Oscar Wilde: Interviews and Recollections,* ed. Mikhail, 2:323.

44. H. Montgomery Hyde speculates that Asquith may well have encouraged Haldane to make this visit. Neil McKenna speculates that Lord Rosebery, the prime minister, encouraged Haldane, while Richard Ellmann suggests that Margaret Brooke, the Ranee of Sarawak, a mutual friend of both Wilde and Haldane, instigated the visit.

45. Haldane, "Oscar Wilde in Prison," 324.

46. Ibid.

47. Hyde, *Oscar Wilde: The Aftermath,* 19.

48. Ibid., 18. Shortly before his release, in 1897, Wilde was to request that he be sent books written and edited by Morrison, including ones by the Italian criminologists Cesare Lombroso and Enrico Ferri, whose English publication Morrison had overseen in his role as general editor of T. Fisher Unwin's Criminology Series, the first series of books ever devoted to criminology in English publishing.

49. Alfred Douglas exhorted his brother Percy to use his political connections to help Oscar, and Wilde's friends Adela Schuster and More Adey may have made efforts to influence prison staff as well. See Robins, *Oscar Wilde,* 26.

50. Harris, *Oscar Wilde,* 194.

51. Constance Wilde to R. H. Sherard, 21 September 1895, quoted in Franny Moyle, *Constance: The Tragic and Scandalous Life of Mrs. Oscar Wilde* (London: John Murray, 2011), 281.

52. Constance Wilde, letter to Hannah Witall Smith, 15 October 1895, quoted in Richard Ellmann, *Oscar Wilde* (New York: Knopf, 1988), 492.

53. The English original of Douglas's defense has been long lost, but Douglas's defense survives in manuscript (not in Douglas's hand) in a French translation at Princeton, as well as in three English-language typescripts, at Princeton, at William Andrews Clark Memorial Library, UCLA, and at the Harry Ransom Center, University of Texas at Austin respectively, that appear to be early twentieth-century retranslations back into English from the *Mercure de France's* French. The Princeton typescript was published in 2002 as *Oscar Wilde: A Plea and a Reminiscence* (intr. Casper Wintermans [Woubrugge, Holland: Avalon Press, 2002], 19–36), but it differs in matters of wording and punctuation from the Ransom Center and Clark Library typescripts, which are preferred here.

54. Quoted in Robins, *Oscar Wilde,* 29.

55. W. D. Morrison, "Prisons and Prisoners," *Fortnightly Review,* May 1898, quoted in Hyde, *Oscar Wilde: The Aftermath,* 21.

56. Sherard, *Oscar Wilde*, 196–98.

57. Robins, *Oscar Wilde*, 27.

58. Quoted in *CL* 665 n.2.

59. Harris, *Oscar Wilde*, 196.

60. Quoted in Ellmann, *Oscar Wilde*, 491–92.

61. Quoted in Robins, *Oscar Wilde*, 33, 29.

62. Ibid., 31, 36.

63. Ibid., 43–45.

64. Robins, *Oscar Wilde*, 44–45.

65. Ibid., 33–34. In his autobiography, Haldane takes credit for persuading the home secretary to make the transfer; see Haldane, *Autobiography*, 179.

66. Quoted in Robins, *Oscar Wilde*, 48, 47.

67. Ellmann, *Oscar Wilde*, 495.

68. *CL* 756–57. Wilde erroneously dated his transfer "November 13th 1895," but Reading Prison's records date it one week later. Robins clarifies that Wilde's bankruptcy proceedings formally concluded on the day before his transfer to Reading; see Robins, *Oscar Wilde*, 47–48.

69. Sherard, *Oscar Wilde*, 211.

70. Ibid., 212–13.

71. Harris, *Oscar Wilde*, 197.

72. Max Beerbohm, undated letter [early 1896] to Ada Leverson [headed "Tuesday, 19 Hyde Park Place, W."], Max Beerbohm Collection 2.4, Harry Ransom Center, University of Texas at Austin.

73. Wilfred H. Chesson, "A Reminiscence of 1898," *The Bookman* (1911), repr. in *Oscar Wilde: Interviews and Recollections*, ed. Mikhail, 2:376.

74. Harris, *Oscar Wilde*, 193.

75. Hyde, *Oscar Wilde: The Aftermath*, 42.

76. [Thomas Martin], "The Poet in Prison" (1906), repr. in *Oscar Wilde: Interviews and Recollections*, ed. Mikhail, 2:332.

77. "In The Depths," *Evening News & Evening Mail*, March 1, 1905, repr. in *Oscar Wilde: Interviews and Recollections*, ed. Mikhail, 2:328–29. Prison rules strictly regulated the order of a prisoner's cell. See Ignatieff, *A Just Measure of Pain*, 8.

78. See "The Poet in Prison," 333–34. Christopher Harding et al. write that the crank "was usually employed as a punishment or as a test of feigned sickness"; see *Imprisonment in England and Wales*, 303.

79. Harris, *Oscar Wilde*, 198.

80. Robert Ross to More Adey, undated letter, in *Robert Ross: Friend of Friends*, ed. Margery Ross (London: Jonathan Cape, 1952), 38–43. Hyde dates this letter to 23 May 1896; see *Oscar Wilde: The Aftermath*, 57.

81. Robert Ross to More Adey, undated letter, 39, 42.

82. Quoted in Robins, *Oscar Wilde*, 53.

83. *Oxford Dictionary of National Biography.* Ruggles-Brise later created the "borstal" system allowing for the separate treatment of young offenders.

84. Quoted in Harris, *Oscar Wilde*, 197.

85. Harris, *Oscar Wilde*, 199.

86. Hyde, *Oscar Wilde: The Aftermath*, 64.

87. Harris, *Oscar Wilde*, 193.

2. From the Depths

1. Wilde, "The Birthday of the Infanta," in his *Complete Shorter Fiction,* ed. Isobel Murray (New York: Oxford World's Classics, 1979), 200. Wilde also echoes here the self-loathing of Dorian Gray when seeing his inner corruption reflected in the portrait that provides the title to Wilde's only novel.

2. Quoted in Ashley Robins, *Oscar Wilde: The Great Drama of His Life* (Brighton: Sussex Academic, 2011), 57, 60.

3. Ibid., 60.

4. A second, more limited petition written by Wilde around this time met a better fate. On July 4, 1896, Wilde petitioned the home secretary to be allowed to have an upcoming meeting with his friend More Adey in the Solicitor's Room, usually reserved for meetings between prisoners and their legal representatives, rather than in "the cage," a pair of hutch-like caged structures in which prisoners and visitors were placed apart, with two prison warders standing between them (*CL* 661). Adey was visiting expressly to discuss the guardianship, education, and future of Wilde's two children, as well as Wilde's life-interest in his wife's marriage settlement. Wilde was "anxious that he should have this important business interview, so vital for wife and children, under conditions that allow of judgment, reflection, and . . . rational decision," rather than in an environment "so degrading, distressing, and inconducive to meaningful communication that many prisoners choose not to see their friends and relatives, rather than to undergo such an ordeal" (*CL* 661, 1047–48). For Sherard's description of "the cage," see p. 51 above. On July 6, the Home Office granted Wilde's request.

5. Quoted in H. Montgomery Hyde, *Oscar Wilde: The Aftermath* (New York: Farrar, Straus, 1963), 77–78. Certain conditions were placed upon Wilde's use of writing materials, namely (1) that Wilde did not employ these materials to communicate with "outside persons otherwise than consistently with the ordinary rules"; (2) that their use did not interfere with Wilde's ordinary prison occupations; (3) that the prison governor supervise the provision of writing materials, with "discretion as to the time during the day when the privilege may be exercised"; and (4) that all writing materials were to be withdrawn at lock-up and all matter written by Wilde made subject to the governor's inspection, ensuring that no improper use was made of this privilege.

6. Robins, *Oscar Wilde*, 63.

7. *CL* 854; Wilfred H. Chesson, "A Reminiscence of 1898," *The Bookman* (1911), repr. in *Oscar Wilde: Interviews and Recollections,* ed. E. H. Mikhail (London: Macmillan,

1979), 2:376. As Wilde writes, the changes wrought under Nelson's governorship were attributable not to any alteration in "the rules of the prison system" so much as to "the spirit in which they [were] carried out" (*CL* 854).

8. [Thomas Martin], "The Poet in Prison" (1906), repr. in *Oscar Wilde: Interviews and Recollections,* ed. Mikhail, 333.

9. Quoted in Richard Ellmann, *Oscar Wilde* (New York: Knopf, 1988), 507.

10. "T. M." [Thomas Martin?], quoted in *The Manchester Guardian,* October 13, 1914, 5. Prison regulations allowed prisoners "to have an interview with the Governor or superior authority to make complaints or prefer requests, and the Governor shall redress any grievance or take such steps as may seem necessary" ("Appendix 1, Abstract of the Regulations Relating to the Treatment and Conduct of Convicted Prisoners," in Philip Priestley, *Victorian Prison Lives* [London: Methuen, 1985], 289–90).

11. "In The Depths," *Evening News & Evening Mail,* March 1, 1905, repr. in *Oscar Wilde: Interviews and Recollections,* ed. Mikhail, 2:329.

12. Ibid., 328.

13. See Ibid., 329, and Robert H. Sherard, *Twenty Years in Paris: Being Some Recollections of a Literary Life* (London: Hutchinson, 1905), 426–27.

14. André Gide, *Oscar Wilde: In Memoriam; De Profundis,* trans. B. Frechtman (New York: Philosophical Library, 1949), 27. Adey sent Wilde the anthology *Poetae Scenici Graeci,* containing the works of Sophocles, Aristophanes, Euripides, and Aeschylus, in February 1896.

15. Haldane sent St. Augustine and Pascal in June 1895, as we have already seen, while Frederic Farrar's *The Life and Works of St. Paul* and Henry H. Milman's *History of the Jews* and *History of Latin Christianity* followed in 1896.

16. Chesson, "A Reminiscence of 1898," 379. Since Wilde also told Chesson that "Longfellow's rhymed translation" was infinitely better than H. F. Carey's "dull blank verse," it is possible that Adey sent *The Divina Commedia* in one or both of these verse-translations.

17. Frank Harris, *Oscar Wilde: His Life and Confessions* (1916; New York, Dorset, 1989), 199.

18. [Martin], "The Poet in Prison," 332.

19. "In The Depths," 329; Sherard, *Twenty Years in Paris,* 430.

20. As noted above in note 5, the Prison Commission stipulated that Wilde should not employ writing materials to communicate with "outside persons otherwise than consistently with the ordinary rules."

21. Prison rules stated that prisoners could only send and receive letters "at intervals, which depend on the rules of the class they attain by industry and good conduct." See appendix A: Prison Regulations Concerning Letters and Visits, in Hyde, *Oscar Wilde: The Aftermath,* 201.

22. More Adey and Arthur Clifton had already been granted visitation rights by the time Sherard applied, and as Wilde informed Sherard, "I am only allowed two visitors."

23. For Wilde's second petition of July 1896, see note 4 above. The substance of this second appeal is repeated in a letter Wilde wrote to the *Daily Chronicle* during the second parliamentary reading of the Prison Bill in 1898. In the course of the letter, Wilde writes that "the mode at present in vogue of exhibiting a prisoner to his friends should be altered. . . . To be exhibited, like an ape, in a cage, to people who are fond of one, and of whom one is fond, is a needless and horrible degradation."

24. See Ian Small, introduction to *De Profundis: "Epistola: In Carcere et Vinculis,"* ed. Ian Small, vol. 2 of *The Complete Works of Oscar Wilde* (Oxford: Oxford University Press, 2005), 10–11.

25. In 1913 at the Ransome Trial, where Wilde's letter was read aloud in court, Douglas testified that Ross had indeed sent him a copy along with an accompanying note, but that he had thrown it into the fire unread. Subsequently, Douglas maintained that Ross had not even sent him a copy. In his autobiography, Douglas does allow that Ross sent him a letter containing extracts from remarks Wilde allegedly made about him in jail, but he says that this letter arrived some time before Wilde's release (so it cannot have contained anything drawn directly from *De Profundis*) and that he tore it up in anger without reading it. See Douglas, *The Autobiography of Alfred Douglas* (London: Secker 1929), 135.

26. Douglas's review is reprinted in Hyde, *Oscar Wilde: The Aftermath,* 208–10.

27. See note 5 above.

28. Wilde's manuscript resides in the British Library (add. MS 50141A). See *Oscar Wilde, De Profundis: A Facsimile,* intro. Merlin Holland (London: British Library, 2000).

29. *Molloy,* in *Novels,* vol. 2 of *Samuel Beckett: The Grove Centenary Edition,* ed. Paul Auster (New York: Grove, 2006), 3. I am grateful to John Kulka for this reference.

30. Wilde instructed Ross to copy "from the fourth page of sheet 9 to the last page of sheet 14," "on page 3 of sheet 18 from 'I am to be released if all goes well' to 'bitter herbs . . . whole' on page 4." He also instructed Ross to extract anything else "good and nice in intention, such as [the] first page of sheet 15" (*CL* 781–82). He can hardly have been citing from memory. His citations imply that he had all of the numbered sheets directly in front of him.

31. See Small, introduction to *De Profundis,* 9. Small posits the manuscript had as many as four stages of composition and concludes that "the process of composition . . . resembles . . . closely what we know of the processes of composition of Wilde's literary works." Wilde may have been striving over many months to bring coherence and unity to several different previous documents, Small suggests, only one or two of which were strictly speaking parts of a letter to Douglas. Far from being a single, integral whole, he concludes, *De Profundis* is quite likely an amalgam of several documents, including (but not limited to) a letter to Douglas that Wilde ended up expanding and developing by interpolating it with other material he had been working on.

32. Rupert Croft-Cooke, *Bosie: Lord Alfred Douglas, His Friends and Enemies* (Indianapolis: Bobbs-Merrill, 1963), 141.

33. Quoted in Croft-Cooke, *Bosie,* 141.

34. Lord Alfred Douglas, "The Wilde Myth" (1916), unpublished page proofs, p. 114, Lord Alfred Douglas Collection, 1.7 Harry Ransom Center, University of Texas at Austin.

35. Lord Alfred Douglas, letter to More Adey, 30 November 1895, in Croft-Cooke, *Bosie,* 138.

36. Quoted in Croft-Cooke, *Bosie,* 139.

37. The news that Wilde wished him to return all tokens of his love "has deprived me of all power of thought and expression," Douglas told Ross in June 1896, but since Wilde wished the dedication to his first poetry collection removed, he would hold back the book, adding that he could not publish it if it were not dedicated to Wilde (quoted in Ellmann, *Oscar Wilde,* 501). Douglas later told Adey that he would never have proposed dedicating the book to Wilde if he realized sooner how Wilde felt about it (unpublished letter to Adey, 8 February 1897 [TS copy], William Andrews Clark Memorial Library, University of California, Los Angeles). As for Wilde's letters, "I cannot give them up to anyone. . . . If Oscar asks me to kill myself I will do so, and he shall have the letters when I am dead. . . . Morning and evening I have kissed them and prayed over them" (quoted in Ellmann, *Oscar Wilde,* 501). At some point in the early summer of 1896, according to Wilde's own later account, Douglas sealed up Wilde's letters and presents in two packages, with the intention of handing them personally to Wilde upon his release (*CL* 776). Shortly after this, Douglas asked Adey to assure Wilde of his own undying love and devotion (unpublished letter to Adey, 20 September 1896 [TS copy], William Andrews Clark Memorial Library, University of California, Los Angeles). By the fall of 1896 Douglas felt deeply hurt by Wilde's rejection. Nonetheless, he did not believe that Wilde was in his right mind, and he was determined to regard Wilde's expressions of contempt as the inevitable and temporary consequences of his sufferings in prison. As Douglas saw it, Wilde had become temporarily possessed by an evil and malignant spirit: even if it proved impossible to exorcise this spirit and Wilde remained hostile, Douglas would continue to love and be faithful to him. See Douglas, unpublished letter to Adey, 27 September 1896 (TS copy), William Andrews Clark Memorial Library, University of California, Los Angeles.

38. This charge was particularly unfair and hurtful to Douglas, who later pointed out repeatedly (and accurately) that Wilde had written large parts of *A Woman of No Importance, An Ideal Husband,* and *The Importance of Being Earnest* in Douglas's company, just as he was to do with *The Ballad of Reading Gaol* in late 1897. *The Importance of Being Earnest* is especially of note, since it makes farcical comedy out of Wilde's life in the years leading up to its composition and is to some extent *about* Wilde's relationship with Douglas. In November 1894, shortly after completing it, Wilde wittily proposed co-writing with Douglas a book titled *How To Live Above One's Income: For The Use of the Sons of the Rich.* As Douglas also pointed out, *De Profundis* is itself a testament to the importance of Douglas upon Wilde's imagination.

39. Douglas later disputed the amount Wilde said he spent over this period, which is roughly equivalent to $700,000 or £460,000 today; he also pointed out that his father stopped his allowance in 1893 as a result of his friendship with Wilde, so "my friendship with Wilde and my refusal to give him up cost me £2450" (*Autobiography,* 82). As

important, and as Wilde's phrase "spent with you" indicates, Wilde enjoyed the fruits of these expenditures and had been profligate with money long before he met Douglas.

40. "My fault was not that I did not part from you, but that I parted from you far too often. . . . I ended my friendship with you every three months regularly" Wilde writes (*CL* 691). Some of the most memorable and painful passages in *De Profundis* recount precise, intimate details of long periods Wilde spent in Douglas's company—at Babbacombe Cliff, near Torquay, in early 1893; at Goring, in Oxfordshire, in the summer of 1893; in London, following his return from Goring and again following Douglas's four-month stay in Cairo during the winter of 1893–94; and perhaps most memorably, at Worthing and Brighton in the late summer of 1894, when Wilde was composing *The Importance of Being Earnest*—only to show how little pleasure Wilde had obtained from them and how painful Douglas's presence had in fact been. According to Wilde, each of these periods was followed by a series of failed efforts to leave Douglas for good, following "dreadful scenes" in which the younger man lurched between selfish rage and childlike penitence. Precise dates, times, and expenditures give an aura of truth to these painful recollections: "my ordinary expenses with you for any ordinary day . . . ranged from £12 to £20"; "for our three months at Goring my expenses (rent of course excluded) were £1340"; "at 12 o'clock you drove up and stayed smoking and chattering till 1.30. . . . Luncheon with its liqueurs usually lasted till about 3.30"; "I refer to your conduct to me at Brighton from October 10–13, 1894"; "the next day, a Monday . . . bored with Worthing . . . you insist on being taken to the Grand Hotel at Brighton"; "Wednesday was my birthday" (*CL* 686–97). Wilde implies that these memories are indisputable, saying that in the fall of 1895 "step by step with the Bankruptcy Receiver I had to go over every item of my life" (*CL* 688). But these "facts" are often wrong. In 1894, for instance, his birthday (October 16) had fallen on a Tuesday, not a Wednesday. Wilde and Douglas had stayed at the Hotel Metropole, not the Grand Hotel, in Brighton—and from October 4 to 7, not October 10 to 13—arriving there on a Thursday, not a Monday. Douglas would later give a very different version of the same events, and so far as forcing Wilde to "brazen it out" in court is concerned, it was Wilde's own mother—who had faced down her own enemies in court on two important occasions—who threatened never to speak to Wilde again if he fled England. Most important of all, Wilde's own correspondence from the years 1893–94 gives a very different color to the events and periods he describes with such pathos in *De Profundis*. For instance, he wrote Douglas from Babbacombe Cliff in early 1893, "Those red rose-leaf lips of yours should have been made no less for music of song than for madness of kisses," adding "come here whenever you like" and signing himself "always with undying love" (*CL* 544). Upon leaving Babbacombe Cliff—when according to *De Profundis* Wilde had determined to break off with Douglas—he wrote to him from London, saying "I must see you soon—you are the divine thing I want—the thing of grace and genius . . . why are you not here, my dear, wonderful boy?" (*CL* 560). "Our love has . . . come out rose-crowned as of old," he wrote to Douglas in Cairo in December 1893: "let us always be infinitely dear to each other, as indeed we have been always" (*CL* 577). "I miss you so much. The gay, gilt and gracious lad has gone away," he wrote Douglas four months later, "and I hate everyone else; they are tedious" (*CL* 588). In July of 1894 he wrote "I want to see you . . . I can't live without you. You are so dear,

so wonderful. I think of you all day long and miss your grace, your boyish beauty, the bright sword-play of your wit, the delicate fancy of your genius" (*CL* 594). From Worthing later that summer—where Wilde says in *De Profundis* that "I was trying to finish my last play . . . by myself" and "had no option" but to entertain the profligate Douglas—Wilde wrote "Dear dear boy, you are more to me than any one . . . has any idea; you are the atmosphere of beauty through which I see life . . . the incarnation of all lovely things. . . . I think of you night and day" (*CL* 602). Clearly missing Douglas, he asked "could you meet me at Newhaven on the 15th? Dieppe is very amusing and bright. Or would you come down here first?" signing his letter "ever devotedly yours" (*CL* 607).

41. "Phrases and Philosophies For the Use of the Young," in *The Artist as Critic: Critical Writings of Oscar Wilde,* ed. Richard Ellmann (1969; repr. New York, Vintage, 1970), 434.

42. Sheet 13 of the manuscript, in which Wilde unfolds and elaborates this argument, is—unlike most other sheets—a pristine and flawless fair copy, suggesting that it is among the most heavily polished parts of the entire text. See also "The Soul of Man under Socialism," in *The Artist as Critic,* ed. Ellmann, 263–66.

3. Release

1. Nelson asked whether Wilde might be allowed to send the letter to Lord Alfred Douglas. But since Nelson's request was dated one day after the letter in which Wilde tells Ross "I send you, in a roll separate from this, my letter to Alfred Douglas" (*CL* 780), Nelson was clearly misinformed about the person to whom Wilde intended to send it.

2. Wilde's contingent stake or "life-interest" in Constance's marriage settlement was listed as one of Wilde's assets at his bankruptcy, in late 1895, and was therefore subject to sale as a way of partially paying off Wilde's creditors. Constance wanted to buy this stake for herself, reasoning that by doing so it would devolve onto the couple's two sons and thereby ensure them an important source of income after her death. But Ross and Adey wanted at least part of Wilde's stake to be (re)settled on Wilde himself, and for this reason they were prepared to bid against her in the bankruptcy sale of this asset.

3. Around this time, Wilde estimated that his wife's income amounted to roughly £1,000 per year (*CL* 676), although it would rise to about £1500 per year upon the death of her mother. Such independent investment income for a Victorian wife had only become possible with the passage of the Married Woman's Property Act of 1882.

4. Constance was prompted to this grave act through Adey's and Ross's acquisition from Wilde's Bankruptcy Receiver—against her wishes, and on Wilde's behalf—of Wilde's life-interest in her marriage-settlement, as well as by the strict terms that they demanded of her in any future financial settlement. It is doubtful whether Constance would have dissolved Wilde's legal guardianship of his children if Ross and Adey had proved more conciliatory (as indeed Wilde had wanted them to be all along), and understandably Wilde was furious at what he rightly perceived to be Ross's and Adey's mismanagement of his affairs. As Robins writes, Wilde's poverty or insolvency was not in itself sufficient grounds for proving his unfitness: "the grounds for interference by the court were gross misconduct and profligacy on the part of the father, who by his behavior had shown that

he was utterly unfit for the upbringing of his children. Moreover if the court was satisfied that the father of young children has been guilty of an unnatural vice (even though not convicted of it) it would be its duty to remove them from him" (Ashley Robins, *Oscar Wilde: The Great Drama of His Life* [Brighton: Sussex Academic, 2011], 93).

5. Constance's main objective in considering divorce proceedings was to dissolve the marriage settlement in which Wilde had, through the agency of Ross and Adey, by now secured his life interest. As Wilde wrote on April 6, 1897, "my wife is now going for a divorce. She has been forced to do so. The purchase of my life-interest against her wishes and interests has left her no option." But obtaining a divorce was immensely complicated in the Victorian period. As Moyle writes, "given the amount of time that had elapsed since Oscar's trial, from a legal perspective Constance could no longer divorce him for the 'crimes' revealed in the cases of 1895. Her reluctance to divorce her husband after such revelations amounted to her condoning them, in legal terms at least" (Franny Moyle, *Constance: The Tragic and Scandalous Life of Mrs. Oscar Wilde* [London: John Murray, 2011], 299). The only grounds on which she could now divorce Wilde was if she proved that he had committed sodomy, a crime of which he had not been charged to date, and of which no evidence had ever been adduced in court. If she proceeded with a divorce suit, Wilde feared, he would be re-arrested, tried for committing sodomy, and returned to prison.

6. According to a warder (Thomas Martin?) who was present when Wilde signed the deed of separation, Constance Wilde had accompanied Wilde's lawyer to see her husband sign the document. But she did not wish to be seen by her husband, so she remained outside in the corridor, except for taking one brief glance through a glass peep-hole, while her husband, unaware of his wife's presence, signed the deed in the room designated for prisoners to meet with their legal representatives. See "In The Depths," *Evening News & Evening Mail*, March 1, 1905, repr. in *Oscar Wilde: Interviews and Recollections*, 2:330. The warder's story received some corroboration from a mourner at the time of Governor Nelson's death, in 1914, who told the *Manchester Guardian* that Nelson "well remembered Mrs. Wilde" ("T. M.," quoted in the *Manchester Guardian* October 13, 1914, 5). Since Nelson only arrived at Reading in July 1896, months after Constance's visit the previous February, his memory of her can only have dated from the visit she purportedly paid in May 1897 to witness Wilde signed the deed. However, "T. M.," the *Guardian's* source, may well have been Thomas Martin, the same warder who anonymously authored the account of Constance's secret visit in the first place. Moreover, Vyvyan Holland writes that his mother "never saw my father again" after her visit of February 1896.

7. Unnamed warder, quoted in Robert Harborough Sherard, *Twenty Years in Paris: Being Some Recollections of a Literary Life* (Philadelphia: George W. Jacobs, 1905), 431.

8. Headlam, *Church Reformer*, 1 June 1895, quoted in H. Montgomery Hyde, *The Trials of Oscar Wilde* (1962; repr. Mineola, NY: Dover Publications, 1973), 220. While Headlam never regretted his stand on Wilde's behalf, it caused estrangements and strains in Headlam's friendships, and led him years later to call it "the most painful" of "all the public difficulties I have been in" (quoted in F. G. Bettany, *Stewart Headlam: An Autobiography* [London, 1926], 130).

9. Ross, unfinished preface to a projected collection of Wilde's letters, partially printed in *CL* 842.

10. *Letters to the Sphinx from Oscar Wilde, with Reminiscences of the Author, by Ada Leverson* (London: Duckworth, 1930), 45.

11. Quoted in Bettany, *Stewart Headlam,* 132.

12. Quoted in ibid. In Leverson's account, which differs from Headlam's in significant details, the note was sent to a Roman Catholic Retreat, asking if Wilde might retire there for six months. Lord Alfred Douglas's contention that Wilde went to the Brompton Oratory to ask for a retreat is hardly credible and is flatly contradicted in an unpublished letter by Reginald Turner to C. J. Renier (22 March 1933, William Andrews Clark Memorial Library, University of California, Los Angeles: "When Oscar came out of prison he didn't go to the Brompton Oratory"), though Wilde had certainly visited the Oratory in 1878, with a view to becoming Roman Catholic. But as Merlin Holland writes, "In view of all the preparations made for his release and his state of mind at the time, it is implausible that Wilde would have considered exchanging one form of confinement for another" (*CL* 842 n.1).

13. *Letters to the Sphinx,* 45–46. Wilde may in fact have been the prison gardener. In their report of October 1895 assessing Wilde's health, Nicholson and Brayne had recommended that Wilde be transferred to a country prison partly in order that he might take up garden work. Shortly before Wilde's arrival at Reading, Colonel Isaacson, the prison governor, assured his superiors that "in fine weather he can be employed daily for about three hours in the garden" (quoted in Robins, *Oscar Wilde,* 47).

14. *Letters to the Sphinx,* 46.

15. In Leverson's account, the Retreat replied that they could not accept him on the impulse of a moment, telling him a lengthy retreat must be thought over for at least a year.

16. *Letters to the Sphinx,* 46.

17. Bettany, *Stewart Headlam,* 132.

18. Ross, unfinished preface, *CL* 842.

19. Reginald Turner, unpublished letter to Christopher Millard, 29 October [191?], William Andrews Clark Memorial Library, University of California, Los Angeles.

20. Quoted in Ross, unfinished preface, *CL* 842.

21. "A Few Maxims for the Instruction of the Over-Educated," *Saturday Review,* November 17, 1894.

22. More Adey, unpublished letter to Adela Schuster, 16 March 1897, William Andrews Clark Memorial Library, University of California, Los Angeles.

23. John Stokes, "Dieppe: 1895 and after," in his *Oscar Wilde: Myths, Miracles and Imitations* (Cambridge: Cambridge University Press, 1996), 149.

24. Stokes, "Dieppe: 1895 and after," 128.

25. Quoted in Stokes, "Dieppe: 1895 and after," 126.

26. Andrew Radford and Victoria Reid, "Introduction: Channel Vision," in *Franco-British Cultural Exchanges, 1880–1940: Channel Packets*, ed. Andrew Radford and Victoria Reid (Basingstoke: Palgrave Macmillan, 2012), 12.

27. Arthur Symons, "Dieppe, 1895," *The Savoy* 1 (January 1896), repr. in *The Savoy: Nineties Experiment*, ed. Stanley Weintraub (University Park, PA: Pennsylvania State University Press, 1966), 23.

28. Reginald Turner, letter to Max Beerbohm, 19 May 1895, in *Max Beerbohm's Letters to Reginald Turner*, ed. Rupert Hart-Davis (Philadelphia: Lippincott, 1965), 117–18 n.4; Reginald Turner, unpublished letter to Christopher Millard, 29 October [191?], William Andrews Clark Memorial Library, University of California, Los Angeles.

29. Ross, unfinished preface, *CL* 844.

30. Stokes, "Dieppe: 1895 and after," 149.

31. Wilde was inconsistent in his spelling of *Sebastian,* occasionally preferring the French *Sebastien.*

32. Jacques-Émile Blanche, from *Portraits of a Lifetime,* trans. W. Clement (1937), repr. as "Oscar Wilde in Dieppe," in *Oscar Wilde: Interviews and Recollections,* ed. E. H. Mikhail (London: Macmillan, 1979), 2:351–52.

33. Richard Ellmann, *Oscar Wilde* (New York: Knopf, 1988), 538.

34. Lugné-Poe's glowing account of the lunch and of Wilde's gratitude duly appeared in *La Presse* on May 28, under the byline "M[onsieur] Oscar Wilde En France."

35. From 1899 onward, children ceased being sent to adult prisons, and nine years later, in 1908, the Prevention of Crime Act introduced a separate system of prisons, known as *borstals,* for juvenile offenders. Ironically for the last twenty-one years of its life, before it was decommissioned in 2013, Reading Prison housed *only* young offenders less than 21 years of age.

36. According to Lord Alfred Douglas, in whose company Wilde was to write the last hundred lines or so of *The Ballad* at Naples in the fall of 1897, Wilde conceived the idea and maybe even the first few stanzas of the poem in prison, although he did not put pen to paper until after his release. See Douglas, "The Wilde Myth" (1916), unpublished page proofs, p. 138, Lord Alfred Douglas Collection, 1.7 Harry Ransom Center, University of Texas at Austin.

37. See too his comment, two months earlier, before the court had passed judgment, that it would be "a sorrow . . . beyond words" if he were deprived of the right to see his children. "I do hope the Court will see in me something more than a man with a tragic vice in his life," he had written movingly to Adey: "There is so much more in me, and I always was a good father to both my children. I love them dearly and was dearly loved by them, and Cyril was my friend. And it would be better for them not to be forced to think of me as an outcast, but to know me as a man who has suffered. . . . It is a terrible responsibility for the Law to say to a father that he is unfit to see his own children: the consciousness of it makes me unhappy all day long" (*CL* 681).

38. Guillot de Saix, "Souvenirs Inédits sur Oscar Wilde," *L'Européen: Hebdomadaire économique, artistique, et littéraire* 1, no. 4 (May 29, 1929): 2.

39. In the late 1950s, following the publication of his own recollections of his father, Wilde's youngest son Vyvyan Holland received from France a letter detailing its writer's memories, from when he was a small boy of ten or eleven years, of seeing Wilde daily around this time, seated alone at a table in a small restaurant on the Rue Jacob, while dining there with his mother. Wilde "ate with his back to the far wall, silent and alone," recalled Holland's correspondent. The boy's mother could see that Wilde was "a model of deportment, elegance and good breeding," and she would have liked to have spoken with him; but he never conversed with his fellow-diners and, without knowing who he was, they could see that "sorrow . . . weighed him down and made him sad." One autumn evening, after the boy had been sharply scolded by his mother for clumsily upsetting something, Wilde turned to the mother and said "Be patient with your little boy, one must always be patient with them. If, one day, you should find yourself separated from him. . . ." Holland's correspondent interrupted, asking "Have you got a little boy?" to which Wilde replied "I've got two." Wilde left unanswered the boy's next question, "Why don't you bring them here with you?" Instead, he drew the boy to him, kissed him on both cheeks, and mumbled something in English before saying farewell. As the boy and his mother departed, they could see that Wilde was crying. The next day, before Wilde arrived, a fellow-customer explained to the boy and his mother that what Wilde had mumbled before they left was "Oh, my poor dear boys!" whereupon Holland's correspondent realized that he had been given the two kisses in lieu of Wilde's sons (Vyvyan Holland, *Time Remembered* [1966], repr. in Merlin Holland, foreword to *Son of Oscar Wilde*, by Vyvyan Holland [1954; repr. New York: Oxford University Press, 1988], 2–4).

40. Wilde, *An Ideal Husband*, ed. Russell Jackson, in *Two Society Comedies*, ed. Ian Small and Russell Jackson (London: Ernest Benn, 1983), 170, 211.

41. Lord Alfred Douglas, *Oscar Wilde: A Summing-Up* (London: Duckworth, 1940), 99.

42. Moyle, *Constance,* 307.

43. Ann Amor, *Mrs. Oscar Wilde: A Woman of Some Importance* (London: Sidgwick & Jackson, 1988), 210.

44. "There is infinitely more peace and happiness coming after this terrible time you have had for 8 years," wrote one intimate correspondent to Constance around the time of Wilde's arrest (Mrs. Robinson to Constance Holland, undated [April 1895], quoted in Moyle, *Constance,* 273). The date at which Constance's marriage to Wilde turned bitter to her remains conjectural. In 1888, on visiting the Wildes on Christmas Day, W. B. Yeats perceived that their home life "suggested some deliberate artistic composition." Three years later, at the commencement of his friendship with Wilde, Lord Alfred Douglas noticed that Wilde "was not very kind to his wife. . . . [H]e was often impatient with her, and sometimes snubbed her, and he resented, and showed that he resented, the attitude of slight disapproval that she always adopted towards him" (59–60). However Douglas also says that Wilde and Constance were "still on terms of great affection" when he first came to know them, that Wilde "adored" his wife, and that the couple only became estranged "a year or two before the final catastrophe" (*Oscar Wilde: A Summing-Up,* 95–96). One recent biographer remarks that the "chasm between Oscar and Constance widened" in the autumn of 1892 and that by the time of Wilde's arrest in

April 1895, the couple had "made a habit of living apart from time to time" (Moyle, *Constance*, 212, 3).

45. Constance's symptoms are now understood to be those of multiple sclerosis, but they were never correctly diagnosed by doctors in her own lifetime. See pp. 225–26 above.

46. More Adey to Adela Schuster, 12 March 1898, William Andrews Clark Memorial Library, University of California, Los Angeles.

47. Amor, *Mrs. Oscar Wilde*, 210.

48. J. Robert Maguire, *Ceremonies of Bravery: Oscar Wilde, Carlos Blacker, and the Dreyfus Affair* (Oxford: Oxford University Press, 2013), 89.

49. Quoted in Moyle, *Constance*, 309.

50. Lady Queensberry to More Adey, 9 June 1897, William Andrews Clark Memorial Library, University of California, Los Angeles.

51. Douglas, *The Autobiography of Alfred Douglas* (London: Secker 1929), 145.

52. Ibid., 146. Douglas later wrote privately that in the summer of 1897, "I knew nothing about . . . his [Wilde's] double-faced letters about me to Ross from Berneval, written on the very days when he was overwhelming me with expressions of love and endearment in letters to myself" (letter to Frank Harris, 30 April 1925, rpt. in Frank Harris and Lord Alfred Douglas, *A New Preface to "The Life and Confessions of Oscar Wilde"* [London: Fortune Press, 1925], 47). In 1936, on being shown the letters that Wilde had written to Alfred Douglas from Berneval, Sherard entirely altered his long-held views on where responsibility lay for Wilde's scandalous reunion with Douglas. Sherard says that these letters showed "alas that Oscar's duplicity was at least as extensive as that of Ross, [Douglas's] bête noire" (Sherard to Hesketh Pearson, 27 June 1936, Hesketh Pearson Collection 10.11, Harry Ransom Center, University of Texas at Austin).

53. Letter from Holman, Queensberry's solicitor, to More Adey, May 1895, quoted in Linda Stratmann, *The Marquess of Queensberry: Wilde's Nemesis* (New Haven, CT: Yale University Press, 2013), 226.

54. Ostensibly Hansell's resignation was due to what he perceived to be conflict between his roles as Wilde's personal solicitor and as a trustee of Wilde's separation agreement with Constance. Henceforth Hansell continued acting in this latter role, telling Wilde in November that he was going to deprive him of his allowance from Constance, according to the agreement's terms, on account of Wilde's continuing association with Bosie.

55. Quoted in Stratmann, *The Marquess of Queensberry*, 226. According to Robert Sherard, during the whole time that Wilde was in Dieppe and Berneval, he was subjected to the espionage of private detectives in the pay of Queensberry. When Sherard visited Wilde that August, "a mysterious individual was ever to be seen hanging about the villa." After observing the detective outside the window one rainy night during his visit, and taking pity on this individual's bedraggled and muddy condition, Sherard even suggested "that we should invite him indoors and give him a cup of tea. But such a proceeding appeared irregular to Oscar Wilde. 'It would look like vulgar bravado,' he said, and the detective was left to amuse himself as best he could under the dripping hedge in a very

muddy lane" (Sherard, *Oscar Wilde: The Story of an Unhappy Friendship* [1905; repr. London: Greening, 1909], 245).

56. Lady Queensberry to More Adey, 13 November 1897, William Andrews Clark Memorial Library, University of California, Los Angeles.

57. Father Cuthbert Dunne, letter to the secretary of the Catholic Truth Society of Ireland, undated, unpaginated holograph, William Andrews Clark Memorial Library, University of California, Los Angeles.

58. Cf. "The three women I have most admired are Queen Victoria, Sarah Bernhardt, and Lilly Langtry. I would have married any of them with pleasure" (quoted in Vincent O'Sullivan, *Aspects of Wilde* [New York: Henry Holt, 1936], 18).

59. *Oscar Wilde, tel que je l'ai connu* by Alin Caillas (Paris: La Pensée Universelle, 1971), partially translated by Padraig Rooney as "Feasting with Cubs: Wilde in Berneval," *The Harp* 11 (1996): 45.

60. Martin Birnbaum, *Oscar Wilde, Fragments and Memories* (New York: Drake, 1914), 24.

61. Christian Krogh, "Fritz Thaulow and Oscar Wilde at Dieppe, 1897," *The New Age* (1908), repr. in *Oscar Wilde: Interviews and Recollections*, ed. Mikhail, 2:350.

62. Krogh, "Fritz Thaulow and Oscar Wilde at Dieppe, 1897," 350–51.

63. See Young, *Apologia Pro Oscar Wilde* (London: William Reeves, 1895). The few other important published defenses of Wilde by Britons, at the time of his trials, include Ernest Newman, "Oscar Wilde: A Literary Appreciation," *Free Review* 4, no. 3 (June 1895): 193–206; and James H. Wilson's privately printed *Some Gentle Criticisms of British Justice* (London: n.p., 1895), which appeared under the pseudonym "I Playfair."

64. *Letters of Ernest Dowson*, ed. Desmond Flower and Henry Maas (Rutherford, NJ: Fairleigh Dickinson University Press, 1968), 384.

65. Ibid.

66. Quoted in W. B. Yeats, *The Trembling of the Veil* (1922), in *Autobiographies*, vol. 3 of *The Collected Works of W. B. Yeats*, ed. William H. O'Donnell and Douglas N. Archibald (New York: Scribner, 1999), 252. Wilde at this time "hoped to conform to British bourgeois pretensions of morality," Robert Sherard later wrote, and to "this hopeless resolution" we must attribute his "agreeing to accompany Dowson to the brothel at Le Légué, Dieppe, where he had his supper of cold mutton" (unpublished letter to A. J. A. Symons, 8 June 1937, William Andrews Clark Memorial Library, University of California, Los Angeles). But see also Sherard's later letter to Hesketh Pearson, in which he writes "Yeats's yarn in *The Trembling of Veil* is a disgusting perversion of the truth. Dowson most certainly did not thus relate the incident at the brothel at the Légué, Dieppe, where Oscar once sacrificed to Venus Meretrix. It is true he did take Oscar hoping to *le ramener au bien* to this lupanar . . . and it is true that Oscar described it to him as supping on cold mutton. I could almost swear that it was O. W. who told me this when I was in Dieppe or Berneval in 1897. But Dowson was a puffick gentleman and would never have embellished the sordid story with such palpable absurdities [as Yeats gives]" (unpublished letter to Hesketh Pearson, 11 March 1940, Hesketh Pearson Collection 10.11, Harry Ransom Center, University of Texas at Austin).

67. Krogh, "Fritz Thaulow and Oscar Wilde at Dieppe, 1897," 349. The French translates as "One must accept a personality as it is. One must never regret that a poet is drunk but that drunkards are not always poets" (Mikhail's translation).

68. *Letters of Ernest Dowson,* ed. Flower and Maas, 387.

69. Letter from Max Beerbohm to Ada Leverson, 20 May 1916, Beerbohm Collection 2.4, Harry Ransom Center, University of Texas at Austin. Unfortunately for posterity, Rothenstein's pastel portrait of Wilde was stolen from Wilde's residence in Naples early the following year, along with others of his possessions, while he was away on a trip to Sicily. See *The Portrait Drawings of William Rothenstein: 1889–1926* (London: Chapman and Hall, 1926), 2.

70. Gide, *Oscar Wilde: In Memoriam; De Profundis,* trans. B. Frechtman (New York: Philosophical Library, 1949), 20–21.

71. Ibid., 22–23.

72. Ibid., 27.

73. Wilde had written to Ross from Reading, on April 6, of his "horror . . . of going out into the world without a single book of my own" (*CL* 790), enclosing a long list of books, in both English and French, that he would like Ross to acquire on his behalf, and asking Ross to inquire whether any of Wilde's literary friends would kindly send him copies of their books upon his release. When Wilde arrived in Dieppe, a shelf full of books was waiting for him, and over the ensuing weeks, numerous friends—Ross, Adey, Turner, Strangman, Douglas, Smithers, Housman—sent him further books. "Bring me a lot of books and cigarettes," Wilde instructed Douglas, when inviting Douglas to visit in mid-June (*CL* 899). Among the books in which Wilde is known to have delighted over the summer of 1897 are Beerbohm's *The Happy Hypocrite,* Pierre Loti's *Aphrodite,* Ernest La Jeunesse's *L'Imitation de Notre-Maître Napoléon,* Laurence Housman's *All-Fellows,* and the recently published poems of Ernest Dowson, Lord Alfred Douglas, and A. E. Housman.

74. Gide, *Oscar Wilde: In Memoriam,* 28.

75. William Rothenstein, *Men and Memories: Recollections, 1872–1938,* ed. Mary Lago (Columbia: University of Missouri Press, 1978), 111.

76. Rupert Croft-Cooke, *Bosie: Lord Alfred Douglas, His Friends and Enemies* (Indianapolis: Bobbs-Merrill, 1963), 156.

77. Robert Ross, unpublished letter to Alfred Douglas, 23 June 1897, TS copy, William Andrews Clark Memorial Library, University of California, Los Angeles.

78. Douglas to Ross, 13 July 1897, quoted in *Daily Telegraph* November 25, 1921; also in Caspar Wintermans, *Alfred Douglas: A Poet's Life and His Finest Work* (London: Peter Owen, 2007), 86.

79. Douglas, *Autobiography,* 148.

80. Sherard, *Life of Oscar Wilde,* 405.

81. Robert Sherard to A. J. A. Symons, 3 June 1937, William Andrews Clark Memorial Library, University of California, Los Angeles. Sherard's phrasing echoes that of Lord Alfred Douglas, who had written to Sherard five years previously: "It is an absolute fact that it was Ross who at Berneval dragged Oscar back to homosexual practices. Oscar told

me this himself. . . . Harris told me at Nice that Ross had told him the same story" (Douglas to Sherard, 26 September 1932, British Library, Add. MS 81705).

82. McKenna, *The Secret Life of Oscar Wilde* (New York: Basic Books, 2005), 434.

83. *Max and Will: Max Beerbohm and Will Rothenstein, Their Friendship and Letters 1893–1945*, ed. Mary Lago and Karl Beckson (London: John Murray, 1975), 38. See also Beerbohm's comment in a letter to Reginald Turner on 20 August 1897, "I hear that ass Oscar is under surveillance—I suppose he is playing the giddy goat" (*Max Beerbohm's Letters to Reginald Turner*, ed. Hart-Davis, 120).

84. John Fothergill's unpublished memoirs, quoted in David Sox, *Bachelors of Art: Edward Perry Warren and the Lewes House Brotherhood* (London: Fourth Estate, 1991), 139–40.

85. Ibid.

86. Fothergill, unpublished letter to A. J. A. Symons, undated, William Andrews Clark Memorial Library, University of California, Los Angeles.

87. Fothergill, unpublished memoirs, quoted in Sox, *Bachelors of Art*, 141.

88. Wilde, handwritten inscription written into presentation copy of Wilde, *Salomé: Drame en un Acte* (Paris: Librairie de l'Art Indépendent, 1893), quoted in Nicholas Frankel, *Oscar Wilde's Decorated Books* (Ann Arbor: University of Michigan Press, 2000), 60.

89. James G. Nelson, *Publisher to the Decadents: Leonard Smithers in the Careers of Beardsley, Wilde, Dowson* (University Park: Pennsylvania State University Press, 2000); Smithers, quoted in O'Sullivan, *Aspects of Wilde*, 102.

90. *Letters of Ernest Dowson*, 390.

91. Laurence Housman to Hesketh Pearson, 4 April, 1944, in Hesketh Pearson Collection 4.6, Harry Ransom Center, University of Texas at Austin.

92. O'Sullivan, *Aspects of Wilde*, 77; *Letters of Aubrey Beardsley*, ed. Henry Maas, J. L. Duncan, and W. G. Good (1970; Oxford: Plantin, 1990), 409.

93. Both Housman himself and Reginald Turner claimed to have given or sent Wilde a copy of *A Shropshire Lad* shortly after its release. *A Shropshire Lad* had appeared while Wilde was in prison, and according to Housman, Robert Ross memorized and recited some of the poems in the volume to Wilde on a visit to him in jail.

94. In fact, this was Smithers's *re*-entry into Wilde's life since, as Smithers may have reminded Wilde, they had corresponded briefly in the late 1880s, when Smithers had complimented Wilde on *The Happy Prince*.

95. Wilde had routinely had his literary manuscripts typewritten since the early 1890s. Like many twentieth-century authors, he found that the order and clarity of the fresh typescript enabled him to see his work anew and gave an impetus to the writing process.

96. Ellmann, *Oscar Wilde*, 547.

97. Douglas, *Autobiography*, 151.

98. I quote here from the amended typescript of *The Autobiography of Alfred Douglas* at the Harry Ransom Center, University of Texas at Austin, not the version published by

Martin Secker in 1929. The phrase "and I did the same," after "Poor Oscar cried when I met him at the station," was deleted by Douglas before publication.

99. Wilde, "The Fisherman and His Soul," in *Complete Shorter Fiction*, ed. Isobel Murray (New York: Oxford World's Classics, 1979), 234.

4. The Pursuit of Love

1. "I saw Oscar once again after the Rouen meeting," says Ross: "then he lied to me by saying he had not any intention of going to Italy with Douglas" (letter to Frank Harris, 17 May 1914, Frank Harris Collection, 4.9, Harry Ransom Center, University of Texas at Austin).

2. Douglas, *Without Apology* (London: Secker, 1938), 275.

3. Gertrude Atherton, *Adventures of a Novelist* (1932), partially repr. as "An Evil Influence," in *Oscar Wilde: Interviews and Recollections,* ed. E. H. Mikhail (London: Macmillan, 1979), 2:344–46.

4. Richard Ellmann, *Oscar Wilde* (New York: Knopf, 1988), 550.

5. Vincent O'Sullivan, *Aspects of Wilde* (New York: Henry Holt, 1936), 180.

6. Ibid., 179.

7. Frank Browning, *A Queer Geography* (1996; rev. ed. New York: Farrar Strauss, 1998), 42.

8. John Pemble, *The Mediterranean Passion: Victorians and Edwardians in the South* (Oxford: Clarendon Press, 1987), 100.

9. August von Platen, *Tagebücher,* quoted in Robert Aldrich, *The Seduction of the Mediterranean: Writing, Art and Homosexual Fantasy* (Hoboken, NJ: Taylor & Francis, 1993), 65.

10. Aldrich, *The Seduction of the Mediterranean,* 168.

11. A. Sper, *Capri Und Die Homosexuellen* (1902), quoted in Aldrich, *The Seduction of the Mediterranean,* 163.

12. Wilde had been thinking about living in the South of Italy as early as May 31, though he ruled it out on two separate occasions (*CL* 869 and 883), saying he preferred to live in Berneval.

13. Lord Alfred Douglas, *Oscar Wilde and Myself* (New York: Duffield, 1914), 126.

14. Ibid.

15. Douglas, *The Autobiography of Alfred Douglas* (London: Secker 1929), 133, and Douglas, *Oscar Wilde and Myself,* 126.

16. Douglas, *Autobiography,* 133. See also Douglas's comments that, since he did not know of the existence of the *De Profundis* MS till years after Wilde's death, "I may have missed references to it which perhaps he made under the impression that I knew of its existence" and "on one occasion when we were together he referred to something he had said or written about me in prison" (*Autobiography,* 134–35). According to Douglas, after he had once reproached Wilde about something, the latter replied "Surely you are not bringing up against me what I wrote in prison when I was starving and half mad. You

must know that I didn't really mean a word of what I said" (135). At the time, Douglas says, he had no idea that Wilde was referring to *De Profundis.*

17. Douglas, *Without Apology,* 75.

18. "The Dead Poet," in Caspar Wintermans, *Alfred Douglas: A Poet's Life and His Finest Work* (London: Peter Owen, 2007), 249.

19. Douglas, unpublished letter to Wilde, 15 May 1895, The William Andrews Clark Memorial Library, University of California, Los Angeles.

20. Douglas, "Oscar Wilde," unpublished typescript, p. 4, Douglas Collection 1.4, Harry Ransom Center, University of Texas at Austin.

21. Alfred Douglas, letter to More Adey, 30 November 1895, in Rupert Croft-Cooke, *Bosie: Lord Alfred Douglas, His Friends and Enemies* (Indianapolis: Bobbs-Merrill, 1963), 138.

22. Douglas to Ross, 13 July 1897, quoted in the *Daily Telegraph,* November 25, 1921, and also in Wintermans, *Alfred Douglas,* 86.

23. Alfred Douglas to More Adey, 4 July 1897 (TS copy), The William Andrews Clark Memorial Library, University of California, Los Angeles.

24. Douglas, letter to his mother, 7 December 1897, quoted in *Without Apology,* 303.

25. Wilde linked this idea to the final line of Anatole France's story "L'Humaine Tragédie" (The Human Tragedy) which runs "Je t'aime parce que tu m'as perdu" (I love you because you have destroyed me).

26. See H. Montgomery Hyde, appendix D, "Lord Alfred Douglas and the Aftermath of the Wilde Trials," in his *The Trials of Oscar Wilde,* 339–48.

27. Douglas, "Oscar Wilde," unpublished typescript, p. 4, Douglas Collection 1.4, Harry Ransom Center, University of Texas at Austin.

28. "Lord Alfred Douglas, "Introduction à mes poèmes avec quelques considérations sur l'affaire Oscar Wilde," *La Revue Blanche* 10, no. 72 (June 1, 1896): 484–85, my translation.

29. "Rejected," in Wintermans, *Alfred Douglas: A Poet's Life and His Finest Work,* 231.

30. Wilde, *The Picture of Dorian Gray: An Annotated Uncensored Edition,* ed. Nicholas Frankel (Cambridge, MA: Harvard University Press, 2011), 246. See too Wilde's comment to Douglas, "Hyacinthus, whom Apollo loved so madly, was you in Greek days" (*CL* 544).

31. "Amoris Vincula" (1893), in Douglas, *The City of the Soul* (London: Grant Richards, 1899), 63.

32. Ibid. A similar sentiment structures "Rondeau," written in 1895 at Sorrento, near Naples, where Douglas's grandmother had lived till her death in 1893 and where Douglas had retreated shortly after Wilde's conviction. Here Wilde's absence only magnifies "my great unrest that will not die," rendering joyless the splendid coastal seascape that the two men were to enjoy together briefly in 1897:

> If he were here, this glorious sky,
> This sweet blue sea, these ships that lie
> On the bay's bosom, like white sheep
> On English fields, these hours that creep

Golden in summer's panoply,
This wind that seems a lover's sigh,
Would make a heaven of peace as high
As God's great love, a bliss as deep.
If he were here.

This great peace does but magnify
My great unrest that will not die,
My deep despair that may not reap
One poppy, one poor hour of sleep,
Nor aught but pain to wake and cry
"If he were here!"

(in Wintermans, *Alfred Douglas,* 231)

33. "The Travelling Companion," in Wintermans, *Alfred Douglas,* 235.

34. By 1897, Douglas had authored a number of ballads, including "The Ballad of Perkin Warbeck," "Jonquil and Fleur-de-Lys," and "The Ballad of Hate."

35. "Sonnet on Approaching Italy," in *Poems and Poems in Prose,* ed. Fong and Beckson, 32.

36. Douglas, *Oscar Wilde and Myself,* 125.

37. *Il Pungolo parlamentare* October 9–10, 1897, quoted in Masolino D'Amico, "Oscar Wilde in Naples," in *Rediscovering Oscar Wilde,* ed. George Sandulescu (Gerard's Cross, UK: Colin Smythe, 1994), 78–79.

38. Douglas, *Autobiography,* 159.

39. Longus's idyllic romance, later transformed into a ballet by Ravel and Sergei Diaghilev, was popular with aesthetes; an exquisite new edition, with decorations by Wilde's close friends Charles Ricketts and Charles Shannon, had appeared in 1893.

40. "A Triad of The Moon," in Wintermans, *Alfred Douglas,* 245.

41. Douglas, *Oscar Wilde and Myself,* 123.

42. See pp. 240–41 above.

43. "He put the poem (far the best poem he ever wrote) into its final shape while I was actually sitting in the same room as him" (Douglas, *Without Apology,* 217).

44. Quoted in *CL* 931 n.3.

45. A misspelled reference to Belgian symbolist painter Fernand Khnopff (1858–1921), whose illustrations to the work of the poets Georges Rodenbach and Grégoire Le Roy emphasized themes of silence, solitude, and secretiveness. For Beardsley's praise for *The Ballad,* see his letter to Smithers, 18 September 1897, in which he writes "I hope Sebastian O'Scar will get his poem in the *Chronicle*" (*The Letters of Aubrey Beardsley,* ed. Henry Maas, J. L. Duncan, and W. G. Good [1970; Oxford: Plantin, 1990], 371).

46. As Merlin Holland notes, Herrmann sent Wilde a sketch for the proposed frontispiece in January 1898. Wilde's description of Herrmann's work anticipates the famous edition of *The Ballad of Reading Gaol* illustrated in 1923 by the Flemish Expressionist Frans Masereel.

47. To this suggestion Smithers replied as follows: "I do not think the poem ought to be over-elaborate with its illustrations; it is on a severe subject and must be treated as such. Its ornamentation, unless perfectly done, will take away from the effect of the poem" (27 September 1897, quoted in Nelson, *Publisher to the Decadents,* 191).

48. Douglas, *Oscar Wilde and Myself,* 123.

49. Douglas, *Autobiography,* 157.

50. See Stanley Weintraub, *Reggie: A Portrait of Reginald Turner* (New York: Braziller, 1965), 89–90.

51. Undated autograph letter to Smithers containing fragment of *The Ballad of Reading Gaol,* October 1897 (AMS [fragment] of *The Ballad of Reading Gaol,* canto 3 with comment, page 3), Free Library of Philadelphia Collection of Literary Manuscripts, Free Library of Philadelphia, Rare Book Department, available online at https://libwww .freelibrary.org/digital/item/51911. Elsewhere in the same letter, Wilde tells Smithers "I am still on literary terms with Robbie."

52. Until 1900, when a special "execution center" was constructed, the execution shed at Reading Prison was in fact the photographic studio. See Anthony Stokes, *Pit of Shame: The Real Ballad of Reading Gaol* (Winchester, UK: Waterside, 2007), 107.

53. *Poésie et Propagande* means "poetry and propaganda." *Dichtung und Wahrheit,* the subtitle of Goethe's 1833 autobiography, means "poetry and truth."

54. "The Devoted Friend," in *Complete Shorter Fiction,* ed. Isobel Murray (New York: Oxford World's Classics, 1979), 124–25.

55. Quoted in Roy Morris Jr., *Declaring His Genius* (Cambridge, MA: Harvard University Press, 2013), 196.

56. Wilde had published in at least one New York–based newspaper previously, having contributed "The Philosophy of Dress" to the *New York Tribune* in 1885, although it is not known how remunerative this had proven.

57. Leonard Smithers to Ross, 23 October 1897, MS, The William Andrews Clark Memorial Library, University of California, Los Angeles.

58. Elisabeth Marbury, *My Crystal Ball: Reminiscences* (1923), partially extracted as "The Last Days of Oscar Wilde," in *Oscar Wilde: Interviews and Recollections,* ed. Mikhail, 2:438.

59. "Some Literary Notes," January 1889, in *Journalism, Part 2,* ed. John Stokes and Mark Turner, vol. 7 of *The Complete Works of Oscar Wilde* (Oxford: Oxford University Press, 2013), 147.

60. As the scholar Rita Severi writes, "if his first Italian translation were carried out on his only French work, he would stand a good chance of obtaining a fair deal and an accurate edition of the play that would begin to establish his fame in Italy" (Severi, "'Astonishing in my Italian': Oscar Wilde's First Italian Editions 1890–1952," in *The Reception of Oscar Wilde in Europe,* ed. Stefano Evangelista [London: Continuum, 2010], 110).

61. Ibid., 111.

62. Chara's translation eventually appeared in 1905.

63. Quoted in Ellmann, *Oscar Wilde*, 353.

64. Quoted in D'Amico, "Oscar Wilde in Naples," 77.

65. The fictitious interview is transcribed, newly translated into English, in D'Amico, "Oscar Wilde in Naples," 78–79.

66. To his great credit, Sherard gave both sides of the argument in his *Oscar Wilde: Story of an Unhappy Friendship* (1905; repr. London: Greening, 1909), which constitutes the only source for Wilde's angry letter rebuking Sherard. Sherard believed that "a lying account of my words was transmitted to Naples," adding that the receipt of Wilde's angry letter "distressed me greatly" (251). According to Sherard, when confronted with the news of Wilde's residency at Naples with Douglas, he had merely said that "it was a great and an unfortunate mistake on his part; that his action would everywhere be miscon-strued; that his traducers and enemies would be justified in the eyes of the world; and many sympathies would be alienated" (250). Sherard later wrote that the loss of Wilde's friendship and respect "never turned me against him. When a man, just like a devoted fox-terrier, is busy with a pack of enemies, the kindest-intentioned interference by a friend to rescue him from the melee is likely to cause that friend to smart and bleed" (letter to Hesketh Pearson, 19 April 1934, Hesketh Pearson Collection 10.11, Harry Ransom Center, University of Texas at Austin).

67. Benjamin Bailey, *Naples Declared: A Walk around the Bay* (New York: Penguin 2012), 160. By contrast, when Douglas was invited for lunch to the Capri villa of the celebrated Swedish physician and philanthropist Dr. Axel Munthe, he said he could not come "without my friend," to which the liberal-minded Munthe replied "that he would be pleased to meet him and hoped I did not think him so ignorant and so brutal as to be unkind to anyone who had suffered so much or been so shamefully treated" (Douglas, *Without Apology,* 299).

68. Douglas, *Oscar Wilde and Myself,* 127.

69. Ibid. Douglas saw the visit of the Embassy attaché as symptomatic of the official pressure being placed on his mother, Lady Queensberry, to effect a split between himself and Wilde (see *Without Apology,* 216). By contrast, Neil McKenna sees it as having "something to do with the fact that Lord Rosebery [the ex-Prime Minister and leader of the Liberal Party] had that year paid £16,000 for the beautiful Villa Delahante [now the Villa Rosebery, an official residence of the Italian President], also in Posilippo" (*The Secret Life of Oscar Wilde* [New York: Basic Books, 2005], 445). Rosebery, with whom Douglas's brother Viscount Drumlanrig may have had a homosexual affair prior to his death (probably by suicide) in 1894, has long been suspected of playing a behind-the-scenes role in the prosecution of Oscar Wilde, as a way of covering-up his own sexual tastes. As McKenna writes, "There was every reason to fear that the unpredictable and passionate Bosie might confront Rosebery with his allegations of a conspiracy in the Liberal Party, or the plot to sacrifice Oscar in order to save Rosebery and other senior Liberals" (445).

70. Adey to Schuster, unpublished letter, 12 March 1898, William Andrews Clark Memorial Library, University of California, Los Angeles.

71. Quoted in *CL* 955 n.1.

72. Quoted by Wilde, *CL* 994.

73. Constance Holland, letter to Carlos Blacker, 30 September 1897, quoted in J. Robert Maguire, *Ceremonies of Bravery: Oscar Wilde, Carlos Blacker, and the Dreyfus Affair* (Oxford: Oxford University Press, 2013), 95.

74. See *CL* 989.

75. Douglas to Adey, 20 November 1897, quoted in Croft-Cooke, *Bosie,* 165–66.

76. See pp. 212–13 above.

77. O'Sullivan, *Aspects of Wilde,* 81.

78. See Douglas, *Autobiography,* 123.

79. Ibid., 155.

80. Douglas to his mother, undated, quoted in *Without Apology,* 297–98.

81. Ibid., 299. Lady Queensberry had suffered greatly at the hands of the Marquess of Queensberry, both before and after her divorce from him in 1887.

82. Douglas, *Autobiography,* 155, 159.

83. Douglas to Strangman, 29 November 1897, quoted in Ellmann, *Oscar Wilde,* 553.

84. Douglas to his mother, 7 December 1897, extracted in *Without Apology,* 304. Douglas felt that his family owed this to Wilde as a "debt of honour," since his brother, Percy Douglas, had pledged—but ultimately not paid—£500 toward the costs of Wilde's libel action against the Marquess of Queensberry.

85. Wilde always maintained publicly that the £200 represented simply partial payment of Bosie's debt of honor. He writes "it is quite untrue that I received £200 from Lady Q. on condition of not living with Bosie. Bosie owed me £500. He admitted this a debt of honour. . . . He paid me £200 of this, but I have had no communication with that mischievous foolish woman; I simply received less than half of what Bosie owes me. I know that Bosie made terms with his mother, but that is not my concern" (*CL* 1038). In fact, Wilde had sent Lady Q. a written pledge that he would not live with Bosie again (Lady Queensberry to More Adey, 18 December 1897, The William Andrews Clark Memorial Library, University of California, Los Angeles).

86. Quoted in Douglas, *Without Apology,* 304–5).

87. Douglas, *Oscar Wilde: A Summing-Up* (London: Duckworth, 1940), 101.

5. *The Ballad of Reading Gaol*

1. Harry de Windt, *My Restless Life* (London: Grant Richards, 1909), 232.

2. Vincent O'Sullivan, *Aspects of Wilde* (New York: Henry Holt, 1936), 60. Wilde had been informed as early as mid-October that O'Sullivan intended to visit, whereupon he had written enthusiastically to O'Sullivan expressing his joy at the prospect of seeing him again. Shortly before this, O'Sullivan had defended Wilde at the Author's Club in the face of Robert Sherard's rebuke. See pp. 152–53 above, and *CL* 963–64.

3. O'Sullivan, *Aspects of Wilde,* 60–61.

4. Ibid., 147.

5. When the journal *The Academy* proposed the founding of an English Academy of Letters in November 1897, it omitted Wilde's name from its list of possible nominees.

While recognizing that the exercise was something of a parlor game, both Shaw and Wells proposed that Wilde should be a member of any such Academy.

6. See Lady Queensberry, unpublished letter to More Adey, 18 December 1897, TS copy, The William Andrews Clark Memorial Library, University of California, Los Angeles.

7. *The Duchess of Padua,* in *Plays 1: The Duchess of Padua; Salomé: Drame en un Acte; Salome: A Tragedy in One Act,* ed. Joseph Donohue, vol. 5 of *The Complete Works of Oscar Wilde* (Oxford: Oxford University Press, 2013), 180; "The Critic as Artist," in *Criticism: Historical Criticism, Intentions, and The Soul of Man,* ed. Josephine M. Guy, vol. 4 of *The Complete Works of Oscar Wilde* (Oxford: Oxford University Press, 2007), 155.

8. "Theocritus. A Villanelle," in *Poems and Poems in Prose,* ed. Bobby Fong and Karl Beckson, vol. 1 of *The Complete Works of Oscar Wilde* (Oxford: Oxford University Press, 2000), 67–68.

9. Stefania Arcara, "Hellenic Transgressions, Homosexual Politics: Wilde, Symonds, and Sicily," *Studies in Travel Writing* 16, no. 2 (June 2012): 142.

10. For the life of Stopford, see William Clarke, *Hidden Treasures of the Romanovs: Saving the Royal Jewels* (Edinburgh: National Museums of Scotland, 2009).

11. Vicki Goldberg, "A Man-Made Arcadia Enshrining Male Beauty," *New York Times,* August 13, 2000, 30–31; Arcara, "Hellenic Transgressions, Homosexual Politics," 137.

12. Arcara, "Hellenic Transgressions, Homosexual Politics," 138.

13. In the postscript to a letter to Wilde dated 26 January, Smithers says "I hear you have a beautiful love in Naples." Wilde's "beautiful love" has never been identified (*CL* 1011–12 n.3).

14. Quoted in Richard Ellmann, *Oscar Wilde* (New York: Knopf, 1988), 557–58.

15. Quoted in James G. Nelson, *Publisher to the Decadents: Leonard Smithers in the Careers of Beardsley, Wilde, Dowson* (University Park: Pennsylvania State University Press, 2000), 199.

16. Quoted in ibid., 195.

17. Marbury to Smithers, 16 February 1898, The William Andrews Clark Memorial Library, University of California, Los Angeles. Marbury's commission and fees are specified in a statement of charges dated 11 February 1898 that accompanied her 16 February letter to Smithers. Her resulting payment of $88.59 to Smithers was the equivalent of just over £18.

18. The sinking of the warship the USS Maine in Havana harbor, one of the events that sparked the Spanish-American War, occurred just two days after the appearance of Wilde's poem.

19. A further thirty copies of a special deluxe edition priced at 21s. were issued printed on Japanese vellum.

20. Unsigned review in *The Academy,* February 26, 1898, repr. in *Oscar Wilde: The Critical Heritage,* ed. Karl Beckson (London: Routledge & Kegan Paul, 1970), 212; *Yale Literary Magazine* 63, no. 9 (June 1898): 443.

21. Wilde originally planned on disguising the identity of the man whose execution the poem commemorates, but he subsequently changed his mind and decided to use Wooldridge's own initials rather than the fictional initials "R. J. M." he originally proposed to use (see *CL* 986). As many commentators have pointed out, as a trooper in the Royal Horse Guards, Wooldridge would have worn a blue coat, not a scarlet one; moreover, he murdered his wife in the street, not in her bed.

22. Healy, *Confessions of A Journalist,* 2nd ed. (London: Chatto and Windus, 1904), 133.

23. *The Ballad of Reading Gaol,* in *Poems and Poems in Prose,* ed. Fong and Beckson, 195, line 3, hereafter cited by line number.

24. Line 160.

25. Lines 4–5.

26. Lines 9–18.

27. Lines 109–32.

28. Lines 24–28.

29. Quoted in Joseph Bristow, "All Men Kill the Thing They Love: Romance, Realism, and *The Ballad of Reading Gaol*," in *Approaches to Teaching The Works of Oscar Wilde,* ed. Philip E. Smith II (New York: MLA, 2008), 246 n.1.

30. Lines 35–36.

31. Lines 53–54.

32. Lines 39–46.

33. Wilde maintained that his mother's ghost visited his jail cell the night she died.

34. Constance Holland, letter to Mrs. Robinson, 19 April 1895, quoted in Franny Moyle, *Constance: The Tragic and Scandalous Life of Mrs. Oscar Wilde* (London: John Murray, 2011), 272.

35. Vyvyan Holland, *Son of Oscar Wilde* (1954; repr. New York: Oxford University Press, 1988), 61.

36. Ibid., 63.

37. Ibid., 134.

38. Ibid., 200.

39. Line 48.

40. Lines 42, 47.

41. H. Montgomery Hyde, *The Trials of Oscar Wilde* (1962; repr. Mineola, NY: Dover Publications, 1973), 272.

42. Line 163. Prison regulations prohibited Wilde from communicating with his fellow prisoners; see p. 37 above.

43. Lines 169–74.

44. Lines 53–84.

45. "In The Depths," *Evening News & Evening Mail,* March 1, 1905, repr. in *Oscar Wilde: Interviews and Recollections,* ed. E. H. Mikhail (London: Macmillan, 1979), 2:331.

46. Lines 535–606.

47. Seamus Heaney, "Speranza in Reading: On 'The Ballad of Reading Gaol'" (1993), in his *The Redress of Poetry* (New York: Farrar, Straus and Giroux, 1995), 87.

48. Arthur Symons, signed rev. of *The Ballad of Reading Gaol*, in *Saturday Review*, March 12, 1898, repr. in *Oscar Wilde: The Critical Heritage*, ed. Beckson, 219.

49. W. B. Yeats, introduction to *The Oxford Book of Modern Verse, 1892–1935* (Oxford: Oxford University Press, 1936), vii.

50. Ibid.

51. W. B. Henley, "De Profundis," unsigned review of *The Ballad of Reading Gaol*, in *The Outlook*, March 5, 1898, repr. in *Oscar Wilde: The Critical Heritage*, ed. Beckson, 217, 214.

52. Ibid., 214. Henley added that the poem as a whole was "a blunder in taste, in sentiment, in art, for it is a mis-statement of fact," and that it ultimately delivered "a taste of unveracity which fouls your mind all through your reading" (ibid., 215–26). Upon reading Henley's "coarse and vulgar" critique, Wilde remarked that "he is so proud of having written *vers libres* on his scrofula that he is quite jealous if a poet writes a lyric on his prison" (*CL* 1032). Some days later, after other reviews of *The Ballad* had appeared, he wrote that "Henley's hysterical personalities have done no harm, but rather the contrary. I am quite obliged to him for playing the role of *Advocatus Diaboli* so well" (*CL* 1041).

53. Heaney, "Speranza in Reading," 85.

54. Unsigned review, *The Critic*, June 1899, repr. in *Oscar Wilde: The Critical Heritage*, ed. Beckson, 224.

55. Lines 337–39.

56. Anthony Stokes, *Pit of Shame: The Real Ballad of Reading Gaol* (Winchester, UK: Waterside, 2007).

57. Unsigned review, *The Academy*, 211.

58. Ibid.

59. Ibid.

60. "The critic . . . being limited to the subjective form, will necessarily be less able to fully express himself than the artist who has always at his disposal the forms that are impersonal and objective" ("The Critic as Artist," in *Criticism*, ed. Guy, 185).

61. William Wordsworth, 1800 preface, in Wordsworth and Coleridge, *Lyrical Ballads*, ed. R. L Brett and A. R. Jones (London: Methuen, 1963), 241.

62. In 1882 Wilde had praised the strength and simplicity of "The Brothers," which he viewed as his mother's "best ballad," and which Heaney argues held a special personal meaning for him, before reciting it in public (*CL* 606).

63. "The Ballad of Perkin Warbeck" (1894), printed as "Perkin Warbeck," in Douglas, *The City of the Soul* (London: John Lane, 1899), 49.

64. Ibid., 56.

65. Albert Friedman, *The Ballad Revival* (Chicago: University of Chicago Press, 1961), 329.

66. Heaney, "Speranza in Reading," 101, 85.

67. Henley, "De Profundis," 214.

68. "A Note on Some Modern Poets," *Woman's World,* December 1888, repr. in *Journalism Part 2,* ed. John Stokes and Mark Turner, vol. 7 of *The Complete Works of Oscar Wilde* (Oxford: Oxford University Press, 2013), 109.

69. Ibid.

70. Lines 145–50.

71. Heaney, "Speranza in Reading," 95.

72. Symons, signed review, 220.

73. Ibid. Symons is referring to canto 4 of the poem, in which Wilde describes how the prison authorities "will not sow . . . root or seedling" in the unconsecrated, "sterile" ground where they bury Wooldridge's corpse, for fear that the red rose might "blow more red" and "the white rose whiter blow" (lines 469–80).

74. Wilde, "The Decay of Lying," in *Criticism,* ed. Guy, 102.

75. Symons, signed review, 219.

6. The Seduction of Paris

1. The date of Wilde's arrival in Paris is not positively known. In a letter written at Naples on February 9, 1898 (postmarked February 11, 1898), he indicated he would be in Paris the following Sunday. If he arrived on the following Sunday, he would have arrived on February 13. He had certainly arrived by February 16, when he received copy from Smithers for a corrected second edition of *The Ballad.*

2. The Hôtel de Nice—"well spoken of," according to *Baedeker's Guide* of 1896—was among the better of the four Paris hotels in which Wilde stayed over the next three and a half years. In late March, 1898, he moved into the Hôtel d'Alsace for a two-month stay on the grounds that it was both cleaner and cheaper. He would stay again at the Hôtel d'Alsace from July to December 1898, from August 1899 till late March 1900, and again from June 1900 until his death the following November.

3. "The Censure and *Salome,*" *Pall Mall Budget,* June 30, 1892, repr. in *Oscar Wilde: Interviews and Recollections,* ed. E. H. Mikhail (London: Macmillan, 1979), 1:188; Maurice Sisley, "La *Salomé* de M. Oscar Wilde," *Le Gaulois,* June 29, 1892, partially extracted and translated as "I Adore Paris," in *Oscar Wilde: Interviews and Recollections,* ed. Mikhail, 1:189.

4. Quoted in Richard Ellmann, *Oscar Wilde* (New York: Knopf, 1988), 346.

5. For the reactions of French intellectuals to the Wilde trials, see Elisabeth Brunet, *Pour Oscar Wilde: Des écrivains français au secours du condamné* (Rouen: Assn. des Amis d'Hughes Rebell, 1994).

6. Gustave Le Rouge, "Oscar Wilde," *Nouvelle Littéraires* (1928), trans. in *Oscar Wilde: Interviews and Recollections,* ed. Mikhail, 2:461.

7. *The Annotated Importance of Being Earnest,* ed. Nicholas Frankel (Cambridge, MA: Harvard University Press, 2015), 149.

8. Jacques Daurelle, *Echo de Paris,* December 6, 1891, trans. as "An English Poet in Paris," in *Oscar Wilde: Interviews and Recollections,* ed. Mikhail, 1:170.

9. Ibid. The Château Rouge was described by *Macmillan's Magazine* as a "meeting-place of thieves and assassins" where "after dark the birds that prey upon society flock to find shelter and companionship" ("Vanishing Paris," *Macmillan's Magazine* 75 [November 1896–April 1897]: 294). The Café Anglais was one of Paris's oldest and most distinguished restaurants: "scarcely any foreigner of distinction visits the French capital," writes one Victorian commentator, "without dining . . . at the Café Anglais" (H. Sutherland Edwards, *Old and New Paris* [London: Cassell, 1893], 123).

10. David Sweetman, *Explosive Acts: Toulouse-Lautrec, Oscar Wilde, Félix Fénéon, and the Art and Anarchy of the Fin-de-Siècle* (New York: Simon & Schuster, 1999), 272–77.

11. Neil McKenna, *The Secret Life of Oscar Wilde* (New York: Basic Books, 2005), 55.

12. See ibid., 166–67. In late 1891, Wilde inscribed a copy of *A House of Pomegranates* for the young French writer Pierre Louÿs with "To the young man I adore," and McKenna writes that the young sexually repressed Louÿs found Wilde's company "revelatory and unsettling" (167). Similarly Wilde once remarked "I love André [Gide] personally very deeply." As McKenna states, there is no evidence that Wilde ever had a romantic or sexual affair with the young André Gide (167), and Gide ripped from his diary the pages covering the three weeks he spent more or less continuously in Wilde's company in late 1891. But there can be little doubt that Gide fell in love with Wilde at this time and, like Lord Henry Wotton with the young Dorian Gray, that Wilde effectively seduced the young Gide by forcing him to confront his repressed homoerotic desires.

13. By the end of the nineteenth century, writes Pascale Casanova, Paris had become "synonymous with literature . . . the capital of a republic having neither borders nor boundaries, a universal homeland exempt from all professions of patriotism, a kingdom of literature set up in opposition to the ordinary laws of states, a transnational realm whose sole imperatives were those of art and literature: the universal republic of letters" (*The World Republic of Letters,* trans. M. B. Debevoise [Cambridge, MA: Harvard University Press, 2004], 25–26, 29).

14. Le Rouge, "Oscar Wilde," 459.

15. Quoted in Ellmann, *Oscar Wilde,* 252.

16. Both "The Harlot's House" and "The Sphinx" were drafted but not completed in Paris in 1883. Upon its publication in 1894, "The Sphinx" was dedicated to the French writer Marcel Schwob in acknowledgement of its French roots. As Ellmann observes, the dedication was also a mark of Wilde's gratitude for Schwob's assistance with the composition of *Salomé,* as well as for Schwob's dedication to Wilde of his own 1892 story "le Pays bleu."

17. As the dedication to Louÿs of the 1893 first edition of *Salomé* indicates, the French symbolist and Parnassian writers who assisted Wilde with the play's composition also constitute its first and earliest readership. Salomé has been called "the icon of the ideology of the decadents" and "the Decadent ideal," and the play is, on one level at least, an act of homage to the French *décadent* writers and painters who had produced earlier

versions of the Salomé story. Wilde was particularly indebted to Mallarme's unpublished poem *Hérodiade*, Flaubert's short story "Herodias," Gustave Moreau's magnificent paintings of Salomé, and Joris-Karl Huysmans's descriptions of Moreau's paintings in his novel *A Rebours* (Against Nature).Some copies of the 1893 French edition of *Salomé* were sold in London, and the imprint of Wilde's English publishers, Elkin Matthews and John Lane, appears on the title page along with that of the French publisher "Librairie de l'Art Independent." But Wilde paid for the book's printing out of his own pocket (*CL* 548), and according to James G. Nelson, Matthews and Lane, on hearing about the proposed French edition, urged Wilde to increase the print run so that they might publish it in London simultaneously (*The Early Nineties: A View from the Bodley Head* [Cambridge, MA: Harvard University Press, 1971], 236). According to Wilde, he only allowed Matthews's and Lane's imprint to appear on the book's title page as "an act of pure courtesy" (*CL* 546).

18. Sisley, "La *Salomé* de M. Oscar Wilde" ("I Adore Paris"), 190.

19. Quoted in *CL* 492 n.3.

20. Arthur Ransome, *Oscar Wilde: A Critical Study* (1912), quoted in Emily Eels, "Naturalizing Oscar Wilde as an *homme de lettres*," in *The Reception of Oscar Wilde in Europe*, ed. Stefano Evangelista (London: Bloomsbury, 2010), 80.

21. Unsigned notice of Wilde, *Salomé: Drame en un Acte*, in *The Times*, February 23, 1893, repr. in *Oscar Wilde: The Critical Heritage*, ed. Karl Beckson (London: Routledge & Kegan Paul, 1970), 133; see also Ellmann, *Oscar Wilde*, 374–75.

22. "The Censure and *Salome*," 188.

23. Letter to Arthur Moore, c. 20 February 1896, *Letters of Ernest Dowson*, ed. Desmond Flower and Henry Maas (Rutherford, NJ: Fairleigh Dickinson University Press, 1968), 343.

24. Bauër, Mirbeau, Adam, de Regnier, Rebell, and Tailhade had all published articles in defense of Wilde shortly after his conviction, while Stuart Merrill had addressed an open letter to Léon Deschamps, editor of *La Plume*, calling on all French writers to petition the English Government for Wilde's release. See Brunet, *Pour Oscar Wilde*.

25. Sweetman, *Explosive Acts*, 391.

26. Ibid., 395.

27. Le Rouge, "Oscar Wilde," 460.

28. Alexander, Waller, and Wyndham were among London's leading actor-managers. All three had been instrumental in Wilde's success as a dramatist: Alexander and Waller had both acted in and produced two of Wilde's plays, while Wyndham, who had journeyed to Berneval to get Wilde writing again, had contracted with Wilde to produce and star in the opening run of *Earnest*. Grundy had publicly protested against the removal of Wilde's name from the billboards and programs of the St. James's Theatre at the time of his arrest. On receiving her copy of *The Ballad of Reading Gaol*, Constance remarked on March 4, "His publisher lately sent me a copy which I conclude came from him" (quoted in *CL* 1035). She had previously seen only the extracts of the poem that had appeared in the

Daily Chronicle on February 15, remarking four days later that "I am frightfully upset by this wonderful poem of Oscar's" (quoted in *CL* 1022).

29. Chris Healy, *Confessions of a Journalist*, 2nd ed. (London: Chatto and Windus, 1904), 134.

30. *The Parliamentary Debates*, 4th series, vol. 61 (April 4–29, 1898), 60.

31. A six-penny edition was never published. With the exception of thirty specially printed copies of the first edition printed on Japanese vellum, priced at one guinea for the collector's market, and a third edition consisting of just 99 copies, priced at 10s. 6d. and each signed by Wilde personally, Smithers sold each edition of *The Ballad* at 2s. 6d. Not till the eighth edition of 1910, priced at 1 shilling, did an authorized cheaper edition appear, although less expensive piracies had certainly appeared before this date.

32. Le Rouge, "Oscar Wilde," 460.

33. Ibid., 461.

34. Henri Mazel, "My Recollections of Oscar Wilde" (1911), repr. in *Oscar Wilde: Interviews and Recollections*, ed. Mikhail, 2:445.

35. Hilton Kramer, "Art, Anarchism & Félix Fénéon," *New Criterion* 7, no. 9 (May 1989). Fénéon was also a leading anarchist, and he is now known to have planted the bomb that injured Laurent Tailhade at Foyot's Restaurant in April 1894. See Sweetman, *Explosive Acts*, 322–23. Fénéon's portrait featured alongside Wilde's in Toulouse-Lautrec's massive two-panel painting for La Goulue's funfair booth at Foire du Trône in 1895. See Sweetman, *Explosive Acts*, 11–18.

36. Antoine was one of Lugné-Poe's two main rivals as France's leading avant-garde stage director. The other was Paul Fort, founder of the Théâtre de L'Art, who like Antoine had wanted to stage Wilde's *Salomé* at an earlier point in time. Fort, who would attend Wilde's funeral in 1900, had attempted and failed to mount a Parisian production of *Salomé* in 1892. Similarly, Antoine had written to the governor of Reading Prison in 1895, shortly after Wilde's arrival there, seeking Wilde's permission to stage *Salomé* at the Théâtre Libre, but Isaacson had returned this letter unanswered saying that "his prisoner was not allowed to receive such a message" (Sweetman, *Explosive Acts*, 414–15).

37. Leblanc had previously sent Wilde complimentary seats to see her performing the lead in *Sappho* at the Opéra Comique, whereupon Wilde had commented that she was "one of the most wonderful artists I ever saw" (*CL* 1083).

38. Georgette Leblanc, *Souvenirs: My Life with Maeterlinck*, trans. J. Flanner (New York: Dutton, 1932), 128.

39. Ibid., 127–28.

40. Ibid.

41. Quoted in Ellmann, *Oscar Wilde*, 565.

42. Quoted in Richard Hibbett, "The Artist as Aesthete: The French Creation of Oscar Wilde," in *The Reception of Oscar Wilde in Europe*, ed. Evangelista, 79.

43. See too Wilde's reference of 20 May 1898 to "a poet who desired to know me" (*CL* 1070). Jill Fell makes clear that this poet was Jarry, whom Davray had invited Wilde to

meet at the Café Rohan, in the Place du Théâtre Français (Jill Fell, *Alfred Jarry* [London: Reaktion, 2010], 125).

44. Vincent O'Sullivan writes that both plays were "impressive as he related them and would doubtless have had a great success if he had written them. But they were both in his old manner—the manner of *Salomé*" (*Aspects of Wilde* [New York: Henry Holt, 1936], 17).

45. Douglas, "Oscar Wilde's Last Years in Paris," *St. James's Gazette,* March 2–3, 1905, repr. in Douglas, *Oscar Wilde: A Plea and a Reminiscence,* intro. Casper Wintermans (Woubrugge, Holland: Avalon Press, 2002), 40.

46. Ibid.

47. See Ellmann, *Oscar Wilde,* 577.

48. Gide, *Oscar Wilde: In Memoriam; De Profundis,* trans. B. Frechtman (New York: Philosophical Library, 1949), 30.

49. Quoted in J. Robert Maguire, *Ceremonies of Bravery: Oscar Wilde, Carlos Blacker, and the Dreyfus Affair* (Oxford: Oxford University Press, 2013), 137.

50. Gide, *Oscar Wilde: In Memoriam,* 31; O'Sullivan, *Aspects of Wilde,* 51.

51. Régis Revenin, *Homosexualité et prostitution masculines à Paris, 1870–1918* (Paris: L'Harmatton, 2005), 51ff.

52. William A. Peniston, *Pederasts and Others: Urban Culture and Sexual Identity in Nineteenth-Century Paris* (New York: Harrington Park, 2004), 79.

53. Peniston (ibid.) writes that, while it was not uncommon for these young men to receive money from homosexual partners, they often viewed such transactions "as tokens of interest and affection," while "the pursuit of pleasure was [their] overriding concern" (118, 91). Perhaps more importantly, these men "formed a community which gave them a sense of belonging and a means of finding emotional and material support. They all shared certain common characteristics in terms of their origin, their ages, and their occupations, which allowed them to form complex and meaningful relationships with one another" (147).

54. Ibid., 99.

55. Julian Jackson, *Living in Arcadia: Homosexuality, Politics and Morality in France from Liberation to AIDS* (Chicago: University of Chicago Press, 2009), 29.

"If you take unfurnished rooms." Wilde maintained, "your visitors go up directly to call on you; the concierge is not seen or consulted; no one can interfere" (1071). But the proprietor of furnished rooms "could turn out any person he chose, at any time," Wilde believed; "that is the French law. . . . So you see that for *me* the only chance I have is to take unfurnished rooms. I don't take them for the purpose of riotous living—lack of money . . . entails chastity and sobriety—but I do not want to be disturbed, and if Edmond comes to see me at tea-time I don't want the proprietor to question me about his social status" (1071). In furnished apartments, "I could not live. I would be asked to go" (1074).

56. Alfred Douglas, letter to Robert Sherard, 17 September 1932, British Library, Add. MS 81705.

57. See *CL* 1077.

58. Quoted in *CL* 1054 n.2.

59. Harris's account of Wilde's parting from Gilbert was subsequently corroborated by Henry Davray, who said that it is "perfectly vain and inane to deny it" and that Gilbert "was seen by all the people who flocked around Wilde at the Calisaya Bar and other cafés on the Boulevard" (Henry D. Davray, letter to Thomas. H. Bell, 6 October 1938, quoted in Bell, "Oscar Wilde Without Whitewash," unpublished TS, The William Andrews Clark Memorial Library, University of California, Los Angeles, p. 128).

60. Frank Harris, *Oscar Wilde: His Life and Confessions* (1916; repr. New York, Dorset, 1989), 271.

61. Ibid., 273.

62. Two months later, in July 1898, Gilbert was working full time as a secretary for Wilde's friend Rowland Strong—the Paris correspondent of the *New York Times,* the London *Observer,* and the *Morning Post*—following the departure of Strong's previous secretary, the journalist Chris Healy, for London. Since this fact contradicts Wilde's joke to Reginald Turner that Gilbert "would not be a good secretary" and that his writing was bad, it is possible that Gilbert had hoped in May to apprentice himself in London to Turner, who at this time was also a successful journalist.

63. See *CL* 1040.

64. Wilde's statement of the "facts" was written in reply to a letter in which Ross enclosed his own draft of a letter to Constance, pleading for a restitution of Wilde's allowance. But Wilde refused to read Ross's draft, saying "I would sooner leave it to you. You have the tact of affection and kindness" (*CL* 1028).

65. See *CL* 1054 n.2.

66. Douglas, *Oscar Wilde and Myself* (New York: Duffield, 1914), 130.

67. Clare de Pratz, quoted in Guillot de Saix, "Souvenirs Inédits sur Oscar Wilde," *L'Européen: hebdomadaire économique, artistique, et littéraire* 1, no. 4 (May 29, 1929): 2.

68. Rupert Croft-Cooke, *The Unrecorded Life of Oscar Wilde* (New York: David McKay, 1972), 171.

69. Douglas to Harris, 20 March 1925, repr. in Antony Edmonds, *Oscar Wilde's Scandalous Summer* (Stroud, UK: Amberley Publishing, 2014), 17.

70. Unpublished letter from Douglas to Frank Harris, 22 March 1925, Harry Ransom Center, University of Texas at Austin.

71. McKenna, *Secret Life of Oscar Wilde,* 188.

72. O'Sullivan, *Aspects of Wilde,* 50; Douglas, *Oscar Wilde and Myself,* 134.

73. For "Uranian," see pp. 13 and 307 n.24 above.

74. Quoted in Ellmann, *Oscar Wilde,* 563.

7. A Confraternity of the Damned

1. Blacker had been living in Paris on and off for the past five years following a hasty departure from England in 1893, the result of having been accused of cheating at cards

by the Duke of Newcastle. In the 1890s, such an accusation brought scandal and warranted flight. Although Blacker had returned to England periodically—he had been married and declared bankrupt there, in swift succession, in early 1895—he determined to settle in Paris. Like Wilde, he would live permanently in France henceforth. See J. Robert Maguire, *Ceremonies of Bravery: Oscar Wilde, Carlos Blacker, and the Dreyfus Affair* (Oxford: Oxford University Press, 2013).

2. Quoted in ibid., 113.

3. Ibid.

4. Ibid.

5. Maguire, *Ceremonies of Bravery,* 117.

6. Quoted in ibid., 118.

7. Ibid., 136, 118.

8. Ibid., 118.

9. Quoted in *CL* 1041.

10. See Maguire, *Ceremonies of Bravery,* 119–20.

11. Quoted in ibid., 119. Doubtless to reassure the Blackers, Constance reiterated on March 26 that "I am going to give Oscar £10 a month"—as Wilde had himself informed Blacker just over a week previously—"and am putting a codicil to my will so that the allowance may continue after my death" (quoted in Maguire, *Ceremonies of Bravery* 121).

12. Maguire, *Ceremonies of Bravery,* 120.

13. Quoted in ibid.

14. Ibid.

15. Healy, *Confessions of a Journalist,* 130, 137.

16. Maguire, *Ceremonies of Bravery,* 124.

17. Quoted in ibid., 126.

18. Ibid., 127.

19. Vyvyan Holland states that "some months before leaving England, she tripped on a loose stair-carpet and fell down a whole flight of stairs, injuring her spine and her right hand, and she never recovered" (*Son of Oscar Wilde* [1954; repr. New York: Oxford University Press, 1988], 73). It is partly due to Wilde's grandson, Merlin Holland, that we know the true reasons for Constance's decline and death. See next note.

20. See Ashley H. Robins and Merlin Holland, "The Enigmatic Illness and Death of Constance, Wife of Oscar Wilde," *The Lancet,* 385, no. 9962 (January 3–9, 2015): 21–22.

21. Robins and Holland speculate that Constance died painfully from a severe paralytic ileus, an acute intestinal blockage, either as the direct result of Bossi's surgery or secondary to intraabdominal sepsis.

22. Douglas, *Oscar Wilde, A Summing Up* (London: Duckworth, 1940), 100–101.

23. "My father shed telegraphic tears of Hibernian sorrow to Robbie Ross, at this fresh misery an unkind fate had brought upon him" (Vyvyan Holland to Frank Harris, 9 May 1926, Frank Harris Collection 4.3, Harry Ransom Center, University of Texas at Austin).

24. Quoted in *CL* 1054 n.2.

25. Leverson, *Letters to the Sphinx from Oscar Wilde, with Reminiscences of the Author,* by Ada Leverson (London: Duckworth, 1930), 43.

26. Quoted in *CL* 1086.

27. See Maguire, *Ceremonies of Bravery,* 137.

28. Wilde's account to Blacker on 28 March 1898 of being "dragged out to meet Esterhazy" and of Esterhazy's "astonishing" talk suggests this was the first occasion Wilde and Esterhazy met. But J. Robert Maguire says that shortly after Strong's introduction to Esterhazy, which Maguire dates to 14 February, "Strong in turn introduced Esterhazy to Wilde . . . in a bar in the Rue St. Honoré" (*Ceremonies of Bravery,* 110). Robert Sherard, by contrast, says that "It was indirectly through me that Wilde may once have met [Esterhazy], for it was I who introduced him to an English journalist called Rowland Strong and it was Strong who introduced him to Wilde at the Calisaya bar" (Sherard, *Bernard Shaw, Frank Harris and Oscar Wilde* [London: T. Werner Laurie, 1937], 244–45). The journalist Chris Healy, who was Strong's assistant and a close associate of Wilde at the time, says that "Whilst the Zola trial was in progress, [Esterhazy] spent most of his evenings at a bar near the Gare du Nord, in company with [Strong,] the correspondent of a well-known Society paper, who for some reason or other was a fierce anti-Semite. . . . On one or two occasions Oscar Wilde was of the party. The epigrams of Wilde used to puzzle Esterhazy. . . . One evening Esterhazy turned to me and whispered 'Do you think he is serious?'" (Healy, *Confessions of a Journalist,* 164–65).

29. Reported conversation between Wilde and Pío Baroja, quoted in José Esteban, "El desprecio de Don Pío," in *Los Amigos Españoles de Oscar Wilde,* ed. José Esteban (Madrid: La Reina de Cordelia, 2013), 26 (my translation).

30. Vance Thompson, "Oscar Wilde's Last Dark Poisoned Days in Paris," *The Sun,* January 18, 1914, 4.

31. Maguire, *Ceremonies of Bravery,* 110.

32. Ibid., 111.

33. La Jeunesse, "Oscar Wilde," *La Revue Blanche* 23 (September–December 1900): 593 (my translation). Fourteen years later, the American journalist Vance Thompson recounted the same incident as if he had witnessed it himself. But since Thompson's account is an almost verbatim echo of La Jeunesse's, right down to the "dialogue from hell" and the comparison with Dante, it seems likely that it is heavily indebted to La Jeunesse.

34. Frank Harris, *Oscar Wilde: His Life and Confessions* (1916; repr. New York, Dorset, 1989), 245.

35. Ibid., 245–46.

36. Like many of Harris's recollections, his account of this meeting needs to be handled with caution. Sherard says that the meeting was wholly "invented" by Harris, while Ellmann says that "it seems likely that Strong . . . was there instead" (Richard Ellmann, *Oscar Wilde* [New York: Knopf, 1988], 564).

37. *Journal of Arnold Bennett,* 3 vols. (New York: Viking, 1932), 1:215, quoted in Maguire, *Ceremonies of Bravery,* 112.

38. Quoted in French, *CL* 1051 n.1.

39. "Pen, Pencil, and Poison," in *Criticism: Historical Criticism, Intentions, and The Soul of Man,* ed. Josephine M. Guy, vol. 4 of *The Complete Works of Oscar Wilde* (Oxford: Oxford University Press, 2007), 120–21.

40. "Aristotle at Afternoon Tea," in *Journalism, Part 2,* ed. John Stokes and Mark Turner, vol. 7 of *The Complete Works of Oscar Wilde,* 35–36.

41. "The Decay of Lying," in *Criticism,* ed. Guy, 74.

42. Wilfrid H. Chesson, "A Reminiscence of 1898" (1911), repr. in *Oscar Wilde: Interviews and Recollections,* ed. E. H. Mikhail (London: Macmillan, 1979), 2:377.

8. The Solace of Spectatorship

1. Richard Ellmann, *Oscar Wilde* (New York: Knopf, 1988), 567.

2. Rowland Strong, *Sensations of Paris* (New York: McBride, Nast, 1912), 186–87.

3. Wilfred H. Chesson, "A Reminiscence of 1898," *The Bookman* (1911), repr. in *Oscar Wilde: Interviews and Recollections,* ed. E. H. Mikhail (London: Macmillan, 1979), 375–77.

4. Ibid., 377–80.

5. Ibid., 380.

6. "The House of Judgment," in *Poems and Poems in Prose,* ed. Bobby Fong and Karl Beckson, vol. 1 of *The Complete Works of Oscar Wilde* (Oxford: Oxford University Press, 2000), 172; Chesson, "A Reminiscence of 1898," 381.

7. Chesson, "A Reminiscence of 1898," 381.

8. See *CL* 1068, 1075.

9. Frank Harris, *Oscar Wilde: His Life and Confessions* (1916; repr. New York, Dorset, 1989), 256.

10. Ibid.

11. Chesson quotes Wilde as saying "I am correcting the proofs of a play, *The Importance of Being Earnest.*" But since Wilde asked Smithers in October "if I am to have proofs of my play" (*CL* 1098) and returned a "second batch of proofs" in late November (*CL* 1101), it seems likely that Wilde was still revising the typed-up copy of the play's script, not correcting the page proofs.

12. Wilde's joke at the expense of the University Extension Scheme had been present in draft manuscripts of *The Importance of Being Earnest* since 1894, but only in 1898 does Lady Bracknell name the title and subject of the lecture.

13. Stanley Weintraub, *Reggie: A Portrait of Reginald Turner* (New York: George Braziller, 1965), 100.

14. *CL* 1098. In Aix, Wilde's mother had given Douglas £30 to go to Venice, but according to Wilde he lost it all at the Casino in Monte Carlo and returned to Paris on the proceeds of his gold cufflinks.

15. The three books whose English publication Douglas anticipated upon his return to England were *Tales with a Twist* (London: Edward Arnold, 1898), *The Duke of Berwick* (London: Leonard Smithers, 1899), and *The City of the Soul.*

16. Vincent O'Sullivan, *Aspects of Wilde* (New York: Henry Holt, 1936), 43; Douglas, *The Autobiography of Alfred Douglas* (London: Secker 1929), 161.

17. According to the writer Gustave Le Rouge, Wilde was "generous down to the last penny" and "popular with the people in the wine cellars because of his generosity in offering drinks to first-comers" ("Oscar Wilde" [1928], trans. E. H. Mikhail, in *Oscar Wilde: Interviews and Recollections,* ed. Mikhail, 2:461–62).

18. Quoted in Immanuel De Rudbeck, "Oscar Wilde, fut-il pensionné par la reine Victoria?" (1933), trans. by Mikhail as "Was Oscar Wilde Granted a Pension by Queen Victoria?," in *Oscar Wilde: Interviews and Recollections,* ed. Mikhail, 2:458.

19. Robert Harborough Sherard, *The Life of Oscar Wilde* (New York: Mitchell Kennerley, 1906), 405.

20. Harris, *Oscar Wilde,* 266–67.

21. H. Montgomery Hyde, Introduction to *Mr. and Mrs. Daventry: A Play in Four Acts, by Frank Harris, based on the Scenario by Oscar Wilde* (London: Richards Press, 1956), 11.

22. Nothing is known about "Sir John" except what can be gleaned from Wilde's own correspondence, but he appears to have eloped to the United States in dubious circumstances in late 1898 or early 1899. In a letter written shortly after his elopement, Wilde says that he was "capital company," a "very astounding person in his capacity for pleasure," "grand in his cups," and had "a heart of gold" (*CL* 1118). The "only thing I never could forgive him," Wilde adds, "was his absurd love of Walter—a plain, crooked, ugly and tedious youth."

23. Quoted in José Esteban, "El encuentro con Galdos," in *Los Amigos Españoles de Oscar Wilde,* ed. José Esteban (Madrid: La Reina de Cordelia, 2013), 14, my translation. Gomez-Carillo's description of the Calisaya Bar as a literary gathering place is corroborated by Alfred Douglas, in *Without Apology* (London: Secker, 1938), 278.

24. Manuel Machado, "La última balada del poeta inglés," in *Los Amigos Españoles de Oscar Wilde,* ed. Esteban, 51, my translation. By a "yankee-style" bar, Machado means that customers were seated or standing at the bar rather than occupying separate tables. Similarly, when Wilde himself refers to the Calisaya as an "American bar," he means that it was an American-style bar, with barmen serving behind a long countertop, not that it was popular with Americans.

25. *Lady Windermere's Fan,* ed. Ian Small (London: Ernest Benn, 1980), 64.

26. Harris, *Oscar Wilde,* 267.

27. Ibid., 264–74.

28. Ibid., 280.

29. A few years later, La Napoule was described by one British visitor as a "village . . . tenanted by poor fishermen, but . . . likely to look up as a bathing place" (Sabine Baring-Gould, *A Book of the Riviera* [New York: E. P. Dutton, 1905], 187).

30. Harris, *Oscar Wilde,* 288, 280.

31. In *Sir George Alexander and The St. James' Theater* (1935; repr. New York: Benjamin Blom, 1969), Alexander's biographer A. E. W. Mason suggests that "either Wilde mistook his bicyclist or Alexander did not see Wilde," as well as suggesting that Harris (in whose

1916 biography of Wilde Mason had read of it) may have made the incident up out of whole cloth. But Wilde had recounted the story directly to Robert Ross in a letter dated December 27, 1898 (*CL* 1112), and in Harris's account, Wilde approaches Alexander, delighted to see him, only for Alexander to turn his head aside and pedal past deliberately. As Mason points out, Alexander's "cutting" of Wilde is hard to reconcile with the warm letter to Alexander written nearly two years later, shortly after a final, friendly meeting, in which Wilde announces that it was "a really great pleasure to see you again and to receive your friendly grasp of the hand after so many years," while noting the "charming and affectionate greeting" with which Alexander's "dear wife" had also greeted him (*CL* 1193). The incident is also hard to reconcile with Wilde's decision, while still in Nice in February 1899, to send Alexander a copy of the just-published first edition of the *Importance of Being Earnest* "with the compliments of the author" (*CL* 1124).

32. Frank Harris quotes Wilde describing "The Ballad of a Fisher" as a "joy-song" in which "I sing of liberty instead of prison, joy instead of sorrow, a kiss instead of an execution" (*Oscar Wilde*, 281).

33. He read Virgil and Henry James's "The Turn of the Screw," marveling at James's "wonderful, lurid, poisonous little tale" and cattily remarking that "James is developing, but he will never arrive at passion, I fear." He also read Smithers's just-published edition of Ben Jonson's *Volpone*, containing the unfinished series of illustrations that Aubrey Beardsley had been working on when he died in March, along with Robert Ross's moving eulogy to Beardsley.

34. Harris, *Oscar Wilde*, 286, 294–95.

35. Ibid., 296.

36. Ibid., 297.

37. *Lady Windermere's Fan*, ed. Small, 57.

38. Leverson, *Letters to the Sphinx from Oscar Wilde, with Reminiscences of the Author, by Ada Leverson* (London: Duckworth, 1930), 43.

39. Evelyn Waugh, *A Tourist in Africa* (Boston: Little Brown, 1960), 14, 16.

40. Leverson, *Letters to the Sphinx*, 43.

41. Gide, *Oscar Wilde: In Memoriam; De Profundis*, trans. B. Frechtman (New York: Philosophical Library, 1949), 11. The story was to be the basis for Wilde's prose poem "The Artist."

42. *Lady Windermere's Fan*, ed. Small, 81.

43. By mid-March, at least, Ross, Adey, and Turner had all written acknowledging receipt of their personalized copies.

44. Quoted in Ellmann, *Oscar Wilde*, 561–62.

45. Wilde's impecuniousness was not alleviated by the publication of *The Importance of Being Earnest* in February 1899 or by his brother's sudden death the following month. Conscious that sales of the play would prove disappointing, Wilde agreed in late February 1899 to sell Smithers his 50% royalty in the play along with his 50% royalty in *An Ideal Husband*, which Smithers had agreed as early as October 1897 to publish. A price of £30 had been agreed, but by March 18 he had only received (and spent) £5 from Smithers, and was urgently insisting that Smithers "let me have £5 *at once*" (*CL* 1130).

The £5 duly arrived within a few days. Wilde had by this point received news of his brother's death, but between Willie and Oscar "there had been . . . wide chasms for many years" (*CL* 1130), and Wilde was sorry chiefly for his sister-in-law's sake, since she had a small child and little left to live on. For his own part, he hoped that his brother's death might alleviate his own poverty somewhat, since the family property at Moytura House was entailed to him upon his brother's death. Moytura produced an income of £120 per year in rents (*CL* 1142), and Wilde hoped that it might be sold for a "fair sum" (*CL* 1130), perhaps "£3000 or a little more" (*CL* 1134). But he knew that his creditors would claim it, and in the event Wilde saw no financial benefit from his brother's death.

46. He had wanted *An Ideal Husband* to be published before *The Importance of Being Earnest,* and Smithers had agreed as early as October 1897 to publish it; see *CL* 975. But nothing more was done about publishing the play until February 1899, once *The Importance of Being Earnest* had appeared and Smithers had bought out Wilde's share of the profits in the planned edition. See James G. Nelson, *Publisher to the Decadents: Leonard Smithers in the Careers of Beardsley, Wilde, Dowson* (University Park: Pennsylvania State University Press, 2000), 213ff.

47. "Would you . . . see that the 'wills' and 'shalls' are not too Hibernian?" (*CL* 1135).

48. Wilde left Gland on April 1 and had arrived at Santa Margherita, near Genoa, by April 7, when he sent Ross four postcards with "specimens of the views to tempt you" (*CL* 1140).

49. "I do not love the lad Edoardo Rolla as much as I did" (*CL* 1141).

50. Smithers to Wilde, 4 May 1899, quoted in Nelson, *Publisher to the Decadents,* 217.

51. See *CL* 1148–49.

52. Wilde had declined dealing with Roberts on the grounds that he lacked experience, tact, and a practical touch, whereas Smithers—who according to his son Jack had interests in a number of theatrical ventures—proposed taking London's Garrick Theatre as early as September 1899 and producing Wilde's play there (Nelson, *Publisher to the Decadents,* 217, 219).

53. During his short trip to Fontainebleu, Wilde ran into his old friend Sir Peter Chalmers Mitchell, who had unwittingly been the model for Alan Campbell in *The Picture of Dorian Gray.* Mitchell says that while he was taking coffee with two English friends at a café near the palace gates, "a heavy-jowled, large grey-faced man, looking as if his suit were too big for him, shuffled past us and sat down at a table near by" (Peter Chalmers Mitchell, *My Fill of Days* [1937], partially extracted as "I Used You in *Dorian Gray,*" in *Oscar Wilde: Interviews and Recollections,* ed. Mikhail, 2:366). When Mitchell recognized this man to be Wilde, his friends got up to go, saying "the hotel should be warned," but Mitchell warmly greeted Wilde, whom he had first met years previously at London's Café Royal, and the two men sat conversing and reminiscing for more than two hours. When Mitchell got up to go, he says, he invited Wilde to dine with them that night, but Wilde replied "Your friends would not stand it. I am going back to my little inn where they don't know me. Good-bye; thank you" (367).

54. Another reason for visiting Le Havre may have been that he wished to meet there with the English actor Kyrle Bellew, with whom he had been in correspondence since April about collaborating on a play. On June 16, 1898, shortly before Wilde's trip to Le

Havre, Bellew sent Wilde a draft to enable Wilde to meet him at the Channel port of Boulogne. Wilde is not known to have met Bellew, either at Boulogne or at Le Havre, and nothing became of their proposed collaboration.

55. Quoted in *CL* 1152 n.1.

56. Ibid.

57. Ibid., 1154 n.1.

58. Ellmann, *Oscar Wilde*, 572.

59. Brehat, *The Romance of Trouville*, trans. Meta de Vere (New York: Bonners, 1892), 7. Trouville had been popular with aesthetes since Whistler, Monet, and Courbet had all painted there in the 1860s, and in Wilde's novel *The Picture of Dorian Gray*, the eponymous hero, Dorian Gray, shares a villa at Trouville with his friend Lord Henry Wotton.

60. "You must not imagine that people in cafés listen to the conversation of others," he told George Ives, who had expressed a wish to converse more privately at Wilde's hotel: "people in life listen primarily to their own conversation, then to the conversation of the person or persons with whom they are" (*CL* 1172).

61. O'Sullivan, *Aspects of Wilde*, 164.

62. Vincent O'Sullivan, undated letter to A. J. A. Symons, speculatively dated "?early 1932" by its editor, in *Some Letters of Vincent O'Sullivan to A. J. A. Symons* (Edinburgh: Tragara Press, 1975), 7. O'Sullivan's account is confirmed by Stuart Merrill, who commented that "Wilde frequented quarters where his presence was extremely disagreeable to those who considered themselves to be compromised in such company" ("Some Unpublished Recollections of Wilde," first published and translated 1954, in *Oscar Wilde: Interviews and Recollections*, ed. Mikhail, 2:470).

63. Leonard Smithers, letter to Oscar Wilde, 29 June 1899, The William Andrews Clark Memorial Library, University of California, Los Angeles.

64. O'Sullivan, undated letter to A. J. A. Symons, in *Some Letters of Vincent O'Sullivan to A. J. A. Symons*, 8.

65. O'Sullivan, *Aspects of Wilde*, 164.

66. Reginald Turner, letter to C. J. Renier, 22 March 1933, The William Andrews Clark Memorial Library, University of California, Los Angeles.

67. Jean Dupoirier, quoted in Robert Sherard, *The Real Oscar Wilde* (London: T. Werner Laurie, 1915), 410; repr. as "Oscar Wilde Worked All Night Long," in *Oscar Wilde: Interviews and Recollections*, ed. Mikhail, 2:455.

68. Merrill, "Some Unpublished Recollections of Wilde," 470.

69. Alfred Douglas, letter to Robert Sherard, 8 March 1937, British Library, Add MS 81705.

70. *Letters to the Sphinx*, 39–40. Jean-Joseph Renaud says flatly that Wilde "did not drink much" and that "in spite of what has been said and written, Oscar Wilde was never a desperate, sinister character, keeping company with the scum of Paris and drinking himself to death." Turner similarly disputes that Wilde "relapsed into bad ways" (letter to C. J. Renier, 22 March 1933): in an unpublished letter to Sherard (3 January 1934,

Reading University) Turner states that "I certainly *never* saw Oscar 'drunk.' . . . Neither did I ever see him stumble in his walk. . . . But though he did drink absinth, and Ross once told me he had got drunk on absinth shortly before his death, he had no Verlaine bouts of drunkenness and I should say was a moderate drinker of spirits and generally drank wine in quite modest quantities unless it was champagne of a good brand, when he no doubt drank as much as was provided. . . . He sat a lot in cafés as Parisians do, especially at Calisaya's. He never sat and soaked." Robert Ross writes similarly that "although Wilde was inclined to take too much alcohol at times . . . he never bore outward signs of it. In fact, owing to his extraordinary constitution he was able (unfortunately perhaps) to take a great deal too much without being affected. He never became incapable" (*CL* 1225).

71. Gide, *Oscar Wilde, In Memoriam,* 31–32.

72. Gold-mounted dentures were among Wilde's effects at his death, although it is unclear when these were made or when Wilde started wearing them. See Robert Sherard, *Oscar Wilde, "Drunkard and Swindler": A Reply to George Bernard Shaw, etc.* (Calvi, Corsica: Vindex Publishing, 1933), 10; also Merlin Holland, "Merlin Holland Muses on Oscar Wilde," in *Artist Dandy Rebel: Men of Fashion,* ed. Kate Irvin and Laurie A. Brewer (New Haven, CT: Yale University Press, 2013).

73. See Sherard, *Twenty Years in Paris: Being Some Recollections of a Literary Life* (Philadelphia: George W. Jacobs, 1905), 449.

74. Many years later, writing under the pseudonym "Louis Marlow," Wilkinson published a detailed account of this correspondence, in which he quoted at length from Wilde's letters to himself. See Louis Marlow [Louis Wilkinson], *Seven Friends* (London: Richards, 1953), 1–25.

75. See Vyvyan Holland, *Son of Oscar Wilde* (1954; repr. New York: Oxford University Press, 1988), 141.

9. Decline and Death

1. William Rothenstein, *Men and Memories: Recollections, 1872–1938,* ed. Mary Lago (Columbia: University of Missouri Press, 1978), 127.

2. Ernest La Jeunesse, "Oscar Wilde," trans. P. Pollard, originally published in French in *La Revue Blanche,* December 15, 1900, in *Oscar Wilde: Interviews and Recollections,* ed. E. H. Mikhail (London: Macmillan, 1979), 2:478.

3. Jean-Joseph Renaud, "The Last Months of Oscar Wilde," unpublished TS, The William Andrews Clark Memorial Library, University of California, Los Angeles. Renaud's typescript elaborates on the account of Wilde's final days that he had given in his 1905 Introduction to his French translation of *Intentions.*

4. La Jeunesse, "Oscar Wilde," 478 ; Pollard's translation modified.

5. In a pair of letters to the actress Aimee Lowther, speculatively dated August 1899 by Wilde's editors, Wilde states that "the little prose-poem, 'The Poet,' appears, with some others by me, in one of the French magazines this month" (*CL* 1164). But this publication has never been traced and, to the best of scholars' current knowledge, Wilde's

prose poem "The Poet," which he recounted orally to numerous listeners, most notably André Gide, was never published in his lifetime.

6. Renaud, "The Last Months of Oscar Wilde." Robert Sherard gives a slightly different version of this anecdote in his *Life of Oscar Wilde* (New York: Mitchell Kennerley, 1906), where he dates it to Wilde's Berneval period and absolves Xau of any indelicacy by saying that his offer was "a plain business-like offer from a very shrewd business-man to a writer of eminent and recognized capacity" (279). But Sherard, who knew Xau well, seems to have derived his version of the anecdote from Renaud's 1905 Introduction (see note 3 above; see also "How Oscar Wilde Died," *Current Literature* 39 [1905]: 394). Renaud's version is preferred here.

7. Laurence Housman, *Echo de Paris* (London: Jonathan Cape, 1923), 15.

8. La Jeunesse, "Oscar Wilde," 478 ; Pollard's translation modified.

9. Shane Leslie, *Memoir of John Edwards Courtenay Bodley* (London: Jonathan Cape, 1930), 18.

10. T. P. O'Connor, "T. P.'s Table Talk," *Cassell's Weekly,* October 27, 1923, quoted in Richard Ellmann, *Oscar Wilde* (New York: Knopf, 1988), 574.

11. O'Sullivan, *Aspects of Wilde,* 27.

12. For Ives's account of this meeting, see his unpublished MS diary, vol. 36, pp. 4079–80, entry dated 6 February 1900, Harry Ransom Center, University of Texas at Austin. Although Wilde enjoyed seeing Ives, he bristled at Ives's mania for privacy, telling him that "it is not necessary to go to a remote cabman's shelter for . . . discussions," that he was "a great baby," and that "one can't help being angry with you" (*CL* 1172).

13. Ashley Robins, a medic specializing in psychiatry, speculates that Wilde was at this time afflicted with septicemia from a streptococcal sore throat and that he recovered fully from this episode (Robins, *Oscar Wilde: The Great Drama of His Life* [Brighton: Sussex Academic, 2011], 101).

14. Elisabeth Marbury, "The Last Days of Oscar Wilde," in *Oscar Wilde: Interviews and Recollections,* ed. Mikhail, 2:438.

15. "Sonnet on Approaching Italy," in *Poems and Poems in Prose,* ed. Bobby Fong and Karl Beckson, vol. 1 of *The Complete Works of Oscar Wilde* (Oxford: Oxford University Press, 2000), 32.

16. To the great delight of the local students who "used to come to the café to talk—or rather, to listen," Wilde denied his true identity and, upon being asked his name, replied only that "every man has one name" and that his name was *Io,* Italian for "I" (*CL* 1183).

17. "Rome Unvisited," in *Poems and Poems in Prose,* ed. Fong and Beckson, 8–9.

18. Quoted in *CL* 44.

19. Ellmann, *Oscar Wilde,* 70.

20. Wilde is alluding to the myth of Venus and Tannhäuser, in which the penitent Tannhäuser, after dallying with the goddess Venus, journeys to seek absolution from the Pope in Rome, where his staff miraculously bursts into bloom. "Grissell" is Hartwell de la Garde Grissell (1839–1907), chamberlain of honor to the pope, whom Wilde had met in Rome in April 1877 and again in Oxford in autumn 1877.

21. On April 21, 1899 Wilde wrote that "I have given up Armando, a very smart young Roman Sporus," adding that "he was beautiful, but his requests for raiment and neckties were incessant" (*CL* 1182). Wilde now liked a young man named Arnaldo, whom he intended photographing. (Within days Armando was "forgiven for the moment," because he "is so absurdly like the Apollo Belvedere that I feel always as if I were Winckelmann when I am with him" [*CL* 1184]). Six days later Wilde had befriended "one Philippo, a student, whom I culled in the Borgia room," remarking "not for many years has Love walked in the Pope's pleasaunce" (*CL* 1186). In early May Wilde befriended a young man named Dario, who "would have kissed me on leaving the Bronze Gateway had I not sternly repelled him" (*CL* 1186). "I have become very cruel to boys, Wilde informed Ross, "and no longer let them kiss me in public." Upon leaving Rome in mid-May, he bade goodbye "with tears and one kiss, to the beautiful Greek boy who was found in my garden," the "nicest boy" to whom Ross had ever introduced him (*CL* 1187).

22. Frank Harris, *Oscar Wilde: His Life and Confessions* (1916; repr. New York, Dorset, 1989), 307.

23. Marbury, "The Last Days of Oscar Wilde," 438.

24. Quoted in Guillot de Saix, "Souvenirs Inédits sur Oscar Wilde," *L'Européen: hebdomadaire économique, artistique, et littéraire* 1, no. 4 (May 29, 1929): 2.

25. Sherard, *Twenty Years in Paris: Being Some Recollections of a Literary Life* (Philadelphia: George W. Jacobs, 1905), 448; and Sherard, *The Real Oscar Wilde* (London: T. Werner Laurie, 1915), 418–19. Wilde's attentive and generous hotelier Jean Dupoirier told Sherard after Wilde's death that his tenant had been a great reader and that Wilde would sit for hours in the hotel's inner courtyard sipping his aperitif and reading. But on closely inspecting the two chests of books that remained in the rooms after Wilde's death—containing about 300 books, Sherard estimated—Sherard found that most of the books were still uncut and showed little sign of use (Sherard, "Oscar Wilde's Tomb," *Reynolds's Newspaper*, 31 July 1904).

26. Henri Mazel, "My Recollections of Oscar Wilde" (1911), repr. in *Oscar Wilde: Interviews and Recollections*, ed. Mikhail, 2:446.

27. Merrill, "Some Unpublished Recollections of Wilde," in *Oscar Wilde: Interviews and Recollections*, ed. Mikhail, 2:470; see also the testimony of Wilde's friends Paul Fort and Madame Fort, who often accompanied him to the *Exposition*, that at this time he seemed "not outwardly unhappy, and interested in everything" (quoted in Arthur Ransom, "Oscar Wilde in Paris," *The Bookman* 33 [1911]: 273).

28. La Jeunesse, "Oscar Wilde," 480.

29. According to Robert Ross, Queensberry bequeathed Douglas £25,000 (Robert Ross to Frank Harris, 17 February 1917, Oscar Wilde Collection, 3.9, Harry Ransom Center, University of Texas at Austin). According to Reggie Turner, Queensberry's bequest to his youngest son was £17,000 (Turner to Harris, 16 May [1925], Harris Collection, 5.2, Harry Ransom Center, University of Texas at Austin); while according to Douglas himself, the bequest was less than £15,000, of which he received only £8,000 at first. See too the letter to Harris in which Douglas says that the inheritance was only about £14,000 (ALS to Frank Harris, 16 August 1930, Alfred Douglas Collection 1.9, Harry Ransom Center, University of Texas at Austin).

30. Douglas, *Autobiography,* 164 and 320. In conversation with Frank Harris (who acted as an intermediary), Wilde reportedly explained that he wanted Douglas "to give me enough to make my life comfortable, to settle enough on me to make a decent life possible to me. It would only have cost him two or three thousand pounds a year" (Harris, *Oscar Wilde,* 302). See as well the reported conversation in which Wilde tells Harris, "I asked him to settle £1500 or £2000 on me to buy an annuity, or to do something that would give me £150 a year" (Harris, *Oscar Wilde,* 308). For Wilde's own account of his falling out with Douglas, see *CL* 1187–88; for Douglas's account, see *Autobiography,* 163–64 and 319–23.

31. Harris, *Oscar Wilde,* 305.

32. Douglas, *Autobiography,* 322. Douglas later claimed he had given Wilde about a thousand pounds shortly after the death of his father (Douglas to Harris, 16 August 1930, Alfred Douglas Collection 1.9, Harry Ransom Center, University of Texas at Austin). See also Reginald Turner's remark to Robert Sherard (unpublished letter, 29 October 1933, University of Reading) that "the only real money of any amount that Oscar got, apart from his allowance and the advances made by various people for possible work, was provided—and provided lavishly—by Bosie Douglas."

33. Douglas, "Oscar Wilde's Last Years in Paris," *St. James's Gazette,* March 2–3, 1905, repr. in Douglas, *Oscar Wilde: A Plea and a Reminiscence,* intr. Casper Wintermans (Woubrugge, Holland: Avalon Press, 2002), 43.

34. Harris, *Oscar Wilde,* 312.

35. Thomas H. Bell, "Oscar Wilde Without Whitewash," unpublished TS, page 33, William Andrews Clark Memorial Library, University of California, Los Angeles. According to Bell, who was Harris's secretary, "Wilde . . . had been hanging around Harris trying to get some money out of him" (31). But Harris had had enough—unknown to Wilde, he was beginning to enter into financial difficulties of his own—so instead of letting Wilde have another check, he urged him "Why don't you write that play of yours, Oscar?" "My play, Frank, I shall never write," Wilde replied, adding "Take it and write it yourself. I give it to you" (32). Harris quite properly declined Wilde's offer, says Bell, but instead of letting the matter drop he got Wilde to agree on the collaboration. Bell says that, if he thought seriously of the collaboration at all, Wilde approached it "as a long luxurious time spent in good hotels, with Harris paying for the dinners and drinks" (32).

36. Wilde's claim is possibly disingenuous. According to Thomas Bell, after diligently writing the second and third acts as agreed, Harris mailed carbon copies of them to Wilde, whereupon "Wilde went up in the air over it" (ibid., 36). An angry correspondence ensued, leading Harris to realize—if he hadn't already realized it—that Wilde would never complete his part of the arrangement and that if he was to seek a return on his own investments of time and energy he would need to complete the play himself. According to Bell, upon receiving the manuscript of the fourth and final act, Wilde wrote Harris, "You have not only stolen my play: you have spoiled it" (41). When the play entered rehearsals, rumors abounded that Wilde was actually the author and Harris simply a front, adopted because the real author was an undischarged bankrupt. But when the play was finally performed, on October 25, 1900, to decidedly mixed reviews and a

few catcalls from the audience, all but the least discerning theatergoers were disabused of this belief. Even still, the production ran for 121 performances before closing in February 1901, two months after Wilde's death. See H. Montgomery Hyde, Introduction to Frank Harris, *Mr. and Mrs. Daventry: A Play in Four Acts* (London: Richards Press, 1956), 7–43. For Harris's own account of the composition of *Mr. and Mrs. Daventry,* see Harris, *Oscar Wilde,* 301–2 and 313–14, and Harris, "The Story of Mr. and Mrs. Daventry," published as an appendix to Brentano's (2nd) 1916 American edition of Harris's *Oscar Wilde: His Life and Confessions,* available online at https://ebooks.adelaide.edu.au /w/wilde/oscar/harris/appendix9.html.

37. The amount of Harris's initial payment is open to conjecture. According to Ross, Harris gave Wilde "£50 on account" (*CL* 1211); according to Harris himself, he had already paid Wilde £50 when agreeing to collaborate back in June, and he now "agreed . . . to give him another £50 down and another £50 later" (Harris, "The Story of Mr. and Mrs. Daventry").

38. See Harris, *Oscar Wilde,* 312–14 for Harris's own account of this correspondence and the effects it had on him.

39. George Bernard Shaw, "My Memories of Oscar Wilde," in Harris, *Oscar Wilde,* 342.

40. See also Reginald Turner's remark to Sherard (29 October 1933, University of Reading) that "Oscar in his last days said that Harris owed him money on account of *Mr. and Mrs. Daventry* . . . But neither Ross nor I were convinced that it was so." Wilde's friend and first biographer Robert Sherard always disputed that Wilde "swindled" Frank Harris over *Mr. and Mrs. Daventry,* and believed that the letter dated 14 December 1900 in which Robert Ross states that "Oscar, of course, deceived Harris about the whole matter" was a forgery, concocted by Harris to support his own account (later endorsed by his friend George Bernard Shaw) of the matter. See Sherard, *Oscar Wilde, "Drunkard and Swindler": A Reply to George Bernard Shaw, etc.* (Calvi, Corsica: Vindex Publishing Co., 1933), 6. To be sure, Ross's letter—which is one of the most important documents in the story of Wilde's life, since it describes Wilde's final decline in intimate detail and gives the only first-hand account of Wilde's death besides Turner's—survives only as a typed transcript or copy, produced to assist Harris in the composition of his 1916 biography of Wilde (Harry Ransom Center, University of Texas at Austin), and was eventually published as an appendix to Harris's biography. But since the typescript contains Ross's handwritten amendments (as well as Harris's) together with intimate details that only Ross or Turner could have provided, it disproves Sherard's assertions. Moreover Reginald Turner told Sherard that he had once seen the original and he took issue with Sherard's suspicions (29 October 1933). Ross's letter, on which I have drawn heavily for my own account of Wilde's final days, is reproduced in *CL* 1211–14 and 1219–23.

41. Robert Ross, unpublished letter to Oscar Wilde, 27 November 1900, The William Andrews Clark Memorial Library, University of California, Los Angeles,

42. Rothenstein, *Men and Memories,* 127.

43. Bernard Thornton, "Oscar Wilde—A Reminiscence" (1918), repr. in *Oscar Wilde: Interviews and Recollections,* ed. Mikhail, 2:442.

44. Nellie Melba, *Melodies and Memories* (125), partially extracted as "After The Débâcle," in *Oscar Wilde: Interviews and Recollections,* ed. Mikhail, 2:372.

45. George Barr Baker, "Criminal Genius in Exile: Picture From His Last Days in Paris," unidentified press cutting, dated 28 November 190?, in an album of press cuttings at The William Andrews Clark Memorial Library, University of California, Los Angeles. I am grateful to Joseph Bristow for passing Baker's account on to me.

46. Anna de Brémont, *Oscar Wilde and His Mother* (1911), extracted as "I Have Lived," in *Oscar Wilde: Interviews and Recollections,* ed. Mikhail, 2:450–51.

47. Shortly after this visitor departed for Naples, Wilde commented how "I miss that brown faun with his deep woodland eyes and his sensuous grace of limb" (*CL* 1196).

48. Ashley H. Robins and Sean L. Sellars, "Oscar Wilde's Terminal Illness: Reappraisal after a Century," *The Lancet* 356 (2000): 1841.

49. Ibid. Today the initial treatment for a cholesteatoma might include careful cleaning, antibiotics, and ear drops. But surgery is required if the cholesteatoma becomes enlarged.

50. W. Wilde, *Practical Observations on Aural Surgery and the Nature and Treatment of Diseases of the Ear* (London: Churchill, 1953), quoted in Robins and Sellars, "Oscar Wilde's Terminal Illness," 1843.

51. In his long letter to More Adey, dated December 14, 1900, Ross states the date of his own arrival as October 17, noting that he had started from London the previous evening (*CL* 1211). However, in a later letter to Adela Schuster, dated December 23, he states that he had arrived on October 15 (*CL* 1226).

52. See too Ross's remark "he was looking extremely well, and seeing various friends at intervals during the day, and sometimes was in the highest spirits" (*CL* 1226).

53. *CL* 1212. According to Frank Harris, Ross's account of this incident is "too timid. . . . The truth is that Oscar stopped the victoria at almost the first café, got down and had an absinthe. Two or three hundred yards further on, he stopped the carriage again to have another absinthe; at the stoppage a few minutes later Ross ventured to remonstrate 'You'll kill yourself, Oscar.' . . . 'And what have I to live for, Bobbie?' he [answered] gravely" (Harris, *Oscar Wilde,* 315).

54. Wilde had bought the eau de cologne and lotion on credit from the parfumerie Jules et Roger in the Rue Scribe at the end of August. Ironically, Jules et Roger only made out and presented their bill on the day of Wilde's death: November 30, 1900 (The William Andrews Clark Memorial Library, University of California, Los Angeles, shelfmark J94Z W6721 1900 November 30).

55. Robert Sherard, *Oscar Wilde, Twice Defended from André Gide's Wicked Lies and Frank Harris's Cruel Libels* (Chicago: Argus Bookshop, 1934).

56. Sherard, *Oscar Wilde, "Drunkard and Swindler,"* 10.

57. Ross, I am afraid, deliberately misled me," writes Douglas of the letter that Ross subsequently wrote: "I got a letter from Robert Ross saying that [Wilde] was ill but that it was 'nothing serious.' . . . He did not . . . want me to see Oscar again before he died. If I had known how ill he was I would have rushed to his side" (Douglas, *Oscar Wilde: A Summing-Up* [London: Duckworth, 1940], 140).

58. Quoted in Harris and Douglas, *A New Preface to "The Life and Confessions of Oscar Wilde"* (London: Fortune Press, 1925), 15.

59. On November 25, Maurice A'Court Tucker, Wilde's attending physician and doctor to the British embassy, called in the specialist Paul Claisse, an expert on meningitis, tertiary syphilis, and skin disorders, among other things. On November 27, when Wilde's symptoms had become much worse, the two physicians jointly issued a statement certifying that "a diagnosis of meningoencephalitis must be made without doubt," that "one cannot contemplate trepanation," and that "surgical intervention seems not to be possible" (quoted and translated in Robins and Sellars, "Oscar Wilde's Terminal Illness," 1842).

60. Turner to Sherard, 29 October 1933 (University of Reading). Although Lord Alfred Douglas was not present at Wilde's death or at the ceremonies performed by Father Dunne just before it, he too later asserted that Wilde was entirely unconscious during Dunne's ministrations (Douglas to More Adey, 17 December 1900, TS copy, The William Andrews Clark Memorial Library, University of California, Los Angeles). Three weeks after Wilde's death, he wrote again to Adey, telling him that he disliked the deceit of pretending that Wilde died a Catholic when he hadn't done so, and that Wilde would not have died a Catholic under any circumstances. See Douglas to Adey, 21 December 1900, TS copy, The William Andrews Clark Memorial Library, University of California, Los Angeles. Four years later still, Douglas—who in 1912 was himself to become a Roman Catholic—wrote unequivocally in print that Wilde "did not become a Roman Catholic before he died. He was, at the insistence of a great friend of his, himself a devout Catholic, 'received into the Church' a few hours before he died; but he had then been unconscious for many hours, and he died without ever having any idea of the liberty that had been taken with his unconscious body" ("Oscar Wilde's Last Years in Paris," 39).

61. Wilfrid Scawen Blunt, *My Diaries; Being a Personal Narrative of Events 1888–1914* (London: Martin Secker, 1932), partially extracted and reprinted as "The Death of Oscar Wilde," in *Oscar Wilde: Interviews and Recollections,* ed. Mikhail, 2:473.

62. Ellmann, *Oscar Wilde,* 584.

63. Reggie Turner's account of Wilde's death, given to Frank Harris years later, differs from Ross's in significant details: Turner (who calls Ross's account an "invention") says that while "the so-called death rattle, or loud roughness of breathing, in his throat" lasted all morning, "towards noon this ceased abruptly, and Robbie and I went together to the head of the bed. Oscar was breathing quite regularly and quietly; suddenly he exhaled a long, deep breath, and then nothing more; silence absolute. I said to Robbie in awe: He's dead, and Robbie nodded his head. That was all: Oscar's end was as quiet and peaceful as that of an innocent child" (quoted in Douglas and Harris, *A New Preface,* 15).

64. "Many thanks for sending the Franciscan Sisters," Ross wrote hastily to Father Dunne on December 1: "He was particularly devoted to St. Francis and deeply read in all his life and literature, so it is very appropriate" (typed copy of petit bleu, in Hyde, correspondence with Margery Ross, Hyde Collection 5.1, Harry Ransom Center, University of Texas at Austin).

65. Quoted in Michelle de Royer, *L'Intransigeant* (1930), trans. as "Oscar Wilde Died in my Arms," in *Oscar Wilde: Interviews and Recollections,* ed. Mikhail, 2:454.

66. *CL* 1221; Turner to Sherard, 9 December 1937, TS, The William Andrews Clark Memorial Library, University of California, Los Angeles.

67. Both children soon quickly discovered the fact of their father's death and were left to mourn privately in shock. Vyvyan was informed just two days after Wilde's death by the Rector of Stonyhurst College, the Jesuit school he attended; the school's teachers and administrators knew Vyvyan's true identity and had probably read of his father's death in the papers. Cyril was left to discover it for himself, in private, from newspaper accounts and from the gossip of his fellow students at Radley School. See Vyvyan Holland, *Son of Oscar Wilde* (1954; repr. New York: Oxford University Press, 1988), 151–53.

68. For Douglas's explanation for his delay, see note 57 above.

69. La Jeunesse, "Oscar Wilde," 480; Miriam Aldrich, "The Burial of a Fallen Poet," unpublished unpaginated TS, Schlesinger Library, Radcliffe Institute, Harvard University, folio 6.

70. But see Ross's (probably exaggerated) assertion that fifty-six people were present, including five ladies in deep mourning (*CL* 1222).

71. Aldrich, "The Burial of a Fallen Poet," Schlesinger Library, Radcliffe Institute, Harvard University, folio 5.

72. Bagneux was "the burial place of the poor of Paris, in which I doubt if there was . . . a single *concession perpétuelle,* and where the modest graves, with their simple headstones and beaded decorations, stand as close together as is possible, and where all the alleys, except the main ones in which the *fourgons* pass, are barely wide enough to let one walk" (Aldrich, "The Burial of a Fallen Poet," Schlesinger Library, Radcliffe Institute, Harvard University, folio 11).

73. Aldrich, "The Burial of a Fallen Poet," Schlesinger Library, Radcliffe Institute, Harvard University, folio 7.

74. "une dizaine d'amis à peine suivaient ce cercueil. . . . A un tournant de rue, les quelques poètes reconnus là s'évanouirent comme un vol de corneilles, et seules demeurèrent le médecin, le chirurgien et le maitre de l'hôtel" (*Le Journal,* 10 December 1900).

75. Arthur Ransome, "Oscar Wilde in Paris," *The Bookman* 33, no. 3 (May 1911), 273; Paul Fort, quoted in Charles Dantzig, Introduction to Wilde, *L'Importance d'être Constant,* trans. Dantzig (Paris: Grasset, 2013), my translation. Two days after the funeral, *L'Echo de Paris* reported that "autour de la tombe, il y avait bien, en tout, quinze personnes" (around the grave there were, in all, fifteen people).

76. On December 23, 1900, Ross wrote: "I shall either purchase the ground outright later on and erect a suitable monument, or remove the remains to a permanent resting-place" (*CL* 1128–29).

77. Aldrich, "The Burial of a Fallen Poet," Schlesinger Library, Radcliffe Institute, Harvard University, folio 15.

78. Ellmann, *Oscar Wilde,* 585.

79. Fort, quoted in Dantzig, Introduction to Wilde, *L'Importance d'être Constant.*

80. "To my words they durst add nothing, and my speech dropped upon them" (Douai version).

81. Holland, *Son of Oscar Wilde*, 196–97. Holland says that, upon realizing his mistake and seeing Ross about to explode, "the undertaker produced a chisel and hacked out the intrusive 'D,' making a bad mess of it" (197).

82. This is a common misapprehension on first viewing a corpse, caused not by continued hair growth but by a withering and retraction of the skin.

83. Harris, *Oscar Wilde*, 316–17. Reggie Turner later disputed this account, which Harris had been given by Robbie Ross personally, leading Harris himself briefly to question it. But Vyvyan Holland, who was present at the disinterment, writes to Harris that "the story as related in your 'Life' is strictly accurate and, if anything, errs on the side of baldness. Robbie did not tell you one quarter of all that actually occurred" (letter to Frank Harris, 24 February 1926, Frank Harris Collection 4.3, Harry Ransom Center, University of Texas at Austin). In a later letter to Harris, Holland clarifies that, although he was "not more than ten yards away" from the grave and "Robbie forbade me to look," Ross "did certainly have my father's head in his hands the only time I looked" and Ross "was certainly covered in earth when it was all over" (to Frank Harris, 30 August 1927, Frank Harris Collection 4.3, Harry Ransom Center, University of Texas at Austin).

Epilogue

1. For my account of the *Exposition Universelle*, I have drawn upon Philippe Julian, *The Triumph of Art Nouveau*, trans. S. Hardman (New York: Larousse, 1974); Richard D. Mandell, *Paris, 1900: The Great World's Fair* (Toronto: University of Toronto Press, 1967); John Allwood, *The Great Exhibitions* (London: Studio Vista, 1977); and Debora L. Silverman's conclusion, "The 1900 Paris Exhibition," in her *Art Nouveau in Fin-de-Siècle France* (Berkeley: University of California Press, 1989), 284–314.

2. Paul Morand, "1900 A. D.," quoted in Allwood, *The Great Exhibitions*, 96.

3. *The Education of Henry Adams*, ed. Ernest Samuels (Boston: Houghton Mifflin, 1974), 382–83.

4. Silverman, "The 1900 Paris Exhibition," 297.

5. Ibid., 303.

6. Julian, *The Triumph of Art Nouveau*.

7. Mandell, *Paris, 1900*, 75.

8. "A Few Maxims for the Instruction of the Over-Educated," *Saturday Review*, November 17, 1894.

9. *The Picture of Dorian Gray: An Annotated Uncensored Edition*, ed. Nicholas Frankel (Cambridge, MA: Harvard University Press, 2011), 192.

10. O'Sullivan, *Aspects of Wilde* (New York: Henry Holt, 1936), 181; Stuart Merrill, "Oscar Wilde" (1900), trans. E. H. Mikhail, in *Oscar Wilde: Interviews and Recollections*, ed. E. H. Mikhail (London: Macmillan, 1979), 2:467.

11. Ives diary, December 1, 1900, vol. 38, 4279. On December 2, 1900, Ives wrote further in his diary that Wilde's death is "the greatest tragedy of the whole nineteenth century." One week later, Ives published a short poetic eulogy to Wilde in the radical *Reynolds's Newspaper*, the only British paper sympathetic to Wilde. See John Stokes,

"Wilde at Bay: The Diary of George Ives," in his *Oscar Wilde: Myths, Miracles, and Imitations*, 82–83.

12. Blunt, "The Death of Oscar Wilde," in *Oscar Wilde: Interviews and Recollections*, ed. Mikhail, 2:472.

13. *North American*, December 4, 1900, quoted in "Oscar Wilde," *The Literary Digest* 21, no. 25 (December 22, 1900), 767.

14. Ellmann, *Oscar Wilde* (New York: Knopf, 1988), xv, 586.

15. Melissa Knox, *Oscar Wilde: A Long and Lovely Suicide* (New Haven, CT: Yale University Press, 1994), 133.

16. Ellmann, *Oscar Wilde*, 548.

17. Neil McKenna, *The Secret Life of Oscar Wilde* (New York: Basic Books, 2005), 465; Emer O'Sullivan, *The Fall of the House of Wilde: Oscar Wilde and His Family* (London: Bloomsbury, 2016), 442.

18. Ellmann, *Oscar Wilde*, 586, 588.

19. "A" [Lord Alfred Douglas], "Oscar Wilde: His Last Book and His Last Years," *St. James's Gazette*, March 2–3, 1905, repr. as "Oscar Wilde's Last Years in Paris," in Douglas, *Oscar Wilde: A Plea and a Reminiscence* (Woubrugge, Holland: Avalon, 2002), 40. He "had his bad moments," admits Douglas, "moments of depression and sense of loss and defeat, but they were not of long duration. It was part of his pose to luxuriate a little in the details of his tragic circumstances" (40). These observations predate by some years the recriminations that crept into Douglas's writings about Wilde after 1912, when he first became aware of what Wilde had said about him in *De Profundis* and turned violently against his one-time lover as a result.

20. "Phrases and Philosophies for the Use of the Young" (1894), in *The Artist as Critic: Critical Writings of Oscar Wilde*, ed. Richard Ellmann (1969; repr. New York: Vintage, 1970), 433; Wilde, *The Annotated Importance of Being Earnest*, ed. Nicholas Frankel (Cambridge, MA: Harvard University Press, 2015), 161.

21. *The Picture of Dorian Gray: An Annotated Uncensored Edition*, ed. Frankel, 192.

22. Wilde, "Pen, Pencil, and Poison," in *Criticism, Intentions, and The Soul of Man*, ed. Josephine M. Guy, vol. 4 of *The Complete Works of Oscar Wilde* (Oxford: Oxford University Press, 2007), 120–21.

23. Wilde, *Lady Windermere's Fan*, ed. Ian Small (London: Ernest Benn, 1980), 42.

24. Wilde, "The Fisherman and His Soul," in *Complete Shorter Fiction*, ed. Isobel Murray (Oxford: Oxford World's Classics, 1979), 234.

25. *Salome: A Tragedy in One Act*, in *Plays 1: The Duchess of Padua; Salomé: Drame en un Acte; Salome: A Tragedy in One Act*, ed. Joseph Donohue, vol. 5 of *The Complete Works of Oscar Wilde* (Oxford: Oxford University Press, 2013), 730.

26. Quoted in Hyde, *The Trials of Oscar Wilde* (1962; repr. Mineola, NY: Dover Publications, 1973), 201.

27. Linda Dowling, *Hellenism and Homosexuality in Victorian Oxford* (Ithaca, NY: Cornell University Press, 1994), 2.

28. See Ellmann, *Oscar Wilde*, 320.

29. Ibid., 15.

30. "Aristotle at Afternoon Tea," in *Journalism, Part 2,* ed. John Stokes and Mark W. Turner, vol. 7 of *The Complete Works of Oscar Wilde* (Oxford: Oxford University Press, 2013), 35.

31. Ibid.

32. Douglas, *Oscar Wilde, A Summing Up* (London: Duckworth, 1940), 138.

33. Robert Ross, "Oscar Wilde," unpublished TS, p. 2, British Library, Add MS 81684.

34. "Phrases and Philosophies for the Use of the Young," in *The Artist as Critic,* ed. Ellmann, 434.

35. For a while, More Adey and Robert Ross tried to keep Wilde supplied with bespoke suits made by Doré. But by June 1898 his "old Doré suit" was tight and "the two lower buttons drag" (*CL* 1081). See too Merlin Holland's description of Wilde's last and only surviving shirt, a bespoke dress shirt made for him in 1899 with the monogram "S. M." embroidered on the left breast ("Merlin Holland Muses on Oscar Wilde," in *Artist Dandy Rebel: Men of Fashion,* ed. Kate Irvin and Laurie A. Brewer [New Haven, CT: Yale University Press, 2013]).

Illustration Credits

Illustration Credits

p. 272   Hôtel D'Alsace, Paris, c. 1898. Published in *Oscar Wilde and Myself* by Lord Alfred Douglas (New York: Duffield and Company, 1914), p. 138.

p. 285   Wilde, photographed on his deathbed. Reproduced courtesy of the William Andrews Clark Memorial Library, University of California, Los Angeles.

p. 293   "Moving sidewalk panorama" of the *Exposition Universelle,* 1900, Paris. Published in *The Parisian Dream City: A Portfolio of Photographic Views of the World's Exposition at Paris* (St. Louis: Thompson Publishing Company, 1900).

Acknowledgments

This book would not have been possible without the generous support of many individuals and institutions. I owe a profound debt to John Kulka, my editor, who commissioned the project and supported and guided me at every stage. Without his sharp, generous mind, fine ear, and infinite patience, this book would be a far inferior production. I am very grateful as well to Joseph Bristow, Jerome McGann, Susan Barstow, and three anonymous readers for Harvard University Press for the generosity and insightfulness with which they read the manuscript. I am also thankful for the many kindnesses on the part of Joseph Bristow, who shared with me the fruits of his own archival research in advance of his much-anticipated critical transcript of Wilde's criminal trials. My thanks as well to Kerry Higgins Wendt, my copyeditor; Christine Thorsteinsson, project manager; John Donohue at Westchester Publishing Services; and Lorraine Janzen Kooistra, Don Meade, Michael Seeney, Steven Halliwell, Kate Nash, Catherine Ingrassia, Phil Cohen, Mark Samuels Lasner, David Latané, Bryant Mangum, and the late Linda Peterson for intellectual and practical support of various kinds.

Research was supported by an Andrew W. Mellon Foundation Research Fellowship from the Harry Ransom Center at the University of Texas at Austin, by the Department of English at Virginia Commonwealth University, and by a travel grant from the VCU Humanities

Center. A Faculty Research Leave from the VCU College of Humanities and Sciences enabled composition to get under way in the fall of 2013. My thanks to David Latané and Kathy Bassard, the present and past chairs respectively of the VCU English Department; to Montserrat Fuentes and her two predecessors as Dean of the VCU College of Humanities and Sciences; and to Richard Godbeer, Director of the VCU Humanities Center. My thanks too to the staffs of the William Andrews Clark Memorial Library, the Bodleian Library, the Harry Ransom Center Library, and the British Library, especially Scott Jacobs at the Clark and Elizabeth Garver at the Ransom Center. Closer to home, my work was facilitated by the Interlibrary Loan Office at VCU's James W. Cabell Library and by the angels in the office of the VCU English Department, especially Ginnie Schmitz and Margret Schluer.

I owe a special debt to Merlin Holland, Wilde's grandson, who generously granted me permission to quote material in which he owns copyright and whose work constitutes the foundation on which much of my own is built. I am grateful as well to John Rubenstein and John Stafford, joint executors of the Estate of Lord Alfred Douglas, for permission to quote from unpublished material in which they own the copyright; to the Harry Ransom Center at the University of Texas at Austin for permission to quote from manuscript material by Douglas in their possession; and to Caroline Gould for permission to quote from unpublished material by Robert Ross in which she owns the copyright.

My largest debt is to my wife, Susan, and my children, Max, Theo, and Oliver, who lived with this book during its lengthy gestation and showed me that, as Wilde says, "to Love all things are easy."

Index

Index

Index

Index